Contemporary Issues in Interpersonal Communication

Mark P. Orbe
Western Michigan University

Carol J. Bruess
University of St. Thomas

Instructor's M
Student Study Gu

Roxbury
Los A

Library of Congress Cataloging-in-Publication Data

Orbe, Mark P.
Contemporary issues in interpersonal communication / Mark P. Orbe, Carol J. Bruess.
p. cm.
Includes bibliographical endnotes and index.
ISBN 1-931719-58-6
  1. Interpersonal communication—Textbooks. I. Bruess, Carol J., 1968- II. Title.

BF637.C45O72 2005
153.6'dc22   200401410

Publisher: Claude Teweles
Managing Editor: Dawn VanDercreek
Production Editor: Carla Plucknett
Copy Editor: Cheryl Adam
Proofreaders: Cheryl Adam and Sacha Howells
Typography: SDS Design, info@sds-design.com
Cover Design: Marnie Kenney
Photography: Gina Gregory

Printed on acid-free paper in the United States of America. This book meets the standards for recycling of the Environmental Protection Agency.

ISBN 1-931719-58-6

ROXBURY PUBLISHING COMPANY
P.O. Box 491044
Los Angeles, California 90049-9044
Voice: (310) 473-3312 • Fax: (310) 473-4490
E-mail: roxbury@roxbury.net
Website: www.roxbury.net

Dedicated to the living memories of my parents:
Theodora Humphrey Marks Orbe (1939–1990)
and Philippe Auguste Orbe (1937–2003)

—MPO

Dedicated to Lisa Anne Benkowski, Ph.D. (1967–2003),
whose endless optimism lives on in me

—CJB

Contents

Part I

An Introduction to Interpersonal Communication

Part II

Interpersonal Messages

Part III

Communication Contexts

Preface

In today's world, many people are reminded that "the one thing that you can count on is change." Each year that we teach interpersonal communication classes, our students force us to recognize that their life experiences are oftentimes drastically different than our own. Sometimes we are surprised to learn that issues, events, artifacts, and memories that are central to our lives are not familiar to most of our students. This presents challenges for us as educators because good pedagogical practice insists that we include relevant applications of concepts and theories—things that our students can easily relate to. Yet, while many of our traditionally aged students focus on the present, we continue to remind them that "the more things change, the more they stay the same."

Consequently, this book was birthed out of the idea that the best textbooks value both the old and the new. As such, we bridge both perspectives: (1) Although particular circumstances may have changed, the core concepts and theories in the field of communication remain applicable to interpersonal communication in the twenty-first century; and (2) new circumstances call for a reexamination of old frameworks, or the creation of new concepts, models, and theories.

We have written an undergraduate textbook on interpersonal communication that introduces the foundational ideas and concepts of our field *and* applies them to issues, events, and concerns that are relevant for today's college-student population. We did not simply reiterate the standard set of core ideas and theories in the field of interpersonal communication; nor did we exclude the traditions and highlight only the most contemporary (emerging) schools of thought. On balance, this book utilizes an integrated approach—both traditional and contemporary—introducing the concepts, models, and theories of the field in a way that will engage and challenge today's most culturally sensitive, technologically savvy, and forward-thinking interpersonal communication students and professors.

In so many ways, *Contemporary Issues in Interpersonal Communication* will appeal to professors and students who desire a basic coverage of interpersonal communication concepts within the context of the key societal issues of today. Although there are any number of issues that we could have focused on, we chose to highlight those that seem to be the most challenging: culture, power, and technology. By focusing on these three, the book represents an introductory text that speaks to today's diverse and technologically savvy student population. *Contemporary Issues in Interpersonal Communication* connects knowledge of specific communication practices to issues of culture, power, and technology in all contexts of interpersonal communication. Becoming aware of, and having a complete understanding of, the breadth to which culture, power, and technology influence all of our interpersonal interactions are essential for students who seek competence and effectiveness as interpersonal communicators.

Organization of the Book

Contemporary Issues in Interpersonal Communication has 12 chapters organized around three major sections. Part I represents "An Introduction to Interpersonal Communication" and covers the most basic concepts for students. Within this section, students will learn about basic principles, models, and theories of interpersonal communication generally, as well as those specifically associated with particular topics such as self and perception.

One unique feature of our foundation chapters is Chapter 2. This chapter focuses on introducing students to three contemporary issues—culture, power, and technology—and explaining how they represent challenges to our communication effectiveness. Unlike other interpersonal communication textbooks that may have separate chapters or sections on culture, power, and technology located throughout the book, *Contemporary Issues in Interpersonal Communication* introduces students to these topics in Chapter 2 and integrates them throughout the remaining chapters. This innovative strategy encourages students to understand how these three issues—independently or collectively—affect various aspects of interpersonal communication. Through this organizational feature, we hope to encourage beginning interpersonal communication students to recognize, and appreciate, the complex ways that our communication is affected by multiple factors.

Part II, "Interpersonal Messages," extends the foundation provided in the first section. Specifically, it focuses on topics such as language, nonverbal communication, listening, communication climate, and conflict. "Communication Contexts," the final section of the text, continues to build upon the framework of core concepts that was established in Parts I and II. However, it also provides different contexts in which this framework can be used to increase understanding. Within this section, students can focus on communicating effectively within personal relationships, the family, and the workplace.

Pedagogical Features

Each of the chapters in this book contains a set of pedagogical features designed to engage students as they learn about new communication concepts. Although various features appear throughout each chapter, many are used in consistent ways to enhance student learning. For instance, each chapter begins with *Contemporary Issues*, a feature that describes a real-life news story that demonstrates how culture, power, and/or technology issues affect interpersonal communication issues. These stories serve as thought-provoking introductory case studies for students, and we provide Web addresses so that students can learn more about the issues raised. Also provided at the beginning of each chapter is a list of *Myths About Interpersonal Communication* that relate to the topic at hand. Many students begin their study of interpersonal communication with several myths about the topic; often, such myths are based upon popular beliefs, distorted perceptions, or misunderstandings. This pedagogical feature encourages students to think through these various statements, and use the information provided in each chapter to ultimately understand and differentiate between statements that are true and those that represent myths. To facilitate this process, we close each chapter with an explanation of each statement and why it is a myth or a truth.

Throughout each chapter, we use a number of different boxed features to help students extend the information that is included in the text. Toward this goal, four different types of boxes are included. *Practical Research* boxes share recent research findings concerning different topics of interest, and ask students to think critically about them. *Self-Reflection* boxes ask students to think through how different interpersonal communication concepts relate to their own life experiences. *Applied Concept* boxes and *Skill Builder* boxes both provide opportunities for students to use concepts in everyday settings.

At the close of each chapter, we also include several pedagogical features designed to maximize student learning. As described earlier, one of these is a *Summary* that highlights the truth behind each myth outlined at the beginning of the chapter. We also include a list of *Key Terms*. In addition, we provide a list of *Suggested Contemporary Readings*. These resources all reflect recent scholarship in various areas of interpersonal communication—ones that we would have loved to include in each chapter, but space limitations prohibited us from doing so. We hope that students and professors will utilize these resources and the other *Chapter Activities* to strengthen and/or extend student learning. Our experiences as interpersonal communication teachers have demonstrated the importance of including opportunities for students to use online databases, access various relevant Web sites, participate in structured small-group activities, and take advantage of suggested media texts for different points of analyses.

We wish you the best as you venture into *Contemporary Issues in Interpersonal Communication*. We invite all of your feedback, comments, and/or questions at any time throughout your course (from both professors and students alike)! You can reach us at *orbe@wmich.edu* and *cjbruess@stthomas.edu*. ✦

Acknowledgments

Mark P. Orbe: *In all thy ways acknowledge Him, and He shall direct thy paths* (Proverbs 3:6). Since I began my doctoral program in 1990, this scripture has remained a permanent fixture in my office. As someone who actively seeks to live life through the divine plan laid out for me, it is important that I first acknowledge God as the constant, unchangeable source of my life. Over the past five years, other scriptures have been added to my Western Michigan University office; one reads: *And He who gave you a good work will be faithful to complete it* (Philippians 1:6). Anyone who has written a textbook understands how the process can represent a seemingly *timeless* journey—through it all, God has remained my constant source of inspiration, motivation, and vision. To Him I give all the glory.

While this book symbolizes a visible manifestation of God's graces, it hardly represents the most important. My beautiful, gracious, and loving wife, Natalie, and wonderfully energized children—Victoria (victorbe), Gabrielle (bobby-elle), and Isaiah (zay)—also deserve recognition for all that they do to support, inspire, and revitalize me! Not a day goes by that I don't acknowledge how blessed I am to have each of you in my life.

Carol, thank you for your faith walk throughout this process. We started the journey of graduate study together in 1990, published our first peer-reviewed article together (with Leda Cooks) in 1993, and now published a textbook together! Without question, what we've produced here is something that neither of us could have done alone. I appreciate our professional and personal relationship.

Lastly, I would be remiss if I didn't acknowledge all of my past and present students. This book is a direct result of your contributions to the learning that has occurred in my interpersonal communication classrooms over the past 10+ years. . . . Dumela!

Carol J. Bruess: I have been thoroughly blessed, both professionally and personally, by the supportive, talented, and loving people in my life. So many of these people have—in large or small ways—made this amazing project finally not only come to be, but also come to be a book of which I am incredibly proud.

I first want to acknowledge the unique and thoroughly amazing work and partnership of my coauthor, Mark P. Orbe. This book is first and foremost the result of your admirable spiritual attenuation. Had you not *Listened* and responded to the *Call*, this book would not be. To you, I say thank you for your encouragement, leadership, wisdom, vision, and guidance.

Second to acknowledge, although always first in my heart, is my darling partner in life Brian, and my precious children Tony and Grace Ellen. Your ability to give, give, give when I need, need, need (time, organization, a clean house, more time, your support, love, prayers, sleep . . . and more sleep) is selfless. For each of you, I am grateful every single day.

Each day I also marvel at the many other people in my life with whom I have been blessed and without whom I couldn't do any of this: my amazing extended family (Sesslers and Bruesses . . . particularly Stephanie Place for your insightful proofreading and college-student perspective), my loyal and brilliant friends (Deb, Suzy, Betsey, Trish, Marla, Sarah, and John and Jeanine—particularly John Sundt, who so frequently would ask, "Got that book done yet?"), my supportive and energizing colleagues (Bernard Armada, Kevin Sauter, Debra Petersen, Tim Scully, Jeff Cook, Julie Friedline, John Cragan, and Lois Dament), and my dedicated research assistant and rising communication star Anna Hoefs. Each of you has contributed to this project in both obvious and not-so-obvious ways, all of which have been appreciated. Your interest and support (Lynn Sessler, Deb, and John) have been uplifting, your practical assistance (Lois, Anna, Stephanie) has been necessary, and your directed expertise and encouragement (Kevin, John, Cragan, Bernard) have been priceless. John Cragan, more than anyone, you likely have no idea how your excitement, advice, and wisdom often came at crucial times along this journey; your interest in seeing this project to its end and your advice in helping it get there are so very much appreciated.

To my friend and former advisor Judy C. Pearson, you have, as you always have, served as a model for my own writing, teaching, and engagement in the field. I acknowledge you here because without you, I'm confident I wouldn't be writing this text. Thank you, as always, for your mentorship, for your positive energy, and for serving as a model for me and so many other women in the field of communication.

To Carol Cortez, my friend, mentor, and the professor who first taught me about the amazing field of interpersonal communication: thank you for such an inspiring introduction as well as for your ongoing support and friendship.

Mark and Carol: Claude Teweles and Carla Plucknett, thank you for believing in us and for your dedicated and focused work on making this book a reality. We have great appreciation for your respect of our vision and your support of our ideas. Special thanks also go to Deirdre Anderson, Eric Carlson, and Elisa Adams for their earlier work on the development of this manuscript.

From the start, this book project has benefited from the expertise, experience, and insight of many reviewers. At each stage of development and production, we were able to utilize your input to create a better textbook. Needless to say, we appreciate all of your time, commitment, and knowledge! Specifically, we would also like to thank the many teachers and scholars of interpersonal communication who reviewed this text in its final stages of development: Andy O. Alali, California State University, Bakersfield; Donald B. Egolf, University of Pittsburgh; Cary Horvath, Youngstown State University; Jon Braddy, Florida Gulf Coast University; Yemi S. Akande, John Carroll University; and Janie Harden Fritz, Duquesne University. We also thank the many other scholars who reviewed earlier drafts of this manuscript: Susan A. Bourke, University of Cincinnati; Marie Griffin, Arizona State University-West; Andrea Leverentz, DePaul University; Eric Ling, Mount Olive College; John Linn, Pennsylvania State University–Altoona; Barbara Sims, Pennsylvania State University–Harrisburg; Chad Trulson, University of North Texas; Gary L. Webb, Ball State University; Robert Weiss, State University of New York–Plattsburgh; and John T. Whitehead, East Tennessee University. ✦

About the Authors

MARK P. ORBE (pronounced "Or-bee") received his undergraduate degree in organizational communication from Ohio University, followed by a master's degree in higher educational administration from the University of Connecticut. After holding several student affairs positions, he returned to Ohio University to complete his doctoral degree in interpersonal/intercultural communication. His first faculty position was at Indiana University Southeast, where he also served as department coordinator and the first director of diversity. Currently, he is an associate professor of communication and diversity at Western Michigan University (WMU), where he also has a joint appointment in the Center for Women's Studies. Born and raised in New London, Connecticut, he currently resides in Kalamazoo, Michigan, with his wife, Natalie, and three children, Isaiah, Gabrielle, and Victoria.

CAROL J. BRUESS (pronounced "Breece," rhymes with "peace") is currently an associate professor of communication studies at the University of St. Thomas in St. Paul, Minnesota, where she teaches undergraduates in the areas of interpersonal, family, and intercultural communication. She received her B.A. in fine art and graphic design at St. Norbert College in Wisconsin and her M.A. and Ph.D. in interpersonal communication from Ohio University. Her current research and writing focus on how couples and families use rituals and private language to find satisfaction in their personal relationships. She is an advocate of service-learning, a teaching strategy that combines meaningful community service with course objectives. She integrates community-based active learning into all of the courses she teaches. In her spare time she enjoys sewing with vintage fabrics, is an amateur photographer, competes in triathlons, and loves reading to her children. Born and raised in Wisconsin, she currently resides in St. Paul with her husband, Brian, and their two children, Tony and Grace Ellen. ✦

Part I

An Introduction to Interpersonal Communication

Chapter 1

An Orientation to Interpersonal Communication

Contemporary Issues: Loving Across Cultural Lines

Tijuana and Michael have been in a long-term dating relationship and hope to marry in the next few years.[1] As Tijuana works to complete graduate school at Yale in the drama department, Michael works as a chiropractor. Although busy with their careers and school, they do the things that most dating couples do: dine out together, enjoy time with friends, e-mail each other notes and photos when they can catch a free moment at work, take advantage of their shared-minutes plan to talk frequently on their cell phones when away on business or simply going about their day, shop for clothes online at Banana Republic, and share a love of digital photography, pop culture, and cooking. Their relationship has faced many of the same challenges that many couples encounter during the dating years. Yet, Tijuana, who is African American, and Michael, who is European American, have faced a somewhat unique set of pressures and questions as one of a growing number of couples who are dating across racial lines.

According to recent studies, approximately four out of ten Americans have dated interracially;[2] five out of ten of those surveyed in one study expressed an openness to becoming involved in an interracial partnership.[3] Researchers suggest that those most likely to date across racial boundaries are males, individuals who are adolescents or young adults, those who are politically liberal and highly educated, and those who attend diverse schools.[4] Because dating is more informal in the United States, there is greater acceptance of interracial dating than there is of interracial marriage.[5]

Interpersonal communication in all of our relationships is shaped by the messages we receive about what is appropriate and acceptable in our culture. Because Tijuana and Michael's relationship exists within a network of peers, colleagues, friends, and family, their interpersonal communication and the relationships that result naturally affect and are affected by the messages they receive from others. As the research reviewed above highlights, couples who date across racial lines are challenged to face, often explicitly, some of the implicit assumptions in U.S. culture about which cultural identities are most powerful and what is right, best, and acceptable when it comes to dating, love, and family relationships. In what ways have your own interpersonal interactions been influenced or challenged by the cultural expectations or ideals of those around you? If you're having a hard time knowing how to answer that question, rest assured that after reading this text you will be very well prepared to examine the many ways that power and culture, and others' perceptions of such, play a role in all of your interpersonal interactions.

Tijuana and Michael's relationship is also influenced, as you saw in the description of their daily routines, by the increasingly technological world in which they live. Many of their daily mundane communication activities are dependent on the use of communication technologies such as e-mail, digital imagery, the Internet, and cellular phones. The impact of the Internet and other communication technologies on interpersonal communication and social relationships is currently under intense investigation. Although contradictory results are emerging, many studies are uncovering the fully integrated way that many of us in the United States are relying on e-mail, cell phones, and the Internet to develop, maintain, and even terminate our relationships.

What has your experience been using communication technologies to communicate interpersonally? Do you think the increase in Internet and e-mail use is enhancing personal relationships or negatively affecting them? Has the Internet, or other communication technologies, changed the way you communicate interpersonally? Although the jury is still out on precisely how individuals' use of the technologies to communicate affects their interpersonal communication, one thing is for sure: People use technology intensely for interpersonal communication. As such, it will be one of the many topics that we explore throughout this text.

Interpersonal communication and the development of personal relationships are the topics of this book. By definition, **interpersonal communication** is *the process of creating and sharing meaning between people who are interdependent, have a relationship between them, and have some knowledge about each other.* Later in this chapter we will fully explore this definition and the components of it. In the chapters that follow, we will be exploring a range of concepts and studies related to the ways that we communicate interpersonally and the ways that our interpersonal interactions affect and reflect the quality of our lives. For instance, we will explore how perception affects how we communicate, the way we use nonverbals to communicate much of the meaning in our messages, how to become a better listener, and even the ways our interpersonal communication directly affects our satisfaction in our personal relationships. As we introduce in Chapter 2 and as you saw in the opening case study in this chapter, we will explore the roles that culture, technology, and power play in all of our interpersonal interactions. By the end of this book and the course you are taking, you should be an effective communicator and better equipped to make informed choices about your own interpersonal communication in the twenty-first century.

Myths About Interpersonal Communication

Our goal in each chapter is for you to learn a great deal. We'll start by getting you to think a bit about what you already know, or think you know, about the ideas in this book. To do that, we'll list some common myths about interpersonal communication. **Myths** are ideas that people believe to be true but are not. In this list of myths, we'll also list one or two items that are actually true. Your job, as you read the chapter, is to figure out which are myths and which are not. You might begin each chapter by making a notation next to each statement on the lines provided below, indicating if you think the statement is in fact a myth (M) or if you think it is indeed true (T). Don't feel bad if you find you believed some myths; most of us do until they are pointed out to us. At the end of the chapter, we will provide the answers.

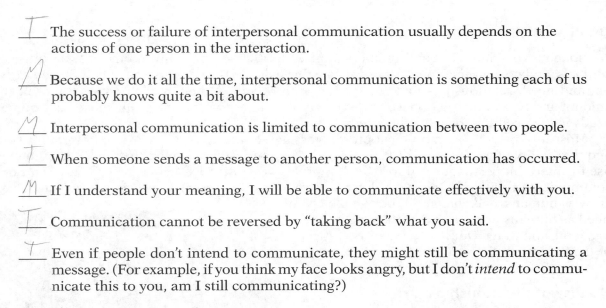

I The success or failure of interpersonal communication usually depends on the actions of one person in the interaction.

M Because we do it all the time, interpersonal communication is something each of us probably knows quite a bit about.

M Interpersonal communication is limited to communication between two people.

I When someone sends a message to another person, communication has occurred.

M If I understand your meaning, I will be able to communicate effectively with you.

I Communication cannot be reversed by "taking back" what you said.

I Even if people don't intend to communicate, they might still be communicating a message. (For example, if you think my face looks angry, but I don't *intend* to communicate this to you, am I still communicating?)

Interpersonal communication is a central part of almost every aspect of our lives. We use it to make connections with others, establish and develop our identities, compare our ideas, check our perceptions, share news, solve problems, give and receive support from others, develop closer relationships, and grow personally. Take a moment to think about the number of times you interacted or communicated with someone today. Most of us spend the majority of our waking hours interacting with others. Many of these exchanges are what we call interpersonal, and they are most often what allows for meaningful relationships to develop.

Why Study Interpersonal Communication?

You come to this class with a lot of experience as an interpersonal communicator. In fact, you probably already know that interpersonal communication is important to study, and you might even have a specific reason for taking this course. For example, you might be taking this class with the goal of having more meaningful friendships. Or maybe you want to better understand your communication with your romantic partner, or manage conflict with friends and family members. Students of interpersonal communication are often delighted to find in the course answers to some of their questions about their own lives and relationships, such as: Why are some relationships joyful, and others difficult? Why do we like certain people and find others more challenging to be around? Why do some people interpret a message completely differently than others? Why do people from other cultures communicate so differently? Why is it that no matter what you do, sometimes you can't change the way others interact with you? How can you have longer lasting relationships? How can you make your relationships happier? Is there a way to interpret others' body language? How can you be a better friend, family member, or coworker? The principles and ideas presented in this text should give you information for developing your own answers to each of these questions, and more!

Let's begin by examining some of the reasons why interpersonal communication is so important to our quality of life, relationships, and even physical health.

Quality of Life

Imagine your life without any interaction with others—no family, no friends, no intimate contacts, and no conversation. It's hard to imagine, isn't it? Humans are social beings who thrive on, and need, relationships and interaction with others. Although each of us differs in the amount and type of interaction we find satisfactory and necessary, one of the most basic human needs is the need for social connection.

Most interpersonal communication scholars agree that the quality of our communication and the quality of our lives are directly related. Communication is more than just something we use to entertain, persuade, or inform; it is a process that literally defines who we are. Through communication with others, we develop a sense of ourselves, reveal ourselves, educate ourselves, grow as humans, and change. To be completely fulfilled as humans, we need more than shelter, clothing, food, and water. Our lives are a direct reflection of the quality of the communication in them.

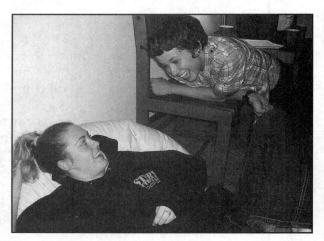

Quality of Relationships

One of the most important things interpersonal communication allows us to do is develop personal relationships. Without it, we would be socially isolated. Imagine not talking to, listening to, or interacting with anyone, in any capacity, for an entire day. No phone calls, e-mails, television viewing, nothing. Solitary confinement, in which social interaction is forbidden, is so abhorrent that it is a form of severe punishment, and its use is limited to short periods of time. We like social interaction, we need it, and we want it. Communication with others helps us meet very important social and psychological needs, particularly those we find in valued and satisfying interpersonal relationships.

Communication with friends and others close to us is a basic human need. In what ways do you think interacting with friends and peers improves your quality of life?

Communication researchers provide volumes of evidence demonstrating how communication is responsible for the way we establish, maintain, and end our relationships. Many researchers in family communication, for instance, have identified good communication as the single best predictor of satisfaction in marriage.[6] Other researchers suggest that the way we interact during conflict is perhaps the most powerful determinant of the satisfaction and quality of our relationships.[7] These researchers propose that learning how to manage conflict—an important set of interpersonal communication skills—can lead us to form stronger, more satisfying relationships. As we will explore extensively through this text, and particularly in Chapter 10, communication is central to the quality of our relationships.

Quality of Physical Health

Although you probably don't think much about it, the quality of your communication and the relationships developed through it also greatly affects the quality of your physical health. Have you ever noticed that when you're really stressed out because you are having an intense fight with your spouse, or when you're feeling lonely because you have just had a falling-out with a dear friend, you tend to get sick more easily or experience signs of physical fatigue or illness? This is not necessarily all in your head. According to researchers who study the relationship between our social connections and our physical well-being, the quality of our relationships and interactions plays a significant role in the quality of our physical health at all ages. For instance, if you are widowed or divorced you are significantly more likely to experience medical problems like heart disease, cancer, and pneumonia, and suffer from clinical depression, than if you are married.[8] Further, researchers report that people who are lonely (including middle-aged women who are childless) tend to die before others who enjoy a satisfying network of family and friends.[9] Other researchers found that people who live with a romantic partner take fewer sick days and were overall less likely to have health problems than those who live alone.[10] Researchers who study the connection between intimacy and health conclude that being isolated is as great a health risk as smoking, being obese, or having high blood pressure.[11] Even the survival rate for women with breast cancer has been shown to increase for women who receive social support from group therapy and friends and family.[12]

Simply put, the quality of our lives, our relationships, and even our health is intimately dependent on our abilities and experiences as communicators. Learning about the processes of interpersonal communication can lead you to a better and healthier life filled with more satisfying and long-term relationships.

The Interpersonal Communication Process

Our interest in this text is specific to one particular type of human communication: interpersonal communication. Before we explain what distinguishes interpersonal from other kinds of human communication, let us review the basic process of communication itself. This basic process serves as the foundation for all types of human communication, including interpersonal communication.

Human communication is the process by which people create and share meaning. When we want to communicate, we create a message we hope will be understood by others. Through the sending of that message and the feedback we receive from the other person or people (Was the message understood? Does the person need more detail? Do follow-up questions indicate interest in the conversation?), we are sharing meaning with others.

All communication begins with meaning. The **meaning** is the message or idea that one person is sharing with another as well as the interpretation of that message by the other person. We express meaning in many and varied ways. We can do it with words, with gestures, through eye contact, in writing, or by the way we dress or look. The process of creating and sharing meaning is ongoing and complex. The word *process* itself means "change," or something that is not static. Communication is definitely a process that is dynamic, never-ending, and constantly changing.

Models of the Communication Process

The way we think about the communication process has changed quite dramatically over the last 50 years.[13] It is helpful to see how, because this evolution reveals a great deal about the nature of interpersonal communication in particular. As you read, think about how you would answer the questions "What is communication?" and "What does communication look like?" Next, we explore how our understanding of communication has changed and improved by examining three models that have evolved over time in our field: from the action model, to the interaction model, to the current transaction model that best represents the communication process.

    Communication as Action. The **communication as action model** views communication as a one-way process.[14] One person creates a message and sends it to another. Think of throwing a ball to another person.[15] The ball is the message and you are the source, throwing the ball and hoping the other person catches it. This model, often called the linear model, is very simple and looks like this:

Figure 1.1   The Action Model

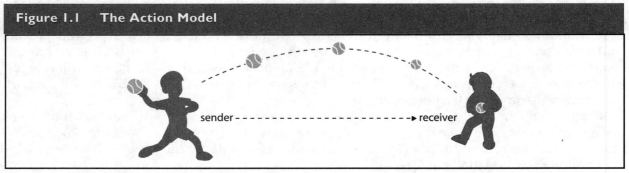

    Later communication theorists realized that more is going on in communication than one person sending a message to another. What the other person does with the ball once he or she receives it is an important part of the process too. Thus, the interaction view of communication evolved next.

    Communication as Interaction. The **communication as interaction model** adds to the action model described above.[16] Viewing communication as interaction recognizes that the person receiving the message responds by sending another message back.[17] Think of a game of catch, in which one person throws the ball, and the other person receives it and tosses it back. The interaction model looks like this:

Figure 1.2   The Interaction Model

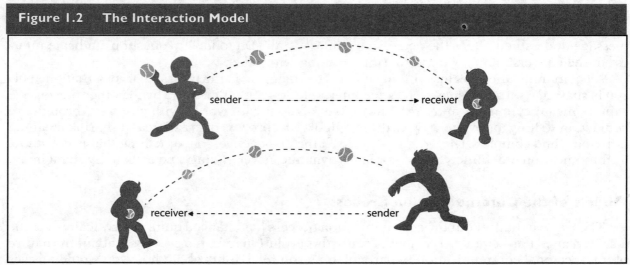

You can see that both participants take turns being speaker and listener, or sender and receiver.

But what other activities occur in the communication process that the interaction model fails to depict? Take a moment right now and see whether you can sketch a model that amplifies the interaction model just a bit and takes into account more complexity in the communication process.

Communication as Transaction. You were right if you decided that the interaction model does not take into account the fact that people are often speaking and listening to multiple messages at one time! The **communication as transaction model** views communication as a transaction, or a process in which the sending and receiving of messages between multiple people is continuous, simultaneous, and unavoidable.[18] In the transactional model, the elements of the communication process are all interdependent, never independent from one another. As an example, read this conversation between you and a friend, which might take place in the span of three minutes:

> *You see your friend approaching on what appears to be a new bike. As he nears, and at the very same time you are saying, "Hey, great bike," your friend smiles, indicating he's pleased to see you and pleased that you recognize his new bike. He says, "Cool, eh?" while he is looking at your new haircut and thinking about where he'll grab lunch. While he's doing all that, he nods a greeting to an acquaintance walking by and points down the street while saying, "Let's grab lunch down there at the bagel café." Noticing that you're holding a juice smoothie that he realizes is your lunch, he moves right along without waiting for an answer: "Oh, you're probably not going to lunch." As he finishes his sentence you nod your head in agreement and shrug your shoulders, then say as he finishes his sentence, "Darn. It would be great to get together for lunch. Maybe next time . . . ?" As you talk, you notice your professor coming down the street and quickly try to appear organized, shuffling to put the book for her class on top of those you're holding. As she walks by, you interrupt your conversation for a moment and smile while holding up the text with a funny grin and raised eyebrows. She gives a gesture of approval, a slight laugh, and a smile, saying, "Nice to see you, and your book, Jill. Happy studying!" Back to your friend, you say, "Yeah, maybe next time. . . ."*

Viewing communication as a transaction recognizes that in every conversation people are simultaneously sending and receiving multiple messages and that all parts of the process are interdependent. *Interdependence* means that changes in one part of the process produce changes in others. Each part of the conversation above is connected to all others. For instance, the observation of the smoothie changes the invitation to lunch. The observation of the professor changes the nonverbal stance and the message being created by the student. The perception by the one friend about the new haircut of the other might generate other topics of conversation or affect the perception of one or both parties. The same is true for the friend who verbally acknowledged the "cool" new bike of the other. Each of these aspects of the interaction is interdependent. As a transactional process, there were also multiple messages being created continuously and simultaneously. How many messages were being created and shared in the interaction you just read? We should be able to count well over 25, all taking place in a matter of minutes. If we had actually been present for the conversation, we could have counted a couple of hundred sources of meaning and messages!

To continue our metaphor of the ball game, both people in a transaction are fielding many balls that are flying all over the room. We catch some balls, miss many that fly right by, maybe get hit on the head by one or two, and return some to the other person immediately. We would be throwing a number of balls simultaneously as some are being tossed our way and even intercepting a number of balls unintentionally that were not being "sent" our way. We would have to reach to catch some, dive to field others, and by no means be aware of all the literally thousands of balls that are filling the room. Both people are throwing, catching, missing, dodging, and retrieving balls at the same time. Although no metaphor or model captures a complex process like that of human communication perfectly, the ball metaphor begins to give you the idea that as a transactional process, human communication is a complex process of interdependent parts where messages are being shared continuously and simultaneously.

In even the shortest communication exchanges, multiple messages are being created and exchanged. How many potential messages are being shared and created just in the nonverbal communication of this pair?

Messages are everywhere, and they are verbal and nonverbal. Everything is part of the transaction process, from what you are saying, wearing, carrying, and riding to where you are looking, what you are doing with your hands and eyes, and even what you *don't* say (silence communicates!). (See Figure 1.3.)

Figure 1.3   The Transactional Model

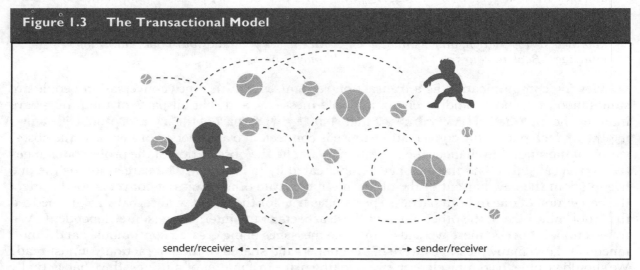

sender/receiver ◀ - - - - - - - - - - - - - - - - - - ▶ sender/receiver

The transactional model is the one we will use as the basis for all our discussions of the interpersonal communication process in this text (see Figure 1.4 for a comparison of all three models). As you will see, there is much to discover about the seemingly simple yet very complex process of creating and sharing meaning.

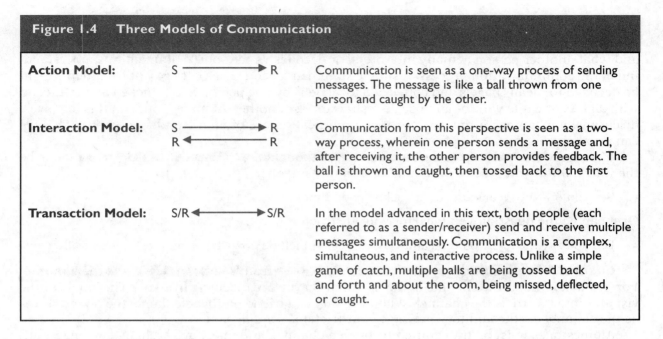

Figure 1.4   Three Models of Communication

Action Model:	S ⟶ R	Communication is seen as a one-way process of sending messages. The message is like a ball thrown from one person and caught by the other.
Interaction Model:	S ⟶ R R ⟵ R	Communication from this perspective is seen as a two-way process, wherein one person sends a message and, after receiving it, the other person provides feedback. The ball is thrown and caught, then tossed back to the first person.
Transaction Model:	S/R ⟷ S/R	In the model advanced in this text, both people (each referred to as a sender/receiver) send and receive multiple messages simultaneously. Communication is a complex, simultaneous, and interactive process. Unlike a simple game of catch, multiple balls are being tossed back and forth and about the room, being missed, deflected, or caught.

The Interpersonal Communication Model

Now that you have an understanding of how communication is viewed from a transactional perspective, it is important to look further at the model and add the basic components that are present in all communication interactions. After we detail the components of a model of communication here, we can explain exactly what distinguishes interpersonal communication from other kinds of communication. Note before beginning that all the elements we mention are interdependent, never independent of each other.

Take a moment to look at the visual model (Figure 1.5) of the communication process, and try to come up with an example of each component. Then compare your examples with the explanations we offer below.

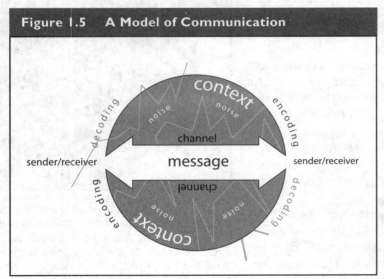

Figure 1.5   A Model of Communication

Participants. Participants in any communication exchange are simultaneously **senders**, those who create messages, and **receivers**, those who interpret messages. Their primary role is to encode and decode messages. **Encoding** is the process of creating a message to convey an idea, feeling, or thought. Typically, we encode a message with words, nonverbal behavior, or both. The other person then decodes the message.

Decoding is the process of interpreting the encoded message.

As you might guess, the difference between what one person is trying to explain, or encode, and what another person actually interprets, or decodes, is the source of much misunderstanding in the communication process. A simple statement encoded as "Let's go out for lunch" might be decoded to mean "bagels and coffee at a local deli" by one person and "chicken and fettuccini with a glass of white wine at an upscale restaurant" by another. At many points in this text, we'll discuss why meanings in interpersonal communication are often misunderstood and what we can do about it.

Messages. The **message** is the idea, feeling, or thought that is encoded and decoded. It can be the information you type in an e-mail to a family member:

See you on New Year's Day for a rockin' good time! :)

Or it can be the question you have for your instructor:

Did you say the test would be all essay, or does it include other types of questions as well?

Channel. The path through which a message travels from source to receiver is the **channel**. For instance, what is the channel of the information you are receiving from us? This book, or the visual printed word, is the channel. When you talk to a friend on the telephone, the phone serves as the channel for the auditory message your friend is sending you.

All messages must be transmitted through a channel, and many are exchanged using multiple channels. When we communicate face-to-face, for instance, there are many channels at work: the visual channel (facial expressions and body movements), the auditory channel (the voices and words of each person), the tactile or touch channel (the touch of the other person who grabs our arm in excitement), and the olfactory channel (the smell of shampoo from our child's freshly washed hair).

With many new technologies available for communication, such as computers and wireless systems, the channels of communication have become quite diverse. E-mail, voice mail, videophone, instant messaging, and other media are channels that mediate our communication with others.

Feedback. **Feedback** is any response to a message. When you ask your friend how he likes your new haircut, you are asking for feedback on your message. When you turn in a report to your boss and she attaches a note to it saying, "Great work! Just make the few changes I've marked," you have received feedback. When you look at your child with a smile and say, "I love you," and immediately get a big hug in return, you have gotten feedback for your loving message.

Feedforward is information we provide about messages before they are sent, such as "This might sound a little confusing, but . . ." or "Get a load of this news!" Because senders and receivers are simultaneously both creating and receiving messages, it is often hard to determine whether

In what ways have new communication technologies changed the channels through which you communicate with others? How many different channels of communication have you used just today that rely on new or evolving communication technologies?

something is feedback (a response to a message) or a new message. However, for practical purposes, feedback tends to be connected in some way to another message and serves as a response to a previous message. Often we don't realize a message is feedback because it takes place a long time after our original message was encoded. Feedback can be intentional, such as the approval your mother seeks after she gives you your birthday gift, or unintentional, such as when you fall asleep during a boring class lecture.

Noise. Think for a moment of all the possible ways that the objects, ideas, and people in our world can interfere with receiving or sending a message: noise from an air conditioner, words or data in the message that you don't understand, the difficult accent or poor handwriting of the sender of the message, a detail you've forgotten from a phone conversation, or your own fatigue, hunger, or other physical distraction. Each of these is an example of what we call **noise**, or the elements in our environment that interfere with the accurate receiving or sending of a message.

All communication takes place amid noise. Early communication researchers realized that noise exists in all communication and takes many forms, including physical, psychological, physiological, and semantic.[19] *Physical noise* includes the loud sounds of traffic, the visual barrier of a large centerpiece on the table between you and your guest, the offensive body odor of the person trying to sell you insurance, or the wheelchair your friend uses (many people tend to focus on the wheelchair instead of on the message). *Psychological noise* includes any kind of mental distraction interfering with the message, such as thinking about how busy you are when you are supposed to be listening to your friend, or making a mental note about an assignment you just remembered while talking on the phone to a friend. Many people even drive or check e-mail while talking on the phone. Each can be psychological noise. *Physiological noise* includes all those aspects of our physical self that might interfere with us fully paying attention to a message, such as the headache we have as a result of our spring allergies, our partial hearing loss, or the hunger that is causing us to not fully pay attention to the message. Finally, it is possible to be distracted by *semantic noise*, which is anything in the actual words that distracts us or interferes with the message. For instance, someone from another culture who uses a word incorrectly creates a kind of semantic noise.

As we will discuss in later chapters, noise can create a great deal of problems in interpersonal situations when it goes unnoticed, is misperceived, or is assumed not to interfere with the success of our exchanges. For now, keep in mind that it is always helpful to reduce the interference that noise can create in any communication interaction.

Context. Finally, all communication takes place in a context. **Context** includes all the physical and psychological elements of the environment in which communication takes place. Think about the difference between greeting friends at a party and greeting the same people at a funeral. You can immediately see that the context greatly influences the communication that will take place. Although most people think of context simply as the physical surroundings affecting the communication, context actually can be physical, cultural, social-psychological, or temporal. **Physical context** includes everything in the physical environment where communication takes place, including the number of people in an interaction. The funeral home in the above example is a type of physical context, as is an electronic bulletin board where thousands of people might read your message. The public context of the bulletin board is very different from the context of a private e-mail sent to a friend, and we communicate differently—or at least we should—depending on physical context.

The **cultural context** is the way the norms, rules, or beliefs of a culture influence communication. In some cultures, for instance, the less you say verbally, the more you are judged as mature and wise. In such a cultural context, if you attempt to talk frequently or offer detailed verbal explanations of your thoughts and ideas in an effort to earn the respect of others, you will be confused and disappointed.

Another type of context is the **social-psychological context**, including such elements as the relationship between communicators and their thought processes. We must consider the status of others, their current thoughts and experiences, as well as our relationship to them when we communicate. For instance, would you use the same tone of voice and words when you talk with your supervisor versus a friend? Would you communicate in a similar way with your grandmother and a 13 year old? How would you monitor your words, choice of topic, and tone of voice when talking with a friend who recently suffered a great personal loss (the death of a child) versus a friend who recently experienced a great personal triumph (graduating with honors)? In each of these examples, the social-psychological context is an important consideration in the overall communication context.

The **temporal context** includes the sequence of events and the timing of an interaction. The temporal context includes, for example, how long it takes someone to provide you with feedback on your new outfit, or the length of time between when you apply for a job and receive a call of rejection or a call inviting you for an interview. The temporal context also takes into account when messages are sequenced in a larger set of events. For example, if your friend Myra discloses information about her health to you and then receives a call later that day from a mutual friend who is concerned about her health, Myra might be suspicious of your trustworthiness because of the timing of such messages. Further, you might choose to not share your own good health news with Myra immediately after she shares with you the bad news regarding her own health.

All communication exists in some kind of context; the context of our communication always affects our messages and the way our meanings are interpreted. When considering how context is affecting your interactions, be sure to consider all the possible factors that might be impacting the message (see Box 1.1).

Box 1.1

Skill Builder

Now that you are familiar with the basic process of communication, the model of communication, and all the components of the communication process, see whether you can apply this model to an interpersonal interaction you had within the last day.

1. Think about and identify an interpersonal interaction you had within the last day.
2. Write a brief paragraph in which you describe who was involved in the interaction, where the interaction took place, what was said, and anything else you perceive as important to the interaction.
3. Use the model of communication depicted in Figure 1.5 to diagram your own interpersonal communication interaction. Label all the parts of the model using your own interaction as the components. You will find that for many aspects of the model, there is a lot to write. For instance, when you think about your interaction, you probably are able to identify more than one kind of noise, many different aspects of the context, and a   ☞

variety of messages that were exchanged. If you selected an interaction with more than two people, the model will be very complex (don't worry if it looks a little messy).

4. Share your model with others in the class and discuss the following: Was drawing the model easy or difficult to do? What does diagramming one simple interpersonal interaction reveal to you about the communication process? Do you think you were able to identify all aspects of the interaction? If you asked the other person(s) in the interaction to diagram the same interaction, do you think your diagrams would be identical? Why, or why not?

Defining Interpersonal Communication

What distinguishes interpersonal communication from other communication? What does it mean to communicate interpersonally? In the past, some researchers identified interpersonal communication as happening only whenever *two* people interacted. If we accept this definition, then a conversation between you and two or three of your best friends would not be interpersonal. We do believe that most often interpersonal communication takes place between two people, but not always. Other scholars have suggested that interpersonal communication happens only in intimate contexts, such as between romantic couples. However, this too would exclude your conversation with a best friend, as well as conversations with many other significant people in your life.

Scholars in the area of interpersonal communication have defined interpersonal communication in a variety of ways. For instance, some scholars suggest that "Interpersonal Communication is a distinctive form of human communication that occurs when you interact with another person and mutually influence each other, usually for the purpose of managing relationships,"[20] or that "interpersonal communication is a selective, systemic, unique, and ongoing process of transaction between people who reflect and build personal knowledge of one another and create shared meanings."[21] Although these are two perfectly acceptable definitions of interpersonal communication, we believe our definition provides a richer and more complete understanding of what interpersonal communication is. As we highlighted at the opening of the chapter, we define interpersonal communication as *the process of creating and sharing meaning between people who are interdependent, have a relationship between them, and have some knowledge about each other*. Let's look in depth at the key features of this definition.

To be interdependent means that each person has an impact or influence on the other, to some degree. For instance, in an interpersonal communication context, what one person says influences what the other will say, even if not directly. If you are the clerk at a grocery store, a comment directed to you from a rude customer will impact you and how you respond not only to that person, but to other customers as well. You and that customer also have a relationship between you that is based on the social roles that each of you has: you as the clerk, he as the customer. You and your best friend probably engage in interpersonal communication all the time; you each influence the other each time you talk about the mundane aspects of your daily lives, and your relationship is obviously one of friends.

To be considered interpersonal communication, therefore, two or more people must be creating and sharing meaning and interacting in an interdependent way, with some relationship between them. The relationship need not be highly "personal" or "intimate" but does exist at least to some degree. For instance, consider the following very different kinds of relationships: between a boss and employee, between the mail carrier and homeowner, between the city employee and the person applying for a driver's license, between you and your best friend, between you and your new baby, between a mother and her teenage son, between the abusive husband and his wife, between the nurse and the patient, between two individuals who work at the convenience store together, and between the student and professor. Each represents a "relationship" in which interpersonal communication takes place.

The last part of our definition suggests that to be considered interpersonal communication, the persons involved have a degree of knowledge about each other. We interact with people every day. But do we interact with all people in the same way? Of course not. Do you talk to the person from whom you are purchasing an airline ticket in the same way, or about the same topics, as when you talk to your spouse, partner, or other loved one? Do you talk to your mother and your teacher in the same way or about the same things? Do you talk to your friends the same way you talk with your soccer coach? Each of these questions represents a type of interaction that is based on a different kind of knowledge of another individual. Each is interpersonal communication, but not necessarily to the same degree.

We believe that an important aspect of defining communication as interpersonal is recognizing *how* we interact with people and the *information* we use to guide those interactions. Although many different kinds of interpersonal communication exist, they require and reflect different degrees of "personalness" depending on the kind of information we have about another person. According to communication scholars, we can interact with people based on social, cultural, or personal information about them.[22] Imagine these three ideas on a continuum (see Box 1.2).[23]

Box 1.2

Continuum of Communication—Levels of Knowledge

Social Knowledge ————————————— Cultural Knowledge ————————————— Interpersonal Knowledge

---

With the majority of the people we see on a daily basis, we interact solely on the most basic information, usually regarding the social roles they play. Think about your day today. A typical day for one of our students might be to get ready for class, stop by the local college café for some coffee, maybe grab a book from the library, purchase a new pen and a birthday card at the bookstore, go to class, head to work at a restaurant, and then take a bus back to campus for an evening class. For much of that student's day, he or she would be interacting with people based on what we call **social-level knowledge**, somewhere on the left side of the continuum. The people selling the coffee, serving breakfast, working at the bookstore, teaching the class, working in food service, and driving the bus are each fulfilling a social role. Although we recognize that each person is a human being, we don't care to know much about that person or interact with him or her beyond the role they play. Engaging in a lengthy or intimate conversation with the checkout clerk at the grocery store is not efficient for either party. Our communication is guided by our knowledge of the social role, but not much else. Hence, communication with such people might be interpersonal, but not to the same degree as would be interactions based on even more personal information about another person.

In the middle of the continuum, you see that the next level of information we have about others is what we call cultural. Although at one time information about one's cultural identity might have been less specific or personal than information based on one's social roles, in our global world today we believe that knowledge of one's cultural identity, background, and worldview is more personal and informative than that of one's social features or social roles. When we interact with people based on **cultural-level knowledge**, we tend to connect with others who have cultural identities we perceive as similar to our own. For instance, on the first day of class you might have carefully selected your seat in the room based on who you saw when you entered. Being a

nontraditional student in your mid-50s, you noticed what you thought might be another person about your age and selected a seat next to that person. You used cultural-level information related to age to guide your connection. The social-level information would have been seeing the room full of people waiting for class to begin as students; using the sometimes noticeable cultural features of others—age, ethnicity, gender—moves us along the continuum to where we rely on cultural-level information. We tend to interact with those who appear to be most like us culturally. Communicating with others based on cultural-level information allows us to communicate in a more interpersonal way than that based on broader categories of social information.

We often communicate with others based only on knowledge of their social role. Have you noticed a difference in the quality and content of your communication when your interactions are based on social-level knowledge versus personal-level knowledge? For instance, how does the amount of knowledge you have about another affect how you would communicate with the clerk at the store versus your friend at your apartment?

Finally, communication becomes the most interpersonal when we have more personal information about a person, or have what we can call **personal-level knowledge**. When you know what your friend likes to eat, what topics will cause tension in your family, and what your spouse is thinking before she even says it, you have knowledge of another that is personal. These are the interactions that fall at the far right of the continuum. You interact with one another *as people*, not merely based on cultural assumptions or social roles. Such knowledge most often develops over time and is constantly in process. When we interact with others using psychological or personal-level information, we are communicating in the most interpersonal way.

We should note that movement along the continuum from social to cultural to interpersonal can happen very rapidly, in a matter of one brief interaction, or might be relatively stable, never leaving one area. Also, our interactions might fall somewhere between points on the continuum or move between points during our exchanges. None of our interpersonal communication can fit neatly into any one category, so interpretation of the continuum is fluid and dynamic. It is important, however, to begin your study of interpersonal communication with an idea of what kinds of interpersonal communication exist and what distinguishes our conversations and interactions as more or less personal. The continuum reveals that interpersonal communication is a matter of degrees, and that interpersonal communication takes place based on varying levels of knowledge about other individuals. As you explore the many concepts in this text and discuss them in your class, keep this continuum and the definition of interpersonal communication in mind.

Key Principles of Interpersonal Communication

Now that you have some insight into what interpersonal communication is and the basic components of all communication situations, we can discuss some key principles for understanding the actual processes of interpersonal communication. These principles will serve as an introduction to many of the concepts we will cover in this book, as well as give you some immediately practical information about your own interpersonal experiences. We will briefly explain how and why interpersonal communication is (1) complex, (2) irreversible and inevitable, (3) rule-based, (4) always related to culture and power, and (5) changing with technology.

Interpersonal Communication Is Complex

Many students think that because we communicate every day, and because we've been doing it all our lives, the topic of interpersonal communication must be simple. However, in reality it is highly complex. The study of interpersonal communication seeks to understand the dynamics of conversations and the nature of meanings and symbols. It seeks to explain why every message in an interaction really has two kinds of meaning, and why there are actually six people in every two-person conversation. Let's explore a few of these complexities here, with more about each of these topics to follow in later chapters.

When we communicate with others, we rely on symbols to help us share meaning. A **symbol** is a representation of something else with many possible meanings and interpretations. Language, for instance, is a complex system of symbols. The word *book* is a symbol we have created to represent a set of pages and a cover with words printed on them providing some kind of information. *Book* has no direct relationship or resemblance to the object it represents; it simply refers to that object. In fact, most symbols do not resemble the objects they represent, and it is not necessary that they do.

The fact that we rely on symbols to communicate makes communication complex and the potential for misunderstanding great. You can probably think of many examples when someone misinterpreted a symbol or word you used. When you tell your friend she looks "phat" (a slang word for "looking good"), she might think you meant she looks "fat" (overweight) and be offended by your comment. One person who says, "I love you," might have a very different meaning for the symbol "love" than the person hearing the message. You tell your parents you will be home "early" only to discover that "early" means midnight to your parents and 2 a.m. to you. The nature of symbols is just one of the ways that interpersonal communication is complex.

Interpersonal communication becomes even more complex when you consider what one communication theorist[24] suggests: In any two-person communication situation, six "people" (or perceptions) actually take part (see Box 1.3). They are:

1. The person you view yourself to be

2. The other person as you see him or her

3. The person that you believe the other person sees in you

4. The other person as he or she sees him or herself

5. The person the other party sees in you

6. The other person as he or she believes you see him or her

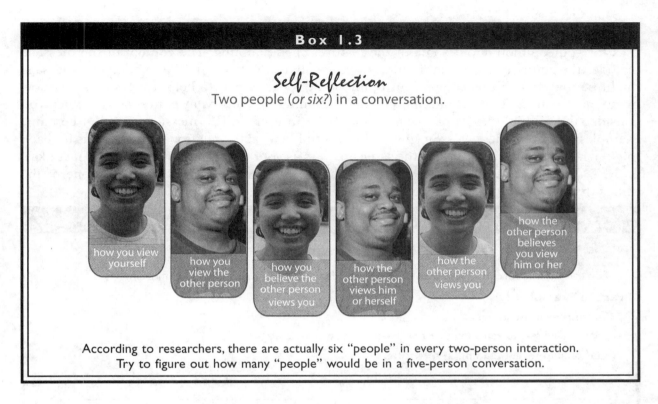

Box 1.3

Self-Reflection
Two people (*or six?*) in a conversation.

how you view yourself

how you view the other person

how you believe the other person views you

how the other person views him or herself

how the other person views you

how the other person believes you view him or her

According to researchers, there are actually six "people" in every two-person interaction.
Try to figure out how many "people" would be in a five-person conversation.

In any conversation, we construct multiple views, like the six above, of others and ourselves. Our interpersonal communication is greatly affected and often limited by the views we have of others and ourselves in a conversation. We will explore concepts of perception as they impact our interpersonal interactions more in Chapter 3.

Finally, interpersonal communication is complex because in every conversation, there are always two types of meaning.[25] For instance, instead of questioning the *meaning* of your father's comments, you actually need to consider the *meanings* of his message. The first is the **content meaning**, or literal meaning. It is usually contained in the actual information communicated. When your father says, "Be home by 10 p.m.," the content meaning is that you should arrive home at or before ten o'clock. Content-level meaning is most often verbal, and is usually easy to determine if you share the same language as the other person.

The second kind of meaning in every interaction is called the **relationship meaning**, or emotional meaning. Relationship meaning reveals the nature of the relationship between the people communicating and is the part of the message that tells us how to understand the content message. For instance, if a father says to his daughter, "Be home by 10 p.m.," what does the relationship meaning say? It says the parent is in charge and has the right to tell his daughter what time he would like her home. Imagine your roommate saying to you, "Be home by 10 p.m." You would understand the content meaning similarly but you would know that the comment must be a joke because, based on your relationship, your roommate does not have the right to tell you when to arrive home. The relationship meaning in this case, because the message is in jest, reveals your status as peers.

Imagine another example: Your friend calls to tell you all about her new kitchen plans and asks for your opinion about some of the features she's planning. The content of the message includes the actual questions and literal message about the kitchen. The relationship message might be that your friend values your opinion and looks to you to help her. It's amazing how much more you can understand interpersonal dilemmas and everyday conversations when you consider the multiple levels of meaning that exist in every single message. Box 1.4 contains examples of content messages. See if you can determine what the relationship meanings for each might be. See if you come up with the same answers as your classmates. If you don't, that's okay. As we'll discover, relationship meanings can be interpreted in many ways. That's one of the things that makes interpersonal communication so complex.

Box 1.4

Skill Builder

For each of the following statements, determine the potential relationship-level meaning.

Practice Example #1:

Content-level meaning:

A close friend says to you: "You sure have been going out a lot lately."

Relationship-level meaning(s) might be:

_____

_____

Practice Example #2:

Content-level meaning:

Your boss says to you: "You'll be at the meeting today, right?"

Relationship-level meaning is probably:

_____

_____

Practice Example #3:

Content-level meaning:

Your significant other says to you: "I learned something at work today that I want to share with you, but you can't tell anyone. It's highly confidential."

Relationship-level meaning(s) could be:

_____

_____

Practice Example #4:

Content-level meaning:

Your mother says to you: "Oh. I see you decided to wear the purple skirt for your big presentation today."

Possible relationship-level meanings:

_____

_____

Interpersonal Communication Is Irreversible and Inevitable

If you've ever baked a cake or some cookies, you know that the process is irreversible. Once you mix the eggs with the butter, flour, and sugar, and bake it in the oven, it is impossible to separate all the ingredients and get them back to their original form. The same is true of our interpersonal communication. *All communication is irreversible.*

Once a message has been communicated, even if we don't like it or wish we hadn't said it, we can't completely take it back. We might try to explain, apologize, clarify, restate, or detract our statement, but we can't fully reverse the process. Once a message is "out there," it cannot be taken back, only commented on further. When the judge instructs the jurors in a criminal trial, "Please disregard the comments of the witness," we know that they have indeed already heard what was said. When your child begins to tell you about getting in trouble at school, and then says, "Oh, forget that I mentioned that. It wasn't a big deal," you might try to forget, but what was said cannot be taken back.

Communication is also inevitable. *Communication is inevitable* because we are communicating all the time. Sometimes we communicate intentionally and mindfully: We yell out the window to ask our neighbor to turn the stereo down, smile at an acquaintance across the room to say "hello" during a lecture, or ask a question in class about the material being covered. These are messages we intend to send.

But even when we aren't intentionally sending messages, we are still communicating. As communication scholars say: We cannot *not* communicate.[26] You might not mean to, but when you fall asleep or choose not to participate in class, you are communicating something (boredom, lack of interest, disrespect) to your professor. Your luxury automobile is communicating something about your personal and/or socioeconomic situation to others, whether you intend to or not. Your silence in the presence of another individual communicates a message, whether it is shyness, anger, or lack of interest. We communicate all the time. It is inevitable. Being aware of this principle is important to learning more about interpersonal communication.

Interpersonal Communication Involves Rules

When you first sit down to play a game, you most likely ask, "What are the rules?" Rules also exist to guide our interpersonal interactions. Communication rules define the appropriate behaviors expected of ourselves and others. For example, you likely had many rules in your family about what, with whom, and how you could talk with others. You probably learned at an early age that you shouldn't interrupt when others are speaking, that expressing anger is not allowed, and that topics such as money or sex are taboo and should not be discussed. All of our interpersonal interactions are based on rules. Without rules to guide our interactions, most of them would feel random, unstructured, bothersome, and unpredictable. Instead, most of our interactions with others are rather easy, enjoyable, and somewhat predictable, and take a similar form.

Most communication rules are implicit, or not clearly stated. For many people in the United States, for instance, an implicit communication rule is to not stand so close to another individual while talking that you can smell his or her breath. Another implicit rule is to allow one person to finish talking before the other begins. Although you were probably never told these rules explicitly—there aren't signs in buildings or on sidewalks that tell you what distance to stand from others or to take turns while talking—you have learned these rules by observing others.

Some rules are explicitly stated. An example of an explicit communication rule might be one in your family such as "Don't use swear words" or "Don't talk back to your parents." These rules have been stated clearly and explicitly, and have been repeatedly told to you. Explicitly stated rules are usually easier to follow simply because we know what they are.

All communication rules are heavily culture-bound, which means that they are specific to particular cultural or co-cultural groups. In many cultures, for example, a communication rule suggests that touching someone you don't know is appropriate and expected; too much distance between communicators is offensive and a sign of disrespect. In other cultures and co-cultures, the use of verbal insults is not offensive, but rather is a form of verbal playfulness and friendship. When we consider communication rules, we must always consider their cultural context.

Rules govern all aspects of our relationships and interpersonal communication in ways that are not simple or obvious. For instance, a complex set of rules develops between two people in an interpersonal relationship, creating a private culture in the relationship. We will discuss the idea of relational cultures at length in Chapter 10. Over time, and based on shared history and experience, couples often develop their own private set of rules that guide everything they do. Their expectations for honesty on some subjects and secrecy on others reflect their jointly constructed rules (See Box 1.5). The private nicknames they use for each other reflect rules about how they will address each other in their relationship and rules about what their relationship should be like. Further, rules about intimacy or friendships outside the relationship are learned over time and jointly negotiated over the course of a relationship. In all ways, rules guide not only our interpersonal communication, but our interpersonal relationships as well.

Box 1.5

Practical Research

What types of information do you keep secret from others? What types of information does your family keep secret? Many people associate keeping secrets with something negative in a relationship. However, according to Anita Vangelisti, a leading researcher in the area of family and interpersonal communication, secrets are a natural and important part of any interpersonal relationship, especially in families.[27] In her research, Vangelisti found that secrets serve a variety of positive functions in the family, such as helping family members form bonds, protecting the family from disapproval and stress, ensuring privacy within the family, and preventing others from taking advantage of family members. According to her findings, family secrets tend to fall into three categories.

Types of Family Secrets

Taboo Topics: These are secrets about issues or activities often regarded as taboo. For example, "My aunt had an affair with her best friend's husband many years ago," or "It's a secret from my grandmother that I'm gay."

Rule Violations: These secrets hide activities that break family rules. For instance: "My sister lives with her boyfriend and my parents don't want people to know," and "I am not a virgin and haven't been since age 16."

Conventional Secrets: These secrets contain information that families do not necessarily view as "wrong" but feel is inappropriate to discuss with some people. For example: "My sister's health problems were caused by a man she had been dating," and "I kept my grades secret all the time because they were not great (unlike my brother's, which were awesome)."

Family members quickly learn the rules that guide what secrets are kept and with whom one can share them. Do you have and keep secrets in some of your close personal relationships or in your family? After reading these findings, can you identify what kind of secrets they are and what functions they might serve in your relationship?

Interpersonal Communication Is Always Affected by Culture and Power

All interpersonal communication is affected by, and a reflection of, the cultural rules and experiences of the communicators. Further, all interpersonal communication is related to issues of power. You might be thinking that of course *some* interactions are affected by culture and issues of power, such as when two people come from different cultural or co-cultural groups (a person of Hmong origin talking with a friend who is African American), or when one person has a position of higher status than the other (a teacher interacting with her student). We contend that even when it is not obvious or explicit, every one of our interpersonal interactions involves power and culture, and being aware of how these structures work in our interactions is extremely important in becoming more effective interpersonal communicators. We have dedicated the next chapter entirely to showing how power and culture, as well as technology, represent defining elements of human existence and thus are central to interpersonal interactions.

Interpersonal Communication Is Changing With Technology

Chapter 2 deals with how cultural systems, power structures, and advancing technologies are changing the way we communicate interpersonally. In order to become the most effective and competent interpersonal communicators possible, we need to think broadly about the way our environment—everything from the way we do our grocery shopping to the way we maintain relationships—is being changed and affected by advances in technology.

You might be tempted to think that only certain communication technologies like e-mail, cellular phones, and the Internet affect our daily interactions. However, technologies of all kinds have the potential to alter not only the methods by which we communicate, but also the way we view relationships, the time we invest in our interactions, and the expectations we have of others and their interpersonal communication choices. For instance, in chat rooms or newsgroups, *flaming* is a negative or hostile response to what someone else has written. Would the same response be acceptable in a face-to-face conversation? How might we respond differently to flaming in writing and flaming in person?

What used to be a handwritten letter is now a quick e-mail; what used to be a long-distance phone call is now a voice message made via cell phone from the car; what used to be a birthday card sent through the mail is now an electronic message linking you to an Internet site where your birthday card sings, dances, and costs almost nothing. How are these changing our interpersonal communication? How are changes in technology changing the very nature of relationships? These are just a few of the questions facing all of us as interpersonal communicators in an age of rapidly growing and changing communication and other technologies. Throughout this book, we will explore these questions and issues further.

The roles that culture, power, and technology play in all of our interactions are important to recognize. How has at least one of these variables played a role in a communication interaction you had today?

Preview of Remaining Chapters and Summary

We know that you're just beginning to explore the concepts of interpersonal communication, so we don't want to overwhelm you here in Chapter 1 with too many more concepts, models, or ideas. You'll have plenty of time to do that in the chapters to come! We do want to give you a quick idea of what you can expect as you read the rest of this text and explore the issues of interpersonal communication with your class. As mentioned, our next chapter will give you an in-depth look at how culture, power, and technology are issues central to all of our interpersonal communication and explain why we have chosen them as a framework for this text. You can expect to see us talk about these issues throughout every chapter in this text. As you will quickly see, each of these is related to all of the interpersonal concepts, from perception to nonverbal behavior, and from family relationships to professional relationships. We will also explore topics such as perception, listening, nonverbal communication, verbal communication and language, gender and communication, intimate and personal relationships, family relationships, relationships at work, and conflict in interpersonal relationships, just to name a few.

As you conclude this chapter, keep in mind the many points about interpersonal communication that we introduced here. We discussed what it means to engage in transactional communication—where each person affects and is affected by the others in the interaction, and where people interact in a complex, simultaneous process of creating and sharing meaning through the use of symbols. We also introduced the components of a model of interpersonal communication, including participants who engage in decoding and encoding, messages, the channels through which messages travel, feedback and feedforward, noise, and context. You should have a solid understanding of these concepts because each serves as a basis for many of the topics and concepts we will discuss in remaining chapters. As you read further in the book, keep in mind the definition of interpersonal communication we offer: *the process of creating and sharing meaning between people who are interdependent, have a relationship between them, and have some knowledge about each other.* Also, recall that interpersonal communication is complex, involves symbols and meanings, is irreversible and inevitable, is based on rules, is always affected by culture and power, and is changing with technology.

We close this chapter by offering explanations to the myths and truths that opened this chapter. Take a moment and look back to see if, after reading this chapter, your answers would be different. Hopefully you can not only easily identify the myths but you can also explain *why* each statement is true or not. Below are the answers and our brief explanations:

Myth: *The success or failure of interpersonal communication usually depends on the actions of one person in the interaction.* Why is this a myth?

Interpersonal communication is transactional and the result of the dynamic process between all people in the interaction.

Myth: *Because we do it all the time, interpersonal communication is something each of us probably knows quite a bit about.*

Interpersonal communication is complex, and understanding it does not occur automatically. Studying the theories and concepts of interpersonal communication can lead to greater awareness and competence as an interpersonal communicator.

Myth: Interpersonal communication is limited to communication between any two people. Why is this a myth?

Although interpersonal communication frequently is thought of and indeed often does take place in dyads, we define interpersonal communication by the kind of knowledge that participants have about one another, not solely the number of people involved in the interaction.

Myth: When someone sends a message to another person, communication has occurred. Why is this not true?

Communication is a more than just sending a message; it is a complex process of simultaneous sending and receiving of messages and meanings.

Myth: If I understand your meaning, I will be able to communicate effectively with you.

There are two levels of meaning in every message exchanged: a content level of meaning and a relationship level of meaning. To communicate effectively, both types of meaning must be considered, but in this case only the content level has been considered.

Truth: Communication cannot be reversed by "taking back" what you said.

Communication is irreversible; you might try to clarify, apologize, or explain further what you have said, but you can never fully undo or "take back" any meaning that has been shared.

Truth: Even if people don't intend to communicate, they might still be communicating a message. (For example, if you think my face looks angry, but I don't intend to communicate this to you, am I still communicating?)

Communication is inevitable; we are communicating even when we don't realize it or don't intend to communicate to others.

Key Terms

Channel	Meaning
Communication as action model	Message
Communication as interaction model	Myth
Communication as transaction model	Noise
Content meaning	Personal-level knowledge
Context	Physical context
Cultural context	Receiver
Cultural-level knowledge	Relationship meaning
Decoding	Sender
Encoding	Social-level knowledge
Feedback	Social-psychological context
Feedforward	Symbols
Human communication	Temporal context
Interpersonal communication	

Suggested Contemporary Readings

E. S. Caplan. "Challenging the mass-interpersonal communication dichotomy: Are we witnessing the emergence of an entirely new communication system?" *Electronic Journal of Communication* 11 (2001).

T. A. Morton and J. M. Duck. "Communication and health beliefs: Mass and interpersonal influences on perceptions of risk to self and others." *Communication Research* 28 (2001): 602–626.

M. E. Roloff and L. Anastasiou. "Interpersonal communication research: An overview." *Communication Yearbook* 24 (2001): 51–71.

A. M. Rubin and R. B. Rubin. "Interface of personal and mediated communication: Fifteen years later." *Electronic Journal of Communication* 11 (2001).

G. H. Stamp. "A qualitatively constructed interpersonal communication model: A grounded theory analysis." *Human Communication Research* 4 (1999): 531–547.

H. R. Walen and M. E. Lachman. "Social support and strain from partner, family, and friends: Costs and benefits for men and women in adulthood." *Journal of Social and Personal Relationships* 7 (2000): 5–30.

Chapter Activities

1. Use one of your college library's databases to locate articles related to health, communication, and relationships (use each as a keyword). What kind of articles did you find? How do they further your knowledge about the way interpersonal communication is related to the quality of your life and the quality of your health?

2. Reflect on the principle in this chapter that communication is inevitable. How often do you think we communicate without intending to? Have you ever experienced someone interpreting meaning from you that you did not intend to communicate? What happened? What are some of the messages you are unintentionally sending right now? Discuss this principle and your experiences of it with others in the class.

3. We rely on symbols to help us share meanings. Can you think of a time when someone used a slang word you didn't understand? Visit the Web site *http://www.ocf.berkeley.edu/~wrader/slang/* for a look at a dictionary of slang. Included here are hundreds of examples of slang words as well as their origins and definitions. Browse the Web and see whether you can find other examples of slang dictionaries. How do words as symbols serve as the basic tools for sharing meaning in communication?

4. Use a database at your library such as Infotrac or CommAbstracts and type in the words *technology* and *relationships*. Select one article that helps you understand the way that new technologies are changing the way we interact within all kinds of interpersonal relationships—from family to work, and from marriage to friendship. Summarize in a paragraph the article you select, and share it with a small group of people in class.

5. Select any conversation you have had with one other person in the last day or two. Try to identify the various content and relationship meanings in the messages shared. What did the relationship messages reveal about the relationship between you and that

person? How does being mindful of the relationship-level meaning in an interaction enhance your skills as an interpersonal communicator?

6. We believe that community-based learning is an important way for you to extend and apply your learning in this class. Community-based learning, or service learning, is an opportunity for you to provide a meaningful service to a community group or individual while enhancing your learning about interpersonal communication. Think about a community-based organization, such as a school, community center, or faith-based program, and spend time volunteering for that organization over the semester. While you do so, observe and note the ways that communication is transactional. To do so, here is your assignment: Keep a journal in which you apply the concepts in each chapter to the communication you observe and participate in while volunteering. After each time you volunteer, write in your journal about how you can apply at least three concepts from this chapter. For example, in your first journal entry you might write about the processes of decoding/encoding, feedback, and cultural-level knowledge. After the second time you volunteer, you might write in your journal about the ways you observed meaning, noise, and symbols at work in the interactions you experienced and/or witnessed. Doing this activity will not only make a positive difference in your community, but will also help you better understand the way interpersonal communication works in the world around you. ✦

Culture, Power, and Technology: Contemporary Issues in Interpersonal Communication

Contemporary Issues: Changing Lives Through the Power of Technology

Don Barrett is lead engineer in the U.S. Department of Education's Assistive Technology Program. Recently he tried to purchase software from a vendor over the Internet. By using his keyboard, he was able to type and use tabs to complete the online form. However, when the Web site required him to click on a "Submit" button, he was unable to complete his order. Why? Don is blind. His screen reader was able to identify all of the fields to fill out the form, but he couldn't see the mouse pointer to submit his order.

Don Barrett is a person with a disability, one of an estimated 60 million in the United States.[1] Advances in technology have allowed people with disabilities to communicate with others without the stigma that may arise in face-to-face interactions. Software companies have developed programs allowing people with disabilities to use computers more efficiently. For example, the visually impaired now have access to voice-activated computers, screen readers, text-to-speech tools, and screen magnifiers. New software programs continue to be developed allowing more people access to computer technologies. These companies realize that accommodating the needs of all people with disabilities brings greater productivity gains. Imagine how future advances in technology could enhance the communication abilities of the 42 million Americans with disabilities who are unemployed or underemployed.

Interpersonal communication, either face-to-face or online, is shaped by the technologically savvy world in which we live. Additionally, the ways in which we communicate with others are also influenced by our cultural identities. In the opening case study, we focused on one part of Don's cultural identity, that being his disability. However, he is also of a certain age, race/ethnicity, sex, sexual orientation, and socioeconomic class.

The opening case study also reveals that Don has power through his technological abilities. Many people believe that knowledge is power, and if nothing else, the capabilities of the Internet represent a wealth of information for users. But what happens to those individuals like Don who don't have access to the vast amount of information available through the Internet? This specific question *can lend itself to more general questions regarding the three issues that are the focus of this chapter, namely, culture, power, and technology. For instance, how do current digital divides—gaps between cultural groups' access and use of computers—impact interpersonal communication effectiveness? Are certain groups rendered less powerful than others because of technological abilities? This current case study serves as a good example as to how the issues of culture, power, and technology are often intertwined.*

This chapter previews three contemporary interpersonal issues featured throughout this book: culture, power, and technology. The opening case study illustrates the subtle and not-so-subtle ways that communication in the twenty-first century is influenced by these three things. This chapter explains why we've chosen to focus on these three issues and provides brief introductions of each. While the basics of culture, power, and technology are described here, discussions for each topic will be extended in other chapters. This will allow you to understand the central role that each plays in different areas of interpersonal communication.

As noted in Chapter 1, there are a number of situational factors that influence interpersonal communication. Some of these include context, time, and function. In this text, we have decided to focus on three specific issues that appear to pose the biggest challenge for interpersonal communication effectiveness in the twenty-first century. In many instances—like in the opening case study—these three issues have clear implications for one another and communication effectiveness. Yet in other interpersonal interactions, the existence of only one of the issues will appear most relevant to the situation. This chapter is written with the underlying assumption that all interpersonal communication is directly or indirectly influenced by issues related to culture, power, and technology. Given the prominence of these elements in the twenty-first century, we argue that a person's interpersonal communicative effectiveness is largely hindered without a clear understanding of how culture, power, and technology influence everyday interactions.

Myths About Interpersonal Communication

Below are seven statements. Read each statement and identify the interpersonal communication myths by placing a "M" in the space provided or a "T" if you think the statement is true. Most of the statements listed illustrate ideas commonly accepted by many people today. Can you identify some of the false assumptions already? By the time you've completed reading Chapter 2, you should understand which are myths and which are not.

_____ Culture and race/ethnicity are the same thing.

_____ The goal of an effective communicator is not to notice cultural differences (that is, to be "color-blind").

_____ Technological advances have expanded the ways we communicate via computers, but they do not affect the way we communicate face-to-face.

_____ Most interpersonal interactions are not influenced by larger societal structures, such as the local community, corporations, government bodies, and so on.

_____ To some extent, power dynamics are present in all forms of interpersonal communication.

_____ In certain situations, people are powerless and can not do anything to gain more power.

Three Evolving Contemporary Issues

Over the years, scholars have presented various theories suggesting that certain issues lie at the core of human existence. Sigmund Freud, the founder of psychoanalysis, argued for example that sex was at the heart of everything we do.[2] The political philosopher Karl Marx, on the other hand, focused on economics as the core of all aspects of society.[3]

Throughout time, a number of different societal elements have been seen as key issues in interpersonal communication. These include such things as economic relations, political agendas, ethical standards, and human rights issues. Some might argue that such issues continue to provide a context from which interpersonal communication must be understood. Yet other issues emerge, largely a reflection of major changes across society. Within this book, we have decided to focus on three contemporary issues—culture, power, and technology—that seem to have particular relevance to interpersonal communication.

One goal for our book is to draw from existing interpersonal communication research, theory, and practice to illustrate how these things can assist us all to be effective communicators in today's world. Because of this, we will attempt to focus on examples, topics, and issues that are most prevalent in the twenty-first century. However, we also draw from some of the well-known research in the field of communication. For example, several scholars have pointed to the issues of culture, power, and technology as core issues of human existence generally, and of interpersonal communication more specifically. For instance, Michel Foucault was a European philosopher who wrote extensively about how power, defined as a complex set of relationships, exists in all interactions. According to one twenty-first-century interpretation of Foucault, you would have to be utterly alone and be free of any hint of socialization in order to escape the power structures that are a part of society.[4] We can look at the existence of sex roles—the belief that women

The cultural diversity within the United States can create communication barriers, but it also can make communication exciting, informative, and meaningful.

and men have clearly defined expectations for their behaviors—in different societies as one example. In order to maintain existing power structures, societal leaders create a system of rewards for those who adhere to expectations. Whether this form of influence is subtle or obvious, our interpersonal interactions with others are situated within certain larger power relationships.

Whereas Foucault and others focused on power, Marshall McLuhan believed that technological inventions had a tremendous influence on human existence. As director of the Center for Culture and Technology at the University of Toronto, McLuhan gained a tremendous amount of popularity because he was an academic who was able to effectively communicate radical ideas to the general public. In short, he believed that changes in modes of communication were the primary force that shaped human existence. McLuhan's premise is that nothing—family life, the workplace, school, entertainment, health care, friendship, recreation, politics, sex, religious worship—remained untouched by communication technologies. While some have criticized McLuhan's ideas as dated and/or overstated,[5] other mass media scholars such as George Gerbner and Stuart Hall have also written on the powerful influence that the media have on interpersonal communication.

Communication scholars have also studied the central role that culture plays within human communication processes. Some point to the inevitable relationship between culture and communication.[6] In other words, you can not talk about one without talking about the other because they are inseparable, forever linked. We learn our culture through communication and, simultaneously, our communication is specific to our cultural background. From this perspective, studying interpersonal communication without acknowledging culture is impossible.

Issues related to culture have received an increasing amount of attention from communication scholars. Given this, our decision to include culture as a core contemporary issue in an interpersonal communication textbook is quite logical. Scholars have also indicated that power and technology—and their relationship to larger culture systems—are issues that are also important to consider when studying interpersonal communication. We do not believe any one of these issues to be the *most* central to interpersonal communication; instead, we argue that all three are central to understanding interpersonal communication in the twenty-first century. The remaining sections of this chapter will provide you with a basic introduction to each issue. The foundation of basic knowledge related to culture, power, and technology found in this chapter will set the stage for additional coverage in subsequent chapters.

Culture and Interpersonal Communication

Culture is like the air we breathe. It is all around us and we can not survive without it, yet often we do not necessarily pay much attention to it. Traditionally, culture has been synonymous with race, ethnicity, or nationality. However, contemporary perspectives view culture as a more inclusive concept. We can define **culture** in the following manner: Culture refers to learned and shared values, beliefs, and behaviors common to a particular group of people. Culture may also include common artifacts, music, customs, food, language, dress, and celebrations. As Figure 2.1 illustrates, what we notice about culture often represents only the tip of the iceberg. What must be understood is that obvious differences between cultures are oftentimes a reflection of cultural values that are less visible. For example, many cultures have different customs as to what food is appropriate for specific holidays. This is fairly obvious, but what must also be recognized are the underlying cultural values and mores that explain food choices. Being an effective communicator requires understanding the subtle means by which culture shapes a group's identity and the ways its members communicate in different settings.

As mentioned in the previous paragraph, communication scholars have historically studied culture by focusing on race, ethnicity, and nationality. However, as recently described by intercultural communication scholar Robert Shuter,[7] parallel research in the twenty-first century will focus on intracultural communication within a society as much as intercultural communication between different societies. For example, we may talk generally about the U.S. culture, but we should not overlook the many different cultural groups that live in the United States.

Figure 2.1   Cultural Iceberg

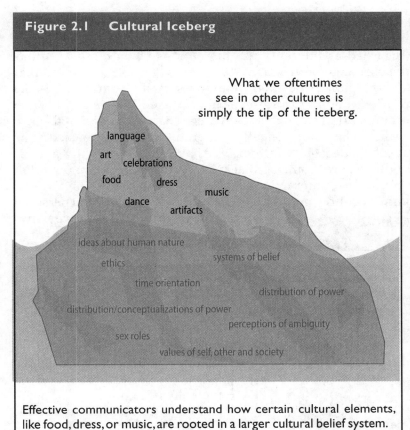

What we oftentimes see in other cultures is simply the tip of the iceberg.

language

art

celebrations

food

dress

music

dance

artifacts

ideas about human nature

ethics

systems of belief

time orientation

distribution of power

distribution/conceptualizations of power

perceptions of ambiguity

sex roles

values of self, other and society

Effective communicators understand how certain cultural elements, like food, dress, or music, are rooted in a larger cultural belief system.

By definition, a **co-culture** is a group of people who are bonded through a system of values, beliefs, and behaviors associated with a common group identity.[8] In the past, co-cultural groups have commonly been referred to as "minorities" or "subcultures," terms with negative connotations that situate them as less important than others. Many cultures exist simultaneously within the United States, including those of Native Americans, the hearing impaired, Generation Xers, gays and lesbians, and the Amish. Think about how each of these groups functions as a culture that is separate from, yet part of, the larger U.S. society.

Whether we are talking about cultural identity generally, or co-cultural identity specifically, one characteristic of culture is that it is omnipresent, meaning that it is all around us.[9] Consequently, we do not often notice how our everyday lives are formed by it. In fact, many aspects of our own culture become apparent only when we observe the differences between it and other cultures. Sometimes we must travel to do this, such as to another part of the United States or another country. Yet sometimes we can experience a different culture very close to home—as when we visit a friend's place of worship or a coworker's home. Once we experience different cultures through this type of exposure, then we typically become more aware of our own cultural norms. For example, an African American child may be raised to believe that you must start each New Year by eating collard greens and by having some money in your pocket—two things that help symbolically trigger financial gain in the upcoming year. If the child is only exposed to other families who participate in similar traditions, she may assume that this is a general belief, and not necessarily one specific to certain segments of the African American community.

This example is just one of many that points to the various ways that a person's culture affects how he or she communicates with others. We all communicate based on the ways in which we have been socialized to think about self, others, and society. Take a moment to think about the different ways that you communicate to others—verbally, nonverbally, or through artifacts like food, music, jewelry, clothes, or arts. You may do many of these things with little thought to how they reflect the cultures in which you were raised. Yet, consciously or unconsciously, each aspect of interpersonal communication does not occur outside of a larger cultural context—typically, the type of community in which you were raised.[10]

Interpersonal interactions are regarded as intercultural interactions when cultural differences exist in ways that influence the exchange of messages. It is important to understand that whenever two people communicate, both similarities and differences exist. **Homophily** is the term used to describe the overlap of common cultural experiences (see Figure 2.2). When homophily exists, interpersonal communication can occur. However, when two individuals have little homophily, then they are also said to be communicating interculturally. Two basic truths about homophily are important to acknowledge: (1) No two people have total homophily, and (2) all people share some homophily. In this regard, some similarities and differences are bound to exist during all interpersonal communication interactions. Typically, the similarities between individuals make interpersonal communication possible. The differences make interpersonal communication interesting, valuable, and sometimes challenging.

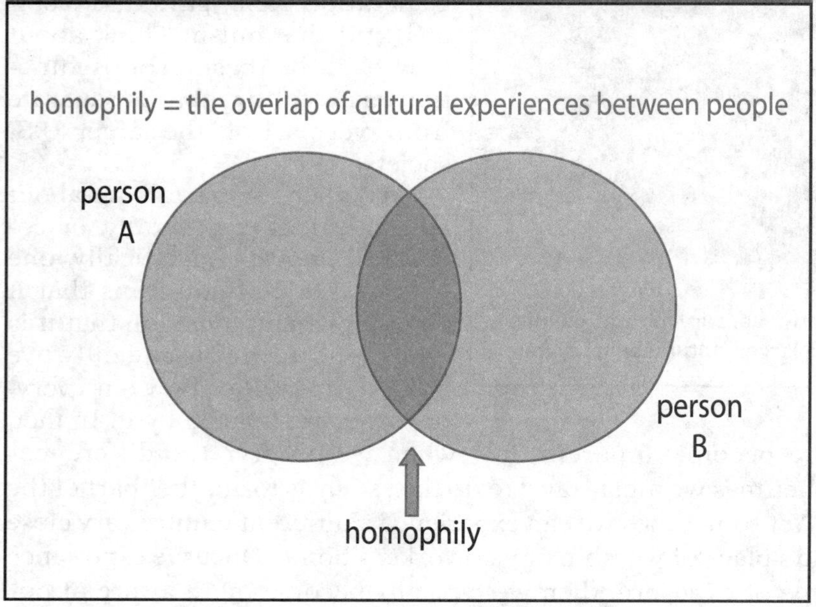

In many societies, like that of the United States, three aspects of culture have the greatest impact on communication: race/ethnicity, sex/gender, and socioeconomic status (class).[11] Cultural differences based on these three elements typically pose the greatest problem for interpersonal communication effectiveness. Therefore, we start by highlighting race/ethnicity, sex/gender, and class issues. Then, we introduce other elements of culture such as age, abilities, regionality/nationality, sexual orientation, and spirituality.

Figure 2.2   The Concept of Homophily

homophily = the overlap of cultural experiences between people

person A

person B

homophily

Race/Ethnicity

As the title of Cornel West's 1993 book puts it, "race matters" in the United States.[12] In fact, differences based on racial and ethnic distinctions continue to be a prominent issue as we proceed through the twenty-first century. Most scholars acknowledge the existence of one human race. However, throughout the text, we use **race** in terms that are consistent with those categories maintained in the United States (African American, Asian American, Native American, and European American) and **ethnicity** to identify a specific set of shared traditions, heritage, and ancestral origins (Hispanics/Latinos, Korean, Hmong, Filipino, or Chinese). The power of racial and ethnic differences lies not in the way biology influences the color of a person's skin or other physical factors. Our physical differences do not themselves represent cultural differences.

Rather, different racial and ethnic groups, over time, have developed specific cultures that sometimes make interracial communication difficult.

If we were to name different racial and ethnic groups, most readers could brainstorm different aspects of culture that are closely associated with those groups. For instance, consider the following groups and think about unique features of their culture as they relate to food, dress, customs, holidays, and music: Mexican Americans, Italian Americans, Caribbean Blacks, Japanese Americans, Irish Americans, and the Navajo people. Are you equally aware, however, of the cultural values that influence the way that each group communicates? For instance, the ways that people use and perceive time are different in different cultures. You may have observed this through your travels, but do you understand the cultural value that is at the root of this form of communication? Michael Hecht, Ron Jackson, and Sidney Ribeau's explanation of "colored people's time" is a good example. In their 2003 book on African American communication,[13] the authors explain that observing that many African Americans are typically late for social events is best understood through recognition of history and economic circumstances (e.g., harvest schedules and market structures). Because of different cultural experiences, what is defined as being late varies among different racial and ethnic groups. Accordingly, it is important to understand that a person's culture is reflected in multiple ways. Throughout the text, we will illustrate how race/ethnicity affects interpersonal communication in different contexts (e.g., in romantic relationships; see Chapter 10).

The communication differences between women and men are as important to recognize as the physical differences between men and women.

Sex/Gender

Many people use the terms *sex* and *gender* interchangeably. It is important, however, to make a distinction between these two terms. **Sex** is a personal trait that is determined by our biology and genes. In comparison, **gender** is a psychological trait that is based on how society attaches certain meanings to sex. Put another way, our sex (being female or male) has to do with the sexual organs with which we are born; our gender (femininity, masculinity, and/or androgyny) is learned through socialization.[14] Traditionally, our sex largely determined our socialization. Young girls were expected to be neat, sweet, nurturing, and soft-spoken. Young boys, on the other hand, were expected to be active, aggressive, independent, and outspoken. More recently, expectations for young girls and boys have changed and may vary greatly. Through the influence of nature (genetics) and nurture (socialization), boys and girls can maintain different gendered identities.

In the last 20 years or so, interactions between women and men have been studied through an intercultural lens. Scholars like Deborah Tannen[15] and Julia T. Wood[16] have studied how females and males are raised to embrace different cultural values that may cause some cross-sex misunderstandings. Best-selling books like John Gray's *Men Are From Mars, Women Are From Venus* are also based on this idea. One point of caution, however, is needed here. It is dangerous to assume that the ways in which all women and men communicate are based solely on their sex. Other factors related to a person's socialization and current situation must also be taken into account. For instance, many women—especially those who were raised in environments where traditional sex roles weren't emphasized or modeled—communicate in ways that are not explained by John Gray's simple division based solely on sex. This is where certain approaches, like those advocated by Gray, become troublesome.[17] Use Box 2.1 to learn more about stereotypical statements.

Box 2.1

Skill Builder

Stereotypes usually exist when individuals have little substantial contact with others not like them or are unmotivated to get to know others as individuals. For instance, the smaller the number of Hispanics/Latinos you know well, the easier it is to hold stereotypes about them. Stereotypes, by definition, are a form of cultural generalization. They are not true for all members of any given group—they may be true for some or even most, but definitely not all. During interpersonal interactions, making assumptions about others based on "general" knowledge can lead to a host of communication problems, many of which are discussed in subsequent chapters.

Think about an incident you were part of in which stereotypes resulted in communication that was unproductive. What statements were made in this situation? What could have been done differently, keeping in mind the principles discussed in this chapter?

Stereotyping Statements:

- _____
- _____
- _____

Nonstereotyping Statements:

- _____
- _____
- _____

Socioeconomic Status (SES)

Socioeconomic status, or class, is another salient cultural marker in the United States. By definition, **socioeconomic status (SES)** refers to both the economic and social standing of an individual. According to some scholars, socioeconomic status influences all aspects of a person's life, including her or his communication with others. "Class is your understanding of the world and where you fit in; it's composed of ideas, behaviors, attitudes, values, and language; class is how you think, feel, act, look, dress, talk, move, and walk."[18] Many of the values we hold are best understood within this context. Understanding socioeconomic status as a cultural marker requires us to acknowledge that it is more than simply how much money a person makes. It also relates to the cultural norms that are associated with a certain social standing.

Beyond your current income, socioeconomic status is also related to your economic security, the importance of family and kinship ties, your interests and leisure time activities, and your communication style.[19] Just because people may suddenly gain or lose a significant amount of money doesn't necessarily mean that they will see themselves or others any differently. For example, you may have known people who suddenly came into a large sum of money, maybe through an inheritance or by winning the lottery. While their economic status changed, their social standing—and the way that they communicated it to others—probably did not immediately change. Like other aspects of a person's culture, socioeconomic status can be dynamic but difficult to change.

Age

Most of us have heard people talk about the *generation gap*, a cause for misunderstanding between people of different chronological ages. The generation gap is best understood as a cultural gap rooted in a different set of lived experiences. In this regard, **age** refers to how old a person is and reflects his or her identification with a particular age cohort of the population. Consider how people who are about the same age share experiences that are unique to the time in which they were born. For example, people who were young adults during the Cold War between the USSR and the United States share a set of experiences that shape their current perceptions of each country. This set of experiences typically includes all the features that were included in Figure 2.1. While we may notice the obvious characteristics of one generation (fashion trends or language use), we must also recognize that these things are grounded in sometimes less obvious philosophies, values, and beliefs. To extend the previous example, certain beliefs related to patriotism and the need for a strong military defense may be best understood within the context of a particular era. Individuals who do not share that history may have a difficult time understanding such beliefs.

Interactions between people of significantly different ages can be difficult because generations often view life differently.[20] For many, the absence of meaningful interaction between different age groups may foster negative stereotypes. For instance, a senior citizen may perceive that a teenage neighbor is "wild" because he has a nose ring, while that teenager may stereotype his neighbor as "senile" because she always asks about the weather. This is most likely in communities where families lack the close intergenerational relationships that are the hallmark of an extended family unit. Intergenerational communication must overcome the same potential problems that plague other intercultural interactions. These problems include key elements of culture and communication that will be presented in future chapters (language differences, negative stereotypes, cultural misperceptions, and ethnocentrism).

Abilities

Another characteristic of interpersonal communication that might define an interaction is the level of abilities of the individuals. By **abilities,** we are referring specifically to the physical, mental, and emotional traits that are related to a person's competency in performing certain behaviors. Communication scholars have studied people with disabilities as a co-culture in the United States,[21] one that operates within a set of distinctive rules, speech habits, and norms. Its members include individuals with congenital as well as acquired disabilities, and those whose disabilities range from severe to mild.

Persons with disabilities recognize that, more often than not, able-bodied people see them as disabled persons first, and as individuals second. Most able-bodied individuals can not imagine what it is like to go through life with a disability, so their communication is awkward, uncertain, and filled with sympathy. Some may decide to completely ignore a person's disability, while others become oversensitive to the point of being patronizing. Generally, effective interpersonal communicators must strike a balance between acknowledging both the similarities and differences between different types of people. In the case of persons with disabilities, this includes acknowledging the particular disability but not allowing it to define your perceptions of the person.

Regional/National Origin

The earliest studies in intercultural communication focused on differences between countries and what problems arose when individuals from different national cultures interacted.[22] Traditionally, **national origin** referred to the country in which a person was born and held citizenship. However, more and more people have dual citizenships and identify with multiple national cultures.[23] This makes understanding the role that national origin plays in human communication more complex and challenging.

In addition to recognizing cultural differences based on national origin, effective communicators must also acknowledge regional differences within countries. Regional origin refers to the location within a country where a person is born. Different parts of a single country, regardless of geographic size, can vary greatly in terms of standard of living. For instance, most U.S. citizens understand the different ways of life for Southerners, New Englanders, Midwesterners, or those living on the West Coast. Cultural differences—sometimes related to the climate, location, and/or size of the region—can be seen in language, dress, time, food, and religious beliefs. For example, people in one part of the United States might ask for soda or the water fountain when thirsty, yet people in another region might use different terms ("pop," "coke," or "bubbler") to ask for the very same things.

Sexual Orientation

All of us have a sexual orientation that is central to our human existence. In the simplest terms, **sexual orientation** refers to the direction of one's sexual interest toward members of the same, opposite, or both sexes. Sexual orientation, however, should not be exclusively defined in terms of sexual activities alone (for this reason, some use the term *affectional orientation*). Because they are in the numerical minority, most gay/lesbian/bisexual individuals see their sexual orientation as more central to their identities than it is for heterosexuals. In other words, when most people learn that someone is gay or lesbian, that fact tends to define who they are. The same is not true when we learn that someone is heterosexual. In either case, sexual attraction is part of everyone's life, and it is counterproductive to define a person solely in terms of sexuality.

Gay, lesbian, and bisexual people have gained more visibility in the recent past and have fostered a greater understanding of gay culture, which typically has its own music, language, literature, symbols, and sense of community. Still, sexuality remains a sensitive topic for some individuals who can only focus on the differences between gay and straight people. As with other aspects of cultural difference, all humans—regardless of sexual orientation—participate in interpersonal communication. While many such interactions are similar for gays and straights, there might be differences. Consider, for example, the relatively mundane process of discussing your weekend plans with classmates or coworkers. For most heterosexuals, this is generally a pretty simple process. For gays, lesbians, and bisexuals, such a discussion might demand a number of conscious choices, such as strategically using generic phrases (significant other, partner) or misleading pronouns (he, she, they) to avoid identifying their sexual orientation when discussing their plans.

Spirituality

A person's **spirituality** is his or her identification with, and belief in, a higher power or set of principles. We prefer using the term *spirituality* rather than *religion* because it is more inclusive and representative of the diversity of thought in this area. Spirituality, then, includes the world's religions (e.g., Christianity, Judaism, Islam, and Hinduism), specific denominations (e.g., Roman Catholic, Baptist, Methodist, Pentecostal), and other beliefs about a set of universal principles (e.g., New Age, Scientology, astrology).

The core of any form of spirituality is a belief system. While this belief system includes a set of principles, traditions, and values, it also is reflected in a number of other aspects of culture including different forms of expression. Anyone who has visited different places of worship can attest to some initial cultural shock when exposed to different forms of worship, preaching/teaching, or expectations for dress or time. For example, Catholics are known for their relatively short, routine worship process, whereas Black Southern Baptists have drastically different norms for the length and flow of their services.[24]

Spirituality is a core element of many individuals' value systems.

Culture Summary

At this point, we hope that you have begun to see the central role that culture plays in different forms of interpersonal communication. Furthermore, it is important to recognize the different ways in which the elements of a person's cultural identity are connected. Yet many people have difficulty when asked to explain why they do certain things the way that they do. Part of this is due to the problems of connecting certain communication behaviors to one particular aspect of identity. Consider, for example, the different communication styles that people use during conflict. Problems might arise because some people use more direct confrontational styles while others opt for less direct ones. Why is this? Can we make a connection between conflict style and one particular aspect of a person's cultural identity (gender, race/ethnicity, age)? Most often, the ways that we communicate are a result of a combination of all of our cultural identities. Therefore, the most productive way to understand the connection between culture and communication is through a more holistic lens, by which we can acknowledge how multiple cultural elements affect communication simultaneously. This will be our strategy throughout the text, as we highlight culture as a significant issue for interpersonal communication in the twenty-first century.

Power and Interpersonal Communication

When we talk about power in interpersonal communication, we mean the ability to influence others and be in control of what happens to you. Remember that we are operating from the basic assumption that *all interactions reflect some form of power*. Sometimes this is obvious, as when a boss is talking to an employee. However, power dynamics exist even in interactions among equals—like best friends. This concept should become increasingly clear as you continue to read this section, which explains different perspectives on power and how power functions at micro- and macro levels.

Perspectives on Power

People have different perspectives on the role of power in their lives. In order to begin our descriptions of power, we highlight three different perspectives on power. Initially, these have been discussed in terms of how women and men view power differently.[25] Yet we believe that gender is only one factor that may influence different perspectives of power. As you read the descriptions below, think about how your life experiences—including gender, age, race/ethnicity, and education level—shape your perceptions of power.

Dominance. Traditionally, most Western societies have functioned within a **dominance** power perspective.[26] In this frame of thinking, power is viewed as a finite quality—meaning that the only way for one person to gain power is for someone else to lose it. Power exists as an advantage because it allows people to control resources, ideas, and/or people. This perspective encourages people to increase their power over others, which usually includes a hierarchy of "haves" and "have nots." The ultimate goal is to obtain enough power to reign over others. Benefits of power relationships are one-sided, and power struggles are natural. As you will see, other perspectives do not cast people in opposing, competitive positions.

Empowerment. A second perspective, **empowerment**, sees power as something to be shared with others.[27] In this regard, power is conceptualized as a means to accomplish your own goals and help others accomplish theirs as well. This perspective sees power as a finite commodity, but centers on compassion to help those who are less powerful. Empowered communicators understand that by helping others, they ensure that everyone wins. However, empowerment is still rooted in unequal relations. For instance, can you understand how empowerment fosters a dependency relationship between those with less power and those with more—given that one person is seen as the helper and the other as the one who is helped?

Synergy. The third perspective of power is the one that we believe is most consistent with interpersonal communication effectiveness. A synergistic perspective sees power as a process rather than as a commodity or an entity.[28] **Synergy** relates to the idea that the whole is greater than the sum of its parts. A clear example of synergy occurs in effective small groups or teams: People working together can accomplish things that are not possible when individuals work apart from one another. People who operate within a synergistic perspective of power are aware of their own resources, as well as their personal strengths and weaknesses. Consider, for example, the Detroit Shock, the 2003 WNBA champions. In one year, this team went from having the worst record to the best record in the league—something that was even more surprising because the Shock didn't have any really high-profile players. While each WNBA team has several talented players, it was the ways in which the Shock came together as a team that resulted in great success. In other words, individual players on the team became better because of the interaction among teammates; by working together, *good* players were able to play as a *great* team. What examples can you identify in which synergy resulted from the collaborative efforts of individuals at your work, in your personal relationships, or in your family?

Some interpersonal communication problems arise when people operate from different power perspectives. In order to understand this issue in practical terms, let's look at a basic introduction to the multidimensional nature of power.

Microlevel Power

We begin our discussion of the nature of power by discussing how power is used at microlevels of human communication, or those levels within an interpersonal communication context. Perhaps the most influential ideas about power and interpersonal communication come from the work of John French and Bertram Raven. In 1959, French and Raven identified five basic sources of power: expert, referent, legitimate, coercive, and reward.[29] They hypothesized that these bases of power are the most common and influential. We offer descriptions, along with two examples, of each power base in Box 2.2, "Applied Concepts."

Box 2.2

Applied Concepts

Do parents have all or most of the power when communicating with their children? As illustrated by the examples below, we would argue that both parents and children have access to each of the power bases discussed in the chapter.

Expert Power

For Parents: Teaching their children new things (e.g., riding a bike, caring for themselves, learning to drive, or preparing for college).

For Children: Teaching their parents new things (e.g., using "new math," navigating a Web site, or understanding the newest dance steps).

Referent Power

For Parents: Children often identify with their parents, and aspire to be like them.

For Children: Parents can also have great respect for the accomplishments of their children and admire certain qualities that they have.

Legitimate Power

For Parents: By law, parents have power over their children until they reach legal age. Parents, however, do not have legitimate power over their children if their children do not respect the laws that give them legitimate power.

For Children: Some parents believe that their role is to please or accommodate the needs of their children; this gives the children some power to draw from.

☞ **Reward Power**

For Parents: Money, gifts, and permission to do certain things (tangible), and giving love, affirmation, support, or praise (intangible).

For Children: Love, respect, attention, positive esteem, and opportunities to be proud (e.g., "The biggest reward in life is for me to see my children happy").

Coercive Power

For Parents: Verbal abuse, physical force, "time outs," extra chores, or taking away certain privileges (e.g., car, phone, or computer).

For Children: Verbal abuse, the "silent treatment," screaming or yelling, or withholding information, attention, or love.

Expert power is based on the knowledge or experience that one person has and others want. Few, if any, individuals have expert power in all areas. A person has **referent power** over someone else when that one person (Person A) has a desire to be like the other person (Person B). For instance, teachers, coaches, and older siblings frequently have referent power over others (students, players, and younger siblings, respectively). **Legitimate power** stems from social structures that give the right and/or responsibility to "control" others to certain people. Most societies recognize the legitimate power of judges, police officers, and professors within certain contexts. However, the legitimate power one person has depends on the respect others have for that position, and not on the position itself. **Reward power** is based on the ability to give others things they desire. In most instances, the promise of rewards isn't enough; some follow-through is necessary to guarantee this form of power. Whereas reward power contains a promise of certain benefits, **coercive power** is based on the ability to punish. Sometimes punishment can take the form of removal of rewards (taking driving privileges away from those convicted of DWI). The overlapping nature of reward power and coercive power makes them hard to distinguish in certain situations.

Like culture, power is an important situational factor when understanding the ways that different people communicate. Whether conscious or unconscious, people draw from different power bases as they interact with others. Those individuals who are most powerful draw from all the power bases described above. However, that does not mean that others are powerless when interacting with them. This, of course, is true for individuals working with others who adopt an empowerment or synergistic power perspective. But even when less obvious, most of us have access to different power bases when communicating with others who, at first glance, appear more powerful. Consider, for example, the power that some students have when communicating with their professors. This could take the form of student evaluations, expertise in a specific topical area, or information regarding university policy.

Macrolevel Power

Thus far, we have discussed how power operates within interpersonal communication contexts. However, it is important to recognize that interpersonal interactions occur within a larger societal (macrolevel) context, one that French and Raven described as "pervasive, complex, and often disguised."[30] Power is pervasive in that it is all around us, even when we do not necessarily recognize it. It is fairly easy to understand how different bases of power function in an example like parent/child communication. Yet power dynamics—the complex ways that different power bases function during interpersonal communication—are multidimensional. In addition, parent/child communication doesn't take place in a vacuum. Therefore, understanding how power operates in everyday situations requires a recognition of larger societal and cultural issues that inform different aspects of interpersonal communication. An example of this can be seen in the ways that societal and cultural norms, parents' legal rights, and child-protection laws influence how parents and children communicate with one another.

In the United States, certain groups have greater access to power than others, whether that power takes the form of political clout, financial standing, corporate leadership, or control over decision making. Most of the time, those in the majority have greater access to power because

Power dynamics and their effect on interpersonal communication can sometimes be hard to understand.

they created those social structures (government, schools, economy, and so on). In terms of our earlier discussion about culture, it is important to recognize that power dynamics are typically affected by majority-minority standing. Historically, those in the majority of decision-making positions created systems that perpetuated the status quo. In other words, those in power created programs and policies that gave advantages to others in the majority. In the United States, this has resulted in a society where European Americans, heterosexuals, Protestants, and able-bodied persons have greater access to power. Co-cultural group members are at a disadvantage. As you will see from the following example, men—although a numerical minority—still hold the reins of power.

Women make up approximately 51 percent of the population in the United States, a fact that would lead some to assume that power is divided relatively evenly between women and men. Yet a quick glance at who is in leadership positions in political, educational, and economic organizations tells us that women largely remain outside decision-making processes dominated by men. Consider the hypothetical example of Rene, a woman whose experiences reflect the reality of many women whose dream is to climb to the top of the corporate ladder.[31] Currently, she is a middle manager in a Fortune 500 company. Her position and reputation in the company provide her with the ability to draw from certain power bases (discussed earlier in this section), yet she is hesitant to exert her power given that the men with whom she works expect her to act "like a lady" while doing her job. This means that her communication is expected to be soft-spoken, respectful, and polite, whereas similar expectations do not exist for her male colleagues.

Rene's everyday interactions do not exist in isolation from other external influences, including what occurs at the board of directors' meeting, the stock market, and the U.S. Supreme Court. In addition, her ability to draw from power bases is influenced by existing stereotypes about how women should behave. Not being able to be assertive (or aggressive) in certain situations without being labeled negatively is a problem that reflects larger male-female power dynamics.[32] This is not to say that all co-cultural group members are affected by macrolevel power relations the same way. However, the point here is that power dynamics exist on multiple levels, each of which affects the other. Think about, for example, how power is used to communicate with people on the individual level. This may be where most of our attention lies. Yet we also must understand that what occurs at the small-group, organizational, and societal levels helps to frame what occurs on the individual level. In other words, the way that we communicate interpersonally (microlevel) occurs in a context that is set by other less obvious influences (macrolevel). The example of Rene, whose communication with corporate colleagues is affected by societal expectations related to gender, illustrates this point.

Technology and Interpersonal Communication

In 1981, media scholar John Wicklein wrote that all modes of communication that humans have created since the beginning of time are coming together into one single electronic system, namely, the computer.[33] More than 20 years later, we can see just how realistic his predictions have become. Computers have become the focus of many lives. In fact, some would argue that almost everything we need to survive is available through our computers. Think about it for a moment. People begin, maintain, and terminate relationships online. Others telecommute and conduct all of their professional work via their computers. Currently, a person can run errands without ever leaving home, including going grocery shopping, paying bills, registering for classes, browsing for a special gift for a loved one, submitting tax forms, mailing a birthday card to a friend, or turning in an assignment to a professor. We can also use the computer to make phone calls, send a fax, watch videos, listen to our favorite CD, and even tune in to a radio station hundreds of miles away.

In this regard, advanced technologies have potentially turned our homes into a communication center of sorts where all our information, work, and entertainment needs are met without much face-to-face human contact. In this book we suggest that all interpersonal communication is affected, directly or indirectly, by advanced technologies. All the capabilities of computers obviously influence the way we communicate when we use them. A good example of this point is seen in the ways that computer users attempt to use symbols, like the multiple variations of smiley faces, in order to communicate nonverbal cues that are a part of face-to-face communication. However, because of the increased reliance on computers, they also influence communication that occurs through face-to-face interactions. Consider the following scenarios, focusing on how the use of technology influences perceptions of the importance of interpersonal communication:

- A company expands its use of online services and starts charging an extra "service" charge for those who place orders in person.

- A friend calls another friend and tells her to check her e-mail and respond as soon as possible.

- A new employee wonders why his boss felt the need to stop by with the answer to his question when he could have easily e-mailed it to him.

- A student is confronted by others who were offended by comments that she posted on the class listserv.

- A man can't understand why his partner reacted negatively to the electronic birthday card that he sent.

Each of these examples illustrates how technological advances, directly or indirectly, influence interpersonal communication. According to a 2002 report by the U.S. Commerce Department,[34] 56 percent of adults in the United States use the Internet. While this number continues to grow, other research indicates that the majority of those who currently are not using the Internet have no interest in going online; most of these individuals are aging baby boomers and senior citizens.[35] Given this reality, how does technology currently impact interpersonal communication in different contexts? How will its influence continue to grow given the predictions that more and more individuals spend some time communicating online? The remainder of this chapter will draw from existing communication research to create a foundation to help us answer these questions.

The Importance of Technology

To explore the idea that technology plays a central role to human existence, we return to the ideas of Marshall McLuhan.[36] According to McLuhan, we are currently living in the **electronic age**. Beginning with the invention of the telegraph in 1850, electronic inventions have transformed the ways that we live and communicate. These include the telephone, radio, phonograph, television, photocopier, answering machine, VCR, cell phone, fax machine, Internet, and PDA (personal digital assistant, such as the Palm Pilot). McLuhan argues that the electronic media foster the creation of one **global village** where everyone is linked (directly or indirectly) through technology with everyone else. In the electronic age, closed human systems no longer exist. Through elaborate communication technologies, like those used by CNN, we know what is happening with others around the world instantaneously.

Not everyone agrees with McLuhan's claims. Yet he never set out to create a communication theory, only to heighten public awareness of the vast influences that media technologies have in all of our lives. It may be a stretch to prove that certain communication inventions *cause* certain societal changes. Still, we believe that the value of McLuhan's ideas is in the ways they prompt us to think critically about the direct and indirect impact of technology.

Like McLuhan, George Gerbner, dean emeritus of the Annenberg School of Communication at the University of Pennsylvania, believed that television was the dominant force in shaping modern society. A great portion of Gerbner's research focused on studying the relationship between television viewing and perceptions of reality, the result of which was the formation of cultivation theory.[37] Cultivation theory is based on the idea that the more television people watch, the greater influence it will have on how they perceive the world. Gerbner's research, for instance, asked people about their perceptions of violence in society (e.g., "How likely are you to be involved in some kind of violent act?"). He found that people's responses to this question had more to do with their television-viewing habits and less with the actual risk in their community. In other words, people living in a community with little, if any, violence were likely to see their community as more violent than it actually was if they watched a lot of television. Accordingly, the ways in which such people communicated with others were influenced by a social paranoia created through and by the media. George Gerbner's ideas, like those of Marshall McLuhan, point to the importance of understanding the influence that technology has on interpersonal communication.

Stuart Hall is another media scholar whose work has been inspired by the relationship between technology, the media, and everyday interactions. A professor of sociology at Open University in England, Hall's work in the area of cultural studies has made significant contributions to critical views of the media. His research is especially important to the focus of this book because it addresses the issues of culture, power, and technology.[38] Specifically, Hall looks at how the media use their influence to maintain the status quo, through which some cultural groups have power and others do not. The concept of hegemony is key to his work. **Hegemony** refers to situations when one group has predominant influence, or domination, over another. According to Hall, hegemony describes the relationship between the U.S. media and the public. He does not see the media as a neutral source for information and entertainment. Instead, he believes the media to be a powerful source where certain ideals, like the "American Dream," are sold to the masses. For instance, cultural studies scholars like Stuart Hall would critique the media's role in communicating unrealistic standards of beauty for women. Specifically, they would describe how these images promote not only certain products (makeup, dieting, exercise, and personal hygiene products) but also certain beliefs, like the idea that a woman's value is in her appearance and not her abilities.

For some, accepting the ideas of McLuhan, Gerbner, and Hall is difficult because they appear pretty extreme. Each, in its own way, points to the powerful influence that technology has on each of our lives. But each set of ideas also tells us that not all people are impacted by the media and technology equally; much depends on the awareness level of the individual. The key point to remember is that technology does impact how we communicate with others, both directly and indirectly. The next section will discuss some of these impacts.

The Impacts of Technology

Year after year, communication technologies continue to become increasingly accessible to the general public. These include enhanced Internet features like instant messaging and wireless Internet connections, PDAs, MP3 devices, and portable laptop computers and DVD players. Each of these technological advances was designed to enhance our abilities to function effectively. But have they actually accomplished this

Technology has both increased and decreased our perceived need to communicate with others.

goal? It is safe to say that they have significantly altered life as we know it, but have some of us become enslaved by the very things that were designed to give us more convenience and freedom? Clearly, there is no simple answer to this question because technological advances have both positive and negative consequences for interpersonal communication effectiveness. At the most basic level, the goal of the effective communicator is to become aware of the consequences of how they do, or do not, use technology to communicate with others.

One of Marshall McLuhan's main ideas was that we as humans shape our communication tools, but they in turn also shape us. For instance, he would suggest that human beings have a dependency on technologies that might be unhealthy. Think about it for a minute. Could you survive without access to a computer? A cell phone or pager? E-mail? Palm Pilot? Cable or satellite television? Communication technologies were created in order to enhance social connectedness and provide convenient access to information. But, in doing so, they have fostered a reliance on technology that may actually hinder effective interpersonal communication.

For example, some would suggest that instead of creating a global village, technologies have allowed for individuals to experience life in relative isolation from others. For some, communication at work (see Chapter 12) consists primarily of e-mail messages, conference calls, and the dissemination of reports via online attachments. Advanced technologies allowed us to write this book despite living hundreds of miles apart and only coming face to face one or two times. Yes, technology has brought the world closer together, but has it really brought us closer in terms of our interpersonal connections?

One way to explore this question is to examine how technology has transformed the traditional office context. Through advanced technology, individuals can now work at any time and any place. People can work in their beds at 3 o'clock in the morning, on the beaches of Hawaii, or while watching their daughter's soccer game on a Saturday afternoon. Yet the capabilities of working "24/7" have some clear disadvantages in terms of quality-of-life issues. What impact does this have on our family and other close relationships? How does it continue to blur the boundaries between work and home? What will be the effects if we continue to work harder and harder? Some might say that some of these questions have been asked for centuries. However, can you see how advanced technology has changed how we respond to them?

In many ways, communication technologies have shaped our expectations for interactions with others. Customer-service relationships are an example that we can use here. We have heard some people, for instance, describe their banking experiences in this way. In the past, they would enjoy the cordial, ongoing relationship with a favorite teller at their local bank. Then, for greater convenience, they would frequently use the "drive-thru" option where they only communicated via an intercom and completed their transactions through a capsule that was shot back and forth. Now, these same people find themselves doing their banking at 11 p.m. on the Internet in the comfort (or confines) of their own home. The result is that some people have very little tolerance for business interactions that do not happen quickly, effectively, and without human error. As companies utilize technological resources to respond to these customer expectations, opportunities for meaningful interpersonal communication are reduced. This is especially true when companies provide incentives, like lower fees or discounts, for customers who choose to use the computer to do their banking, purchase airline tickets, or pay their bills.

To date, technology has had many direct, and not-so-direct, impacts on different forms of human communication. For this very reason, we include it here as one of the three key issues for interpersonal communication in the twenty-first century. Future chapters will extend what is offered here, and highlight how technology influences interpersonal communication in different contexts.

Summary

This chapter was designed to give the reader a foundation for three contemporary issues—culture, power, and technology—that will be woven into the different interpersonal communication topics covered in upcoming chapters. At this point, it is important to recognize that effective communication in the twenty-first century involves recognizing the direct, and indirect, ways that each influences how we communicate with others. Throughout the remaining chapters, we will extend our discussion of each issue and highlight the ways that each affects different aspects of the interpersonal communication process.

We began this chapter by listing several statements about interpersonal communication, most of which were myths. Below you will find a corresponding "truth" for each myth listed at the beginning of the chapter. The fifth statement was the only correct one listed.

Myth: Culture and race/ethnicity are the same thing. Why?

A person's race/ethnicity is just one aspect of a person's cultural identity.

Myth: The goal of an effective communicator is not to notice cultural differences (that is, to be "color-blind"). Why?

Being aware of cultural differences is important for effective communication.

Myth: Technological advances have expanded the ways we communicate via computers, but they do not affect the way we communicate face to face. Why?

All forms of interpersonal communication, directly or indirectly, are influenced by advanced technologies.

Myth: Most interpersonal interactions are not influenced by larger societal structures, such as the local community, corporations, government bodies, and so on. Why?

Interpersonal communication does not occur in a vacuum; therefore, we must understand how it is influenced by the larger society.

Truth: To some extent, power dynamics are present in all forms of interpersonal communication.

Issues of power exist at both macro- and microlevels and influence how we communicate with others.

Myth: In certain situations, people are powerless and can not do anything to gain more power. Why?

Sources of personal power vary from situation to situation, but effective communication skills can work to increase these levels.

Key Terms

Abilities	Ethnicity	Referent powerRace
Age	Expert power	Regional origin
Co-culture	Gender	Reward power
Coercive power	Global village	Sex
Culture	Homophily	Sexual orientation
Dominance	Hegemony	Socioeconomic status (SES)
Electronic age	Legitimate power	Spirituality
Empowerment	National origin	Synergy

Suggested Contemporary Readings

D. Charlesworth. "Transmitters, caregivers, and flowerpots: Rhetorical constructions of women's early identities in the AIDS pandemic." *Women's Studies in Communication* 26 (2003): 60–87.

J. W. Chesebro. "Gender, masculinities, identities, and interpersonal relationship systems: Men in general and gay men in particular." In *Women and men communicating: Challenges and changes*, edited by L. P. Arliss and D. J. Borisoff. Prospect Heights, IL: Waveland, 2001.

L. S. Clark. "Challenges of social good in the world of Grand Theft Auto and Barbie: A case study of a community computer center." *New Media & Society* 5 (2003): 95–116.

S. A. Fox. "The uses and abuses of computer-mediated communication for people with disabilities." In *Handbook of communication and people with disabilities: Research and application*, edited by D. O. Braithwaite and T. L. Thompson. Mahwah, NJ: Lawrence Erlbaum Associates, 2000.

T. Kanayama. "Ethnographic research on the experience of Japanese elderly people online." *New Media & Society* 5 (2003): 267–288.

P. M. Leonardi. "Problematizing 'new media': Culturally based perceptions of cell phones, computers, and the Internet among United States Latinos." *Critical Studies in Media Communication* 20 (2003): 160–179.

A. Mitra. "Marginal voices in cyberspace." *New Media and Society* 3 (2001): 29–48.

T. Obilade. "Oppositional codes in students' narratives about new information technologies." *Howard Journal of Communications* 13 (2002): 191–206.

D. V. Tanno. "Names, narrative, and the evolution of ethnic identity." In *Our voices: Essays in culture, ethnicity, and communication*, edited by A. Gonzalez, M. Houston, and V. Chen. Los Angeles: Roxbury, 2000.

M. Valo. "Workmates, friends, or more? Perceived effects of computer-mediatedness on interpersonal relationships." *Electronic Journal of Communication* 13 (2003).

Chapter Activities

1. According to *http://test.thespark.com/gendertest,* this Web site "will predict, with 100% accuracy, whether you're a guy or a girl" simply by analyzing your responses to a series of questions. Take the test and then discuss your perceptions of the accuracy for yourself and other students. For instance, you might discuss the value of the test, or whether or not you believe that it only relies on traditional stereotypes of women and men.

2. Reflect on the various aspects of culture that were described in this chapter. Of all these things, which seem to have the most importance to you as an individual? For example, think about when you communicate with others. Which parts of your cultural identity (race/ethnicity, sex/gender, socioeconomic status, age, abilities, regional/national origin, sexual orientation, or spirituality) are most important? What other elements of your identity are also central to who you are? Share your responses with other classmates via small-group discussions, and note any similarities and differences.

3. The Job Accommodation Network (*http://www.jan.wvu.edu*) provides information about job accommodations, the Americans with Disabilities Act, and the employability of people with disabilities. Visit the Web site to learn more about what companies are doing to maximize the productivity of their employees with disabilities. Take special

note of specific strategies that use technology as a way to make organizations more equal for people with disabilities.

4. Use a database in your campus library (e.g., InfoTrac) to locate articles that deal with culture, power, and technology. What types of articles were located using these three words? How do they relate, directly or indirectly, to interpersonal communication issues?

5. You can peruse various stories about the 2000 U.S. Census on the following Web site: *http://www.usatoday.com/news/census/index.htm*. For instance, you will find stories about gay households, ways that people of color are reshaping the suburbs, people with multiracial backgrounds, grandparents raising grandchildren, white supremacists' reactions to the increases in racial/ethnic diversity, as well as specific statistics about the demographics for individual states and cities. Select one or two stories that are of particular interest to you and discuss how these shifts in demographics might potentially affect interpersonal communication in the twenty-first century.

6. One of our goals for this book is that students should be able to seek out specific opportunities to use what they are learning in their own communities. Think about a community-based organization that might benefit from some of the information shared in this chapter. Then, use your knowledge of the organization (this may involve meeting with some of its members or observing a typical day in the organization) to respond to the following questions: Which of the three contemporary issues featured in this chapter are strengths or weaknesses for the organization? What recommendations might you offer to the organization on how to more effectively highlight their strengths and improve upon their weaknesses?

7. Within this chapter, and throughout the book, we cite statistics related to technology use. Unfortunately, these statistics are oftentimes outdated by the time you end up reading them. But we've found a solution to this problem! Visit *http://www.cyberatlas.internet.com*, where you can read about the most up-to-date Internet trends, and then compare them with the statistics included in this book. ✦

Chapter 3

Self and Communication

Contemporary Issues:
Self-Esteem–Based Pregnancy-Prevention Programs

Natalie Johnson is a young female student who participates in a pregnancy-prevention program in New York. Trying to prevent teen pregnancy—whether by preaching abstinence or handing out condoms—can be a complex and controversial issue. One method exists, though, that seems to get universal support: building self-esteem. Experts report that teenagers who feel good about themselves are more likely to remain abstinent or practice "safe sex." With this in mind, programs across the United States are incorporating lessons on self, self-esteem, and assertiveness into teen pregnancy-prevention efforts. Some lessons, for example, involve using assertiveness to politely return food at a restaurant. While this may sound trivial, experts agree that such everyday encounters help build young girls' self-confidence and thus their ability to be assertive in other situations. Dr. Michael Carrera, who works at the Children's Aid Society in New York, praises what he calls "above the waist" pregnancy-prevention programs. He understands the difficulty in teaching self-esteem with a preset curriculum, but sees the value in providing opportunities for teens to understand the role that self-perceptions and self-value play in decision making. "If you feel like you are going someplace and some good things are going to happen, then you will avoid risks, you will control impulses," he said.[1]

This opening case study illustrates one of the ways that building self-esteem has been linked to different forms of interpersonal communication. As you read the brief description provided above, did you think about your own experiences with communicating about sex or other difficult topics in personal relationships? How might these experiences be different for women and men, people from different cultures, or those from different generations? This chapter focuses on the concept of self. As you will see, a person's self-concept is central to how she or he communicates.

Not all communication is about self, but a person's sense of self is central to all communication. Our sense of self and how we communicate are two things that are so closely intertwined that it is difficult understanding one without including the other. It is important to realize that our sense of self is not created solely from within. Instead, we rely on others around us to help us understand who we are. All interpersonal communication begins with self, and subsequently, our communication affects our sense of self. As we will discuss in this chapter, we gain a sense of who we are through our communication with others. Furthermore, we use interpersonal communication to express ourselves to others.

Myths About Interpersonal Communication

As you have seen already in Chapters 1 and 2, we list several statements about interpersonal communication here at the beginning of each chapter that relate to the particular topic at hand. We understand that all students begin studying interpersonal communication with some degree of communication knowledge. Some of this knowledge is learned from school, but most of it was gained from past experiences, reading, media sources, and/or friends and relatives. Given your vast experiences of communicating with others, you are bound to have different assumptions about what makes someone an effective communicator. And while these experiences will undoubtedly make it easier to apply course material, it is important to note that many myths about interpersonal communication exist. In many instances, what makes many of these myths untrue is that they reflect simplistic answers or principles unable to capture the complex process of interpersonal communication. So, one of our goals with this book is to build upon your existing knowledge but also simultaneously show you that there is a great deal to learn about our communication with others.

Below are six statements about self and communication. Can you identify which statements are myths and which are not (M = myth, T = truth)? If some seem unclear and you aren't sure, don't despair. By the end of this chapter, the answers should be clear.

_____ The self is the most important social unit.

_____ Changing your self-concept is not easy.

_____ High (and low) self-esteem comes from within.

_____ Complete openness is the key to effective relationships.

_____ People typically communicate about themselves consistently regardless of communication context.

_____ The choice to share personal information with others is the same for all people.

Self-Concept

Take a few minutes right now to think about who you are by completing the well-known "Who Am I?" exercise.[2] Write "I am" 20 times down the left side of a piece of paper. Then fill in something about yourself to complete each statement. Assume that no one but you will see the list. The key is not to take a lot of time on this exercise; just write down whatever pops into your mind.

The "Who Am I?" exercise is a great way to identify various aspects of your self-concept. By definition, **self-concept** is the mental image you have of yourself, including your traits, character, abilities, skills, knowledge, and personality. Our self-concept is relatively stable over time, but it can change gradually over the course of our lives. Some people might believe that to "know thyself" is relatively easy; for most of us, however, trying to understand who we are is a lifelong process. As you read this chapter, keep your 20 "I am" statements close at hand. We will refer back to them several times throughout the chapter.

Self-concept actually includes two ways we see ourselves: our self-image and our self-esteem. **Self-image** describes the way you see yourself and includes your various roles as student, daughter or son, spouse, friend, and so on. Self-image is the general descriptive picture that we have of ourselves. In comparison, **self-esteem** is an evaluative measure of how we feel about ourselves, and therefore includes some value judgments. Self-esteem is the degree to which you have a favorable impression of your self-image, or of who you have become. Refer back to your "I am" list. Some of your statements might reflect self-image ("I am a student," "I am 35"), while others represent your self-esteem ("I am overweight," "I am a good student"). Because self-image and self-esteem are so closely intertwined, other statements might include both, for example, "I am just a freshman." Can you see how this comment reflects both self-image ("freshman") *and* self-esteem ("just")? Did you include any statements like this in your exercise?

Self-Concept Development

How does a person's self-concept develop? Certain personal characteristics may be genetic, meaning that they were present since birth. However, babies aren't born with a clear idea of who they are and what their value is. The process by which we develop and then maintain or change our self-concept is a complex one. Three major sources of information exist that contribute to our sense of self: self-perceptions, interactions with others, and social comparison. As you will see in the following descriptions, each of the sources for information is directly and indirectly tied to our interpersonal communication.

Self-Perceptions

We form ideas about who we are through our attempts to understand why we behave the way we do. These ideas are **self-perceptions**. We usually interpret our behavior to mean something specific about ourselves. Yet it is important to recognize that our interpretations are tied to our past communication with others. For instance, a parent helping her second-grade daughter complete an assignment may find herself getting angry with her daughter for not taking the assignment seriously. The mother immediately catches herself and then tries to understand why she reacted the way she did. What does her anger say about her as a person, as a mother? Does it mean she has unrealistic expectations for her child, or does her reaction indicate her willingness to push her daughter to live up to her potential? Or could it reflect other personal characteristics: a lack of patience, strong belief in the importance of education, or need for perfection? How were these things reflective of past or current communication interactions with others? Obviously, the meaning of this behavior depends on the particular person and her set of circumstances. Note, though, that we are constantly evaluating our own thoughts and behaviors as an information source for our self-concept. Box 3.1 offers an activity that will help you to apply the complex nature of changing self-concepts.

How we perceive ourselves has a lot to do with how we communicate with others.

Box 3.1

Applied Concepts

When we talk about self-perceptions, it is important to recognize that several dimensions of self exist, all at the same time. For many of us, these are so intertwined that it is difficult to see how each one operates. Still, self-perceptions are guided by a person's:

- *Idealized Self* (the person that you aspire to be)

- *Perceived Self* (the person you think you are)

- *Actual Self* (the person you actually are)

In order to understand how these dimensions of self coexist, read the following statements and select the appropriate response.

1. One of my greatest strengths is my ability to listen when others need me.

   Strongly Agree   *Agree*   *Uncertain*   *Disagree*   *Strongly Disagree*

2. I like making new friends.

   Strongly Agree   *Agree*   *Uncertain*   *Disagree*   *Strongly Disagree*

3. When working on an important project, I am not normally bothered by interruptions.

   Strongly Agree   *Agree*   *Uncertain*   *Disagree*   *Strongly Disagree*

4. I am competitive, but not to a point where it is destructive or unhealthy.

   Strongly Agree   *Agree*   *Uncertain*   *Disagree*   *Strongly Disagree*

5. During times of conflict, I maintain an open mind.

   Strongly Agree   *Agree*   *Uncertain*   *Disagree*   *Strongly Disagree*

Review your responses and think about how each might reflect your actual, perceived, or idealized self. Don't be too quick to assume that you have described your actual self. In some instances, people respond to self-assessment instruments (like this one) with answers that reflect what they think they should say (idealized self). Other people are more critical of themselves in their responses (perceived self) than is actually necessary. Have 2–3 friends and/or relatives respond to each item in terms of how they see you. Then you can see just how close your self-perceptions match the perceptions others have of you (which may or may not be representative of your actual self!).

Once established, self-perceptions play an important role in maintaining our self-concept. One way they do so is through the self-fulfilling prophecy. A **self-fulfilling prophecy** is a prediction you accept about yourself in such a way that it becomes more likely to be true. Although self-fulfilling prophecies can be either self-created or imposed on us by others, the most powerful ones are those we reinforce within our own minds. Self-fulfilling prophecies become true through two different means: selective perception and triggering behaviors. **Selective perception** occurs when you focus on messages that are meaningful for you. In the case of a self-fulfilling prophecy, selective perception occurs when an individual gives attention to those things that support the existing prediction. **Triggering behavior** refers to verbal and nonverbal cues that provoke specific reactions from others.

Here's an example of how both these means operate. Suppose Mr. Jones was your favorite ninth-grade teacher, so much so that you were sad when he left to go back to graduate school. But then you couldn't believe your luck to find out he had been hired as a faculty member at a local community college—the one that had just accepted you. Upon enrolling in his class, you were amazed to discover how many of the other students disliked Mr. Jones' teaching style because they felt he was condescending! How could this be? Your positive perceptions of Mr. Jones can be explained through:

Selective Perception. Because you expected Mr. Jones to be a good teacher, you unconsciously gave more weight to his positive traits. When you did notice some poor teaching qualities, you tended to ignore them or see them as less frequent or important than other students did.

Triggering Behaviors. Your excitement about being in Mr. Jones' class again was evident the first day of class. Your enthusiasm while interacting with him prompted more positive behaviors from Mr. Jones. Although you didn't notice, Mr. Jones' excitement when talking with you did not match the way he interacted with other students.

As you can see from this example, not all self-fulfilling prophecies have negative consequences.

Interactions With Others

A second major source of information that contributes to self-concept is our interactions with others. In both direct and indirect ways, people communicate their perceptions to us. Some of these images relate to the way they view us, and subsequently these perceptions of theirs become a key source of information for the development of our self-concept.

Throughout our lives, family and friends directly guide our self-perceptions. Think back as far as you can remember: What direct messages were you sent in terms of your self-concept? Some of you might have heard comments regarding your spirituality ("You are a child of God made in His image"), race/ethnicity ("Your grandmother came to the United States from Cuba in 1971, so that makes you a second-generation Cuban American"), or other personal characteristics ("You are smart and beautiful, and don't let anyone tell you otherwise!"). Without question, these types of direct expressions contribute to the development of self-concept. However, of equal if not greater importance are the indirect ways that others communicate their perceptions *of* you *to* you.[3]

Symbolic interactionism is a theory that helps us to understand how direct and indirect messages contribute to a person's self-concept.[4] As you can probably tell by the name of the theory, the focus is on the symbolic—or less obvious—effects of our interactions with others. In its most basic form, symbolic interactionism suggests that we gain an understanding of who we are through our interactions with others.[5] Although this theory was initially studied in the field of sociology, communication scholars have embraced it because of its focus on the importance of interpersonal communication in the process of self-concept development.

The effects of the symbolic nature of our interactions with others seem especially strong in the case of young people.[6] Several years ago, a public service announcement flashed a series of young faces on the television screen while adult voices said things like, "How could you have done that?" "What are you, stupid?" "I wish you were never born," "Why can't you be like your sister?" and "What good are you?" This dramatic presentation vividly illustrated the important role that adults' comments play in children's self-concept. While the negativity associated with these statements is clear, it is important to note that equally damaging messages can be sent in less direct ways like a punishing silence and lack of attention. Children come to understand who they are based on how others interact with them. In less obvious ways, so do adults.

According to the ideas associated with symbolic interactionism, each of us has an idea of how others generally see us. This idea is known as our **generalized other**.[7] Knowledge of our generalized other creates a looking-glass self whereby we develop, through our interactions, an image of how others see us.[8] In other words, we develop a sense that allows us to see ourselves through other people's eyes. The term **significant other** is used to describe a person whose interactions are more likely than the generalized other to influence our sense of self.[9] Many of us are familiar with the use of this term to describe romantic partners. However, with symbolic interactionism, the term is broader and includes any individuals with whom we have an established relationship such as parents, family members, close friends, and teachers.

You probably remember vividly some specific comments people have said to you that had a direct impact on your self-concept. Sometimes these things are said by strangers or acquaintances (gained from our generalized other); at other times they come from family and friends (significant others). A person's self-concept is affected by both types of messages; however, the influence of one source may be greater depending on the power and repetition of the message. For instance, the media historically have been criticized for presenting limited images of male and female behaviors.[10] The influence of these messages is weighted against those that are received from significant others. For example, imagine the impact on the young boy who hears things like, "Don't throw like a girl," "Big boys don't cry," or "You're acting like a sissy." Young girls may hear similarly restrictive messages about their behaviors: "Little ladies don't climb trees," "You're sitting like a little boy, not a little girl," and "Let's go comb your hair so that you will be pretty for school." Comments like these can create sex-based expectations with negative consequences. For instance, in terms of the last example, research indicates that girls are judged in school based on their physical appearance and the "neatness" of their work, while boys are evaluated primarily on their accomplishments.[11]

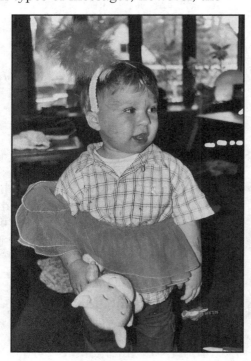

Self-concept is affected by the messages that we receive from others.

Some of us may have heard some of these comments when we were younger—directed either at us or at others. Others of us might recall saying them to children. Think about how comments meant to shape our roles influence our self-concept. Not meeting the expectations of others can have a drastic impact on a person's self-esteem; it can result in an uncomfortable gap between our self-concepts and our ideas of what others want us to be. As effective communicators, we need to acknowledge the impact that others have on our self-image and self-esteem. Being honest with yourself, think of instances when another person has said or done something that caused you to reflect on how others might see you. By answering this question, you have an idea of how symbolic interactionism works.

To say that we gain an understanding of who we are through our interactions with others does not mean that they have the ultimate power to define us. Each individual has the power to accept, ignore, or reject the images of ourselves that others reflect to us. Consider, for example, the case of Vickie Bye, a 40-something mother of two teenagers who is considering attending college. She has the support of her immediate family. But when she shared her plans with her parents, her mother asked her, "Aren't you a little old to start college? I don't understand why you want to do this; it's not like you need to get a job with the money your husband makes!" While this comment might affect Vickie's self-concept, it doesn't have to. She could do a number of things, including:

Accept the comments and incorporate them into her current self-concept, which revolves around her primary roles as mother and wife.

Ignore the ideas her mother has about her plans to attend college. While she understands her mother's view and that others might share her perspective, Vickie does not allow it to alter her new self-image.

Reject her mother's ideas as wrong and old-fashioned. Instead of discouraging Vickie, her comments may actually give her additional motivation to attend college.

Thus far, we have discussed two major sources of information that contribute to our sense of self: self-perceptions and others' perceptions. The next section discusses social comparison, the third and final influence on self-concept development.

Social Comparison

All of us compare ourselves to others to some extent as a means to understand who we are. We measure our own accomplishments and value by using others as points of comparison. For example, we may notice what others scored on a test we took, compare the make and model of our cars, or assess the relative status of our career choices. Thus, in addition to our self-perceptions and our interactions with others, comparison to others, known as **social comparison**, also provides us with information that affects our self-concept.

Consider the following scenarios:

Tyray is not different than most college students. The first thing that he does when he gets a test or paper back from his professor is to look for the grade. The next thing that he does is to check how his grade compares to others in the class.

Dawn is a single parent of two girls, one of whom (Larissa) just entered junior high school. Dawn is concerned because Larissa has begun getting detentions for minor offenses such as repeated tardiness. When she attempts to talk to her daughter about it, Larissa claims it isn't a big deal and she is making too much of it. After all, she told her mother, "My friends, Crystal and Ebony, got suspended and their mothers didn't trip out at all."

Although she's not like some students who create their class schedules around certain television programs, Mary does like to watch all of the different "judge shows." Her favorites are *Judge Hackett, Judge Judy,* and *Divorce Court.* She thinks the people on these shows are too funny. Plus, hearing them talk about their problems helps her realize that her life is pretty good!

These examples help demonstrate social comparison's role as an information source for our self-concept. Tyray evaluates his performance on class assignments, in part, based on what grades others received. In comparison, Larissa feels her behavior is acceptable because her friends' behavior is worse. Mary compares her life to the lives of people in the courtroom dramas and finds the result comforting.

The examples also show the crucial role that reference groups play in the process of social comparison. Larissa used friends who had gotten into more serious trouble as her reference group. However, if she had used another reference group, such as honor students, her perceptions about her behavior, and as a result the level of her self-esteem, would have been different. Who do you use as a reference point? Is it your siblings? Coworkers? Fellow students? Perhaps you have your own standard of excellence against which you measure your level of self-esteem. Still, it is important to identify with a group of like-minded people you can use for support and inspiration.[12]

You should also be aware of *how* you use reference groups. Listening to the guests on *Divorce Court* might be therapeutic, for example, but do they serve as a realistic, positive reference group to guide our self-concepts? Box 3.2 provides additional reflections of how media images become a reference group for many people.

Box 3.2

Self-Reflection

Do you think some people use actors, sports figures, and other celebrities in the media spotlight as reference groups? We may not always use specific people such as significant others. Instead, we may compare ourselves generally to images that we see in the media. Think about what type of images are provided by the media. Many scholars have criticized the role that the media plays in fostering unrealistic images of beauty, fitness, and life in general.[13] For instance, scholars[14] have found that, on average, women who spend a couple of minutes looking through a fashion magazine become more self-conscious—if not more depressed—about their bodies. As you can see, using media images as a reference group to measure your self-worth is a dangerous practice. However, many of us—if we are honest with ourselves—can recognize times when we did just that.

The Importance of Social Identities

As discussed in Chapter 2, one assumption that many Americans have is that the individual self is of primary importance. While this may be true in some aspects of U.S. society, it is certainly not true for all. In other cultures, discussions about self-concept are not as important as acknowledging one's family, community, profession, or other type of social unit.[15] Let's now take a different look at the relationships between self, society, and communication. Within this section, we focus on perspectives that place these various social units—not the individual—at the core of self-concept. Box 3.3 summarizes the research of two scholars interested in exploring the relationships between the self-concept, self-esteem, and academic success of individuals with diverse social identities.

Social identity is a product of the groups or categories to which a person belongs (or aspires to belong). Social identity is best understood in terms of the ways that different group memberships come together to form a complex sense of self. For example, in 1998 communication scholars Dreama Moon and Garry Rolison wrote about socioeconomic status as an identity marker.[16]

Box 3.3

Practical Research

For many undergraduate students, the connections between academic research and everyday practice are difficult to make. Because of this, we will provide Practical Research boxes throughout this text to help students understand how research can be used to help us become more effective communicators in our everyday lives. This box focuses on a study that examined the effect of alcohol consumption and self-esteem on flirtatious behavior.

In a 2000 *Human Communication Research* article, Jennifer Monahan and Pamela Lannutti[17] reported the results of a study that they conducted that looked at an everyday topic—flirting. In particular, they wanted to explore the effect that social drinking had on women who had low and high self-esteem. In order to do this, they gave 50 women a self-esteem measure and randomly provided an alcoholic or nonalcoholic beverage. Then they had each woman talk to an attractive, flirtatious man who they had trained specifically for the experiment.

The results of their study revealed that alcohol consumption had little effect on women with high self-esteem. However, women with low self-esteem were less anxious and self-disclosed more when drinking than when sober. Think about these results for a minute. Do they surprise you, or are they what you expected? More importantly, what type of practical guidance does this research provide in terms of our interpersonal communication? How might you use this information to provide advice for women who are social drinkers?

Their research focuses on specific sites where socioeconomic values are communicated (trailer parks, suburbs, high-rise apartments, housing projects). They also discuss how other groups to which individuals belong, including those based on race/ethnicity and gender, also make up their social identities and influence communication with others.

Each of us has different parts of our social identity, but how central each aspect is to our self-concept varies from person to person and from culture to culture. For many co-cultural group members (such as Mexican Americans), racial/ethnic identity is central to self-concept; in fact, many children of color are taught at an earlier age to identify with and take pride in their heritage.[18] However, the same is not true for most members of dominant cultures in the United States.[19]

For instance, let's look at possible responses to the "Who Am I?" exercise at the beginning of this chapter. Experts predict that co-cultural group members would be more likely to include social/cultural identity statements than would group members from dominant groups.[20] In other words, a student who is visually impaired would be more likely to list "I am a person with a disability" than another student would be to list "I am able-bodied." In the same way, African Americans would be more likely than European Americans to include statements about their race/ethnicity.

What this boils down to is that some people find it difficult to identify their self-concept apart from their social identities.[21] Figure 3.1 illustrates two different perspectives on self-concept. Typically, this distinction is associated with primary differences related to culture.[22] An **individualistic self-concept** appears as a separate entity, one that is loosely connected to several social identities. A **collectivistic self-concept** also is surrounded by various social identities. Unlike an individualistic self-concept, the collectivistic self-concept is *embedded* within different social identities. Those that are most central to a person's sense of self are located in the middle of the concentric circles. Those that are not as important are positioned in the outer layers.

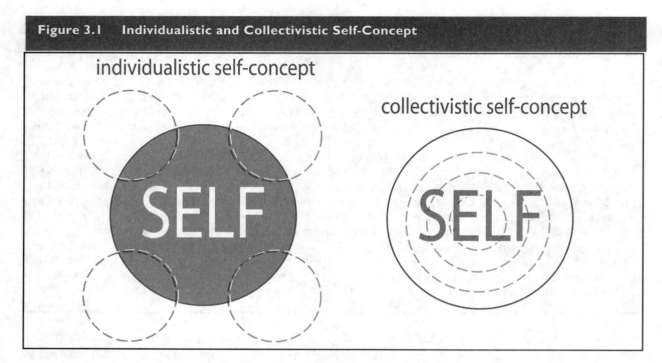

Figure 3.1   Individualistic and Collectivistic Self-Concept

individualistic self-concept

collectivistic self-concept

SELF

SELF

Think back to our discussion about culture in Chapter 2. What are some different types of cultural groups with which you identify? Were some of these listed when you completed the "Who Am I?" exercise? Refer back to your list of 20 statements and take special note of which group memberships you listed first. Scholars suggest that the ordering of statements indicates the relative importance of the many aspects of your social identity.[23] For instance, note which cultural marker you listed first (if at all)—was it your gender, race/ethnicity, age, sexual orientation, or spirituality? Everyone has multiple parts of their social identity. Yet, each part might be seen differently by individuals when they are asked about their self-concept.

Core identity markers are those group memberships that are most salient, or most central, to a person's self-concept. Scholars suggest that persons from co-cultural groups are likely to maintain core identity markers that are related to the aspect of their identity that is in the minority.[24] For instance, think about two African American men who attend the same traditionally Black Baptist church, Jeffrey and Rob. While neither may think much about the power that comes with being a man, both see their race as a core identity marker that others react to. Why? Research indicates that people of color are constantly aware of their marginalization in the United States because of the dominance of European American culture.[25] This is not to say that all core identity markers reflect aspects of co-cultural status. Both Jeffrey and Rob also see their spirituality as centrally important to their self-concept. While Jeffrey and Rob share several core identity markers, at least one key difference exists in terms of sexual orientation. Jeffrey is a heterosexual man who is married with two children; he would never think to list "I am straight" within his 20 "Who Am I?" statements. Rob, on the other hand, is a gay man who, although childless, has been in a committed relationship for over 10 years. Because Rob lives in a society that refuses to recognize his significant other along the same lines as others' spouses (ability to marry, share insurance, show public affection), he is constantly reminded of his co-cultural status.

Therefore, he would be more likely to include sexual orientation in one of his 20 "I am" statements.

Within this example, you can see how two persons share some, but clearly not all, core identity markers. What is also important to recognize is that in addition to these more central aspects of social identity, each person's self-concept also includes situational identity markers. **Situational identity markers** refer to those group memberships that are not generally central to how we describe ourselves, but do become important in certain situations. For example, age is a situational identity marker for our hypothetical friends, Jeffrey and Rob. Both are in their early 30s and maintain friendships with others of similar age. However, when they were both invited to speak at a Young Black Male Think Tank that their church was sponsoring, age became a crucial aspect of their sense of self.[26] Speaking to a large group of teenagers, they couldn't believe it when one asked, "Who is Desmond Tutu?" What they had to remind themselves was that, while they had direct memory (and interest) in the role the Bishop Tutu played in ending apartheid in South Africa, most of these young men were not born when this occurred. Accordingly, both men realized that their communication with the male teenagers would not be effective unless they used examples that were more relevant to their experiences.

Another example can also illustrate the "situationally salient" nature of social identities. For instance, let's imagine that Rob invites Jeffrey to a gathering at his house. When Jeffrey arrives, he discovers that he is one of only a few straight men. As described earlier, Jeffrey normally does not give much attention to his heterosexuality. However, in this context, his sexual orientation seems to take center stage as he constantly finds himself making references (directly and indirectly) to his heterosexuality—something that he does so that others won't assume that he is gay.

Communicating Self

The next step in understanding how self-concept is developed, maintained, and/or altered is discussing how we communicate our self-concept to others. Therefore, our attention turns to the topic of self-disclosure.

Self-Disclosure

Self-disclosure is the act of sharing information about oneself to others. The information is perceived to be true and can be provided verbally (by saying, "I am married") or nonverbally (by wearing a wedding ring). Most self-disclosures are intentional, but some are not. For instance, some self-disclosures can be communicated through "slips of the tongue."

One way to understand the relationship between self-concept and self-disclosure is through the Johari Window.[27] The Johari Window (see Figure 3.2) includes four boxes—or quadrants—each of which represents a combination of self- and other-awareness in terms of what specific information is shared. Each box is described below.

Open Self: The **open self** contains all information that is known by both you and others. Examples can be demographic information (age, family income, hometown), as well as psychological information (religious beliefs, political affiliation, attitudes). The size of your open self will vary depending on a number of things including your desire and/or need to self-disclose, the situation, and the relationship you have with the other person. Although you may seek total openness with another person, the sheer volume of information you

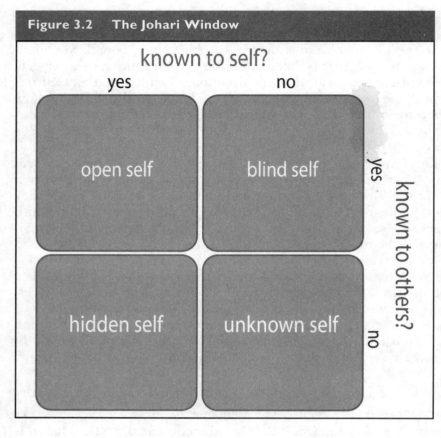

Figure 3.2   The Johari Window

known to self?

yes   no

open self   blind self

hidden self   unknown self

known to others?

yes

no

possess makes it impossible to share everything. Consequently, some information is not relevant, appropriate, or necessary to share.

Blind Self: Your **blind self** represents information that is known to others but not to you. This can include things you are not conscious of, like nervous habits such as spinning your pen between your fingers or biting your lip. Listening to yourself on tape or watching yourself on video helps to identify different aspects of your blind self. Through the exercise described in Box 3.1, you also might have a relative or friend share information with you that decreases your blind self. This new insight, should you accept it, increases your open self. Can you see how communication generally, and the disclosures of others specifically, alter the Johari Window?

Hidden Self: Information you are aware of, but decide not to share with others, is part of your **hidden self**. Depending on the situation, we refrain from disclosing certain types of information with others. For example, during the first few weeks of the term we may not share certain information, even if it is positive (such as our GPA, awards, or scholarships), until we have developed some sort of relationship with our classmates. One factor in the size of a person's hidden self is his or her personality and culture. Some individuals are raised to maintain a certain level of privacy, especially as it relates to topics like family problems, sex, religion, or finances. For others, these topics are not "off limits."

Unknown Self: What is in the **unknown self**, the final quadrant that includes information not known to the self or to others? We are constantly learning new things about our selves. Until we become aware of these things, they reside in the unknown self. For example, many students are required to take general education requirements in college. The exposure that they receive through these different classes may facilitate a new awareness of what they want to do with their lives. In this example, an experience (taking a class) caused a reduction in a person's unknown self (career uncertainty) and an increase in the open or hidden self (depending on if the person shares the epiphany with others).

The Johari Window provides a basic framework to help us understand what parts of our self-concept are visible to others. Generally speaking, when we disclose a bit of information to someone else, we increase our open self while decreasing our hidden self. When we learn something about ourselves from someone else it also increases our open self, but it is our blind self that is reduced. These general rules help to illustrate a major principle regarding the Johari Window: *All four quadrants are interrelated.* As illustrated in the examples provided earlier, no one quadrant can change without a change also occurring in another quadrant (see Figure 3.3).

Figure 3.3   Understanding Relationships via the Johari Window

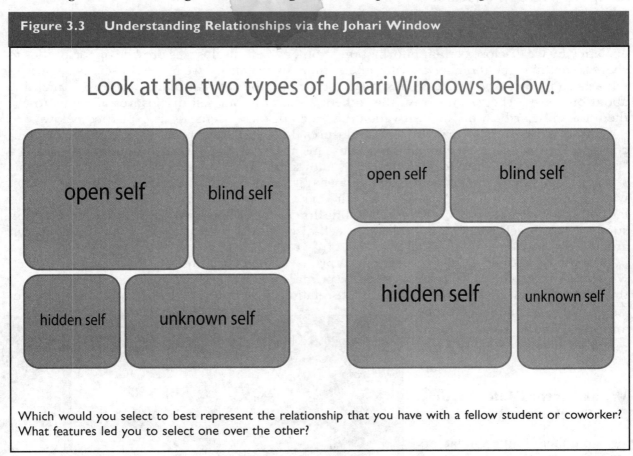

Look at the two types of Johari Windows below.

open self

blind self

hidden self

unknown self

open self

blind self

hidden self

unknown self

Which would you select to best represent the relationship that you have with a fellow student or coworker? What features led you to select one over the other?

Given its basic nature, the Johari Window is not without its limitations. It does not give any attention to the impact that power, culture, or technology has on the relationship between self and communication. This framework also does not pay any attention to possible differences between self-perceptions and the perceptions of others. Let's say, for example, that Shaun comes home late one night after going to a party that he was not allowed to attend. He begins a general conversation with his father successfully avoiding any specific discussion about the evening's activities, keeping the information part of his hidden self. But what Shaun doesn't realize is that his father received a phone call a half an hour earlier asking him to tell Shaun that he had left his coat at the party. So, Shaun thinks the party is part of his hidden self and communicates accordingly, but his father sees it as part of his open self—although he doesn't plan on letting Shaun know quite yet! Could this scenario be illustrated using the Johari Window? Or would the current framework need to be extended to allow for instances when a person falsely thinks that he is hiding certain information? Our next chapter, which focuses on the central role that perception plays within the communication process, will assist in generating some insight to this example. First, though, we need to provide some more information about the self-disclosure process.

Why Do We Self-Disclose?

One of the things that makes human beings different from most animals is our ability to be expressive, reflective, and emotionally close to others. Each of these characteristics helps to explain why we disclose certain information to others. Self-disclosures provide opportunities to share something about ourselves with others. In many instances, we make conscious choices to tell a friend, coworker, or stranger something for no other reason than to express something about ourselves. The various ways that others respond to our self-disclosures allow us to use them for self-clarification and self-validation. Each of these scenarios is explained below.

Self-clarification occurs with self-disclosures that we share in order to help define our self-concept. For instance, someone might disclose his newly found political affiliation by wearing a "George W. Bush for President" button. This allows him to openly express a specific part of his self-concept as well as to further understand what it means to him as people respond in different ways. Along the same lines, this self-disclosure may serve as a way to get validation for a particular political stance. In other words, **self-validation** occurs when we use self-disclosures to gain support for our self-concept. In both cases, self-disclosures are healthy ways to express oneself and develop greater self-knowledge.

Without question, self-disclosures play a primary role in relationship development. In fact, we would suggest that self-disclosures are the primary means to achieve intimacy. In order to test this principle, think about your most intimate relationships. Can you identify specific self-disclosures that you shared with one another at each stage of your relationship?

What Factors Affect Our Self-Disclosures?

A number of different factors affect our decisions to self-disclose information to others.

Self-disclosures of Others: Generally, self-disclosures follow a principle of reciprocity; self-disclosures typically mirror other self-disclosures. Therefore, if a person discloses something to you such as, "I love you," then you are

Some topics, like those related to sex, sexual pleasure, and sexual fantasy, are difficult because they are taboo.

likely to respond with a similar self-disclosure.

Topic: In any society certain topics are *taboo,* meaning that they are generally not discussed openly. What is considered a taboo topic, however, may vary depending on things like culture and situation. In the United States, we may avoid taboo topics related to sex/sexuality, drugs, abuse, money, and death. When deciding whether to self-disclose or not, we will also take into account how others might perceive the appropriateness of a self-disclosure on the topic.

Relationship: As mentioned earlier, our current relationship status influences our willingness to self-disclose. Typically, we consider the following: Is this disclosure something that is appropriate to share with this person? Are we close enough? Will this self-disclosure help or hurt our relationship?

Personality: All people have certain personality traits, many of which impact their willingness and ability to self-disclose information to others. One example of this is how shy a person is. For some persons, self-disclosure is a natural part of their outgoing personality. For others, it is a more difficult process.

Risk Factor: Some disclosures, like your favorite color and profession, are typically low risk in terms of the potentially negative effects that might result from sharing such information with others. Other disclosures, like your financial status or a romantic interest in someone, carry greater risk. It is important to note that all self-disclosures contain some potentially positive rewards as well. For instance, the person who reveals a romantic interest may be doing so to someone who was waiting for a sign to do the same! Both potential risks and rewards influence self-disclosure decisions.

Past Experiences: A well-known saying tells us that "once bitten, twice shy." In terms of self-disclosure, this phrase allows us to understand how reactions from others in the past influence future decisions to self-disclose. For instance, if you lost a friend when you shared your emerging interest in witchcraft, that may affect future disclosures about this aspect of your self-concept.

Context: Certain topics are more appropriate for certain situations. For example, sharing your current relationship problems may be appropriate at church but not at work. The number of other people present is another aspect of context. Are you more likely to share information one-on-one, in a large group, or among family and friends? Think about the impact that computer-mediated communication has had on self-disclosures. How does the context of communicating online affect what and how people self-disclose to others?

General Self-Disclosure Patterns

Within the list of factors that we just provided were several ideas that pointed to general self-disclosure patterns. For instance, one was reciprocity. **Reciprocity** refers to the tendency for self-disclosures to mirror the self-disclosures of others. Another idea had to do with relationship status. **Relationship status** refers to the type and quality of connections or associations that we have with others. In many ways, our self-disclosures with others reflect the status of our relationships with them.

Remember that a principle or a pattern is not an absolute; it is a general rule. Obviously, exceptions exist for any rule. For instance, have you ever been in a confined place for a certain amount of time, such as when taking a plane trip or waiting for a doctor's appointment, and had a complete stranger self-disclose intimate details about his or her life? This documented phenomenon is known as *stranger-on-the-plane* and clearly does not follow established patterns for self-disclosures.

Another factor regulating self-disclosure is **impression management**.[28] According to this idea, we use self-disclosures strategically as a way to communicate favorable images of ourselves to others. During initial interactions, like a first date or interview, we disclose only those things that provide the most positive image possible. That way, potential romantic partners and colleagues will want to get to know us better. Once this image has been established, we continue to consciously choose self-disclosures that will help maintain that image. Some scholars even believe that self-disclosing is a form of "marketing" by which we sell ourselves to others.[29] That is not to say, however, that we maintain one image for all the contexts in which we communicate. We may have different images at school, work, and home. Our self-disclosures are then chosen accordingly.

Social penetration theory provides another framework that helps us to understand the process of self-disclosures in relationships.[30] According to this theory, self-disclosures have two dimensions: breadth and depth. **Breadth** refers to the range of subjects included in your self-disclosures. Some relationships, like that of a mother and daughter, may contain self-disclosures of great breadth. Other relationships might only focus on one area, such as a professor and student's concentration on academic achievement.

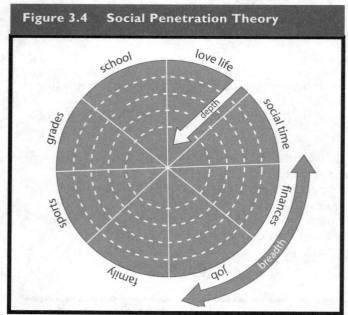

Figure 3.4   Social Penetration Theory

Figure 3.4 will help you visualize how self-disclosures can include a wide variety of topics. Within this illustration, each topic is represented by a slice of the larger circle. Figure 3.4 also includes an illustration of the amount of **depth** in each self-disclosure, or the amount of intimacy that is associated with it. Initial interactions may have a small, moderate, or great amount of breadth. However, they typically have little depth. They allow others to have only basic, nonthreatening information that scratches the surface of the social penetration model.[31] As relationships grow, we usually share more intimate information that reveals our inner layers, those circles near the core of the model.

Contemporary Issues and Communicating Self

So far we have discussed a number of basic ideas about self-disclosure. These provide a valuable foundation to understand how (and why) individuals communicate their self-concept to others. But, in doing so, we have presented models that give no specific attention to the significant roles that culture, power, and technology play in how we communicate self to others. Thus far, we have attempted to integrate some discussion regarding these topics into our explanations. The following sections discuss how greater attention to these contemporary issues provides valuable insight into interpersonal communication effectiveness.

Cultural Similarities and Differences

If all cultures communicated exactly the same way, then the concepts and theories we have presented so far would be enough for us to understand how all people use communication to understand themselves and others. However, different cultures operate within different sets of values that directly and indirectly affect the way that group members communicate. Let's take a look at how cultural difference affects how people communicate about themselves to others.

Research has demonstrated that all cultures do not place the same value on self-disclosures.[32] Therefore, the expectations for self-disclosure—who does it? when? how? why? and to whom?— may differ from culture to culture as well as within a specific culture. For instance, studies have shown that in the Japanese culture, a significantly low level of self-disclosure is viewed as most appropriate for initial interactions.[33] In addition, other important considerations exist that must be recognized. These include the situational context, the power dynamics between the two individuals, and the nature of self-disclosure between same-sex individuals.

Think about the various cultures of which you are a part. These could be based on your particular race/ethnicity, age, sex, or nation of origin. Does each group have similar or different rules regarding self-disclosure? Can you identify any patterns that seem fairly unique to one group?

While the dominant cultural value in the United States expects self-disclosures to occur at every level of interaction, remember that such values are not necessarily shared with other cultures in other countries.[34] And even within the United States, differences among groups exist. For example, men have been shown to use self-disclosure less than women and for different reasons.[35] This information is interesting and valuable in increasing our awareness about cultural differences. However, it is also a conclusion based on research that generalizes to the "average" female or male. Therefore, the research should be viewed with an understanding that women and men are both similar and different in their self-disclosure patterns. In fact recent research, collected by communication scholars Daniel Canary and Kathryn Dindia, suggests that knowing the sex of a person provides little predictive power in terms of self-disclosure and other communication behaviors.[36] The most productive way to try and predict how and why a person might self-disclose is to take into account several aspects of their core identity (not just whether they are female or male, *or* Japanese or French, *or* 20 or 50 years of age).

Communicating self involves both verbal and nonverbal forms of expression.

Power Dynamics

Power also provides an interesting lens through which to understand self-disclosure. At the surface level, we might assume that each person has the same amount of power in terms of what he or she chooses to share about him- or herself. No one can force someone else to share information that they do not wish to, or can they? Of course, upon deeper analysis, we can identify any number of scenarios where power influences greater or reduced self-disclosure.

Those with power based on their position at work or in a family, for example, have greater flexibility in their choices to self-disclose. Teenagers typically have less power than their parents to refuse to answer questions about where they are going. Similar power dynamics occur between professor and student, employer and employee, and police officer and civilian. Interactions between siblings and between sales clerks and customers have less obvious power dynamics. However, all these examples help illustrate the fact that power differences exist in interpersonal interactions—especially when your self-disclosures could have potentially serious consequences in interpersonal communication generally, and in interpersonal relationships more specifically.

Let's consider, for example, a discussion about safe sex between two sisters.

Older sister: "So, are you excited about going to your senior prom?"

Younger sister: "Yes."

Older sister: "Well, you don't sound excited. What's the matter? You and Chris aren't having problems, are you?"

Younger sister: "No, we are fine. But I have a question for you. . . . "

Older sister: "What?"

Younger sister: "What type of birth control do you use?"

Older sister: "What!?! Are you thinking about having sex with Chris the night of the prom???"

Younger sister: "Yes. We've talked about it. You better not tell mom!"

In this example, these two sisters—who are only two years apart in age—are very close and don't see power differences as a big issue in their relationship. However, in the conversation shown above, you should be able to see how certain power bases (as discussed in Chapter 2) are evident. Can you see how the older sister has more referent, expert, and information power than her younger sister?

A closer look at how power is related to self-disclosure reveals an inverted-U shape (see Figure 3.5). In other words, those with the smallest and greatest amount of power may have the least amount of choice when it comes to their personal self-disclosures. Those individuals in the United States with less power are constantly forced to disclose information with little choice. For example, to receive food stamps, people must periodically disclose highly detailed information about their finances, children, job, and even romantic relationships. On the other end of the power spectrum, top politicians, entertainers, and leaders also have little

Power dynamics between individuals can affect what (and how) self-disclosures occur.

choice about self-disclosures. Their choice to be in highly visible professions that also grant them a great deal of power ultimately reduces their self-disclosure choices. To illustrate this point, think about how many celebrities choose to self-disclose about personal matters—such as information regarding their health, personal relationships, and financial matters—to the public in order to avoid having these matters uncovered and highlighted by the media.

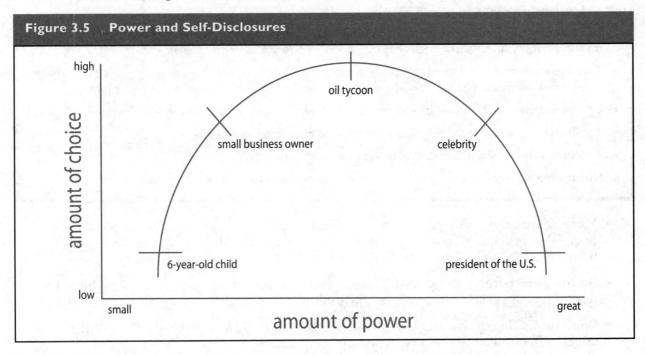

Figure 3.5   Power and Self-Disclosures

Self-Disclosure and Technology

Traditionally, most discussions regarding self-disclosures focus on face-to-face interpersonal communication. Yet, the growth of the Internet and e-mail provides another context in which to discuss how people communicate about themselves to others. Research has found that different rules about communication generally, and about self-disclosure specifically, seem to apply in computer-mediated interactions.[37]

Communicating via the computer is different from face-to-face communication in at least three significant ways. First, it can be done in the comfort of home or work and allows communicators to transcend space and time. Second, individuals are forced to rely much more heavily on verbal communication with few nonverbal cues available. Third, communicating online provides a certain degree of anonymity; people do not have to use their real names and have greater opportunity for deception. What additional differences can you identify that influence how individuals communicate to one another online? Box 3.4 provides guidelines for effective self-disclosure.

How do self-disclosures online differ from those that are communicated face to face? Based on our experiences, we have identified some clear patterns about communicating via the computer. Read each general rule below. Based on your experiences of communicating online, do you agree? Why, or why not?

Box 3.4

Skill Builder

As discussed earlier, effective self-disclosures are crucial to the development of healthy, fulfilling interpersonal relationships. The following guidelines are offered to foster the necessary skills to effectively use, and respond to, self-disclosures.

- Consider your own motivation for self-disclosing information. When responding to others, attempt to discern their motivation for self-disclosing particular information to you.

- Take into account what it is generally viewed as appropriate for that specific situation (e.g., consider the culture of the other person, current relationship status, mode of communication, and situational context).

- Understand the role that power differences potentially play—directly and indirectly—during self-disclosures.

- Attempt to identify all of the potential consequences of your self-disclosure.

- Anticipate how others might respond to your self-disclosure.

- Monitor the reactions of others and take these into account for future self-disclosures.

- More self-disclosures are prompted by more assertive direct questions from others (e.g., what is deemed "polite" or "appropriate" to ask is different when communicating online).[38]

- Because of a perceived decrease in risk, people are more likely to self-disclose information that is of great depth more quickly online.

- Communicating online allows some individuals to avoid self-disclosures that may negatively affect face-to-face interactions (race, age, sex, or physically disabilities/disfigurements).[39]

- Detecting deception is more difficult while communicating online compared to face-to-face interactions.

Given the increased use of computer-mediated communication in both our personal and professional lives, additional research is needed to find out more about how we use these channels to communicate images of self to others. In fact, some scholars have already started to combine issues of power, culture, and technology in their studies. Susannah Stern, for instance, has explored the Internet's potential as a new "safe space" for girls' self-expression.[40] As we outlined in Chapter 2, these three contemporary issues promise to become increasingly important to becoming an effective communicator in the twenty-first century.

Summary

This chapter focused on the relationship between our self-concepts and interpersonal communication. Our self-concept is developed through self-perceptions, our communication with others, and social comparison. In addition, social identities play a role in self-concept development in different ways. Individuals communicate about themselves to others through self-disclosure, a process influenced by various elements. Finally, contemporary issues such as culture, power, and technology affect how we communicate our self-concept to others.

We close this chapter with several points of insight that should help you correctly identify interpersonal communication myths. Of the six statements listed at the beginning of the chapter, five were myths. Below are corresponding truths for each of the myths; our second statement (which was the only truth) is repeated.

Myth: *The self is the most important social unit.* Why?

The self is generally an important concept related to interpersonal communication, but in some cultures the self is regarded as less important than collective social identities.

Truth: *Changing your self-concept is not easy.*

Altering the result of years of socializing messages from family, friends, and the media is possible, but difficult.

Myth: *High (and low) self-esteem comes from within.* Why is this a myth?

According to symbolic interaction theory, we gain our self-concept—including both our self-image and self-esteem—through our interactions with others.

Myth: *Complete openness is the key to effective relationships.* Why is this not true?

Being an effective communicator in personal relationships has less to do with being completely open and more to do with making informed choices about *what* to share, *how* to share it, and *when*.

Myth: *People typically communicate about themselves consistently regardless of communication context.*

Actually, communicating about self, like other forms of interpersonal communication behaviors, is affected by the communication channel that is used.

Myth: *The choice to share personal information with others is the same for all people.*

Power dynamics, to some extent, are present in all forms of interpersonal communication and consequently have an effect on each person's ability and/or willingness to self-disclose information to others.

Key Terms

Blind self	Self-disclosure
Breadth	Self-esteem
Collectivistic self-concept	Self-fulfilling prophecy
Core identity marker	Self-image
Depth	Self-perceptions
Generalized other	Self-validation
Hidden self	Significant other
Impression management	Situational identity marker
Individualistic self-concept	Social comparison
Open self	Social identity
Reciprocity	Social penetration theory
Relationship status	Symbolic interactionism
Selective perception	Triggering behavior
Self-clarification	Unknown self
Self-concept	

Suggested Contemporary Readings

M. Andrejevic. "The work of being watched: Interactive media and the exploitation of self-disclosure." *Critical Studies in Media Communication* 19 (2001): 230–248.

M. W. Baldwin and J. R. P. Keelan. "Interpersonal expectations as a function of self-esteem and sex." *Journal of Social and Personal Relationships* 16 (1999): 822–833.

S. D. Boon and C. D. Lomore. "Admirer-celebrity relationships among young adults: Explaining perceptions of celebrity influence on identity." *Human Communication Research* 27 (2001): 432–465.

J. E. Campbell. "Always use a modem: Frames of erotic play and performance on cyberspace." *Electronic Journal of Communication* 13 (2003).

V. L. DeFrancisco and A. Chatham-Carpenter. "Self in community: African American women's views of self-esteem." *The Howard Journal of Communication* 11 (2000): 73–92.

A. Duggan and R. Parrott. "Research note: Physicians' nonverbal rapport building and patients' talk about the subjective component of illness." *Human Communication Research* 27 (2001): 299–311.

L. A. Ford and R. D. Crabtree. "Telling, re-telling and talking about telling: Disclosure and/as surviving incest." *Women's Studies in Communication* 25 (2002): 53–87.

K. Ijams and L. Miller. "Perceptions of dream-disclosure: An exploratory study." *Communication Studies* 51 (2001): 135–148.

K. Prager and D. Buhrmester. "Intimacy and need fulfillment in couple relationships." *Journal of Social and Personal Relationships* 15 (1998): 435–469.

K. Voss, D. Markiewicz, and A. B. Doyle. "Friendship, marriage, and self-esteem." *Journal of Social and Personal Relationships* 16 (1999): 103–122.

Chapter Activities

1. Go to *http://www.queendom.com* and go to the link that features the "Top 5 Tests." Select the self-esteem option and complete the assessment. As reported on the Web site, this self-assessment tool has been used by over 100,000 people to measure their feelings of self-worth and how their beliefs may affect their communication with others. Complete the test, review the results, and see what advice is provided to you. Then reflect on what was learned, and how—if at all—this differed from what you already knew about yourself.

2. Review the statements from your "Who Am I?" exercise. Divide those that relate to your self-image and self-esteem. Then see if you can identify the source for each self-esteem statement. For instance, if one of your statements read, "I am a fun person to be around," attempt to explain how you know that about yourself. This exercise should serve as an excellent illustration of the basic ideas associated with symbolic interactionism.

3. Use a library database, like Infotrac or CommAbstracts, to locate articles related to the main topics in this chapter (self-concept, self-esteem, self-disclosure). Once you've found a number of articles on one of these topics, analyze them to see how many directly or indirectly relate to culture, power, and technology. Do most of them include information about these topics, or are they other contemporary issues that communication scholars should be focusing on?

4. Think for a minute about how your family communicated to you about certain topics, such as sex and drugs. What types of self-disclosures were used by your relatives to help you make informed decisions about your personal choices? How might you use some of the concepts discussed in this chapter to help understand why certain types of information were shared in certain ways? If time permits, break up into small groups in order to share your experiences and insights with others.

5. Spend some time volunteering with young people in your community. This could be reading to students at a local elementary school, mentoring teenagers at a community center, or simply spending time with some children currently residing at a local homeless shelter. During this time, pay close attention to how the young people describe themselves (in terms of their self-concepts). Then make a conscious attempt to interact with them in ways to nurture a more positive self-concept. Document what you did, and any changes that you observed over time.

6. Review your local newspaper and locate one or two articles that discuss a self-disclosure made by a politician, entertainer, athlete, or otherwise public person. Then analyze the article to determine the circumstances of the self-disclosure. For instance, you might discuss the context of the self-disclosure and the reasons why the person decided to share the information with the public. Then determine if the case matches the inverted-U model related to power and self-disclosure featured in Figure 3.5.

7. In his book, *Therapeutic Communication,* Paul L. Wachtel addresses the ethical questions regarding therapist's self-disclosures with clients. Do you think that counselors should use self-disclosures as a means to create a level of intimacy with clients, or should therapists avoid self-disclosures in order to remain an objective source for information? Break up into small groups and discuss the advantages and disadvantages for counselors who self-disclose about themselves during counseling sessions. Then, see if the group can generate some general guidelines that counselors should follow. ✦

Chapter 4

Perception and Communication

Contemporary Issues: The Power of Self-Perceptions

From all accounts, Jordan is a healthy, well-adjusted 12 year old. He does well in school, loves to swim, and listens to music. However, if given the choice, his favorite thing to do is play video games on his Play Station 2—sometimes up to three or four hours a day. His mother attempts to limit the time he spends playing video games, but as a single mother it isn't always easy. For a recent birthday, Jordan asked his mom for a new game, Resident Evil. *She got it for him, but was concerned about the explicitly violent content of the game.*

Advancing technologies continue to enhance the graphics of video games, so much so that individuals like Jordan's mom, who was raised on Pong, *are in constant amazement. Yet many parents and educators are voicing concern about the increasingly violent content of some video games. They argue that constant exposure to harmful images—even those that are not the focus of the game itself—will have a negative impact on how young people perceive themselves and others. According to some recent research, they may be right.*

In late 1999, newspapers around the United States reported that negative stereotypes about aging have a counterproductive effect on how senior citizens function. One social psychologist from Yale University Medical School, Becca Levey, has found that stereotypes can affect a person's memory, self-confidence, handwriting, and even will to live. Eliminating the negative stereotypes of seniors has been known to increase both mental and physical health.

For instance, researchers[1] chose 47 healthy, independent-living women and men with an average age of 70. Both groups played a series of computer games. While one group was playing, words like "wise," "experienced," and "sage" were flashed on a subliminal level. The other group was exposed to words such as "senile" and "forgetful." When researchers measured walking speed and agility for both groups, the group that had been exposed to the positive messages increased their average walking speed by 10 percent. In addition, these individuals showed an improved "foot swing time" that was similar to what occurs after 12 weeks of strength training!

This research provides some scientific support to the popular belief that negative self-stereotypes and positive thinking can, and do, affect people's lives. Given the findings summarized above, what impact do you think that constant, repeated exposure to violence might have on young girls and boys? Think about your own experience with mediated images. How are they tied to the perceptions that you have about yourself and others? How are these perceptions created, maintained, and/or changed over time? How do they affect interpersonal communication processes? By providing answers to these questions, this chapter will highlight the central role that perception plays in human communication interactions.

Myths About Interpersonal Communication

Read the five statements below. Each represents a commonly held belief about how perception operates in interpersonal communication processes. We present them here as a way to get you thinking critically about some of the assumptions that you have about how perceptions work. See if you can detect which statements are myths and which are true.

_____ Perceptions are formed in a linear, objective, straightforward process.

_____ Our current perceptions are independent from other perceptions.

_____ Perception (what people think happens) is just as important as reality (what actually happens).

_____ Some stereotypes are positive and enhance our communication effectiveness.

_____ Given its heavy reliance on verbal codes, our communication on the Internet is not really influenced by perception-related problems.

Understanding Perception as a Process

The perception process is central to communication. By definition, **perception** is the mental process through which we come to understand the world around us. Perceptions are not objective, fixed in time, or consistent from person to person. They are also not formed in a vacuum. Perceptions develop through the three stages of selection, organization, and interpretation. They then become part of a larger mental framework that guides our future perceptions.

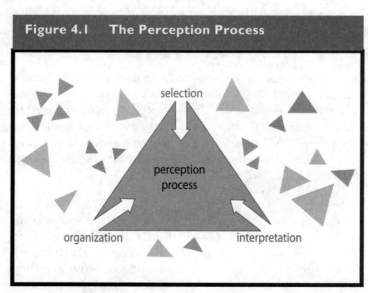

Figure 4.1   The Perception Process

selection

perception process

organization   interpretation

We describe each of these stages below. However, before reading the descriptions, you should understand that the stages overlap considerably. In order to present these ideas in a way that is easy to understand, we discuss each step in a linear fashion. But, as illustrated in Figure 4.1, the three stages occur simultaneously within a larger framework. One perception (larger triangle) develops amid existing perceptions (smaller surrounding triangles).

Selection

Right now, there are countless stimuli around you. We hope your attention is focused on your textbook: the words that make up sentences, pictures that illustrate ideas, and figures and diagrams that help you to understand the various concepts. Still, if you took a quick break, you could sense all the other stimuli. First, explore all the visual stimuli around you right now. There are no doubt hundreds, if not thousands, of things to see. Now use your ears to listen. What sounds can you hear? Shift your listening focus to different sounds; you may be surprised at all of the sounds around you. Other stimuli reach you through your other senses (smell, taste, and touch). From this brief exercise, you will probably realize just how many stimuli surround us at any given moment.

We constantly are being exposed to more information than we can handle. The perception process, then, begins when we select certain stimuli to attend to. We typically select stimuli that are of particular interest to us at the time. These could be things that are enjoyable, interesting, or central to fulfilling a need. **Selective attention** describes the reason why we choose certain stimuli over others: We simply do not have the capacity to attend to everything around us. We might be exposed to some things on a daily basis, yet not pay any attention to them. Then, because of some particular motivation or interest, we selectively attend to those things. For instance, suppose you are buying a new car. Are you the type of person who tries to purchase a car whose model, design, or color is atypical? We know several people who do, and are surprised at how many similar cars they notice after their purchase. These cars have always been on the roads around them; however, the buyers did not recognize them until after they had bought a similar car. Box 4.1 explores how this principle is used in advertising.

Box 4.1

Perceptions of TV Commercials: An Advertising Perspective

Research completed in the 1990s suggests that the average person is exposed to close to 1,800 advertising messages each day.[2] Given the increase in technology (e.g., the Internet), this number has undoubtedly continued to increase. Consequently, the success of television commercials lies in their ability to get and keep our attention. Many use familiar strategies like increasing the volume (which explains why the commercials always seem louder than the programs) and using stimulating visual images, music, and/or vibrant colors.

Think about those TV commercials that seem to do the best job at capturing the attention of millions of TV viewers around the world. A great point of reference is those that appear during the Super Bowl; advertisers pay *hundreds of thousands of dollars per second* for these ads. What are some that always grab your attention? Why do some people perceive them in different ways? Is it correct to assume that the "best" commercials are those that are out of the ordinary, are related to one of your particular interests, or fulfill some personal need or desire? Based on what you've learned about selective attention, how do these commercials compare to the basic ideas presented thus far?

What we attend to is also influenced by our existing beliefs, needs, or desires. This phenomenon is known as selective exposure, an idea that is closely related to selective attention. **Selective exposure** refers to the tendency for people to expose themselves to those things that support their current belief systems and avoid stimuli that challenge or contradict them. For instance, think about the choices you make in terms of the media. The type of newspaper, radio station, CD, Web site, television program, or magazine that you select most likely supports your ways of thinking. Some media forms, for example, are more liberal or conservative than others. More politically conservative persons typically expose themselves to media sources that match their beliefs. Consequently, they would listen to James Dobson's *Focus on the Family* (a conservative Christian program) every morning rather than Don Imus's *Imus in the Morning* (a liberal radio program out of New York).

Organization

We don't simply collect perceptions and leave it at that. Stimuli are selected through one or more of your five senses, but then need to be organized in ways that make sense. Those things that you select often are organized and interpreted rather quickly. Your brain simply draws on existing experiences to quicken the perception process. However, for new or different stimuli the process of organizing is more lengthy.

In general, we organize stimuli based on patterns. For instance, we group things that are close to one another. A proximity pattern exists when we organize all stimuli that exist close together as one unit. As illustrated in Figure 4.2, how we perceive individual stimuli is influenced by other things that surround it. We also organize stimuli according to their similarities and differences. Similar stimuli are grouped together and contrasted with stimuli that are different. For example, things are either good or bad, productive or unproductive, tasteful or distasteful, or right or wrong. As we grow older and are exposed to a greater number of stimuli, these groupings may become more complex and less static.

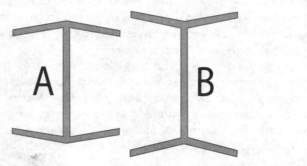

Figure 4.2 : **Which Lines Are Longer?**

Look at the middle lines in each of these illustrations. Which set of middle lines is longer?

A   B

If you were to actually measure the lines with a ruler, you would find that both are the same size. At a glance, however, it doesn't seem to be true. The reason is that the lines are surrounded by other lines that influence our perceptions.

Schemata are mental blueprints that help individuals structure their thought processes and organize and interpret the things around them. **Scripts** are a type of schema that guide behavior. Similar to a script for a play, they tell you how to act, what to say, and what happens when. **Prototypes** represent the ideal form of something. Think about your ideal car, house, pet, or career. These are prototypes; they help you evaluate stimuli in relation to your greatest expectations. **Stereotypes** are generalizations that we assume are true for all things belonging to a certain general category. We will explore how stereotypes affect human communication in a later section of this chapter. Until then, the example below will help demonstrate how schemata work together to organize stimuli.

Each of us has different perceptions for what should happen on "the first day of class." Your script provides you with information about what should happen when. For example, the professor will provide an introduction to the course and distribute the syllabi. A few students might *not* attend the first day of class; their script tells them that it is not important.

Each student has a prototype of what they perceive as a great professor. They also have ideas about the ideal time, size, and structure of a class. During the first day of class, students organize and evaluate the situation based on their prototypes. Very quickly, they also place various elements of the class into stereotypical categories that provide guidance as to what they can expect throughout the semester. For instance, all some students need to see is the age, gender, race, or dress of a professor and they immediately relate it to a stereotype they hold.

Professors also have schemata related to the first day of class. Like those of students, these can vary greatly depending from campus to campus, department to department, and person to person. As you might guess, students and professors who have different sets of schemata may start the class on the wrong foot. Box 4.2 provides the schemata of one communication professor. How are these perceptions similar to, or different from, those of your communication professor?

Box 4.2

Schemata for the First Day of Class: One Communication Professor's View

Script

1. Rearrange class into a semicircle (if possible).
2. Introduce yourself to students.
3. Make sure everyone is in the right place.
4. Distribute and explain the syllabus.
5. Facilitate an ice-breaking activity that helps students get to know one another and understand what the class will entail.
6. Create a dialogue about student expectations of the class.
7. Cover basic introductory information (time permitting).

Prototypes

The ideal student:

- checks schedule and the classroom location prior to the first day of class;

- purchases the textbook prior to the first day of class and flips through it in order to learn about the class content;

- comes to class a few minutes early;

- brings the textbook, a notebook, and at least two writing utensils;

- sits in the front, or middle, of the classroom and participates when appropriate; and

- is ready to ask questions about the course.

The ideal classroom:

- is clean, bright (natural light), and decorated with contemporary fashions;

☞
- has chairs and/or tables that can be moved into different configurations;

- is large enough to have all students sit in a semicircle;

- has minimal audiovisual equipment (VCR/monitor overhead project, computer access) that is built in; and

- has heating and cooling mechanisms that the professor can control.

  The ideal class meeting times:

- Two times a week, either Monday/Wednesday or Tuesday/Thursday

- Midmorning, preferably beginning at 9:00–9:30 A.M.

Stereotypes

- Students who do not attend the first day of class are minimalists, meaning that they do just enough to get by in the class.

- Students who come unprepared (without any materials to take notes, for example) will not do well.

- Students who sit in the back of the room and do not participate, or who participate in disruptive ways, are not committed to learning.

Interpretation

As we organize stimuli, we also interpret them. Interpretation assigns meaning and value to the stimuli that we have selected and organized, usually by comparing and contrasting them. For instance, when you receive an assignment back, you probably look at the grade and place it into a category in your mental grade book. The professor may have used *B* to signify that your work was good, but your mental schemata may place a B in a not-so-positive light. This brief example illustrates how closely tied the organization and interpretation processes are to one another. However, imagine how the interpretation of your grade may change once you learned that a B was the highest grade in class. We are constantly comparing and contrasting stimuli as a means to understand their meaning and value.

Finally, we might use closure to complete the perception process. With **closure**, we fill in the gaps with stimuli in order to make sense of them. Whenever you "read between the lines" to better understand what someone is saying, you are using closure. For example, on the first day of class students may use closure to assume that the middle-aged person who comes into class is the professor and not a student, and that someone who looks very young is a student and not the professor.

Once the selection-organization-interpretation process has been completed, perceptions then become part of a larger framework. Because of selective exposure, these perceptions often-times simply reinforce ideas (schemata) that already exist. Yet, perceptions of new stimuli—or familiar stimuli seen in a different light—can add new dimensions to the ways that people select, organize, and interpret things around them. The remainder of this chapter discusses two things: (1) why differences in perceptions occur, and (2) what perceptual patterns exist. This information is important given that as we develop perceptions, they become part of our memory and act as guides for future perceptions.

Why Do Perceptions Differ?

The three-step perception process is consistent from person to person. Yet the ways in which individuals select, organize, and interpret stimuli around them vary greatly. Four factors can help us understand why different perceptions occur: cultural differences, individual differences, past experiences, and situational context.

Cultural Differences

Culture, as defined in Chapter 2, is about more than simply sharing some characteristic—like skin color, chronological age, or a language—with others. In many instances, it also encompasses a set of experiences that influences how you come to understand the world around you. Differences in perceptions, then, can be related to your cultural background. Let's take, for example, Katherine, who is an 18-year-old first-year student at a large state university. She was hesitant about attending such a large school, but relieved when she met her roommate, Erika, and found out that both were Christians. Katherine and Erika spent a lot of time talking about their faith, so much so that they arranged to visit each other's church during break. However, the visits were awkward because both perceived each other's service as "kinda weird." For a devout Catholic like Katherine, visiting Erika's church—a full gospel Pentecostal church where people shouted, danced, and "got full with the holy spirit"—was shocking. Katherine couldn't understand how people could worship God like that. Erika was equally disturbed by her visit to Katherine's church. She couldn't imagine how people could be so low-key and routine in their worship experiences.

In this example, two women shared a common identity marker but had drastically different perceptions as to how it should expressed. Seeing spirituality as a cultural element helps explain the differences in their perceptions. Both had been attending church since they were little. Yet they never realized that their church membership reflected a particular culture that had specific norms about dress, time, music, and presentational styles.

Age differences can often be the cause for different perceptions of the same stimuli.

Individuals who share a common culture typically share a common set of experiences that influences how they see the world. This idea is at the heart of **standpoint theory**, a body of theories grounded in the field of sociology and recently adopted by a growing number of communication scholars.[3] Standpoint theories are based on two simple ideas. First, the world looks different depending on your social standing. Second, your social standing is largely influenced by cultural elements like race/ethnicity, gender, class, and sexual orientation.

As an example, think about how you feel about holding hands with your significant other in public. Many individuals see this as an important step to signal the status of your relationship to others. However, different cultures have varying norms about *who* should show affection to *whom* and *when*. Cultural norms, then, will influence how you perceive hand-holding. In addition, standpoint theorists would point to how social standing affects your perceptions. From the vantage point of most U.S. citizens, holding hands with your significant other in public is nothing more than a simple display of affection. But in many communities, holding hands with your partner is something that is only accepted if you are heterosexual. Gays or lesbians who hold hands are generally taking a huge risk that might result in physical abuse or verbal assaults. In this example, standpoint theory allows us to understand how one group could perceive hand-holding as innocent and romantic, while another sees it as a radical political statement. Box 4.3 describes research on MTV's *The Real World* to further illustrate this point.

Box 4.3

Practical Research

Cultural Perceptions of "Real-World" Conflict

With the success of *Survivor, Big Brother, Temptation Island, The Bachelor,* and *Boy Meets Boy,* reality-based television has become increasingly popular. Researchers Mark Orbe and Kiesha Warren used a clip from one of the early reality-based television programs, MTV's *The Real World,* to study the perceptions of individuals from different cultural groups.[4] Specifically, they presented a video clip from the first season of the show (New York) to diverse groups of people (mostly African American and European American). The clip showed an argument between Julie, an 18-year-old European American woman from Alabama, and Kevin, a 24-year-old African American man from New Jersey. Participants in the study were then asked to discuss their perceptions of what happened, who was at fault, and what could have been done to avoid the conflict.

The results were extremely interesting, especially for what they revealed about perception differences between cultural groups. African American women saw *race* as the main factor in the conflict. Specifically they pointed to the potential role that interracial sexual attraction and racial stereotyping played in Julie and Kevin's argument. In comparison, European American women saw *gender* as the distinguishing marker in the conflict. Their perceptions focused on how a man, Kevin, attempted to aggressively use his body and voice to intimidate Julie.

European American men saw the conflict as a result of *personal* differences. Race and gender were only addressed in limited ways. Instead, the focus of the discussion was on how Kevin and Julie's personalities were at the root of the conflict. And what about African American men? Many defined the conflict as one where race played a role; however, they also saw how *other factors*—like age, socioeconomic status, and upbringing—came into play as well.

This research provides a clear example of the way cultural standpoints can lead to varying perceptions of the same stimuli. Within their article, Orbe and Warren also discuss how some individual differences were noted within each cultural group. Follow-up research on this topic also compared Latinos'/as' perceptions to those of African Americans and European Americans.[5]

Individual Differences

Standpoint theory also gives us a way to understand the individual differences that exist within and between social groups. In other words, we must see people not only as members of one or more cultural groups. We must also see them as individuals whose particular life experiences make them unique.

Individual differences can be based in specific personality traits, personal attitudes, and particular preferences. Think about how these three things can generate different perceptions.

Humor is a good example. A joke that one person finds extremely funny may be highly offensive to others. Can you think of a funny joke or story that you recently heard? How did it mesh with your particular personality? Did others have different ideas about the appropriateness or the topical focus? In general, what types of things do you find funny? Are there certain things that you consider to be in poor taste? Your perceptions of humor—as well as other stimuli in the environment—are tied to your individual personality traits, personal attitudes, and particular preferences. Given the wide variety of individual differences, it should not be surprising that different perceptions of a single stimulus exist.

We can also study how certain physical traits influence the perceptions of individuals. All of us, for example, have a certain height, weight, and body type. Dianna, for example, is a 20-something woman who just had her first baby. Although the child weighed just over 7 pounds, Dianna gained about 40 pounds. She only weighed 110 pounds before her pregnancy, so this was a significant change for her. Just two months after the birth of her child, she weighs 125 pounds but still feels, as she puts it, "like a big, fat blob." Do you think her self-perceptions might be different than how others perceive her? Consider the perspectives of the following individuals:

- Her husband, a former college standout athlete who is now 30–40 pounds overweight

- Her older sister, who, in her adult life, has never weighed less than 175 pounds

- Her best friend, who has three children and has unsuccessfully struggled to maintain her "ideal" weight range, 140–150 pounds

- Her younger cousin, who has never weighed more than 100 pounds

Can you see how individual differences, in this case a person's own weight and other experiences, might prompt different perceptions of Dianna? Research, like that of Peggy Orenstein, has long established that perceptions of weight are not the same for different cultural groups. For example, maintaining a certain weight is generally more important to women than men. European American women, as compared to African American women and Latinas, are less accepting of a healthy, rounded body type.[6] Of course, these are generalizations and not true for all women or men. But they do provide another interesting example as to how culture can affect perceptions. They also remind us how important it is to recognize individual differences among any one cultural group.

Past Experiences

As discussed in Chapter 1, one element in all interpersonal communication encounters is field of experience. All of us have had a lifetime of experiences that make us who we are. Consciously or unconsciously, we rely on them to determine the way we communicate with others.

Think about, for instance, your current relationships with friends and/or romantic partners. You have a complex set of past experiences that influence how you interact with these persons. These include your observations of others' relationships as you were growing up, your personal needs and desires, as well as your past relationships. Some people think that they can start a relationship anew—almost like having a blank slate. But it is important to recognize that all of us bring "baggage," in the form of our past experiences, to our current relationships. In a general sense, how we come to define friendship, love, and what it means to be in a relationship is affected by these past experiences. On a smaller scale, perceptions of everyday interactions—like what gifts, if any, are exchanged on partners' birthdays—are also influenced by past experiences. Did you expect a gift? Did you like the gift? Did you think that it was appropriate and/or meaningful? Or was it something that you perceived as ineffective in capturing the status of your relationship? The answers to these questions, in part, are influenced by your past experiences with gift-giving, relationship expectations, and other relational partners.

As you can see with this example, our past experiences work to influence our current perceptions. **Perceptual constancy** refers to the tendency that perceptions remain consistent over time. In other words, once we develop a particular perception of some form of stimuli, any future perceptions of that stimuli (however defined) will be similar to the first one and difficult to change. To extend the previous example, our past experiences with birthday gifts influence how we perceive whatever current gifts we receive. You may come from a household where birthdays were acknowledged but not a big deal. You might have had a cake for some "special" birthdays but few, if any, presents. In comparison, some people are raised to believe that birthdays deserve huge celebrations. Each and every birthday includes a party with lots of people, food, and gifts. According to perceptual constancy, changing your perceptions of how a birthday is celebrated is difficult. Imagine the potential problems when two people start dating, don't discuss their past experiences, and behave as if everyone has the same expectations about a birthday gift.

Situational Factors

Perception differences can also exist based on situational factors. The same individual, for instance, might perceive the same exact stimuli in different ways depending on the context. A good example of this is seen in Figure 4.3. Surrounded by letters, the stimuli (13) is most likely perceived as a *B*. However, when surrounded by numbers, it is more likely to be perceived as *13*. Being an effective interpersonal communicator includes understanding that situational factors influence the way we perceive both verbal and nonverbal codes. Remember that the perception process involves three overlapping phases: selecting, organizing, and interpreting stimuli. Situational factors affect what goes on during each of the phases.

Figure 4.3 Perception in Situational Contexts

Read each of the symbols below.

11 12 13 14 15

* A 13 C *

Can you see how natural it is to interpret the same symbol, 13, in two different ways based on the situational context? Our perceptions are not developed in isolation. Instead, we look to other stimuli in the context to provide clues to guide our perceptions.

What are some situational factors? Consider location. Seeing a couple in skimpy bathing suits at the beach prompts one set of perceptions; having them knock on your door at Thanksgiving prompts a whole different set. In addition, our perceptions are influenced by any other stimuli that are present. These stimuli often serve to help contextualize our interpretations. For instance, if the Thanksgiving couple in bathing suits were also carrying a bunch of tropical props—in addition to a brochure about winter vacation specials to Aruba—our perceptions would probably be different.

An individual's feelings and circumstances at the time of interacting with the stimulus can also impact his or her perception of it. Do the ways that you see things change depending on how you feel? Of course they do. Perceptions of everyday activities (driving to class, taking notes, caring for family members or friends) change drastically when a person has a headache, experiences fatigue, or has a hangover. If you are tired or sick, something as relatively simple as getting out of bed and into the shower becomes difficult and you may perceive stimuli differently than when you are well rested and healthy. In a similar way, perceptions of things to eat and drink will probably differ depending on how hungry or thirsty you are.

Another situational factor that influences how people perceive the world around them is the weather and season. As we wrote this section of the book, both of us were experiencing a wonderful sunny day that had a clear impact on how we perceived everything around us. It was mid-January and we had just gone through a two-month period where all we saw were snow and clouds, and more snow and clouds. A single day of bright sunshine—even though it was no more than 20 degrees—suddenly made everything in our lives a little more pleasant. The same kind of day two months early, or three to four months later, would have been perceived differently. The stimuli that we were interpreting didn't change, but a shift in their context did. The result was a change in our perceptions.

Finally, the time of day, and possibly even the day of the week, can also influence how you perceive stimuli. Consider the following example. Most people would assume that for a parent, nothing is as beautifully sweet as hearing your child say, "I love you." While this is generally true, your perceptions of this message will probably not be positive when it comes at 3:00 a.m. after you just spent the past two hours trying to get that child to sleep! Imagine that this scenario occurs on a Wednesday morning amidst a hectic week of juggling work and final exams. Such vivid examples should make it relatively easy to see how situational factors affect our perceptions every day.

Common Patterns in Perception

People move through the same three phases (selection, organization, and interpretation) in the perception process. However, we experience these phases differently based on things like cultural identity, individuality, field experience, and situational context. In spite of these differences, several common patterns do exist. These are tendencies that all humans share in terms of how they perceive themselves and others. Next, we'll describe five common patterns.

Our Perceptions Are Ethnocentric

Ethnocentrism is the belief that your cultural group is superior to all other groups. To some extent, all individuals are ethnocentric in that they are raised to believe that their values, customs, dress, food, and other cultural norms are "ordinary." As people learn about how other cultures function, a common pattern is to use your own ways of doing things as the standard to interpret the stimuli. In many ways, ethnocentrism operates on an unconscious level. Even when we recognize a tendency to be ethnocentric in our perceptions of others, it can be difficult to avoid this pattern.

Let's use food for an example. What are your perceptions of each of the following foods?

- Rabbit
- Raw fish
- Ostrich
- Snail
- Beetle
- Pig
- Cow

The perceptions that you have for each of these things—all of which are examples of different foods that people eat around the world—is grounded in what you view as appropriate. People who were raised eating rabbit would see that as "normal," but other foods like ostrich or snails as "weird." Interestingly, some cultures limit what they view as appropriate food to certain parts of an animal. For instance, many people in the United States eat pig (pork chops or sausage), but can't understand others who eat pig feet or chitlins (a pig's small intestines). For others, the idea of eating *any* type of meat is unacceptable.

Different cultures have different norms about food. They also have varying expectations in terms of dress, time, holiday celebrations, music, and what constitutes appropriate communication (both verbal and nonverbal). These differences can be based on our race/ethnicity, age, region, nation of origin, or spirituality, or a combination thereof. During our interactions, we typically assume that others are like us. Consequently, our perceptions are based on the standards that guide our personal lives, even though others may operate from a different set of standards. This tendency leads us to be ethnocentric in our perceptions of others.

We See What We Want to See

Do you know people who want a satisfying relationship so badly that they ignore signs that indicate otherwise? For example, some of us may wonder how a person could ignore signs of cheating or rationalize these signs in order to maintain the image of a happy couple. Yet some partners do not seem to notice that their significant others are spending long

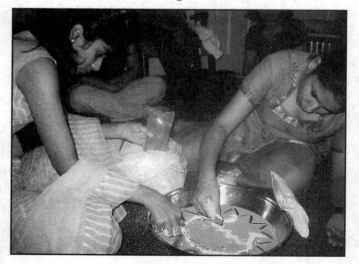

Ethnocentrism occurs when we perceive different cultural rituals as weird, uncivilized, or just plain wrong.

amounts of time away with no concrete explanations. When they do notice some clues, they explain them in ways that allow them to maintain the idea that their relationship is stable. Thus, personal desires influence the perception process.

In similar ways, our expectations also influence our perceptions. For example, Karen is a person who likes to start each day reading her horoscope. Although critics say these are too general to be meaningful, Karen proceeds with her day with a particular expectation that her horoscope will provide some direction. One day, Karen's horoscope said:

> *There's a strong possibility you could see someone at work in a fresh light today and gain a new friend in the process. The door is unlocked. Walk through with an open heart.*

Throughout the day, she saw a couple of examples of things that were relevant. A new classmate invited her to lunch, and an old friend appeared a little more flirtatious than usual. It would be safe to say that Karen might not have seen the connection between these events and her horoscope if she didn't read the newspaper that day. On some level, she wants the predictions to be true, which guides her observations. The tendency to see what you expect or want to see is known as **perceptual accentuation.** For Karen, a keen interest in her horoscope influenced her perceptions.

Self-fulfilling prophecy also relates to this idea. By definition, a **self-fulfilling prophecy** happens when people make a prediction that ultimately becomes true, in part, because they behave as if it is true.[7] Sometimes roommates fall into this trap. Based on first impressions, they expect that they will not get along with someone, and those predictions become true because of preconceived ideas. In other words, roommates can unconsciously find exactly what they expect to find, even though other positive cues exist (see Box 4.4 for another application).

Box 4.4

The Thinking Behind Keeping a Gratitude Journal

Through her popular talk-show program, Oprah Winfrey has popularized the idea of keeping a gratitude journal. From her own accounts, Oprah has always seen the value of keeping a journal filled with personal reflections of her daily life. Accordingly, she has been journaling since she was a young girl. However, in recent years she noticed that those journals seemed to focus on negative struggles in her life most often related to her personal relationships, weight, professional accomplishments, and public image. This recognition prompted a change in the way she journaled. Instead of focusing on what struggles she was experiencing, she would concentrate on describing five specific things that she was grateful for each day. These things did not necessarily have to be momentous things; they could be relatively small. The shift of focus, according to Oprah, has been life changing. And, in true Oprah style, she has passed along the empowering strategy to her viewers.

Not surprisingly, many viewers have also shifted the way they journal. Others have started keeping a journal for the first time. Many viewers have shared how this simple process has changed their outlook on life. Each person now looks for things throughout the day that can be documented in his or her gratitude journal. Some days are easier than others, but most are constantly amazed at how many positive things they notice now that they are actively searching for them.

What do you think about keeping a gratitude journal? Can it actually change the way that you experience life? Think about how different concepts discussed in this chapter relate to your perceptions. Can an increased awareness of the perception process actually change how you view things around you? What do you think?

Consider an exchange between a state trooper and someone who has been stopped for speeding. Say, for instance, that the driver anticipates that the trooper is a jerk who has stopped him to meet some kind of quota. Regardless of whether this perception is true or not, a self-fulfilling prophecy occurs when the driver interacts with the state trooper as if his perceptions were true. The driver's tone, body position, and choice of words all communicate his disrespect. In response, the state trooper's communication is affected and becomes more abrupt and authoritative. The driver picks up on this and his initial perception—state troopers are jerks—has been reinforced.

Initial Perceptions Can Be Difficult to Change

First impressions last a lifetime. How many of us have heard this saying before? Whether accurate or not, initial perceptions establish a foundation from which future perceptions are launched. If you think about it for a minute, it makes sense. The first time you encounter a new stimulus, you go through a process of selection, organization, and interpretation. Then this perception becomes a part of your mental imagery. The next time you encounter the stimulus, the perception process will be quicker because you can take a shortcut using the perceptual template that was established earlier. In this regard, your first impression acts as an anchor for future perceptions. Even when different, future perceptions are perceived as closer to the anchor than they necessarily are.

Organizing schemata helps to facilitate a smooth, less strenuous interpretation process. By creating categories, we are able to make quick judgments on stimuli that are similar to those we have encountered in the past. For instance, our initial interaction with Brett, a coworker, may suggest that he is friendly, outgoing, and sociable. Once this perception has been established, these three characteristics help to form a mental blueprint for him. Whenever we encounter Brett, our initial perception is triggered and shapes how we interpret his current behavior. We may even see him in another context and notice that he isn't as friendly as normal. However, our initial perceptions are not likely to change. Instead, we will most likely fit our perceptions of his behaviors into our existing schemata. We will, in other words, see his behaviors as friendly—just not as friendly as normal, or caused by some rational explanation. This adjustment is known as **selective distortion**, a process whereby we alter our perceptions of stimuli so that our existing ideas remain intact.

What typically does *not* happen is that our existing perceptual constructs change with exposure to contradictory stimuli. In the case of Brett, we are more likely to selectively attend to cues that support our initial impression that he is sociable and outgoing. This is an example of selective exposure. Or we may notice that his current behaviors contradict our initial perceptions. Instead of altering or changing our initial perceptions, we are more likely to view his behaviors as an exception or isolated case. If Brett continues to act in an unfriendly, nonsociable way, our perceptions may change. Yet we will still see his

First impressions set the stage for all future interactions.

behaviors within an existing perception that contradicts these characteristics, so any change will be slow and gradual.

This perceptual pattern is one that most people acknowledge. We spend considerably more time when meeting someone important (prospective client, new boss, or future in-laws) for the first time. There are certain instances when we find that our initial perceptions were inaccurate and change them accordingly. However, this does not happen without some significant amount of mental energy.

We Judge Our Own Intentions, but Others' Actions

Have you ever been driving on a busy street and been cut off by another driver who suddenly switches lanes? Most people perceive such drivers as careless and irresponsible (and a whole host of other characteristics not appropriate to print here!). What happens, though, when *you* suddenly have to change lanes and accidentally pull out in front of another car? In this instance, we understand that our behavior was a result of something out of our control; perhaps there was something in the road that we had to avoid. We know that we didn't intend to cut anyone off, and we judge our behavior accordingly. However, we typically are not aware of others' intentions, so we judge their actions more harshly. In short, we can see how a perceptual pattern emerges: We judge our own *intentions*, but others' *actions*. In addition, we chalk up the good things we do to something internal; the bad things are caused by some external factor that was out of our control. This is known as a **self-attribution bias**. This concept does not reflect a universal truth, but it is a general pattern that is important to understand how we perceive self and others.

Self-attribution bias is a concept associated with **attribution theory**, a set of ideas that explains how people understand the causes for human behavior.[8] Attributions are explanations that we use to understand events or occurrences. For instance, when trying to determine why a specific person acted in a specific way, we ask ourselves several questions:

- In similar situations, do others behave in similar ways?

- Is the person's behavior consistent over time?

- Does the person's behavior reflect a general pattern or a specific case?

- Is the person able to control the behavior or not?

The answers allow us to create perceptions that include the reasons a person has for acting in certain ways.

Let's take an example from an organizational meeting of a new sports team. Our perceptions of a new team member (Michaela) who becomes angry during an orientation meeting will vary depending on our attributions. We most likely will ask ourselves the following questions: Did others attending the meeting become angry, or was she the only one? Is Michaela angry often, or simply in specific situations? Our ultimate perceptions, and the way we interpret her behavior, will be determined by our responses that will lead us to certain conclusions. For instance, if Michaela was the only person who became angry, we would likely conclude there was some internal reason for her behavior. A perception that Michaela is an angry person might also explain her behaviors if they are consistent from situation to situation. If this were an isolated expression of anger and/or if others in the meeting also were angry, we would form a different perception.

Note that the attribution process includes a number of concepts discussed earlier, especially past experiences and situational context. Our tendency to attribute human behavior to certain causes does not occur in a vacuum. Instead self-attributions, as well as those we process for others, are affected by different communication elements.

We work to maintain balance among our perceptions. Earlier we discussed the importance of initial perceptions and how they set the stage for the way we select, organize, and interpret similar stimuli. One of the reasons why our initial perceptions are so influential is that we typically strive to maintain balance in our perceptions. In other words, once we establish a perception we make assumptions that are consistent with it. This is a largely unconscious process. But it allows us to avoid any uncomfortable feelings that may occur when our perceptions contradict one another.

Maintaining consistency, or a balance, among perceptions is difficult because we attach some sort of positive or negative value to our perceptions. Very few, in fact, are neutral. The idea that a larger system of perceptions affects our judgment of additional, individual perceptions was first proposed in the 1940s.[9] Over the years, it has become known as the **implicit personality theory**. In short, this theory suggests that as soon as we obtain information about a person, we form a mental catalogue of traits for him or her. We then use closure to assume that other traits consistent with this mental picture must apply to the person. In this way, we keep our perceptions of an individual in balance.

A specific example may help illustrate how this pattern functions. For instance, think about Dr. Brown, a favorite professor of many students on your campus. Dr. Brown challenges her students, but she makes learning fun, exciting, and meaningful. Students most enjoy all the wonderful stories she tells. Based on what you know about Dr. Brown, how would you describe her in terms of the following?

Attractive - - - - - - - - - - - - - - - **or**- - - - - - - - - - - - - Unattractive
Romantic - - - - - - - - - - - - - - **or**- - - - - - - - - - - - - Unromantic
Honest - - - - - - - - - - - - - - - **or**- - - - - - - - - - - - Dishonest
Generous - - - - - - - - - - - - - - **or**- - - - - - - - - - - - Stingy
Reliable - - - - - - - - - - - - - - **or**- - - - - - - - - - - - Unreliable
A great mother - - - - - - - - - **or**- - - - - - - - - - - - A horrible mother

According to the implicit personality theory, most individuals—given her positive reputation with students—would assume that Dr. Brown is also attractive, romantic, honest, generous, reliable, and a great mother. Within the implicit personality theory, using existing positive perceptions of a person to assume that he or she has other positive characteristics is known as the **halo effect**. A reverse "halo effect" also occurs; if we believe that a person has a few negative traits, then a mental catalogue is formed and we will assume that the person has other negative characteristics as well.

We Tend to Maintain Perceptions That Are Balanced

We also work to maintain a balance in the way our perceptions relate to one another. For instance, let's say Alejandro, Brittany, and Charisse are high school students. If Alejandro is really good friends with Brittany and Charisse, he will assume that they would also be good friends with each other. But if he was good friends with Charisse and really disliked Brittany, he might assume that Charisse also would dislike Brittany. Figure 4.4 illustrates the types of relationships between these three people that would be balanced. What do you think typically happens when Alejandro experiences imbalance? For instance, what might occur when he discovers that Charisse is a good friend of Brittany, a person he considers an enemy? According to this perception pattern, Alejandro would need to reevaluate his perceptions of Brittany and/or Charisse so that they would be consistent (e.g., like Brittany or dislike Charisse).

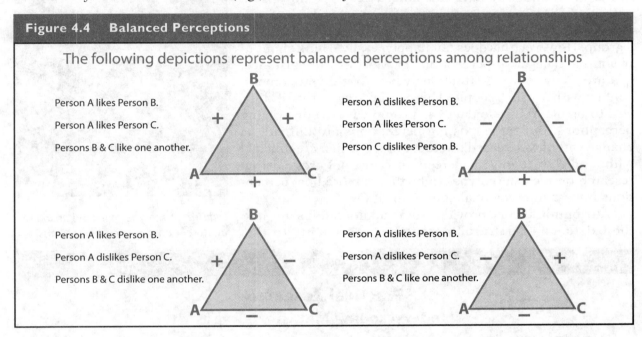

Figure 4.4   Balanced Perceptions

The following depictions represent balanced perceptions among relationships

Person A likes Person B.

Person A likes Person C.

Persons B & C like one another.

Person A dislikes Person B.

Person A likes Person C.

Person C dislikes Person B.

Person A likes Person B.

Person A dislikes Person C.

Persons B & C dislike one another.

Person A dislikes Person B.

Person A dislikes Person C.

Persons B & C like one another.

Cultural Stereotypes: A Form of Overattribution

Cultural stereotypes are preconceived ideas that we have about a person based on one or more cultural groups to which that person belongs. Many cultural stereotypes exist: Women are emotional. Men don't stop and ask for directions. Whites can't dance (or jump). Blacks can. People from the East Coast are rude. Southerners are slow. Midwesterners are conservative. If we had time, we could generate literally thousands of stereotypes for different groups.

Traditionally, stereotypes have been regarded as either negative (gay men are promiscuous) or positive (Asian Americans are good at math). However, "positive" cultural stereotypes are just as dangerous as those that are negative because they represent assumptions based on one aspect of a person's identity. All cultural stereotypes are unproductive, in fact, because they include a false supposition. Having a fixed impression as to what you assume about a particular person based on one identity marker leads to misunderstandings. It is more productive for your communication to acknowledge the person as an individual who is a part of a number of groups than to make assumptions about the person based on one group membership.

How are cultural stereotypes formed? We can draw from our earlier explanation of common perception patterns to answer this question. Typically, our initial perceptions of other cultural groups are based on limited knowledge of that group. Because we don't have much contact, we form schemata that represent generalities we have gained through what others have told us or from what we have seen in the media. Our initial perceptions, while incomplete and general, then serve as a guiding force for our future interactions. Through selective exposure and selective distortion, we reinforce these initial perceptions.[10] This is not to say that our initial interactions remain unchangeable. Over time—and with increased interactions with different members of cultural groups—we can move beyond our initial perceptions of a group. However, this does not happen easily. Think about it. If you have negative perceptions of Muslims, for instance, you are likely to avoid situations where you might come in contact with Muslim people. This creates a cycle that is difficult to break. Your avoidance is prompted by your existing perceptions, but these existing perceptions are difficult to change without increased interactions . . . which are unlikely without a change in your perceptions. Box 4.5 uses existing research on metastereotypes to further explore how perceptions impact interpersonal communication.

Cultural stereotypes can lead an individual to act on distorted perceptions.

Attribution theory provides some additional insight into the existence of cultural stereotypes. According to this

Box 4.5

Practical Research
Understanding Metastereotypes

Historically, researchers have spent considerable time studying the existence of stereotypes and their impact on human communication. The result has been a considerable body of literature that includes a significant amount of research and theory on racial stereotypes. Only recently, however, has attention been paid to the existence and relevance of metastereotypes. **Metastereotypes** are the perceptions that one group has of the stereotypes that other groups have of their group.

In 1997, Lee Sigelman and Steven A. Tuch published a study on metastereotypes that focused on African American perceptions of European Americans' stereotypes.[11] As exploratory research in this area, their study compared the percentage of European Americans who endorsed a particular racial stereotype with the percentage of African Americans who *perceived* that most European Americans endorsed the stereotype. Below we have listed five summaries of their findings. The left column describes stereotypes of African Americans, the middle lists the percentage of European Americans (EA) who hold that stereotype, and the right column the percentage of African Americans (AA) who hold that metastereotype.

Stereotype	EA Stereotype (%)	AA Metastereotype (%)
Prefer to live off welfare	59	75
Violent	54	82
Lazy	47	69
Unintelligent	31	76
Unpatriotic	18	44

☞ Notice that in every case, the percentage of African Americans holding a particular metastereotype is higher than the actual percentage of European Americans who report endorsing the stereotype. Sigelman and Tuch concluded that the actual percentage of European Americans who hold racial stereotypes is probably higher than reported, given that some would not feel comfortable admitting such beliefs. In some cases, however, the difference is quite large. So, what is the impact when African Americans overestimate how many European Americans believe in racial stereotypes? Can you see how these complex sets of perceptions impact the daily interactions between individuals of different racial and ethnic groups? Existing research on metastereotypes, such as what is highlighted here, helps us further understand how multiple perceptions—all of which affect communication—exist simultaneously.

approach, cultural stereotypes can be understood as a form of overattribution. Remember that attributions are explanations we use to understand human behavior. Overattribution occurs when we focus on one or more obvious characteristics of a person to explain *all* their behaviors. Take, for example, the experiences of Kala, a young African American student who was raised in a household headed by a single mother. Kala is generally an outstanding student. However, several recent instances of misbehavior have prompted the staff at her school to assume that her behavior is related to her current family situation. Kala's behaviors could have been linked to any number of elements. She could be having difficulty with the teaching style of a particular teacher or being teased by a few of her classmates. Maybe a recurring illness has triggered her actions. Overattribution occurs when others, especially those who do not notice other possible factors, assume that behavior can be explained by an "obvious" factor (her "dysfunctional" home). In fact, researchers have used the term *the ultimate attribution error*[12] to describe the tendency to attribute negative acts of outgroup members to an aspect of their culture.

For those persons in the minority, overattribution can occur frequently. The perceived cause of a woman's behavior may be tied to characteristics associated with being female (such as her menstrual cycle). Everything that people of color say or do may somehow be linked to their racial and/or ethnic background. In many ways, we identify microcultural group members by that which makes them a minority. People are not able to simply be people; instead, they become the "African American accountant," "gay brother," "disabled student," or "Jewish neighbor." Remember that for many, these identity elements are important to recognize. However, overattribution is likely to occur when others focus on one human characteristic and ignore others. The "Jewish neighbor," for example, is a complex person who may also identify strongly in terms of his race/ethnicity, age, socioeconomic status, and sexual orientation. It is rare when a person's behavior can be traced directly back to one factor. By remembering this point, we can avoid overattributing a person's behavior.

Perceptions of Technology

A couple of years ago, an e-mail was circulated that provided a link to a Web site with a unique service. It could take your picture while you sat at your computer and allow you to send it to people all over the world. Many people were amazed at how advanced computer technology had become and wanted to take advantage of this opportunity. After making sure that they had their best smile on, they went through the necessary steps only to discover that when "their picture" appeared on the screen, it was of a cute monkey!

How many people do you think that this e-mail prank fooled? It stands to reason that those who believed it also understood that recent advances in technology have made many things that were unimaginable 20 years ago a distinct reality. Currently, most Internet use is limited to stimuli that we can see and hear. But can you imagine computer technology that allows us to also use other senses like touch, smell, and taste? Wouldn't it be great to be able to feel a sweater before we purchased it online? Or sample the smell and taste of a meal from a restaurant that we plan to visit on an upcoming trip? These are things that seem only possible in science fiction. However, efforts are currently underway to provide such sensory stimulation via the Internet. Some companies, in fact, already have these basic capabilities (see Box 4.6). According to reports published in early 2001, many others hope to add similar features in the near future, including computer games and online adult Web sites that will include touch and smell.[13]

Box 4.6

Touch, Smell, and Taste via the Internet

Most of us are accustomed to basing our Internet experience on sight and sound stimuli. However, advances to also include touch, smell, and taste are already in the works. Below are a few examples, along with corresponding Web sites. The technological advances described here excite some people, while others remain skeptical. What are your perceptions of the potential to increase our sensory perceptions on the Web?

- Logitech began selling iFeel computer mice in 2000. The devices use touch technology from San Jose–based Immersion. (*http://immersion.com*)

- Trisenx of Savannah, Georgia, is developing technology that allows individuals to sample foods with both smell and taste via the Internet. The company already has a separate smell-only device with 20 different fragrances. (*http://trisenx.com*)

- A company based in Oakland, California, DigiScents, is working to enhance smell attachments for computers. They are also trying to develop a consumer version so that "scent cameras" may complement personal Webcams or video recorders. (*http://digicents.com*)

The Power of Perceptions

Do you see a familiar pattern here? Personal perceptions influence human behavior. Those individuals whose initial perceptions of the Internet were unfavorable are unlikely to get online, which is the only way they could discover the benefits that come with Internet access. Looking at perceptions of the computer-based technology, then, can help you understand why certain individuals, or groups of individuals, are less likely to get online.

This idea might provide some insight into the differences in Internet use for various racial and ethnic groups in the United States. Research consistently reports that Asian Americans and European Americans have much greater access to the information superhighway than do African Americans, Latinos/as, or Native Americans. Some reports have indicated that the gap is closing;[14] others point to a growing disparity between specific groups.[15] For instance, one study conducted in 1999 found that 47 percent of European Americans own computers, but fewer than half as many African Americans do. Only about 25 percent of Latinos/as own computers. However, over 55 percent of Asian Americans have one, and 36 percent have Internet access—the highest of any racial and ethnic group. Remember, we don't want to fall into the trap of overattribution and assume that Internet use is solely related to a person's racial and/or ethnic identity. Other factors, such as socioeconomic status, are just as important to consider. However, the 1999 study indicated that children in lower income European American families are three times more likely to have Internet access than children in a comparable African American family and four times more likely than those in a Latino/a household.

Many Internet companies are working diligently to strive for greater equality in Internet access. Some are concerned with leveling the playing fields within the information superhighway, while others have more money-making interests at heart. Yet their strategies are similar: to show reluctant users how easy and beneficial Internet access can be. Hundreds of Web sites exist for this particular purpose: Attract a select group of individuals and provide an array of services geared specifically for them. One example is *HispanicOnline.com*. The Web site is directed toward Hispanics/Latinos/as and provides guides to estate and financial planning, health information, and online discussion of various topics. It is also linked to *HispanicMagazine.com*, a site that includes new stories on issues relevant to Latinos/as including business, technology, culture, and entertainment. By showing this diverse ethnic group all that the Web has to offer, marketers hope that they can influence their perceptions and utility on the Internet. Other similar efforts are geared at groups—such as senior citizens—whose Internet use is low.

Expectations regarding the potential to succeed and actual performance are impacted by personal perceptions.

The effect that personal perceptions have on our interpersonal communication interactions is quite real. Remember the idea of a self-fulfilling prophecy? It was supported by research that found that teachers' expectations were central to student achievement. When teachers were led to believe that students were high achievers—but in actuality were average or below-average students—the students performed like high achievers. Our perceptions also affect how we evaluate others. For instance, one study provided three essays to participants and asked them to rate each one.[16] Participants were told that one was written by a female, one by a male, and one by a source whose sex was unknown. Overwhelmingly, the "male source" was rated highest, followed by the "unknown source" second, and "female source" third. What participants didn't know was that all essays were actually written by the same person.

What does this study suggest in terms of how we view the writing competencies of women and men? The power of our perceptions derives, in part, from our inability to recognize that these perceptions even exist. Ideally, this chapter has increased your awareness of the central role that perceptions play in interpersonal communication interactions.

Summary

We develop, maintain, and sometimes change our perceptions through a three-step process of selecting, organizing, and interpreting stimuli. Many communication misunderstandings are rooted in perceptual differences based on cultural and individual differences, past experiences, and situational contexts. Effective interpersonal communicators recognize that these differences are likely. However, they also realize that certain patterns exist that help us understand how perceptions are formed.

We close by articulating the "truths" and "myths" about perception and interpersonal communication. How many did you get right from your answers at the beginning of the chapter?

Myth: *Perceptions are formed in a linear, objective, straightforward process.* Why is this not true?

The perception process involves three stages that overlap and oftentimes occur simultaneously.

Myth: *Our current perceptions are independent from other perceptions.*

Our perceptions do not function in a vacuum; instead, they are formed by other—past and present—perceptions.

Truth: *Perception (what people think happens) is just as important as reality (what actually happens).*

People communicate based on their perceptions, which may or may not be accurate.

Myth: *Some stereotypes are positive and enhance our communication effectiveness.*

Actually, all stereotypes are dangerous because they represent assumptions based on unidimensional generalizations.

Myth: *Given its heavy reliance on verbal codes, our communication on the Internet is not really influenced by perception-related problems.*

Actually, perception is central to all forms of human communication, including that which occurs online. Consequently, perception plays an important role in decoding both nonverbal and verbal codes.

Key Terms

Attribution theory

Closure

Ethnocentrism

Halo effect

Implicit personality theory

Metasterotypes

Perception

Perceptual accentuation

Perceptual constancy

Prototypes

Schemata

Scripts

Selective attention

Selective distortion

Selective exposure

Self-attribution bias

Standpoint theory

Stereotypes

Suggested Contemporary Readings

T. H. Feeley. "Evidence of halo effects in student evaluations of communication instruction." *Communication Education* 51 (2002): 225–236.

S. Henderson, R. Taylor, and R. Thomson. "In touch: Young people, communication and technologies." *Information, Communication & Society* 5 (2001): 494–512.

D. Ifert. "Resistance to interpersonal requests: A summary and critique of recent research." *Communication Yearbook* 23 (2000): 125–161.

M. A. Jaasma and R. J. Koper. "Out-of-class communication between female and male students and faculty: The relationship to student perceptions of instructor immediacy." *Women's Studies in Communication* 25 (2002): 119–137.

D. E. Mastro and C. Atkin. "Exposure to alcohol billboards and beliefs and attitudes toward drinking among Mexican American high school students." *Howard Journal of Communications* 13 (2002): 129–151.

D. M. McLeod, B. H. Detenber, and W. P. Eveland, Jr. "Behind the third-person effect: Differentiating perceptual processes for self and other." *Journal of Communication* 51 (2001): 678–695.

D. Merskin. "Winnebagos, Cherokees, Apaches, and Dakotas: The persistence of stereotyping of American Indians in American advertising brands." *Howard Journal of Communications* 12 (2001): 159–169.

S. Mills. "Caught between sexism, anti-sexism, and 'political correctness': Feminist women's negotiations with naming practices." *Discourse & Society* 14 (2003): 87–110.

D. Niven and J. Zilber. "Elite use of racial labels: Ideology and preference for African American or Black." *Howard Journal of Communications* 11 (2000): 267–277.

M. Sotirovic. "How individuals explain social problems: The influences of media use." *Journal of Communication* 53 (2003): 122–137.

Chapter Activities

1. Eye Magic (*http://www.harmsy.freeuk.com/eyemagic.html*) is a Web site containing 10 different optical illusions, including one that we included in Figure 4.2. Click on each link, and try to correctly answer the questions posed. Once you've completed each item, click on their answer/explanation, and see how they include different concepts that have been discussed in this chapter.

2. Create your own schemata for the first day of class (similar to those in Box 4.2). Be sure to include descriptions of the different scripts, prototypes, and stereotypes that you have. If time permits, compare and contrast with other classmates.

3. Complete the Ethnocentrism Scale found at *http://www.jamesmccroskey.com/measures/ethnocentrism_scale.htm*. After completing the measure and reflecting on your own responses, answer the following questions: Are you more or less ethnocentric since attending college? Do you think that younger or older people are more ethnocentric? What are the best ways to reduce a person's ethnocentrism?

4. Select two to three people from work, school, or home. Ask them about their first impressions of you, and how (if at all) they have changed over time. How does this insight affect your self-perceptions?

5. Conduct an informal analysis of a court show (*Judge Judy, Divorce Court, Texas Justice, People's Court,* and so on). Pay particular attention to how both sides describe their perceptions of the series of events that led to the court case. How, if at all, do you think the judge's particular standpoint—based on gender, race, age, marital status, and so on—affects his or her decision?

6. Select one of the studies cited in this chapter—either in the Contemporary Readings list or endnotes—and locate it in your campus library. Once you've read its findings, conduct a small informal (replication) study to see what you find. This may involve doing a small survey, interview, or media analysis—what you find might surprise you!

7. Select a local community-based organization and conduct an informal perceptual assessment of the organization. Specifically, conduct interview or survey research that explores how organizational leaders, employees, clients, and the larger community perceive the organization (i.e., in terms of its mission, strengths, weaknesses, and effectiveness). Compare and contrast the results of your perceptual assessment, and present them to the leaders of the organization. ✦

Part II

Interpersonal Messages

Chapter 5

Language and Meaning

Contemporary Issues: The Importance of Language Choices

In May 1999, Valentin S. Krumov received his doctorate in political science from the University of Georgia in Athens, Georgia. Five months later, the 38-year-old Bulgarian man started working for the United Nations in Pristina, the capital of Kosovo. His goal: to devote himself to establishing peace and rebuilding Kosovo. After his first day at work, he and two female colleagues were going to dinner when he was mobbed, beaten, and shot. The October 19, 1999, news headline read: "U.N. staffer in Kosovo was killed for 'speaking wrong language'."

According to police officials, Valentin Krumov was near his hotel when a group of ethnic Albanian teenagers asked him for the time (in Serbian). He responded in Serbian, and was attacked by the teenagers. "One individual . . . hit him with his fist, and others kicked him," reported one official. "A large crowd [then] gathered around the altercation. All of a sudden, a shot was heard, the crowd dispersed and the body . . . was on the ground, lifeless." Valentin Krumov had been killed by a single shot to the head. This attack prompted officials to emphasize the potential danger of speaking any Slavic language, such as Serbian, in parts of Kosovo. One Polish police officer admitted that he never speaks his own native language for fear that he may be the target of ethnic Albanians.

This case study[1] powerfully illustrates the important role that language can play in terms of a person's identity, culture, and overall communication effectiveness. Our daily language choices are not typically a matter of life and death. But you can probably think of several instances in which your choice of words has had undesirable or at least unintended effects. The language that we choose directly affects our ability to communicate effectively with others, whether at work, in school, or with friends and family.

Language is a powerful resource that serves multiple functions in our everyday lives. Throughout this chapter we will explain a number of key concepts related to language use in interpersonal communication. As with every chapter, we will highlight the influences that culture, power, and technology have on language. Our ultimate objective is twofold: (1) to demonstrate the importance of language during interpersonal interactions, and (2) to make you more aware of the potential effects of particular language choices. In short, we want to make sure that you understand that interpersonal communication is more than simply passively using words.

Myths About Interpersonal Communication

For most people, a person's native language is like the air that they breathe: They use it all the time without much thought. This casual use of language is based on several assumptions that are oftentimes unchallenged and, in many instances, false. Below we have listed six statements about language. Take a moment to see if you can identify each statement as a "myth" or a "truth."

_____ Words have one specific meaning attached to them, that which is found in a dictionary.

_____ Multiple potential labels exist for each person, place, or thing.

_____ The key to any language system is that the meanings of words are consistent from person to person and place to place.

_____ Personal definitions of what a word means are not as important as the official definitions.

_____ It is the other person's responsibility to understand the language we use.

_____ Due to the dynamic nature of language, language development is an ongoing process that continues until death.

The Nature of Language

The power and richness of effective communication are largely due to the nature of language. However, many contemporary communication problems are also primarily caused by the nature of language itself. Communication, as you will come to understand, is much more than simply the language we use. Effective interpersonal communication requires understanding the role of many different aspects of the communication process including context, nonverbal cues, and perception. We have been and will continue discussing these three, as well as many others, in other chapters. Our focus for this chapter, however, is language and the crucial role that it plays in effective interpersonal communication.

Language is central to human communication processes. Before we explore specific concepts related to language use, let us identify the different functions that it plays. Specifically, we use three analogies—those of a tool, lens, and exhibition—to explain the functions of language.

Language as a Tool

Most people understand that language is a tool used to communicate with others (sometimes it is used effectively; sometimes it is not). Not everyone understands, however, that language systems are not simply made up of words. They also include grammatical and semantic patterns that provide rules for using words. Language systems allow us to express our ideas, thoughts, and feelings to others who understand and use that particular language system. This process is central to human communication, as we can see from the origin of the word *communication* itself. Communication comes from the Latin **communicare**, which means "to make common." Without any common language systems, human communication would be impossible.

In many ways, a language system is similar to a toolbox. Try and picture your native language system as being made up of a set of tools that you use at different times. No limitations are put on the number of tools that a person is capable of acquiring, nor is any one person restricted from learning how to use any one set of tools. In fact, we would guess that many people effectively use different sets of tools to achieve different objectives in various settings. Figure 5.1 demonstrates that the number of people in the United States who use a language other than English in their homes continues to grow. In fact, many individuals have mastered different toolboxes (languages), as well as the particular tools within each box (words, grammar, syntax). Many are so skilled that they can change toolboxes without hesitation or use two or more at the same time!

If U.S. Census 2000 statistics are accurate, most people reading this textbook have one primary toolbox (use one primary language). You might, however, use different sets of tools in different settings. For instance, Julie might draw from one set of tools when interacting with family members and another when discussing a chemistry test with her professor. It might be necessary to use different tools when in the company of friends, professional colleagues, or those with a common interest or hobby. In short, a well-stocked toolbox (language system) is essential to getting the job done (communicating effectively). The following "tool tips" are offered to help the "less skilled."

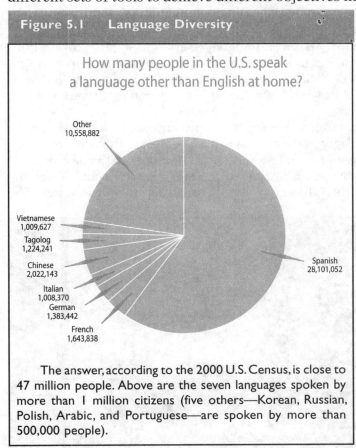

Figure 5.1   Language Diversity

How many people in the U.S. speak a language other than English at home?

Other 10,558,882
Vietnamese 1,009,627
Tagolog 1,224,241
Chinese 2,022,143
Italian 1,008,370
German 1,383,442
French 1,643,838
Spanish 28,101,052

The answer, according to the 2000 U.S. Census, is close to 47 million people. Above are the seven languages spoken by more than 1 million citizens (five others—Korean, Russian, Polish, Arabic, and Portuguese—are spoken by more than 500,000 people).

- Not everyone has the same tools in their toolbox (e.g., words, phrases, and so on). Some toolboxes are pretty empty; others are overflowing with hardly used gadgets!

- Trying to work without the proper tools is possible but difficult. (Have you ever used a kitchen knife as a screwdriver, or a high-heeled shoe as a hammer?) Can you think of times when you couldn't find the right words to express what you were feeling?

- People may have the tools in their toolboxes and still not know how to use them properly (not using language choices effectively to adapt to the situation).

- Some people use their tools in innovative ways that others cannot understand or replicate. (Do you know people who use duct tape or a glue gun to fix just about anything?) In terms of language, have you seen instances when people's creative use of language has confused others?

• Even when all the right tools are available, some jobs are more difficult than they initially appear to be. Some scenarios, like parents and children having "the sex talk," are a challenge even for the most well-trained communicators!

Language as a Lens

Without question, language is a tool used to communicate effectively. However, language is not neutral and the process of using it is hardly passive. Language serves as a guide for an individual's mental activity.[2] In other words, the language that we use functions as a lens through which we view the world around us. The Whorf-Sapir hypothesis (sometimes also referred to as the Sapir-Whorf hypothesis or simply the Whorfian hypothesis) is a key concept related to this idea.

The **Whorf-Sapir hypothesis** says that language helps to shape our reality. In other words, language is necessary in order to express thoughts. This hypothesis suggests that different language systems—like English, Spanish, Japanese, and so on—affect the way native speakers of those languages interpret the world.[3] Likewise, according to the theory, even speakers of the same language can perceive reality differently if they consistently use different words to describe the world around them. What does the Whorf-Sapir hypothesis tell us in a nutshell? The words that we use shape the way we see things. Some communication scholars even believe that our understanding is limited to the language that we have to describe certain things. In other words, complex understanding requires complex language. Maybe that is why your professors "force" you to learn complex terms in all of your subject areas!

Let's look at some examples. For many people who have little, if any, experience dealing with Christmas trees, differentiating between the different types of trees can be difficult.

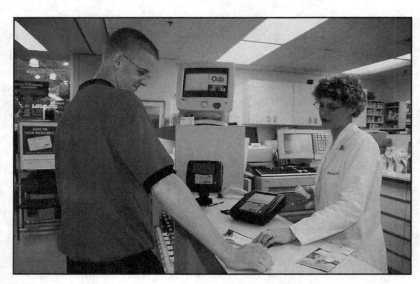

The most effective communicators use language that others can easily understand.

They typically don't have a set of complex words to describe them: A Christmas tree is a Christmas tree, no more, no less. They are all basically the same. Now imagine bringing these individuals to a Christmas tree farm that has multiple types of Christmas trees. With the introduction (and explanation) of new terms like Frasier fir, Douglas fir, pine, blue spruce, and so on, they can begin to understand the differences between various types of Christmas trees. In this example, new language helps develop a more complex understanding and a new reality of the things around them because they now are labeled. The same could be said for the complex terms used to differentiate between various colors (see Box 5.1).

Box 5.1

Color Complexity

In order to see how language functions as a lens, do a simple experiment with your friends and/or family. Locate a clothing catalog, box of crayons, or collection of paint samples. Then ask several people to identify the different colors. Record their responses to compare and contrast. Take special note of how complex each person's words were. Do you think that it is safe to assume that if a person only has basic color terms (red, blue, orange, and so on), he or she only sees in these colors?

Based on this small experiment, you will probably discover a related idea: When provided with explanations of different terms, most people begin to see the small differences between related colors. According to this idea, they did not see the color differences earlier, because they did not have the language to describe it. Imagine how a person's perceptions can change when they learn new language to describe a couple of sweaters that are "light brown." Now they realize that they could actually be tan, camel, honey, champagne, taupe, khaki, oatmeal leather, ivory, beige, cement, wheat, sand, stone, chestnut, jute, or ecasame!

Young children also serve as a great illustration for the Whorf-Sapir hypothesis. One of the challenges that parents face is trying to communicate effectively with young children who do not have the words to describe complex things. What makes this even more frustrating is that, according to the Whorf-Sapir hypothesis, the children can not fully understand what they are experiencing until they learn language that helps them structure their thoughts. Read over the following conversation between a father and his 5-year-old daughter, and think about how a lack of language ability affects this interaction.

Father: Why did you write on your sister's homework?

Daughter: She was bothering me. Why aren't you punishing her?!?

Father: What do you mean, "bothering" you?

Daughter: Bothering me!!!! You know, just bothering me.

Father: And that's why you wrote on her homework?

Daughter: Yes.

Father: Well, that's no reason to do that.

Daughter [Frustrated that Dad doesn't understand]: Yes, it is. She was bothering me all day . . . singing that song that I hate and looking at me.

Father: And you think that I should punish her for that? Singing a song??? Looking at you???

Daughter: Yes, she was doing it to bother me!

Father [In a more frustrated tone]: How? How was that bothering you?

Daughter: AAARRRGGGHHH!!! You don't understand!!! I'm so mad!!!

According to the Whorf-Sapir hypothesis, the daughter's lack of language ability shaped the way that she saw her sister's behaviors. A more complex set of words would have allowed her to more fully understand what was going on and also help her father understand as well. Over the next several years, she will learn new words that will foster an understanding of the differences between bothering, harassing, joking, tormenting, disturbing, and teasing. Without these words, says the Whorf-Sapir hypothesis, such a differentiation of feeling is difficult.

Language as an Exhibition

Language serves another important function: to exhibit or display our thoughts. The language choices that we make to communicate certain ideas do more than simply represent those ideas. Sometimes unintentionally, they provide additional information—about how we feel about certain things. According to linguist Del Hymes, language is a reflection of our internal thoughts.[4] Consider the following example to see how individuals' language choices sometimes communicate more about them than they recognize.

Rob applied for a hall director position at a university that prides itself on a comprehensive Residence Life Program. Throughout the interview, Rob did a good job at answering questions but described residence halls as "dorms," students as "kids," and local residents as "townies." This pattern troubled the selection committee because they suspected that while Rob had been coached on all the "right" answers, his true feelings about the job didn't match the philosophy of the university (that residence halls represent a total living-learning environment for adults). Their perceptions were primarily based on his language during the interview. And while their conclusions may or may not be completely accurate, this example provides a vivid illustration of how Rob's language choices were treated as an exhibition of his unspoken thoughts. Another example related to this idea is the use of "politically correct" language (see Box 5.2).

Box 5.2

Using "PC" Language

In the early 1990s, the idea of being "politically correct" (PC) gained national attention. Part of the PC movement was the adoption of new terms used to describe underrepresented groups in more accurate and empowering ways. For instance, people were encouraged to use the terms *sexual orientation* and *gay/lesbian/bisexuals* instead of *sexual preference* and *homosexuals* (both terms that situated same-sex attraction as a form of clinical deviancy). Other emerging terms included Native American (replacing Indian), Asian American (replacing Oriental), person with disabilities (replacing handicapped or disabled), international students (replacing foreign students), and first-year students (replacing fresh*men*).

Some perceived using politically correct language as a threat to the freedom of speech on college campuses. Others saw it as a necessary step in the elimination of outdated terms used to describe different underrepresented groups. They rejected the media criticism of PC language and asserted the need to use terms that were more culturally sensitive and appropriate. While some of the PC furor has died down some in recent years, it is still common to hear references on and around college campuses (i.e., "I know that isn't PC, but . . .").

What impact has this controversy had on the communication that goes on inside and outside the classroom? Some people are quick to point out that a person who is racist, sexist, or homophobic can use politically correct language. He or she can adopt certain words and still maintain his or her personal biases. Others believe that learning to use less derogatory terms helps to facilitate a more complete understanding of diversity and the ultimate reduction of existing prejudices. Think about how this applies to the three functions that language plays in human communication. What is your opinion of politically correct language? How does it function as a tool, lens, and/or exhibition on your campus?

How conscious are you of the way others draw conclusions about you based on the language that you use? Of course, these assumptions are not always accurate. But people assume that the language you use reflects (and/or shapes) your perceptions. Remember that this is the main idea associated with the Whorf-Sapir hypothesis. Again, the assumptions that people make about language choices may not always be correct, but they do affect the communication that takes place.

Characteristics of Language

In order to increase communication effectiveness, several characteristics of language need to be reorganized and understood. We highlight five specific characteristics in this section that help to describe the nature of language as symbolic, subjective, rule-governed, contextual, and creative. Throughout the chapter, we also talk about other characteristics, but highlight these five central characteristics here first.

Language Is Symbolic

Words are symbols; they stand for something else. Speakers of a language agree in general terms about what each symbol stands for. Yet specific words do not have any inherent meaning. The **arbitrary nature of words** is a concept that states that meanings are in people, not in the words themselves. What exactly does that mean? When people hear words, they create meaning based on their interpretation of the words. The words themselves do not create meaning for people. For instance, let's say a person from Indiana requests a "coke." In her mind, she is naturally connecting that specific word with the type of beverage she wants. "Coke" in certain parts of Indiana, however, is the generic term for a "soft drink," "pop," or "soda." What did you visualize when you first read the word *coke*? If words were not symbolic, everyone would have pictured the same image. The way that some people from different parts of the United States passionately defend which term is correct shows how we tend to forget that language is symbolic.

Even though we recognize that language is symbolic, we often use language with an assumption that words do have a specific meaning naturally tied to them. Can you think of an instance when the arbitrary nature of words led to a misunderstanding? If you think hard enough, you are probably able to identify several examples. Just think about how many people use the same word but are operating with a drastically different meaning. For instance, would you describe yourself as "old"? Many people in their early-mid 30s would not, but as defined by an 18 year old, a 33 year old is *old!* Remember, however, that language is symbolic, so age is simply a symbol and has no inherent meaning tied to it.

Language Is Subjective

The way that we use and interpret language (symbols) is not neutral; it is influenced by our personal experiences. Because we have different levels of homophily (as explained in Chapter 2), people attach different meanings to the same word. They can also attach the same meaning to different words. For example, individuals describe their romantic partners in multiple ways (significant other, boyfriend or girlfriend, life partner, soulmate) based on their preference for certain terms over others. As established earlier, these terms can mean different things to different people, but it is important to know that the process by which one term is chosen over others is highly subjective. No one "official" term exists.

To help explain this concept, we should explore the difference between the denotative and connotative meanings of words. **Denotative** refers to the direct, explicit meaning that is generally accepted for a word. One way to remember this definition is to link "D for *d*enotative" with "D for *d*ictionary." Denotative meanings are those listed first in the dictionary. **Connotative** refers to a less formal, more subjective meaning for a particular word. In many interpersonal interactions, it is important to recognize both denotative and connotative meanings. Do not make the mistake of assuming that the person is using a denotative meaning, because people oftentimes personalize the words that they use.

In addition to being subjective, language is also dynamic. The meanings of words are constantly changing, especially with the influence of new generations. Some words, like *cool*, tend to stand the test of time. But many idioms (*groovy*, *hip*, *fresh*, *phat*, *tight*, and *sweet*) quickly find themselves outdated and new words (*slammin'* or *off the chain*) take their place.

Language Is Rule-Governed

Language may be symbolic and subjective, but that does not mean it is random. The way we use it is guided by various rules. These rules vary among different types of language that make learning some languages more difficult than others. In general, the easiest languages to learn use rules most similar to those of your native language.

We might also have different rules for the same language. Ebonics, also known as "Black English," is an example of the way users can develop different rules for different versions of the English language. While some perceive people who use this form of language as ignorant or unintelligent, Ebonics has rules that must be followed just like any other language system. If this point is not clear, try and picture someone who is not well versed in Black English—including some African Americans—attempting to use it! For instance, popular comedians such as Eddie Murphy, Cedric the Entertainer, and Chris Rock have long used this scenario in their stand-up comedy routines. The bottom line is that without a keen understanding of the rules of a language, it is not possible to effectively use it.

All languages have certain basic types of rules. **Semantic rules**, for example, help us understand the meaning of individual words. General acceptance of meaning for a particular word (e.g., *home* is a place where you live) is necessary for any understanding to occur. This is sometimes difficult, though, because meanings can be ambiguous. For some, home is a four-bedroom house with all of the amenities. For others, home is a loft, a one-bedroom apartment, or a more temporary form of shelter.

Syntax rules address how words should be used in relation to other words. Without proper syntax, groups of words are not able to generate meaning. Read aloud the

Different language systems are governed by different sets of rules.

following words: *Before class to doing well is crucial reading your textbook in this course.* Doesn't make much sense, does it? A more effective placement of words, however, makes the meaning clear: *Reading your textbook before class is crucial to doing well in this course.* The rules that govern such tools as word order are the rules of syntax.

Pragmatic rules also exist. These help reduce ambiguity by drawing attention to the way your relationships with others affect meaning. Hearing a friend tell you, "You're so stupid!" probably has different meaning than when a professor tells you the same thing. This is because the relationship that you have with a friend, compared to a professor, includes different rules on how one is to communicate—and interpret the communication—with others. In short, rules help us make sense of the language that we use.

Language Is Contextual

In many situations, context is the key to meaning. What you say, the language that you choose to represent your message, is important. But language holds little meaning all by itself. In fact, classic communication research estimates that only 7 percent of a message is communicated through verbal language.[5] While some argue that the percentage is two or three times that amount, the fact remains that other communication elements provide greater meaning than the words we use. These include facial expressions, vocal qualities, and other nonverbal cues (such as those discussed in Chapter 6). Language, then, only generates meaning in the context of other communication aspects. The old saying, "*How* you say something is more important than *what* you say," captures this idea.

Whenever you try to understand the language choices that are being used, you should ask yourself a number of questions: Who is using this language? To whom are they speaking? What is their relationship? How is it being said? What is the setting in which the language is being used? Again, all these questions help us to accurately create shared meaning. This is important because the same verbal codes can generate drastically different sets of meanings depending on context. Think about the meaning of "Shut up!" in these three examples:

- During quiet reading time, two young students are talking. The teacher asks them not to talk, but they continue. In frustration, he tells them, "Shut up!"

- One student is constantly being teased by other students because of his weight. He usually tries to ignore them. One day, at recess, the teasing becomes unbearable and he screams for them to "Shut up!"

- Two best friends are working together on a tough math challenge that is designed to take at least five minutes. They finish the problem in less than one minute and show their teacher, who responds by saying, "Shut up!" The girls are tickled that their work has amazed the teacher.

Each of these examples is set in the same general context, a middle school. As you can see, though, each particular context generates a somewhat different meaning for the same two words. This reminds us not to take things out of context. We must remember that meaning is created by looking at other informational cues in the communication context.

Language Is Creative

One of the fun things about language is how creatively it can be used. Over the years, people have created new words and used existing words in new ways in order to communicate. These words keep language alive and expressive. However, they also raise unique challenges for those trying to learn the language. For instance, groups often create language that is common to their shared experience (see Box 5.3). Physicians understand that a "subcutaneous hematoma" is a bruise. Tennis players know that "being bageled" isn't good (losing every set without winning a single game). Young people (or people around them) realize that "livin' large" is not a comment about someone's size, but describes how well they are doing in general.

Box 5.3

Different Types of Co-Languages

Co-languages are specialized languages used by different co-cultural groups in a given society. Since these co-cultures are united by a common element, their members have developed sets of terms that are used when communicating with one another. Co-languages help to facilitate effective communication and also provide a sense of identity to the group. Four examples of co-languages are:

- *Argot:* A specialized vocabulary used by a particular group of nonprofessionally related people. Argot in its purest form is not understood by people outside the group. Examples include language that is used by drug dealers, some teenagers, and some music cultures.

- *Jargon:* A technical language used by a particular trade, profession, or group. College professors, investors, computer technicians, doctors, and lawyers all use jargon when communicating with one another.

- *Slang:* Terms that were derived from argot but have become more widely known to the general public. Examples of slang include the growing number of terms made popular by young people ("She's on the pipe"). Despite its general recognition, slang is still not acceptable in most formal settings.

- *Idiosyncratic Language:* Personalized terms that are generated, used, and accepted by a small group of people. Idiosyncratic language is highly unique and can not generally be understood by people outside the group. Each family or group of friends typically has different levels of this type of language.

These examples illustrate how people who are part of a community (professional, social, or cultural) use language to express themselves in unique ways. People also creatively use language to label things that might be offensive or uncomfortable for others; using an inoffensive substitute is called using **euphemisms**. In order to soften the blow, employers talk about "downsizing," "terminating," or "restructuring" instead of firing their employees. We use euphemisms related to death, love, drugs, alcohol, and sex all the time. Even the act of going to the bathroom has been creatively renamed by some as:

- "Going to the little girls/boys room"

- "Needing to powder my nose"

- "Doing #1 or #2"

- "Paying the water bill"
- "Going to see a man about a horse"

Some of you may view some of these phrases as outdated or have never heard of others. Yet each of you reading these examples could probably add several more to this list. Because of this, attempting to keep track of the creative ways that we use language can be very difficult!

Language and Meaning

Language has one additional characteristic: *Alone, it is insufficient for understanding.* On the surface, using language to communicate looks like a straightforward process. We think about what we want to communicate, select the necessary language to represent those thoughts, and then deliver them. However, remember all of the characteristics that describe language. Language is governed by rules that everyone (supposedly) understands, but it is also symbolic, subjective, contextual, and creative. In this regard, the very nature of language works to create a number of challenges for effective communicators. We identify several of them here (see Box 5.4) and present specific practices to assist in overcoming each.

Box 5.4

Overcoming Potential Barriers

Potential Barrier	Solution
Polarization	Use middle terms and qualifying language.
Static Evaluation	Date comments and foresee the possibility of change.
Intensional Orientation	Minimize impact that labels have on defining others.
Fact-Inference Confusion	Differentiate between facts and inferences.
Bypassing	Use active listening, paraphrasing, and feedback.

One barrier to the effective use of language is polarization. **Polarization** occurs when a person uses language that describes things in "either-or" terms. When people use polarized language, they see things as either good or bad, right or wrong, or beautiful or ugly. Western society tends to promote an either-or approach to the world, and this is reflected in our language. We learn about opposites early in our lives, and our ability to master these terms is used as an indicator of our educational progress. In order to avoid polarization, we must recondition ourselves to recognize how most things have some good *and* bad, right *and* wrong, and beauty *and* ugliness. Our language choices should reflect this recognition. We can also use middle terms and qualifiers to resist the tendency to use polarized language (e.g., "Although the incident was horrible, some good came out of it"). This may include a necessary increase in vocabulary, and a commitment to change our everyday talk.

A second barrier, **static evaluation**, refers to the tendency to use language that is fixed, rigid, or not open for change. Everything and everyone in the world—including each of you who is reading this book—are constantly changing. However, in many instances our language does not recognize this important point. Instead, we use language that does not differentiate between any changes that may occur over time. For example, think about how older family members describe you. Can you see specific examples of how their language is outdated and no longer appropriate? Many of us are still fighting off childhood nicknames that reflect less mature personalities. In other ways, relatives describe us as if we were still children even though we have changed tremendously. We suggest two strategies to avoid static evaluation. First, mark specific comments with dates that allow others to understand the context of particular comments (e.g., "When Tara was 7, she was an extremely emotional child"). Second, use language that recognizes the distinct possibility that change is likely (e.g., "Tom is currently overweight").

Intensional orientation is another barrier. **Intensional orientation**, or the practice of relying on labels for your perceptions, is something that everyone does to some extent. In order to understand all of those things we come in contact with, we place them in categories and label them. A theory known as **constructivism**[6] says that we make sense of the world through a system of mental blueprints (schemata) that we create in our minds. The problem occurs when we allow these constructs to define what we see, not the other way around. For instance, we might see a student on campus that we label, because of her age, as "nontraditional." Intensional orientation occurs when that label limits how we see that person. If we allow it, our existing schema guides our thinking of every person we place in the category of *nontraditional student*. The solution to intensional orientation is easy to identify, but more difficult to actually do. We have to avoid unnecessarily labeling things and people and putting them into neat little categories. By doing this, we will begin to see just how unique the world is and how limiting labels can be.

Another barrier to language effectiveness is fact-inference confusion. **Fact-inference confusion** happens when individuals do not distinguish between things that are true and those that are assumed. Facts can generally be defined as statements reflecting specific observations, something presented as objectively real. Inferences, in comparison, are based on assumptions drawn from observations. In largely unconscious ways, we often treat inferences as if they were facts. "I saw Michael in a gay bar" is a fact. "Michael is gay" is an inference. While this distinction is easy to see, we often allow inferences to be passed along to others as facts. What can we do to avoid fact-inference confusion? Most importantly, we can use language that helps to differentiate between our use of facts and inferences. We can also question when others make potentially false assumptions based on inferences. In the example offered earlier, this might mean that we clearly state that we don't know that Michael is gay, but we do know that he was in a gay bar.

Differentiating between facts and inferences is key to effective understanding.

Our last description allows us to identify the specific barrier associated with the arbitrary nature of words. **Bypassing** occurs when people incorrectly assume that words have inherent meanings. Instead of recognizing that meanings are specific to individual interpretation, they use words as if they actually contain meaning; they bypass the fact that meanings are in people, not words. Just think of how many problems bypassing has caused with the use of the three simple words "I love you." This one phrase does not have one definitive meaning; instead, people use it to communicate different things ("I am dedicated to you for life," "You are my soulmate," "I like you very much," or "I want you to do what I want"). Overcoming the barrier of bypassing is relatively easy if we use effective communication practices such as active listening, paraphrasing, and feedback. These strategies will be discussed in greater detail at the end of this chapter. Although we describe the strategies to overcome language barriers in fairly simple terms, human nature can make using them effectively a challenge (see Box 5.5).

Box 5.5

Practical Research
How to Resist an Idiom

Idioms are expressions that capture a general idea with little attention to specific circumstances. Some examples of idioms used in the United States are "tit for tat," "You have to face the music," and "Absence makes the heart grow fonder." Idioms are used successfully to communicate around a sensitive or uncomfortable topic; many times they are used when people are having difficulty finding the right thing to say. Since idioms capture an idea that is largely taken for granted, they are hard to resist.

But how can you counter an idiom when needed? Researcher Celia Kitzinger analyzed group conversations among women with breast cancer to explore this question.[7] She found that in several contexts, these women needed to resist the idiom of positive thinking (as in "You have to think positive") that they oftentimes heard from others. From their perspectives, maintaining their mental health included an understanding that sometimes they were *unable* to think positive or, indeed, that thinking positive was not always productive.

Kitzinger found three strategies that breast cancer survivors used to resist the "think positive" idiom. First, they resisted by using vocalized pauses (um, ah, or mmm), silence, or token agreements (an unconvincing "yeah"). A second strategy involved responding with their own idioms. So, when told to "think positive," the women might respond by saying, "It's not mind over matter," or, "Reality sucks." The last strategy focused on using specifics to show how the idiom was not effective. One women, for instance, was told that "Mr. Fell said think positive." In resisting the use of this idiom, she responded by pointing out, "Mr. Fell says that to everyone," "Everybody's not as strong as one another," and, finally, "Some people just can't be positive."

Like other forms of language, idioms play an important function in communication. However, sometimes their use silences, disempowers, or marginalizes others. Kitzinger's research on the communication of women with breast cancer helps remind us of this. Can you think of similar situations when people have used idioms that you felt were ineffective? Did you resist? If so, how?

Becoming more aware of the barriers that hinder effective communication is a key first step to overcoming them. Throughout this chapter, we have discussed the importance of language and the number of functions that it plays in interpersonal communication. We also described the nature of language and related barriers. Next, we discuss how culture affects language.

Language and Culture

The way we use language is directly related to our cultural backgrounds. In Chapter 2, we introduced a broad definition of culture. Remember that your cultural background includes your race/ethnicity, age, nationality, sex/gender, socioeconomic status, physical abilities, family structure, spirituality, health status, and sexual orientation. Take a moment and think about how each of these things individually influences the way you use language. You probably recognize that certain words, phrases, and nonverbal elements are connected to certain aspects of your cultural background.

Earlier in this chapter, we explained how specialized languages develop within groups that share a common element. In Box 5.3, we explained how argot, jargon, slang, and idiosyncratic language are used by people who share certain professional or nonprofessional interests and status. In similar ways, people who share common cultural experiences also develop particular terminologies. In fact, these language systems are even more significant given that they also include specific rules on how and when to use such terms. In addition, they are largely multigenerational, passed on from generation to generation. Communication scholars have studied the language of different cultural groups and concluded that many have different norms.

Speech Communities

Any discussion about language and culture would be incomplete without an explanation of the way different cultural groups function as speech communities. According to Gerry Philipsen, a leading scholar in the area, a **speech community** exists when a group of people understands goals and styles of communication in ways not shared by people outside the group.[8] Speech communities, then, function in unique ways that are oftentimes misunderstood by nongroup members.

Speech communities can vary from country to country and sometimes from region to region. In the United States, however, numerous speech communities coexist within the same areas. Some examples are the language systems used by Puerto Ricans, people who are deaf, gays and lesbians, or those from high socioeconomic groups. In fact, we can see how speech communities are maintained around each aspect of culture described earlier. Some—like those based on race, ethnicity, or nation of origin—are fairly obvious. Others, however, may be less so. Recently, Julia T. Wood has revealed how women and men function within different gender speech communities.[9] Traditionally, women have been socialized to follow feminine communication rules, including using language to include others, talking with emotion, and building relationships through talk. Men, in comparison, are often taught to communicate via masculine communication rules, like asserting yourself and using talk to accomplish certain goals. We discuss these gender speech communities in much greater detail in Chapter 10.

Recognizing the existence of speech communities helps us to understand why certain communication problems between different cultural groups occur. As you might imagine, effective communication is difficult when people who come from different speech communities continue to use the codes and rules specific to their cultural group. Ideally, both people can adapt their communication to become more like the other person's, meeting somewhere in the middle. According to **communication accommodation theory** (CAT),[10] this pattern is called **convergence**. Individuals can also practice **divergence**, however. Divergence is a conscious effort to use language and nonverbal cues to emphasize differences between individuals. In any two-person situation, we can have any one of three primary scenarios: (1) Both people practice convergence; (2) one person practices convergence, the other divergence; or (3) both people practice divergence. Box 5.6 uses the example of Spanglish to demonstrate how convergence and divergence can also be combined in certain situations. As we discuss later in this chapter, intergroup communication is related to issues of power, and this is one of the factors that influences who converges and who diverges in different situations.

Box 5.6

Have You Ever Heard Someone Speak Spanglish?

With the growing number of Latinos/as in the United States, Spanish is more commonly heard in many different contexts. This is especially true in certain geographical areas where Spanish-speaking people are a sizable minority—or even the majority. One form of communication adaptation that is used by native Spanish speakers is known as *Spanglish.*

What exactly is Spanglish? It is a form of hybrid language where both Spanish and English are mixed together, but where the Spanish language and Latino culture remain most dominant. It is an interesting example of partial convergence and divergence because going back and forth between Spanish and English can happen within a particular sentence or phrase. People who are bilingual, then, can switch between speaking Spanish, English, and Spanglish.

Some people, as described by Ed Morales in his 2002 book *Living in Spanglish,*[11] criticize the use of this form of hybrid language. Yet this form of vernacular is commonly seen alongside Spanish and English. Two popular magazines, *Latina* and *Moderna,* illustrate this strategy. Some of the articles are primarily in English, some primarily in Spanish. Advertisements are even more diverse. In addition to texts that are available in only Spanish or English, other ads use Spanglish. Both these magazines demonstrate how natural blending these languages can be to bilingual people.[12]

Ingroup Use of Language

Women sometimes use *girl* or *bitch* to refer to themselves and other women. Gays and lesbians use *queer* in empowering ways. Some racial and ethnic groups also use seemingly degrading terms to describe themselves in nonoffensive ways. Yet when outsiders to the group use these terms, they are considered offensive. The distinction between *intragroup* communication, such as these examples demonstrate, and *intergroup* communication is helpful because it points to how communication rules operate differently in different contexts. Communicating with others who share a common set of experiences is different from communicating with those who do not.

The idea of **reappropriating language** helps us illustrate this point. Historically, some words or phrases—like the ones listed above—have been used to degrade particular cultural groups. Most have been identified as highly offensive and are no longer commonly used. Instead, they have been replaced with more suitable descriptors that empower those groups that have been historically disenfranchised. Some group members, however, consciously use traditionally offensive words to describe themselves and others. This is done as an effort to reclaim and redefine the terms in positive ways. So, instead of having a negative connotation, the terms reflect a positive statement about their identity and cultural pride. Redefining the term works to gain control of the very language that has been used to degrade them. In some instances, reappropriating language also involves small, but distinct, changes. For example, many non-African Americans hear some African Americans referring to each other as "niggers." What they often fail to recognize is that *nigger* is seldom, if ever, used. An alternative pronunciation, "niggah,"[13] is actually what is being said. This slight but significant difference strengthens the reappropriation that has taken place. The way that it has been used has been changed, and so has the way it is pronounced.

Reappropriating language maintains "cultural ownership" over certain terms and phrases. Being a part of a certain group, it is reasoned, gives you license to reappropriate language and use it to refer to yourself and others like you. Outgroup members can not "own" the term because they have not experienced all of the hurt, pain, and oppression associated with it. This makes their use of the term especially offensive to those who can more fully appreciate the power of this form of language. Not all members of underrepresented groups, however, agree on the usefulness of this practice. Because of the history of certain terms, some can not understand why anyone would continue to use them, especially when other, more acceptable terms are available.

Language and Power

Power is directly tied to the ways that language is used, perceived, and validated over time. Earlier in the chapter, we described language systems as toolboxes. Extending this analogy can assist us in understanding how power relates to language. Different types of tools are contained in each toolbox. Those who are the most skilled have mastered how to use each tool in the appropriate ways. These people have the most power. Others may have the proper tools but not be able to use them effectively. This makes them less powerful. Yet others may have tools that work for them, but are not allowed to use them in some settings because they are not "approved" as meeting certain regulations. The result is that these individuals might have power in certain contexts, but considerably less in others.

Language functions as a tool that can work to increase or decrease one's personal power. It largely depends, however, on how language is used. Table 5.1 describes different types of "powerless" language forms. Read each example and reflect on how they work to lessen the power of the speaker. Those of you who find yourselves using powerless language might consider adopting more empowering alternatives. Over time, you will find that your levels of personal power will be enhanced. However, it is also important to understand how "powerless" language operates within certain situations.

Table 5.1 Identifying "Powerless" Language		
Type of Language	***Example***	***More Empowering Alternative***
Qualifiers	Well, I *sort of,* want to, you know, go to the party.	I want to go to the party.
Hedges	*I think that* we should do it this way.	We should do it this way.
Disclaimers	*You don't have to listen to me,* but I feel that you are losing control.	You are losing control.
Tag Questions	We should shut the door since it's getting noisy, *shouldn't we?*	We should shut the door since it's getting noisy.
Intensifiers	I love her *soooooooo much.*	I love her.
Compound Requests	*Won't* you please call your mother today?	Call your mother today.
Ultra-Politeness	Excuse me, *sir, may I bother you for a second* and ask you a question?	Excuse me, I have a question.

For instance, we mentioned earlier that some "tools" are not approved as meeting certain regulations. The same goes for some forms of language. The question we must consider is, "Who determines what forms of language are acceptable and which are not?" The answer to this question is easy: Those who have power determine language standards. Quite logically, these individuals approve language systems that are most natural to their ways of communicating. Over time, certain standards are established that evaluate some ways of speaking as acceptable ("Standard English," for example) and others as unacceptable (e.g., slang or powerless language). This has clear consequences for how language is used.[14]

First, those individuals whose language most closely matches what has been set as the "standard" have an advantage over others. They are not forced to learn a new language, nor are they taught that their way of communicating is "substandard." Second, when others learn standard language systems and use them effectively, they reinforce existing standards. The result is a catch-22 of sorts. If people refuse to adopt the standards, and continue to use their own language, they are regarded as ineffective. The only way to be effective is to adopt standard language. Using a common language is instrumental for effective communication to occur, but it can also work to maintain a language hierarchy where one language is viewed as better than others. Can you see how this operates in the United States? Standard English is maintained as the norm, and other forms of speaking (Spanish, Black English, slang, and so on) are deemed as inappropriate in most contexts.

With this in mind, we suggest an alternative way of understanding powerless language. The examples provided in Table 5.1 are not forms of language that cause people to have less power. They are, instead, ways that less powerful people get their ideas across. This is a small, but important, distinction to make. For instance, gender and language research has traditionally reported that women, on average, are more likely to use powerless language than men. This research leads people to draw the conclusion that powerless language is what hinders women's success in different areas. However, other more recent research[15] reveals that these forms of language are used strategically to communicate in settings where traditional sex roles influence language choices. Consider the following example:

> Sarah was interested in joining the Intra-Greek Council because she felt that it was a good place to put her communication skills to work. However, she became increasingly frustrated when the council president seemed to ignore or ridicule any suggestions that she made. She focused on using more empowering language, but it didn't matter. It was clear these men thought that sorority women didn't have any brains! Then Sarah began to watch other women on the council who seemed to be more effective in getting their ideas heard. She noticed that instead of saying something like, "I have an idea that will help this problem," they would say, "This is one idea; what do you think?" The men seemed to be less threatened by this approach.

This case scenario occurs in a number of organizational settings. As you can see, a woman's use of language is affected by how sex roles are viewed. If traditional sex roles are accepted, certain forms of language are not accepted for women to use. Therefore, women in these settings might adopt alternative forms of language that allow them to function most effectively.

Language Bias

Language can serve as a bridge between people. It can also be something that constructs a wall between people. It all depends on how you use language in your communication with others. In this section, we discuss language bias as a way to increase your awareness of the importance of using inclusive and nonoffensive language. It should go without saying that effective interpersonal communicators should avoid offensive language. This includes language that is considered to be sexist, racist, or homophobic, or otherwise works to oppress others. Avoiding blatantly offensive language is the easy part. Identifying and eliminating less obvious forms of language bias are more difficult.

Unfortunately, we can't offer you a comprehensive list of what terms to use in every situation. Because of the subjective and contextual nature of language, no list would ever be complete and could potentially cause more harm than good. People are simply too different in their personal preferences to create such a list. Consequently, the objective of this section is to raise your awareness to the subtle ways that language bias creeps into our everyday interactions. While no specific universal "commandments" are offered, we believe that the guidelines described here will serve as an excellent foundation for your language choices.

Be Sensitive to the Power of Labels

It is part of human nature to use labels to refer to others as well as ourselves. Labeling helps us make sense out of a complex world. In order to increase our communication effectiveness, however, we must recognize the power associated with labels. For instance, let's look at how diverse groups in the United States are described. Historically, certain groups with minority status have been labeled by those with dominant group status. Many of these labels were convenient for the dominant group, but inaccurate or offensive to the group themselves. An example of this is using the term *Indian* to describe hundreds of nations indigenous to the Americas. Groups that self-identified as Oneida, Sage, Pequot, Mohegans, Blackfeet, Sioux, Cherokee, Potawatomi, and so on were now labeled as Indians (a misnomer in itself since Columbus mistakenly believed he had actually landed in India).

Therefore, one of the first guidelines that must be used is to acknowledge the power to label. Have you ever noticed that certain groups of people get labeled more often than others? The ability to label—and force others to use these labels to function in dominant society—belongs to those in power. Most often, this is the majority group. Take a look at any daily newspaper for examples of this phenomenon. You frequently see headlines that read "Black Scholar to Speak on Economic Issues," "Is Gay/Lesbian Adoption the Answer?" or "Female Astronaut Receives Award." In comparison, it is unheard of to see headlines that include phrases like "White scholar," "straight adoption," or "male astronaut." Without labels we assume the "norm": that scholars are European American, families are headed by heterosexuals, and astronauts are male. These examples point to another advantage of the power to label others: Those doing the labeling remain unlabeled.

The next section deals with determining what, if any, labels are necessary in different situations. But before ending this discussion, we want to illustrate the complex nature of this issue. Imagine glancing at a headline that read, "Scholar to Speak on Economic Issues." What image will most likely pop in your mind? Was it of a European American—maybe a man in his late 40s or early 50s? Many would make specific assumptions based on their perception of the label *scholar.* Because of this tendency, some see the necessity in labeling African American scholars as such—even while European American scholars do not carry any specific racial label. Becoming sensitive to the power of labels does not necessarily provide any concrete answers to these questions. However, it does lay a valuable foundation for making well-informed choices.

Determine What, if Any, Labels Are Necessary

Once you become sensitive to the power of labeling, you may wonder why we use labels at all. Isn't everyone first and foremost human? This is certainly true, and in certain circumstances, labeling others is not necessary. Recognizing our commonalities as human beings does not mean that we should ignore those things that make us all different. Think about our language and all the labels that we unconsciously use to describe ourselves and others. Boss. Christian. Student. Athlete. Filipino. Single parent. Sorority member. Thirty-something. Midwesterner. Cancer survivor. In many situations, we find ourselves using a label to provide some relevant information about a person. In these situations, labels are productive. Choosing which labels to use sometimes is a challenge, though.

One guideline for using language to describe others is simply to respect their personal preferences.[16] In other words, refer to people by the labels that they prefer you to use. A number of language choices are available at any given time. For instance, instead of using *cancer survivor* (above) we could have used *cancer patient*, *cancer victim*, or possibly *someone in remission*. As you can see, each label is similar yet communicates a different meaning. Some people have strong preferences for the labels that others use to describe them. In part because of the way that labels work to define people, others might not. Listening to what labels others use to describe themselves is helpful.

Another guideline is to describe the person at the most appropriate level of specificity. Ask yourself, "How specific do I need to be with the label?" For instance, is it most appropriate to use "Filipino," "Filipino American," "Asian American," or the person's name? How about "Christian," "Baptist," "believer," "pastor," "Sister Brown," or simply "Mrs. Brown?" Remember that language is contextual. Therefore, the answers to these questions likely depend on the situation. Some situations call for more specific labels than others. Can you think of different situations where the same person might prefer one of these labels but not the others?

Use Inclusive Language

A significant element in effective interpersonal communication is using language that includes, not excludes, others. In certain instances, the terms or phrases that we are accustomed to using in our everyday interactions are not inclusive. Instead of treating everyone equally, they only refer to certain groups of individuals. Some specific examples of man-linked terminology can help illustrate this point.

Man-linked terminology refers to words or phrases that include the word *man* in them. They came into use at a time in history when only men occupied certain positions. However, many remain in place despite the fact that women also are in these positions. Ironically, both women and men continue to use these terms even in the midst of obvious contradictions (e.g., *female chairman*). Using language that acknowledges that both men and women are in positions of power is important. Consider the examples included in Table 5.2. Sometimes it takes a while to adopt to new language, especially given how long our society has embraced certain terms as acceptable.

Table 5.2 Alternatives to Man-Linked Terminology	
Man-Linked Terminology	**Inclusive Language**
Anchorman	Anchor
Congressman	Representative; senator
Fireman	Firefighter
Freshman	First-year student
Man of the house	Homeowner
Salesman	Salesperson
Sportsman	Sports enthusiast

You might be amazed at the impact that relatively small changes in your language will have on others. Many will see inclusive language as an indication of the value you place on all human beings. For instance, we have found that using *significant other* or *partner* in our interpersonal classes makes a lot more sense given that not all our students are romantically involved with someone of the other sex. Using these terms (as opposed to *girlfriend/boyfriend* or *spouse*) seems like a minor adjustment. However, doing so actively works to avoid excluding others in ways you may or may not have been aware of.

Some might say that the small distinctions being made here are trivial and not meaningful. Remember, however, that language functions as a tool *and* as an exhibition. Adopting inclusive language communicates a sense of affirmation to those who might otherwise feel alienated. Creating an environment of tolerance, respect, and affirmation is crucial for communication effectiveness.

Avoiding language bias that we have described here is an important first step in eliminating terms that hinder effective interpersonal communication. However, we must also recognize how our biases creep into our language in other, often more subtle, ways. The next section on the semantics of prejudice will help shed light on how this happens.

Shifts in language are a key source for changing existing perceptions.

Semantics of Prejudice

Many times we unconsciously use words that carry metameanings. The **semantics of prejudice** is an idea that suggests that language choices can unintentionally reveal information about our unspoken thoughts. In other words, our use of certain words—over other possible alternatives—reflects subtle judgments about what we are describing. In many cases, these judgments are not recognized by the speakers themselves, nor are they overtly communicated to others. However, their impact is still felt within interpersonal interactions.

For instance, most human characteristics can be described in several different ways. Read through the list of six sets of words below. As you read through each set, think about the subtly different meanings that people have for each word.

Careful	Meticulous	Fussy
Passionate	Emotional	Hysterical
Realistic	Suspicious	Cynical
Youthful	Young	Immature
Courageous	Bold	Reckless
Economical	Thrifty	Cheap

These specific examples should help you recognize how the semantics of prejudice work. Those words in the left column have a favorable metameaning. The words in the right-hand column have an unfavorable meaning; the ones in the middle are more neutral. Can you see how each set of words is describing a generally similar characteristic, yet in subtly different ways? When describing someone, we choose those words that best fit our own implicit value judgment of them. For example, consider a woman in your class who shares her experiences in a verbally abusive relationship. The way you might describe her actions is tied to how highly you value her as a person, women in general, and women who have been in abusive relationships specifically. Those with a favorable attitude might describe her actions as *passionate;* those with a less favorable attitude, *hysterical.* As you can see from this example, our language choices are oftentimes a reflection of our thoughts—even when we are not conscious of it.

This is not to say that the use of certain phrases is a direct reflection of certain thoughts, beliefs, and/or values. Nor is it accurate to conclude that everyone who uses a specific term has similar thoughts. Remember, however, what the Whorf-Sapir hypothesis suggests: Our language structures predispose us to think in certain ways (language functions as a lens). People who are interested in becoming more effective interpersonal communicators must become more conscious of their language choices. Some terms might be used with no malice or intention to offend. But it is important to recognize that others' perceptions of you may be largely informed by the words you use.

The Dynamic Nature of Language

It would be great if, as children, we could learn all that we needed to know about language in order to function in society. In the 1940s, some language scholars[17] promoted the idea that mastering as few as 850 words ("Basic English") would enable people to communicate effectively in any context. Unfortunately, as you realize after reading the language characteristics described earlier, the possibility of that happening is slim. The dynamic nature of language makes it an even more remote possibility.

Language systems are constantly changing. One area that reflects the dynamic nature of language is computer technology. Think of all the terms that are commonly used today but were virtually unheard of 10 years ago. World Wide Web. Internet. Web site. URL. E-mail. CD-ROM. Modem. Listserv. DVD. Ethernet. Zip disc. E-commerce. Without question, advanced technology has changed the way we communicate. We can chat online with friends, family, and strangers any time of the day. We can also shop, take classes, pay bills, and work via the computer. Cyberspace romances and/or sexual relationships are becoming increasingly common. In essence, we are now able to function in society without ever leaving our homes and coming face to face with another human being!

Some might say that a computer speech community has developed in the past few years. Communicating via the computer also has its own set of rules. People who spend a lot of time surfing the Net have mastered these rules. For them, communicating online is like second nature. But for Internet newcomers ("newbies"), not understanding the rules can greatly hinder their communication effectiveness. For instance, newbies oftentimes don't understand all the different symbols and abbreviations used. Read the interaction below and see if you can understand what is being communicated.

GR8FUL4HM: r u there?

MPOnMI: yep. w'sup?

GR8FUL4HM: n/m. u?

MPOnMI: just getting ready to head home . . . .

GR8FUL4HM: i'm trying to go out but having my usual problems &:(

MPOnMI: again? :-)

GR8FUL4HM: stop! ;-(it's ruining my love life

MPOnMI: lol

GR8FUL4HM: I'm thinking about shaving my head . . .

MPOnMI: roflol

GR8FUL4HM: :-@ IT IS NOT FUNNY

MPOnMI: j/k

GR8FUL4HM: k, i'm out

MPOnMI: :-*

GR8FUL4HM: :-*

How effective were you in following this brief conversation? Some of the symbols and abbreviations were relatively easy to interpret: :-) communicates smiling, "r u there" is shorthand for "Are you there?" and "lol" means "laughing out loud." But you probably couldn't understand the context of the conversation unless you knew that &:(= a bad hair day, ;-(= feels like crying, roflol = rolling on the floor laughing out loud, :-@ = screaming, j/k = just kidding, or :-* = a kiss. The conversation was an actual one between a woman and man involved in a long-distance friendship.

Virginia Shea has published a book on **netiquette** that details different rules on how to communicate via the Internet.[18] One strategy to communicate effectively while online is to "lurk" before communicating. Lurking is reading the existing posted messages in order to learn the rules of that particular group. As you might imagine, this kind of exposure is extremely helpful in understanding different communication contexts on the Internet. Remember that different chat rooms might have different rules. In Internet communication, then, lurking can be a good thing to do!

Summary

Not only does language function as a tool to communicate with others, but it also serves as both a lens and an exhibition. Language can be described as being symbolic, subjective, rule-governed, contextual, and creative. These characteristics illustrate how potential barriers can make effective language use a challenge.

In many ways, language is inextricably linked to culture, technology, and power. Language bias, speech communities, semantics of prejudice, and ingroup communication reflect how these three things are seen in everyday interactions. The Internet is another context in which to illustrate the dynamic nature of language. Based on what was covered, you should now be able to distinguish which of the opening statements were myths and which were truths.

Myth: Words have one specific meaning attached to them, that which is found in a dictionary. Why is this a myth?

Words have multiple interpretations, including both denotative and connotative meanings—an important consideration for effective communication to occur.

Truth: Multiple potential labels exist for each person, place, or thing.

Assuming that every concept has one precise label that is consistently used by others is dangerous.

Myth: The key to any language system is that the meanings of words are consistent from person to person and place to place.

One key to effectively using a language system is to recognize that meanings are co-constructed between people.

Myth: Personal definitions of what a word means are not as important as the official definitions. Why is this not true?

People use words in both formal and informal ways; effective communicators, therefore, need to be aware of various ways that words are used.

Myth: It is the other person's responsibility to understand the language that we use.

All people in an interaction should take some responsibility to ensure that shared meaning occurs. Mutual responsibility enhances the likelihood of success.

Truth: Due to the dynamic nature of language, language development is an ongoing process that continues to death.

While the core of our language is developed by adulthood, language systems are constantly changing; this should be reflected in an individual's ongoing language development.

Key Terms

Arbitrary nature of words

Bypassing

Communicare

Communication accommodation theory (CAT)

Connotative

Constructivism

Convergence

Denotative

Divergence

Euphemisms

Fact-inference confusion

Intensional orientation

Man-linked terminology

Netiquette

Polarization

Pragmatic rules

Reappropriating language

Semantic rules

Semantics of prejudice

Speech community

Static evaluation

Syntax rules

Whorf-Sapir hypothesis

Suggested Contemporary Readings

L. Chong-Yeong. "Language and human rights." *Journal of Intergroup Relations* 29 (2002): 57–65.

N. Fairclough. " 'Political correctness': The politics of culture and language." *Discourse & Society* 14 (2003): 17–28.

C. R. Groscurth. "Dialectically speaking: A critique of intergroup differences in African American language research." *Journal of Intergroup Relations* 30 (2003): 47–63.

S. O. Hastings. "Social drama as a site for the communal construction and management of Asian Indian 'stranger' identity." *Research on Language and Social Interaction* 34 (2001): 309–335.

M. S. McGlone and J. A. Batchelor. "Looking out for number one: Euphemism and face." *Journal of Communication* 53 (2003): 251–264.

A. Mulac, J. J. Bradac, and P. Gibbons. "Empirical support for the gender-as-culture hypothesis: An intercultural analysis of male/female language differences." *Human Communication Research* 27 (2001): 121–152.

A. K. Ojha. "Humor: A distinctive way of speaking that can create cultural identity." *Journal of Intercultural Communication Research* 32 (2003): 161–174.

D. J. Phillips. "Negotiating the digital closet: Online pseudonymity and the politics of sexual identity." *Information, Communication & Society* 5 (2002): 406–424.

R. Ribak. " 'Like immigrants': Negotiating power in the face of the home computer." *New Media & Society* 3 (2001): 220–238.

F. Trix and C. Psenka. "Exploring the color of glass: Letters of recommendation for female and male medical faculty." *Discourse & Society* 14 (2003): 191–220.

A. Weatherall. "Towards understanding gender and talk-in-interaction." *Discourse & Society* 13 (2002): 767–781.

Chapter Activities

1. Reexamine the information presented in Figure 5.1. Then think about your own particular state. What is the percentage of people who speak a language other than English at home? Of this number, what languages are most common? Once you've mentally completed this exercise, compare your predictions with actual data from the U.S. Census 2000 (*http://www.census.gov/population/www/cen2000/phc-t20.html*, Table 5. "Detailed List of Languages Spoken at Home for the Population 5 Years and Over by State: 2000").

2. Think about the different co-languages that you use in different contexts and with different groups. Select one of these contexts (e.g., related to your school, job, sports team, or cultural group) and create a 5–10-item co-language test. Each item can follow this example taken from a co-language test for soccer players: A banana kick refers to when a player: (1) kicks the ball so that the other player slips, (2) kicks the ball so that it curves around the defense, (3) jumps into the air and bends his or her leg like a banana, or (4) attempts to kick the ball but slips and misses. (Correct answer: 2.)

3. Create a list of personal *red-flag words*—words or phrases that trigger a mental alarm when dealing with potential or current significant others. Think about those things that others say that send up red flags during different stages of relationship development (e.g., when your romantic partner asks, "How exactly do you define cheating?"). If time permits, share your items with others in the class, and compare and contrast lists.

4. Visit the "Online Slang Dictionary: A Collaborative Project," which is located at *http://www.ocf.berkeley.edu/~wrader/slang/*. Read through some of the recent additions to test your own level of current awareness. You can even add some of your own slang terms to this growing source.

5. Seek out an opportunity to do some volunteer work with an organization that serves individuals from a culture different from your own. During your time working with this community, pay particular attention to what (and how) language is used. Based on what you've learned from this chapter, did you see examples of divergence and convergence? How, if at all, did the communication change over the course of your volunteer experience?

6. Conduct a brief review of today's newspaper, paying particular attention to news stories that focus on language barriers, problems, or conflicts. Clip any articles that you find, and attempt to offer solutions to the situation based on different concepts included in the chapter.

7. Break into small groups and discuss the importance of free speech in the United States. Why is free speech so important? Do similar rights exist in other countries? What, if any, limitations should be placed on a person's right to free speech? Within your discussions, think about how what you learned from this chapter might affect your opinions on this topic. ✦

Chapter 6

Nonverbal Communication

Contemporary Issues: Use Caution When E-Mailing

Janna is the marketing director of a large public relations firm in Dallas, Texas. She is discussing the details of some work her firm is doing for a client in Houston. Janna writes in an e-mail message: "We'd like to continue working with you. We need to propose a rate hike of 12 percent to cover the costs of the project." The client fires back an answer: "I assume you're joking? We can't afford that. Send me another message when you have more reasonable figures for us to consider."

Would this interaction have been the same across a conference room table? Would a smile, the tone of voice, or the gesture or body lean of Janna have prompted a different answer? Did the lack of eye contact create a defensive and unnecessarily hostile reaction from the client? According to a Stanford University study reported in a recent news headline,[1] "Face-to-face negotiations certainly have their place. . . . An [e-mail] message that's especially direct can come across as rude; and one intended to be humorous can come across as hostile." Michael Morris, author of that study and associate professor of organizational behavior at the Stanford Graduate School of Business, has completed a number of studies to examine the development of trust through different communication media, including e-mail. He has found that negotiations over e-mail can often break down because of vague and confusing nonverbals.[2] Although e-mail is an excellent way to send a document quickly, it is not necessarily the best way to discuss that document. Because many nuances of a conversation are lost when communicating via e-mail, we should consider limiting them, especially in the business setting, to rapid-fire notes and information, not to emotional, in-depth, or heated discussions or negotiations. In Janna's case, a face-to-face interaction might have resulted in a more productive conversation with the client. Have you had an experience when your written communication (e-mail or otherwise) has been misinterpreted? Do you think that such a message might have been more accurately interpreted if the other person could have seen your face, heard your voice, and/or observed other aspects of your nonverbal communication?

The development of new technologies for communicating and the ever-increasing presence of mediated interpersonal communication (e-mail, voice mail, instant message, and Internet chatting) have made us look more closely at how having limited nonverbal codes affects the interaction and the relationship between communicators. In this chapter, we consider the way nonverbal communication plays a role in *all* of our interactions, those face-to-face *and* those mediated. We will also consider how our increasingly diverse society demands that we are more aware of the culturally based nature of nonverbal communication, and the way that nonverbal behaviors often reflect, create, and/or reveal the power dynamics of an interaction or relationship. If you haven't thought about it already, you should be significantly more conscious after reading this chapter how a smile : -) or RAISING YOUR VOICE (!), as well as other aspects of your nonverbal behavior, play a significant role in creating the meaning in any interpersonal interaction.

Myths About Interpersonal Communication

Before we begin, take a minute to consider the following common myths and truths about nonverbal communication. Identify which of the following you believe are myths (M) and which are actually true (T):

_____ You can read a person like a book.

_____ Most people are unaware of the extent to which their nonverbal behavior is communicating to others.

_____ Nonverbal communication often accounts for a majority of the meaning in interpersonal interactions.

_____ Most of the nonverbals we use (facial expressions like a smile, and hand gestures like a wave) are the same around the world.

_____ We can diagnose problems in relationships by specifically observing nonverbal communication.

Even though you have been communicating all your life, and nonverbal communication is something you use everyday, we are guessing that until you read this chapter in full, you might not be able to fully articulate why and how some of the above statements are or aren't true. If you can, good for you! If not, you'll have some important ideas to consider as you read on.

What Is Nonverbal Communication?

Nonverbal communication refers to all types of communication that do not rely on words or other linguistic systems. For instance, American Sign Language is not nonverbal communication because ASL is a linguistic system; nor is the use of written words. Nonverbal communication does include the way we use gestures, touch, tone of voice, body positioning, space, time, facial expressions, and all types of body language to communicate. Take a look at Figure 6.1 and examine how much you can learn from just the nonverbals (the touch, proximity, gestures, dress, and facial expressions) of the people in these pictures.

Nonverbal communication can tell us a lot! Many people assume that because nonverbal communication lacks words, it does not include sound. However, sound is a very important aspect of nonverbal communication. The qualities of sound that surround our words, such as how loudly we speak, how fast we speak, or how we emphasize certain words or phrases with our inflection and pitch, are part of the message we send. Figure 6.2 depicts an easy way to begin to think about nonverbal communication and its relationship to verbal communication. As you see, the chart identifies the vocal, nonvocal, verbal, and nonverbal aspects of the ways we communicate; the ways in which nonverbal and verbal communication work together; and the available message systems we have for creating meaning in our interpersonal interactions.

Figure 6.1   Nonverbal Communication

Just by examining the nonverbal communication of the people in these photos, we can gather a great deal of information. Take a moment to reflect on just how much gestures, facial expressions, the distance between people, and the touch, dress, and body positions of people communicate to us what is happening, or the emotions of the people, in any situation.

Figure 6.2   Verbal and Nonverbal Communication

	Verbal	Nonverbal
Vocal	Spoken words	Laughs, "hmmmm," "ahhh," voice pitch, rate of speaking, inflection, voice quality, accent, volume of speech, and so on
Nonvocal	Written words, American Sign Language	Touch, eye contact, space, facial expressions, body movements, use of time to communicate, artifacts, and so on

As this chart reveals, nonverbal messages can be both vocal and nonvocal. Verbal communication, too, can take vocal or nonvocal forms. American Sign Language is considered "verbal" because it is a linguistic system (a "language") communicated by the use of hands and body movements. It is different from other nonverbal communication because of its linguistic qualities. We will discuss each of the types of nonverbal communication in this chapter.

Studying and Understanding Nonverbal Communication

Both professional researchers and the popular press have paid a lot of attention to nonverbal communication in recent years. You have probably seen articles entitled, "How to Read Your Boss's Body Language," "How to Know if Someone Is Lying," or "Baby Sign Language: The Secret to Helping Your Baby Communicate." Although some of the information in these articles is interesting, and some is based on scholarly research, much of it is based on misinterpretations and overgeneralizations of research findings. Communication researchers know quite a bit about nonverbal communication; hundreds of scholars in the communication field are doing research on topics such as lying, touch, eye contact, appearance, and even the importance of nonverbal behavior in the physical and social development of infants. We have decades of research on nonverbal communication in relationships, among family members, in the health-care context, in organizations, as it is used in persuasion, and in small groups, to name just a few research areas. In this chapter, we will try to provide you with a basic understanding of the types of nonverbal communication that are most common, the characteristics of nonverbal communication, and its relationship to verbal communication to help you become a more informed and skilled interpersonal communicator. Here are some important suggestions to consider as you read this chapter.[3]

Engage in Self-Reflection. Reflect carefully on the information provided here and in the other popular or scholarly sources about nonverbal communication, particularly if you are going to use it to change your own behaviors. Be honest with yourself about the areas in which you do well and in which you need improvement. As you read, keep those in mind as you begin to make more informed and critical choices about your own nonverbal behaviors and make choices to change those behaviors.

Be a Conscious Observer. Raise your awareness and observe the world of nonverbal behavior all around you: Look. Watch. Listen. By beginning to be more aware of the everyday behaviors of those around you—your family members, your classmates, strangers, and your friends—you will be better able to make sense of what you read about in this chapter.

Avoid Erroneous Conclusions. Be careful about drawing conclusions from isolated bits of nonverbal behaviors. Nonverbal communication takes place in "packages" of behavior. Each "package" is made up of a variety of different nonverbal cues, and has meaning based only on the other cues in that "package." So, be careful about concluding that the position of someone's arm means they are cold or angry, or that a lack of eye contact means someone is rude. You need to consider more about the nonverbal context, such as how that person usually holds his or her arms and the person's cultural rules for using eye contact, before drawing a conclusion about just one part of a person's nonverbal behavior.

Apply New Information Thoughtfully. Resist the temptation to apply new knowledge about nonverbal communication in a rigid, absolute way. Also, resist the temptation to give advice on others' nonverbal behavior. You *should* use the information in this chapter to better understand your own and others' nonverbal behaviors and choices, but be careful about assuming you know everything there is to know. The information in this chapter can only begin to introduce just a few aspects of nonverbal communication. Thousands of books and articles have been published that can tell you more about nonverbal communication.

Avoid Overgeneralizations. Remember that most of the results and conclusions presented here are "true" from a statistical standpoint: They apply to the average or typical person, or in the context in which they were studied by researchers (limited to certain ethnic or cultural populations, for instance). However, the information may not apply to you, your friends, or your family members as individuals. Be careful about overgeneralizing the conclusions, as well as dismissing conclusions because you can identify at least one exception.

Learn the Vocabulary. Learn and try to use the new vocabulary of nonverbal terms that we will introduce in this chapter. By doing so, you will open yourself up to a whole new world of communication and become aware of interpersonal dynamics you might normally have overlooked.

Using Nonverbal Cues

Consider the following scenario:

Marissa's alarm buzzed loudly at 7 a.m. As she slowly dragged herself out of bed and turned on the small light on her dresser, her roommate covered her head with the blankets on her bed and sighed loudly as she turned over. Marissa was getting up earlier so she could get a front-row seat in her 8 a.m. class. She was the first person on the wait-list for this class, and hoped that if she came early, greeted and smiled at the professor before class, and sat in the front row, she might up her odds of getting into the class. This was the first day of class for Marissa at Carver College. As a transfer student from a local community college, Marissa was a little nervous about how she might fit in. Even though she didn't know anyone and wasn't even sure where her class building was, she set out on her first day trying to appear confident, walking with a fast stride and looking around at the signs and the campus with a slight smile, humming a quiet tune, and holding her book bag over her right shoulder.

As she walked toward the cafeteria, she saw a group of three young women coming toward her, laughing and giggling as they walked and chatted. With their long, blonde hair, their updated clothes—probably from the Gap or Abercrombie—she was sure they were probably sorority "chicks" and wouldn't be friendly to her. They almost looked like sisters, she thought to herself, with the same makeup, nail polish, and hairstyles. They are probably all wealthy, she thought. She was hoping they weren't going to be in her class, because she didn't want to deal with the "triplets" who probably wouldn't take the class seriously anyway.

As Marissa entered the cafeteria, she tried to smile at the server behind the counter. He looked like he was in his mid-30s, and didn't look showered. His shoes looked old and he didn't look at any of the students or smile, even when someone said hello. "He's probably unhappy about having this job, and not making much money. Look at his shoes and clothes . . . wonder how you can make a living working in a college cafeteria," she thought to herself. She picked up a tray and grabbed her breakfast. As she headed out to find a table, she nervously walked toward a table with a few people sitting alone, each with about four chairs in between them. The guy on the end had on a baseball cap pulled down almost over his face. He was reading the sports section of the campus newspaper. Marissa was sure he was a "jock" and probably not a good conversationalist. The guy sitting a few chairs away was dressed in nice but plain clothes. He was glancing through a new textbook that still had the price on it. She didn't think he was really reading it, but nervously paging through the book to look as if he was busy and not wanting company. Probably a "geek" who would be boring to talk to, she thought to herself. Behind him was a group of two young women, sitting close to one another and talking quietly to themselves. "I'll bet they're roommates, probably friends from last year. They probably aren't interested in meeting a new transfer student, since they already have friends." Marissa was hoping to herself that they'd invite her to sit with them anyway.

After finishing breakfast, Marissa headed for class. She saw a few students waiting outside the class, chatting with each other. "Is that a tattoo on that guy's neck?" she thought to herself. He wore a black leather jacket and had a chain from his wallet to his belt loop. "Wonder what he's doing in college?" He didn't look like the typical college student. Marissa was a bit ashamed that she was thinking that. As she entered the room, she wasn't surprised that most students were taking seats in the back; the back row was already full, mostly with guys who wore new Levis and polo shirts. "They'd be good friends with the three blondes I saw this morning," she thought. One guy was sitting in the second row, booting up his laptop computer and checking his schedule on his handheld Palm IV. He was dressed in khaki pants and had a pressed shirt. He even had two pens neatly placed in his shirt pocket. "He looks like he'd be a great person to be in a group project with." Marissa made a mental note of him, in case they were assigned such a project. She selected a seat in the front just as the professor came in. Dressed in wrinkly corduroys and a sweater vest, his hair matted from the previous night's sleep, Professor Gorman placed his large, overstuffed, tattered brief case on the front table. He didn't look at the students, and began writing something in sloppy writing on the board. "This should be interesting," she said sarcastically to the woman sitting next to her. To herself, she finished her thoughts: "Look at him. He can't even wash his hair in the morning. Hope he's more interesting than he is attractive." As he wrote on the board, Marissa decided to approach Professor Gorman and asked him if she could add the class. . . .

Maybe you don't want to admit that you use nonverbal cues to evaluate and understand your surroundings to the extent that Marissa did. Most of us do, however, observe the nonverbal behaviors of others to make judgments and draw conclusions. Often without even thinking about it, we observe facial expressions, gestures, how people sit or stand, what they wear or drive, or the items they carry with them in order to make decisions about how we should communicate in a situation, with whom we want to develop relationships, and how to behave. Although most of us are aware that nonverbal communication plays a large role in our everyday interactions, many students of interpersonal communication are surprised, after reading and studying the topic, just how influential nonverbals are, and just how much we do use them— every day, all day—to judge people and situations.

How Much Meaning Is in Nonverbal Cues?

Nonverbal communication accounts for much of the meaning in any interpersonal interaction. Some researchers suggest that 65 to 93 percent of all meaning communicated in any situation is attributable to nonverbal behaviors.[4] Some communication scholars suggest we can't really know how much of meaning is in the verbal or nonverbal aspect of our messages, because both are so intricately interwoven.[5] Yet we know that both verbal and nonverbal elements are important in all interpersonal interaction, and that communicating meaning usually requires both verbal and nonverbal elements, not either one alone.

Characteristics of Nonverbal Cues

Before we begin to explore the different kinds of nonverbal communication possible in our interpersonal interactions, it's important to look at characteristics of nonverbal cues and understand some of the things that we know about how nonverbal communication functions in our interpersonal interactions. Below we overview five essential characteristics of nonverbal communication, summarized based on much research on this topic.

Although some kinds of nonverbal behavior are more obvious or intentional than others (like waving to say goodbye, or kissing someone to indicate liking), we often communicate nonverbally without even realizing it. We do this by choosing what we wear, the kind of car we drive, or how we arrange our homes and apartments. We even communicate something by the gifts we select for others. You might give your grandparents a computer and Internet access (hoping to be able to communicate with them via e-mail), give your partner a membership to the gym (telling him you want him to get in shape and lose some weight), or give your friend's baby girl a pink dress and your new baby nephew a toy truck (communicating culturally defined, sex-specific roles). In all of these ways, we are communicating, even though not all of our communication is intentional.

Nonverbal Communication Occurs in a Context. One of the most important results of studying nonverbal communication is understanding that it always takes place in a context. Context includes the physical environment (a bar versus a funeral home), the nature of a relationship (a stranger versus a former intimate partner), the culture or ethnic heritage of the communicators (what are the rules for nonverbal behavior assumed and used in that particular cultural context?), or a host of other contextual factors (the political, historical, or economic issues of a situation, for example). As we cautioned above, be careful about drawing conclusions from bits of nonverbal behavior without considering the context in which it occurred. For instance, if you wink at a person in one context it might signal interest or liking; in another, it might indicate you are telling a lie. Raising your hand in the classroom indicates a question or request; raising your hand on the side of a busy New York street might indicate that you need a cab. A sign of peace (two fingers raised and slightly apart) is a friendly gesture in the United States, but is a highly offensive gesture in other cultures.

Nonverbal Messages Are More Believable Than Verbal Messages. Common sense tells us, and communication researchers confirm, that actions speak louder than words. This principle applies to nonverbal communication, too. In fact, nonverbal communication is generally more believable than verbal communication. When our verbal and nonverbal messages contradict one another, people tend to believe the nonverbal. When Janet received a birthday present from her friend Tamica, she said, "I love it," without looking up, without raising her voice with excitement, and with a blank look in her eyes. Do we really think that Janet loved the present Tamica selected for her? Probably not, because her nonverbal behavior spoke more loudly than her words of praise. When you enter the kitchen in the morning wearing your new brightly colored, Hawaiian-style shirt and your wife says, "Nice shirt," with downturned lips and a tone of sarcasm, do we really think she means she thinks the shirt is "nice," or do we interpret her verbal message to mean she doesn't like it because her nonverbals suggest otherwise? Probably the latter. Take a moment to think of a time when you looked to the nonverbal behavior of a person to figure out whether the verbal message was true. We're guessing you can think of many examples.

On the other hand, research on liars and deception offers interesting information to consider, cautioning us to not rely too heavily on nonverbal cues when attempting to spot deception. Most of us think we're pretty good at knowing whether and when someone is lying to us, especially a significant other. We often look for nonverbal "leakage" cues, those behaviors that we think are signs that someone is lying, such as longer pauses before answering a question, reduced eye contact, reduced smiling, slower speech, or unfilled pauses. However, communication researchers Buller and Burgoon argue in their interpersonal deception theory that we should doubt our ability to detect deception because generally people are not as good at lie detecting as they think.[6] They found that most people have a "truth bias," believing that others are generally honest, complete, direct, and clear—even when they are lying. Further, according to this theory, liars often are better able to sense suspicion than detectors are at sensing deception, and quickly change their suspicious behaviors to heighten their partner's belief in their lie. Further, other researchers have found that in laboratory conditions, people are rarely more than 60 percent accurate in their abilities to spot deception; the average person has about a 50 percent chance of accurately pointing out a liar.[7] So, even though we tend to, and should, believe the nonverbal over the verbal, we need to be cautious about overestimating our ability to detect when others are deceiving us.

Nonverbal Communication Is Important in Interpersonal Relationships. Nonverbal behavior can indicate the power dynamics in relationships, is guided by and reflects the rules of a relationship, and can reveal the intentions of those in a relationship. Nonverbal cues are also responsible for most of the impressions that are first formed in an interpersonal interaction. In so many ways, nonverbal behaviors are central to interpersonal relationships.

How do you communicate aspects of your power in your relationships? Do you purchase more expensive and thoughtful gifts for those you like or care for more than others (a card for a casual friend, tickets to a pricey concert for a partner or significant other)? Are you less worried about being late for a meeting with someone who has equal or lesser power (such as a friend) than with someone who has more power (such as a boss)? As we will discuss in detail throughout this chapter, your nonverbals are used in many ways to indicate power dynamics in relationships.

Similarly, your nonverbal behavior is guided by the rules in your relationship. Whether you use a private gesture to indicate a loving message, or you know that being "on time" actually means you both expect to arrive about 30 minutes late, you are coordinating your nonverbal cues with another interpersonally. The use of nonverbals can also signal intentions of individuals in relationships. The use of intimate touch is a rather clear sign of affection when used in an intimate relationship. Smiles, eye contact, and leaning toward another can signal interest. Other ways in which we indicate our intention to have less interaction or to end a relationship are through nonverbal cues such as distance or silence. Finally, most of the first impressions others have of us—and we have of others—are based on nonverbal cues, sometimes exclusively. Our appearance, smile, hairstyle, clothing, body type, posture, and artifacts we carry or surround ourselves with communicate a great deal about our interests, desires, and worldviews. The power of our nonverbal cues to invite others to communicate with us and to make impressions of us is striking. We will discuss this too, in much greater detail, throughout this chapter.

Nonverbal Communication Is Culture Based. Does a smile mean "happy" in every culture around the world? Do young children in every culture suck their thumbs for comfort or raise their arms to be picked up? Some researchers suggest that these are just a few of the nonverbal expressions similar in most cultures. Others argue that there are no universal nonverbal behaviors. Regardless, most scholars do agree that culture does indeed influence, to a significant degree, our use and interpretation of nonverbal behavior. The way one culture greets is the way another culture insults. The way one culture expresses negative emotions is a forbidden expression in another. The distance one appropriately stands from another in a social conversation is perceived as an invasion of space in another culture. In some Inuit cultures, for instance, banging the other party on the head or shoulder is a common greeting; in India, you shouldn't touch another's head, for it is considered a great invasion of space and an insult. In many areas of China, you should point only with an open hand. For many in England, it is generally seen as impolite to talk with your hands in your pockets. In most of the former Yugoslavia, it is an obscene gesture to bend the arm at the elbow, make a fist (with knuckles away from face), and shake the fist once. In much of Colombia, you should clap your hands lightly to beckon another person.[8] If you have traveled or encountered people from a culture other than your own, you have probably experienced some misunderstanding based on different culturally specific rules for communicating nonverbally. Throughout this chapter, we will discuss more about the role culture plays in our nonverbal communication.

The Relationship Between Nonverbal and Verbal Communication

In most contexts, we use nonverbal and verbal communication together seamlessly and naturally. We usually need both to communicate clearly, effectively, and completely. There are six common ways that verbal and nonverbal communication work together.

Accenting

Nonverbal communication often accents, emphasizes, or enhances what we say verbally. You might remember when your father wanted to emphasize a point about mowing the lawn or coming home too late. He might have raised his voice, squeezed your shoulder, or looked at you with glaring eyes. Each nonverbal was an attempt to accent the seriousness of his verbal message. Your teacher might emphasize her message about reading the assigned chapter before class by banging her hand on the desk while scolding the unprepared students. Your partner might accent his happiness to see you when he smiles as he greets you. Read the following sentences, noting the differences in how the accent changes or highlights different parts of the message:

I *love* chocolate ice cream!

I love *chocolate* ice cream.

I love chocolate *ice cream.*

Italicizing or highlighting written words, and using different kinds of punctuation, emphasizes them and indicates where the spoken word should be accented—a type of nonverbal communication using the qualities of our voice. These kinds of nonverbal communication are important parts of accurately communicating meaning.

As more and more of us become active Internet users, we have begun to learn the nonverbal language of e-mail messages. Many of these serve to accent what we want to say. A smiley face :-) typed within or at the end of a message (read with your head tilted slightly left) accents that the message is lighthearted or friendly. Similarly, we can express a look of shock :-o or even stick out our tongue at someone :-p to accent our verbal message when using electronic messaging. Read the information in Applied Concepts (Box 6.1) for a more complete list of what experienced e-mailers know as *emoticons*, the clever signs you can type that allow you to communicate the nonverbal nuances of your verbal messages. Similar to studies of female-male verbal communication, one study found that females were more emotionally expressive and frequent in their use of emoticons than were males participating in an online newsgroup.[9]

Box 6.1

Applied Concepts
Electronic Nonverbals: Emoticons

As most e-mailers know, you don't have to just stick with verbal messages when you're communicating electronically. You can emphasize your POINT! by using punctuation, *italics*, or **highlights**. Or, as even some of the most novice e-mailers quickly learn, there are a variety of ways to use just your keyboard to smile :-) or frown :- (or even share a kiss :-* in an e-mail message. Known as *emoticons*, these nonverbals have been used by millions of

☞ electronic communicators for almost a decade.[10] Emoticons allow you to more accurately communicate the non-verbal aspect of your verbal message. Below is a sample of some of the most commonly used and recognized emoticons:

: -) Smile	;-) Winking, wry	8-) Smile wearing sunglasses; too cool for words	:-| Indifferent
:D Big happy smile	:-C Bummed out	: -} Embarrassed smile	:*) Drunk
:-o Surprise	:'-(Crying	:-C Really sad	:-& Tongue-tied
:- Mad	:——D Laughing	:-@ Extremely angry	:-O Yelling
= :0 Scared	|-O Yawning	:-p Sticking tongue out	:-)~ Drooling
: -# Censored or told to be quiet	:-x Lips are sealed	:-$ Person with braces	:-~) User has a cold
:-)}/// Smile with a tie	{:-) User wears a toupee	== Fish or fishy message	=:-) Into punk rock
:——) Happy	(-: Left-handed	:——) Happy and bearded	

New communication technologies might soon make emoticons a thing of the past. A new "imagemorphing" program called Facemail allows an e-mailer to insert the animated face of a model into her or his e-mail to simulate a wink, smile, nod, or look of surprise.[11] Plans are for users to eventually be able to substitute their own pictures for the generic models.

Complementing

Along with accenting, our nonverbals can also complement—reinforce, add to, or clarify—our verbal messages. The more we can complement our verbal messages with reinforcing or additional nonverbal messages, the more accurately someone might be able to interpret our meaning. For instance, if a close friend approaches you to apologize for not keeping information private as you asked her to, you are much more likely to interpret her apology as sincere if she moves close to you, looks you in the eyes, and in a sincere and serious tone of voice says, "I'm *really* sorry about what I did." Compare that apology to that of a friend who shouts across the front lawn while laughing and smiling with some friends, "I'm really sorry for what I did!" The first message is complemented by the addition of the nonverbals that accompanied the verbal communication. The second is not. Remember that when messages are in opposition to one another, we tend to believe the nonverbal cues over the verbal.

Contradicting

Sometimes nonverbal messages don't accent or complement the verbal message, but contradict it. When we smile and say we're sad, when we keep reading the paper when we say we're listening, when we say to our clients that they are important to us but don't respond to their e-mails for over a week or return phone calls for days, or when we sneer when we assure our mother we won't walk on the carpet with our shoes on, our nonverbals contradict our verbals. Sometimes we intentionally contradict our verbal message with our nonverbals. When you say to your friend in a sarcastic tone, "Nice shirt" (because you know he got it as a gift from his girlfriend but does not like it), you are intentionally using contradictory nonverbal and verbal messages.

Regulating

One of the most common and overlooked uses of nonverbal behavior is to regulate or help coordinate the verbal interaction between people. Consider how you know it is your turn to speak when having a conversation with friends. Do you have to raise your hand and be called on before speaking? Does one person say, "It is now your turn to speak"? Usually not. Rather, our subtle and implicitly understood use of nonverbal communication works to indicate when we should or can speak. We generally know that when people look our way, or when there is a pause or silence, it is "our turn" in a conversation. When we would like to continue our turn in a conversation, we often used "vocalized pauses" such as *ummmm* and *ahhhh* to indicate that we have more to say, but just need a moment to think of what it is. Further, we often indicate our interest in what someone is saying by leaning forward and encouraging them with our body stance and eye contact. You can probably think of examples of people who aren't as skilled at regulating interactions, or aren't as aware of how nonverbal behavior serves to regulate their behaviors. The person who frequently interrupts, who dominates the conversation without a pause for others to participate, or who is nonresponsive ("like talking to a wall") is an ineffective communicator.

Repeating

A nonverbal message that serves to repeat or reiterate the verbal message is one that could stand alone if the verbal message were not present, although it is used in conjunction *with* the verbal message. For instance, if you are in an elevator and the person by the control panel asks what floor you would like pushed, you say, "Five, please," while holding up five fingers. When you say, "Good job," to your preschool son who is learning to swim while also giving him the "thumbs-up" sign from the side of the pool, your gesture is repeating your verbal message and could even substitute for it.

Substituting

As mentioned above, our nonverbals might not only repeat what we say verbally, but can also actually substitute or be sent in place of verbal messages. You might wave your hand in the air to a friend walking on the other side of the parking lot in place of yelling, "Hello!"; shrug your shoulders when your spouse asks you where his wallet is, instead of saying, "I don't know"; raise your hand in class instead of yelling out, "I have something to say"; or walk by someone silently with a frown or while staring at the floor to substitute for the message "I'm in a bad mood today; please leave me alone." All day long, we use nonverbal communication to substitute for what we could say verbally.

Types of Nonverbal Communication

Now that we've explored the basic foundation of nonverbal communication and its relationship to verbal communication, we can begin looking more closely at the categories or different types of nonverbal communication: facial expressions, body movements and gestures, eye contact, voice, the use of space and territory and our environment, the use of time, touch, and our personal dress and appearance. Figure 6.3 provides an overview of each type of nonverbal cue. We will examine each below, followed by a closer look at how each varies across cultures and co-cultures.

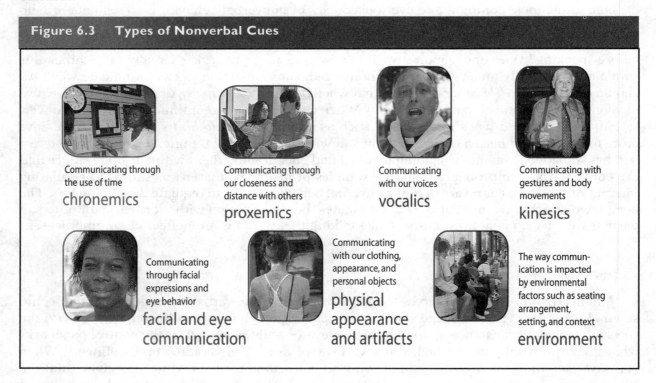

Figure 6.3   Types of Nonverbal Cues

Communicating through the use of time
chronemics

Communicating through our closeness and distance with others
proxemics

Communicating with our voices
vocalics

Communicating with gestures and body movements
kinesics

Communicating through facial expressions and eye behavior
facial and eye communication

Communicating with our clothing, appearance, and personal objects
physical appearance and artifacts

The way communication is impacted by environmental factors such as seating arrangement, setting, and context
environment

Kinesics

Kinesics is the study of the way we use body movement and gestures to communicate. Kinesic behavior includes all behavior of the body including gestures, eye behavior, head movement, posture, facial expressions, and movement of the arms, legs, hands, fingers, and trunk of the body. When we lean slouched against a doorway with our head hanging, or when we stand erect with our head held high facing forward or slightly up, our bodies are communicating something about how we feel. Kinesics is the study of the many ways our body movement communicates nonverbally.

When you encounter someone from another culture and do not speak his or her language, you often rely on gestures to help you communicate. We might point or use our hands to depict an object to try and make our point. People have used gestures to communicate since ancient times, even before using verbal communication. Some current communication researchers suggest that gestures frequently come before verbal communication in interpersonal interactions, "framing" the conversation before it begins.[12] If asked to keep a log of all the gestures you use during a day, you'd most likely be able to document thousands of hand movements, both large and obvious, small and subtle, in just a few hours. As you recall, they serve to accent, complement, contradict, regulate, repeat, or substitute for what is said verbally.

Gestures and Body Movements. Gestures and body movements, a category of kinesics, can be categorized into five types (as depicted in Figure 6.4): emblems, illustrators, regulators, affect displays, and adaptors.

Figure 6.4 Types of Nonverbal Communications.

An index finger pointing upward says, "We're number one" or "We're great."
emblem

Moving your hands apart can illustrate the length of the object you are describing.
illustrator

A large smile with a laugh can reveal your joyful mood.
affect display

A nod with raised eyebrows can tell another speaker when it's her time to talk.
regulator

Constantly scratching your head during a speech might be a personal adaptor, a sign of nervousness.
adaptor

Emblems are a type of gesture that can take the place of a word or a phrase, and often have a direct verbal translation. They are known as "speech-independent" gestures because they can easily exist independently of speech. Before reading on, try to think of a few gestures or body movements you use that would be easily understood by most people in your culture to mean a word or phrase. Can you think of any? Common examples of emblems in U.S. culture include the hitchhiking emblem (arm extended with a closed first and the thumb extended upward), the "A-OK" sign (first finger and thumb together creating a circle with other fingers extended), "no" (shaking your head side to side), "you're dead" (using hand or finger to slit throat), "up yours" (extending one's middle finger), or "he's nuts" (using circular finger motion next to one's head). Generally, emblems are known by most or all of a group, class, culture, or co-culture. The emblem has more in common with verbal communication than any other kind of nonverbal behavior.

Illustrators are arm or hand movements that accompany speech, but usually cannot stand alone. They are often used to literally "illustrate" our verbal messages, or to complement or emphasize what we are trying to say. We illustrate with gestures or body movements when we point on the map to the place we're talking about, when we illustrate the shape or size of a present under the tree ("It's about this long, and this high"), or to emphasize a point (stomping your foot while saying, "Get yourself up the stairs this instant"). Each illustrator provides additional meaning to the verbal communication.

Regulators are gestures or facial expressions that are used to control or regulate the flow of a conversation. As skilled communicators, we become aware of how to raise our eyebrows, lean slightly forward, raise a finger, open our mouths a small amount, nod our heads, or shift our eye contact when we want to tell another communicator we would like to take a turn in a conversation. We also use regulators to tell others to hurry up, continue, elaborate, or conclude what they are saying. Regulators are important nonverbal cues that help us interact effectively in interpersonal interactions.

The fourth category of gestures and movement is **affect displays**. These are the nonverbal cues that allow us to express our emotion, or affect. We often use facial expressions to display how we are feeling, although we also do so by our posture, the way we walk, the movement of our arms and hands, and other behaviors. Affect displays are important indicators of not just *what* we are feeling, but also how *intensely* we are feeling a particular emotion. For instance, when you get back a test from your professor with a large "F" written on the front, you might have a confused or depressed look on your face, but the slump of your shoulders and the way you walk slowly and solemnly back to your desk might indicate the intensity of your despair. On the other hand, if you receive a paper that you worked on all semester with an "A+" on the top, you might automatically smile wide; the way your lift your head, raise your eyebrows, hold your paper in front of you, and walk confidently and swiftly back to your seat might indicate the intensity of your happiness. Affect displays are often called *displays* because we generally express such nonverbal behaviors unconsciously and automatically, displaying without awareness of how or what we are communicating. Take a look at the pictures in Figure 6.5. Can you determine the emotions of the woman in the photos? What kinds of affect displays can you identify that would indicate not only what the emotion is, but also its intensity?

Figure 6.5 Affect Displays

Skill Builder

Can you determine the affect of the woman in these photos? After doing so, identify specific aspects of her expressions that indicate the intensity of her emotions. In photo 3, is she really happy, or just somewhat happy? How can you tell? In photo 1, is she somewhat sad, or really depressed? What is it about her body position, posture, facial expressions, or other nonverbal behaviors that would indicate the affect being displayed?

When you're uncomfortable or nervous, what do you do? Do you twist a strand of your hair around your pointer finger, tap your foot back and forth, jingle the coins in your pocket, or squeeze your hands tightly together? Maybe you scratch your head, rub your nose, tug on your ear, or snap gum in your mouth. As a child, you might have been attached to a favorite blanket or certain animal or toy; all of us need to comfort ourselves from time to time. When we're nervous, anxious, uneasy, or upset, we engage in nonverbal behaviors called adaptors. **Adaptors** are those nonverbal behaviors, often habitual or automatic, that help us adjust to our environment. Take some time today and notice what adaptors you tend to use. Do you tap your pen, pick at your nose, rub your arms, or doodle in your notebook? If so, you might be using an adaptor. We are often unaware of adaptors until someone points them out to us or we become mindful of them.

Posture. Your posture is the position and movement of your body and is one type of kinesic behavior. But how does it communicate? According to researchers, we communicate a great deal through the positioning of our body.[13] Think about how you use your body position and posture to indicate that you are uninterested in someone who is looking at you from across the room. You use your posture to communicate to your professors each day you sit in class; your slouched posture, tightly crossed arms, head down, and lean back into the chair might indicate boredom and disinterest. One well-known nonverbal communication researcher suggests that we communicate openness and a willingness to communicate by a slight forward lean, a direct body orientation, and a relaxed but open posture.[14]

Some communication scholars believe posture is one of the most revealing cues of gender.[15] Females tend to position, hold, and orient their bodies differently than males. For instance, young girls in U.S. culture tend to be socialized to exhibit "shrinkage" cues; they are more likely to keep their heads and eyes low, tip their heads to one side, and keep their arms and legs closer to their bodies to take up less space. Young boys, however, are often socialized in U.S. culture to engage in "expanding" nonverbal cues, or those that take up more space. Common masculine nonverbal behaviors include legs positioned apart when sitting or standing, taking longer strides when walking, and carrying arms away from the trunk of the body.

Body movements are very important in interpersonal relationships, especially in creating perceptions of how assertive and powerful we are. According to Dale Leathers, a well-known communication scholar, if we wish to be perceived as assertive, we must take special care to monitor our nonverbal cues.[16] Table 6.1 lists those behaviors associated with assertiveness, the majority of which involve kinesics such as body position and body movement. The lists are compiled from a number of studies on nonverbal behavior that Leathers suggests will either increase or decrease our chances of being perceived as assertive and powerful. Note that these findings apply to assertiveness and power in the U.S. culture only. Perceptions of power and assertiveness vary greatly among cultural and co-cultural groups.

Table 6.1 Power and Assertiveness in Body Movements
Nonverbal Behaviors Associated With Assertiveness:
1. Having a relaxed posture with a slight forward lean; relaxed use of gestures
2. Having deliberate but not expansive gestures
3. Sustaining eye contact without staring

Table 6.1
Power and Assertiveness in Body Movements (*Continued*)

4. Using illustrators and appropriate inflection of the voice to emphasize key words
5. Using an appropriate voice volume (loud, but not too loud)
6. Using touch appropriately (firm handshakes, appropriate touch on the arm)

Nonverbal Behaviors Associated With Nonassertiveness:
1. Nervous gestures such as touching the hair, tapping fingers on the table, and pulling on clothing
2. Smiling when the smile is not expected (in the middle of an argument or crisis)
3. Slouching or hunching of the shoulders
4. Putting the hand over the mouth to cover it
5. Maintaining a stiff or rigid body posture
6. Clearing one's throat frequently or making small coughing noises
7. Not making appropriate amount of eye contact, or averting of eyes
8. Using vocal fillers in place of silence (ah's and um's)

Nonverbal Indicators of Power:
1. A relaxed posture
2. A posture that is upright (not slumped)
3. Dynamic and purposeful gestures
4. Steady and direct eye gaze
5. Variety in the rate and inflection of the voice
6. Using a variety of postures
7. Postures used are relatively expansive (but not overly so)
8. Having the option to touch, stare at, interrupt, and stand or approach someone closely

Nonverbal Indicators of Powerlessness:
1. A tense and overly rigid body posture or use of body movements
2. Smiling excessively or inappropriately
3. Staring at someone or using intensely inappropriate eye contact
4. Inability to look directly at others
5. Looking down at the floor frequently
6. Arriving early for meetings, parties, or other social events
7. Nervously or continuously moving the feet
8. Having a closed body posture
9. Avoiding touch in all instances

As Leathers points out, communicating powerlessness and unassertiveness is not always undesirable or dysfunctional. In some instances, taking a less powerful position might be warranted or desirable, particularly in the context of a personal relationship. Can you think of some examples?

Facial and Eye Communication. Another type of kinesic behavior is facial and eye communication. When you're trying to determine how your child feels about hearing his grandfather passed away, how your boss feels about your request for extended vacation, how your spouse feels about the new sofa you purchased, or how your roommate feels about your new boyfriend, you most likely look at the other person's face for your answer. The face has long been known as a primary, and perhaps the richest, source of information about how others are feeling. Even as infants, we focus intensely and foremost on the face of those feeding us, peering into our cribs, and talking to us. Some scholars suggest that the face is second only to verbal speech as a source of information.

We pay a great deal of attention to the face because it is very visual. When we communicate with others, where do we look? At their feet, knees, or back of the head? When we try to identify others, do we look at their hands and elbows? Of course not. Most often, we recognize others by their faces and look at faces when communicating.

Did you know that your face is capable of producing over 250,000 different facial expressions? Did you know that you have only three sets of facial muscles that allow you to form all of those expressions? According to researchers,[17] the three sets of facial muscles used to form facial expressions are (1) the brow and the forehead; (2) the eyes, eyelids, and root of the nose; and (3) the lower face including the cheeks, remainder of the nose, mouth, and chin. Most researchers agree that facial expressions are both innate and learned.[18] As babies, most of us are able to express our primary emotions through seven common facial expressions: sadness, anger, disgust, fear, interest, surprise, and happiness (the acronym SADFISH might help you remember them!). As we are socialized into adulthood, our expression of emotions and our facial expressions become a little less innate and more a result of social learning. For instance, we might learn that we shouldn't express sadness in certain contexts, or to hide our anger and smile instead. Figure 6.6 depicts these three areas of facial muscles in use.

Figure 6.6 . Facial Zones and Expression

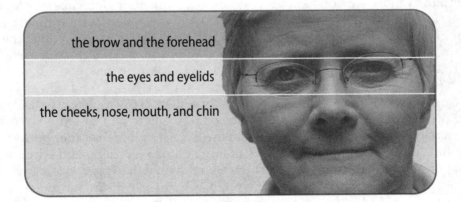

Did you know that it takes only 3 sets of facial muscles to make thousands of facial expressions?

the brow and the forehead

the eyes and eyelids

the cheeks, nose, mouth, and chin

The three zones of facial muscles we use to make facial expressions are (1) the brow and the forehead; (2) the eyes, eyelids, and root (or base) of the nose; and (3) the lower face, including the cheeks, remainder of the nose, mouth, and chin.

We can accurately and consistently identify a range of emotions by looking at specific areas of the face.[19] For instance, look to the eyes and eyelids to determine if someone is expressing sadness; the same is true for fear. If you are trying to distinguish disgust from surprise (which are very similar facial expressions), you should look to the lower half of the face where disgust is most obvious. You can most accurately judge happiness by looking at the eyes and eyelids; the second most accurate region of the face for judging happiness is to look at the mouth and lower facial region. Anger is one of the more complex emotions to accurately judge, because most often anger is expressed in at least two regions of the face simultaneously (mouth, cheeks, brows, and forehead).

Much of the work on nonverbal facial communication has focused on eye behavior, or aspects of eye contact. Eye contact is defined as looking directly at someone. The eyes have been known as "the windows to our soul" and as deep and intimate sources of emotional information. Many cultures maintain strict rules about communicating with the eyes—direct and strong eye contact connotes respect in one culture, whereas averting eye contact is a sign of respect in another. We spend more time looking at eyes (43 percent of our time) than looking at any other part of the body. The mouth is the second most common place we look at others, gaining our visual attention about 13 percent of the time. Dale Leathers[20] points out the many expressions in U.S. culture used to describe eye behavior: the person is "shifty-eyed," "bug-eyed," or "cross-eyed"; the person "gave me the eye," he's "making eyes" with me, and we "see eye to eye"; you "have an eye for that," that's "an eyesore," and what an "eye-opener." Communication with eyes has great significance in our culture.

Eye behavior serves a number of important functions in our interpersonal interactions; it regulates interactions, helps us monitor feedback, assists us in expressing emotions, and generally communicates the type and nature of interpersonal relationship in which we are engaged.[21] Some researchers even argue that eye behaviors are more important than any other kind of nonverbal behavior in initiating, establishing, and developing intimate relationships. We use our eyes to indicate attention and level of interest, and look more and longer at people we like and are intimate with than at those we don't know. Avoiding eye contact or gazes also serves a number of important functions in relationships. Think about what you try to communicate to another if you avoid looking at them or "catching their eye." You might be trying to reduce the intimacy of the relationship, communicate to the other that you're not interested in them or what they are saying, limit the amount or length of communication, and/or protect your own privacy in the interaction. On the other hand, most of us tend to look at those people and things we like or those things we perceive as providing a potential reward. In general, you are likely to use more eye contact when you predict that you will use more eye contact: when the topic you are discussing is a lighthearted, easy, or impersonal topic; when you are in love or like the other person a great deal; when you are interested in the other person's comments or reactions; and when your status is lower than that of the other person.[22] On the other hand, you will likely use less eye contact when you are in a discussion that involves challenging, conflictual, or intimate topics; when you are embarrassed or trying to hide something; when you have little interest or investment in the topic or the reactions of the other; and when you believe your status is higher than the status of the other.

Over the next few days, pay attention to your nonverbal communication and try to decide whether the above conclusions seem to be true for you as you communicate interpersonally. Because we often make first judgments of someone by looking at their eyes, and others "size us up" with their eyes and by our eyes, we need to be aware of the many ways eyes communicate and the ways we communicate with our eye behavior.

Proxemics

The study of the way we use space to communicate is **proxemics**. It comes from the word *proximity*, which means the distance between people or things. Our use of space and the way we create and protect our own spaces (our territories, private spaces, personal space, and environments) communicate volumes to others. You can probably think of times when you felt your "space" was violated by someone who stood too close, touched your arm when you felt it was inappropriate, or chose to sit in the chair right next to you when there were many other chairs available at a further distance. You create your own territories, or protect your personal space, in a number of ways. These include putting your coat over the chair next to you in the movie theatre, or stretching your feet over the chair across from you in the library. You even communicate something about your personality or interests by the way you arrange and decorate your apartment or bedroom, the size and style of your bedroom or apartment, and whether you leave the door open or always close it.

Personal Space. Imagine you're standing alone in the elevator at a local mall, waiting for the door to close so you can get to the third floor and check out the sale at Bath and Body Works. Before the door can close, a person of your same sex enters the rather large elevator and stands directly next to you, their shoulder touching yours. What do you think? You are probably uncomfortable because with so much empty space in the elevator, you wonder why this person invaded *your* space.

Each culture has fairly clear rules regarding how much personal space we prefer when communicating interpersonally, with strangers, and in a variety of social situations. Edward T. Hall helped define four spatial distances we use in our interactions with others in the dominant U.S. culture.[23] Each distance defines the type of relationships between people, as well as the type of communication they are likely to engage in. Figure 6.7 depicts these distances.

Intimate distance: Touching (0 inches) up to 18 inches. Intimate distance is reserved for intimate touching, love-making, conversing with close friends, or comforting or protecting others. Most people do not consider this distance appropriate for public use in U.S. culture.

Personal distance: From 18 inches to 4 feet. Personal distance is most commonly used in casual conversations where you still desire to maintain and protect your personal "space" from those you're interacting with. It is the private "bubble" that surrounds a person that we try not to enter without permission. Personal distance allows you to touch another person if you extend an arm or reach for them, but does not allow for close contact, to smell another's breath or the scent from another's body or clothes. We most often use personal distance when communicating with friends, family, or other loved ones.

Social distance: 4 feet to 12 feet. We conduct much of our professional and impersonal business conversations (like a job interview), as well as some social interactions (like a small group conversation at a cocktail party), at a social distance. When you use social distance, you are far enough away from a person that you begin to lose some of the detail in facial and body features, but you are still close enough to have a face-to-face interaction without difficulty. Being at a social distance results in a more professional and distanced relationship, such as you would find in an office where the desk of the manager is positioned so that a visitor would sit in the guest chair probably about 6 feet away from hers. Think about times when you find yourself most

Figure 6.7   Personal Distances

intimate distance (0–18 inches)

personal distance (18 inches–4 feet)

social distance (4 feet–12 feet)

public distance (12 feet–25 feet or more)

In the United States, we generally use four approximate spatial distances in our interactions with others. The distance we choose is usually a reflection of the type of relationship we have with the person we are communicating with. Have you ever felt like your personal space was violated because someone did not observe an appropriate social distance? How did you respond?

comfortable using a social distance for communicating, and compare them to those times when a personal distance is more appropriate. As you can begin to see, space can be a subtle but powerful communicator.

Public distance: From 12 feet to 25 feet or more. Public distance allows you to protect yourself from others in a public context. You can probably think of many times when such a distance from others, usually strangers, is preferable, such as in a public space like a bus or an airport. Most public speakers use public distance between themselves and the audience, as do teachers or others who are communicating in public. Public distance does not allow for interpersonal interactions, but is still close enough so that visual cues of the situation are available.

The type of personal space we use and prefer is affected by a number of variables. As you might guess, you will stand or move closer to those you like, allow those of higher status to stand closer to you, and stand closer to people when you're in a larger room than in a smaller space. Can you think of other factors that affect the way you use your personal space? Take the Nonverbal Space Quiz in Box 6.2 and consider what some of those variables might be. There are a number of others, some of which we'll discuss next as we explore the concept of our personal territory.

Territoriality. Beyond our personal space, as described above, most of us also have types of "space" we consider our own, often called our **territory**. Territory refers to the space we often nonverbally claim ownership of, even when we are not present in that space. For instance, our territory includes the spot at the library table where we put our books, bag, and coat. Even when we temporarily leave that space to get a drink of water or use the restroom, we expect our

Box 6.2

Skill Builder
Nonverbal Space Quiz

(The following quiz is adapted from J. DeVito's *Nonverbal Communication Workbook*.)[24]

Look at the following drawings of tables and chairs. Imagine that you are at the library and for each situation you must select a chair at the table described because it is the only table left. In the space marked with the dark circle is seated the person described. Indicate by placing an X in the appropriate chair where you would sit. After completing each, answer the questions below. Discuss your answers with others in your class.

1. The person at the table is a young man or woman you are physically attracted to. You've never spoken to this person, but you have a class together and know each other by sight.

2. The person at the table is someone you find physically unattractive and a person to whom you've never spoken.

3. The person at the table is a person of the opposite sex you are not attracted to, but do not find unattractive. You have never seen this person before.

4. The person at the table is a person you have dated a few times and would like to date again. You would currently consider yourself very good friends.

5. The person at the table is an instructor you had a class with last year. You earned a "C" in the class and weren't too happy because you thought you should have received an "A."

6. The person at the table is your favorite professor, someone you'd like to get to know a little better. You had him for class last semester.

Questions for thought and reflection:

A. Why did you select the position you did? For example, does the position you selected better help you achieve your goal in the interaction?

B. If you were the one already seated in the position marked with the dark circle, do you think the person described would make the same seating choice you did? Why, or why not? Does the level of perceived power in the situation make any difference?

C. What do you think the position you select communicates to the other person at the table? In what ways might these nonverbal messages be misinterpreted? What other nonverbal cues might you use to communicate your message and intention more clearly?

territory to remain—that no one will have sat down and started studying in our spot—before we return. Most of us stake out our territories with a "marker." A sign on our bedroom door that says, "DO NOT ENTER!" is an obvious marker. Other ways we mark our territories include positioning our desk and chair in our small dorm room so that our "study area" is clearly delineated, placing the plastic bar between our groceries and the next person's at the supermarket, putting down the arm rest between your seat and your companion's on an airplane, spreading your feet out on the couch, and writing your child's name with permanent marker on his bookbag, toys, and other personal objects to indicate ownership. In so many ways we use nonverbal cues to protect and "mark" our territories, an extension of our personal space.

Both the ways we use space and the way we occupy and protect our territories reflect intricate power and status differences.[25] For instance, the following tends to be true:

- The higher our status, the more personal space we tend to have.

- The higher our status, the more we can invade others' personal space.

- Those with higher status and power tend to have more territory.

- Those with more power are granted more rights to protect their territory.

- Those with higher status and power can invade the territory of others of lower status and less power.[26]

You can probably think of many examples of how the people around you who have more status or power use space and territory to communicate such power nonverbally. For instance, your parents or the elders in your home probably occupied the largest bedrooms, those at the highest level of the house, and those with the greatest number of comforts (private bath, personal television, personal phone). The head of a company is usually the person with the largest, best-furnished office, and is likely on the top floor and most protected (by a receptionist in the outer office, security codes, a long hallway, or closed doors). Your parents and your boss are also likely to be allowed to enter your private space (your bedroom or office) without invitation or warning, but the reverse is generally unacceptable and inappropriate.

Vocalics/Paralanguage

As we mentioned earlier in this chapter, nonverbal communication *does* indeed include the voice. The study of the way we use our voice and vocal qualities to communicate nonverbally is known as **vocalics**. We call the vocal, but nonverbal, dimensions of our speech, such as the pitch, volume, and tone of our voice, **paralanguage**. For the remainder of this chapter, we will use the term *paralanguage* when we refer to these vocal aspects of our nonverbal communication.

Try the following exercise: Say the first seven letters of alphabet ("A, B, C, D, E, F, G") in sequence, while trying to communicate each of the following emotions or feelings one at a time:

Anger

Disgust

Joy

Sadness

Fear

Love or attraction to another

Don't be shy. Really try it! Our students are often surprised, after completing this exercise, how much of the emotions and the feelings that we communicate are articulated by the way we use our voice. When we do this activity in class, our students are able to correctly guess almost every time the emotion being communicated with just these seven letters of the alphabet and vocal qualities of the student.

Paralanguage includes the manner in which we say things, and a wide range of vocal qualities: rate, volume, pitch, pausing and hesitations, and rhythm. Try saying the word *great* in response to the question, "How are you doing?" first in a happy voice and then in a sad or sarcastic voice. The way you use your voice gives the word meaning. When your spouse asks if you're interested in checking out the home and garden show that is in town, your same verbal response ("sounds really interesting") could be said, depending on your vocal qualities, to mean you are really excited and interested ("sounds really great!"), or to mean you think it sounds boring and uninteresting ("sounds *really* interesting" in a sarcastic and monotone voice). Again, it is the vocal, nonverbal aspects of what you said that allow for the true meaning of your words to become clear.

You are all probably very aware of the way your professors use their voices to get you excited and interested in a topic or lecture (by talking faster or louder to emphasize a point, or by making dramatic swings in their pitch or tone to indicate interest in the idea). Other professors, as you have likely experienced, could use some training in using paralanguage more dynamically (less monotone) to increase interest in their lectures. When you watch public figures and professional speakers, such as President George W. Bush or Dr. Martin Luther King Jr., notice how they use each aspect of paralanguage (changes in volume, rate, pitch, and rhythm) to more clearly and effectively communicate their messages. Try tuning in to a televised religious service on a Sunday morning and observing for just five minutes the way paralanguage is used extensively by the ministers preaching their sermons to an audience of thousands.

We use paralanguage not just to increase the interest and effectiveness of our meanings, but also to make judgments of others' emotional states, intelligence, and even personalities. We tend to be perceived as more persuasive and intelligent when we speak quickly, and we also tend to see other people as more believable and objective when they speak at a slightly faster than normal rate. Based solely on paralinguistic cues, most of us could correctly identify the sex, status, and approximate age of a speaker most of the time.[27]

Environmental Factors

An often overlooked aspect of nonverbal communication is the environment, or the physical context in which our communication takes place.[28] The architecture, lighting, wall and décor colors, noise level, and room arrangements not only communicate something about the people who create such environments, but also affect the mood and communication of the people in such environments. Restaurants with bright lighting, loud music, and hard-plastic seating do not encourage lengthy conversations; they communicate that you should eat fast and move on. Environments with these qualities are considered "high-load environments"; they arouse emotions and involve participants visually.[29] High-load environments force people to deal with a lot of stimuli at once. Restaurants with comfortable chairs, dimmer lighting, and softer, more relaxing music invite longer conversations and encourage people to stay longer (and spend more money). Such environments are considered "low load," inviting people to feel more relaxed and comfortable. One study found that when students studied in an area painted in a red color, their performance was lower than those students who studied in a study area painted blue or white.[30] This might be due to the fact that red is one of the most arousing colors; blue is one of the more calming colors. What kind of choices did you make in structuring your own personal environment: a room, part of a room, apartment, or home? Did you decide to make the lighting bright and the colors bold, or to have dim lighting, large, comfortable furniture, and art collected from your travels around the world? What is the mood you tried to create with the color you painted the walls, the rug you selected for the floor, or the temperature you prefer in the room? Is your house or apartment neat and clean or messy and cluttered? What do these aspects of your environment communicate about you and your preferences? Many aspects of our environment affect our moods, communicate to others, and reflect aspects of our life that are important to us.

Think about the classes you have been in where the students feel open and willing to discuss. Compare those to the classes where students never talk. Is there a difference in the physical environment of those classes? Most likely, the classes with dynamic discussion by students are those where desks are arranged in a nontraditional way (not in rows, not all facing forward). The traditional classroom arrangement actually has been shown to discourage active participation of students (see Figure 6.8), and when students are allowed to choose, they most likely will select a U-shaped arrangement of desks.

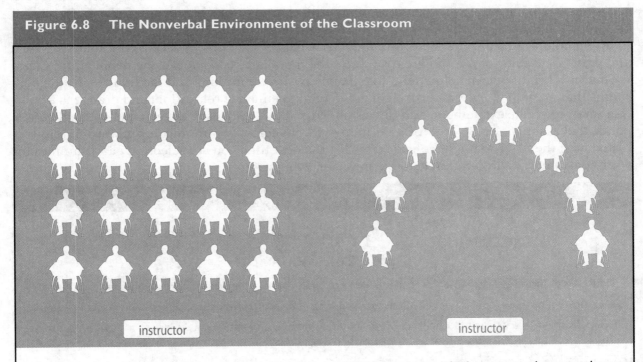

Figure 6.8   The Nonverbal Environment of the Classroom

Which seating arrangement do you prefer in the classroom? Which do you think promotes better and more effective communication between students in the class, and between students and the instructor?

A number of environmental factors encourage or facilitate communication, and some discourage or inhibit it.[31] Both kinds of factors serve important functions, depending on the context. For instance, airports are designed in such a way as to limit interaction and inhibit communication among visitors. The long, straight lines of immovable chairs allow for travelers to maintain some privacy by not being forced to make eye contact with others as they wait for arrivals and departures. Living rooms that are structured with couches and chairs placed closely (within 3–4 feet) around a small table tend to encourage communication and interaction among family members and guests. On the other hand, more than three people sitting on a couch together have a difficult time interacting because of diminished eye contact. Small areas with semicircular or circular seating in large hotels invite guests or visitors to sit and interact. Even the temperature of a room can encourage or discourage interaction and activity. When temperatures rise above 77 degrees, students in one study showed significantly slower comprehension and reading speeds.[32] A study of the nonverbal environments of McDonald's and Burger King revealed that customers at McDonald's were less comfortable (due to seating types and arrangements, noise, lighting, and color) than their counterparts at Burger King.[33]

Even the color of your environment can affect your communication and behavior. The color of the packaging used for products greatly affects consumer behavior[34] (sugar doesn't tend to sell well in green packages; beauty aids don't tend to sell well in brown jars) and raises safety concerns (green cars are not as safe in summer months because they blend with foliage). Studies of children's emotional reactions to colors revealed distinct trends; children had positive reactions to bright colors such as pink, blue, and red, but negative reactions to dark colors such as brown and gray.[35] The color of a room greatly affects the mood and behavior of the people in it. Classrooms with bright, warm colors tend to enhance positive emotions and facilitate learning; bedrooms that are white, light blue, or light green tend to enhance relaxation; and orange is a color that tends to create excitement, and thus is often used in stimulating environments like theatres, parks, and casinos. See Box 6.3 for a sampling of what colors communicate and the moods associated with them.[36] You might consider this list the next time you are selecting paint samples for your apartment, bedroom, kitchen, business, or living room.

Box 6.3

Self-Reflection
Color Communicates

Red: Red is bold and aggressive. It is associated with fire, heat, courage, patriotism, anger, blood, sin, and danger.

Blue: Blue is serene, pleasant, and cool. It is associated with devotion, truth, justice, sadness, and discouragement.

Yellow: Yellow is touchy, friendly, cheerful, warm, irritating, hostile, and unpleasant. It is associated with sunshine, glamour, sickness, and jealousy. It is associated with having little value and being temporary. Yellow is the fastest color for the eye to see.

Green: Green is almost always pleasant. It tends to be peaceful, calm, and leisurely. It is always natural. Green makes people feel tended to and secure. It is associated with freshness, youth, vigor, prosperity, envy, and inexperience.

Orange: Orange indicates informality and affordability. It is lively, exuberant, bright, noisy, irritating, and unpleasant. It is associated with fruitfulness and harvest.

Purple: Purple is rich, stately, dignified, lonely, and nostalgic. It is associated with victory, authority, royalty, passion, and memory.

White: White symbolizes delicacy, refinement, and purity. It is sparkling, cold, and clean. It is associated with innocence, chastity, joy, and hope.

Black: Black signifies mystery, authority, dignity, and sophistication. It is melancholy, profound, and sad. It is associated with night, death, wickedness, sorrow, and despair.

Color communicates mood and emotion and can affect the communication of others. Reflect on the above descriptions of what colors mean. Do you think that the color of a room, object, or environment communicates a message? Does the color of a room ever affect the way you feel or communicate? Reflect on choices you might have made regarding the dominant colors in your personal territories, such as a room, office, or home. After reading the above descriptions, what do you think the colors in your personal environment are communicating to others?

Haptics/Touch Communication

Think about how the *way* you touch someone communicates a message. If you hit your friend in the face with a tightly closed fist, you are clearly communicating something different than if you pat him lightly on the shoulder. If you gently nudge a stranger on the bus with your elbow, you communicate something quite different than if you shove that person with both arms. The study of the way touch is used to communicate nonverbally is called **haptics**.

Touch is important for our health and well-being. It is well known that infants who are not touched or held do not develop well physically, psychologically, or socially. Babies in orphanages who are not held or touched can actually die from lack of touch. Some research suggests that the amount we hug our kids, other things being equal, could affect their success later in life. Box 6.4, entitled "Hugging Kids = Happy, Successful Adults?" discusses an interesting study about the connection found between how much you hug your kids and how happy and successful they might be as adults. Touch has become more recognized as an important form of nonverbal communication in a variety of contexts, beyond its most basic importance in the development of physically and socially healthy children and adults. No other nonverbal form of communicating has the same potential to communicate love, warmth, and intimacy, or to inflict harm and injury. Consider the following list of ways you can touch. You might hit, kiss, kick, rock, embrace, jab, bite, hug, brush, poke, tap, groom, push, rub, pinch, pat, caress, shake, pull, guide, tweak, nibble, slap, tug, punch, hold, tickle, grab, shove, stroke, grasp, lick, tackle, restrain, or nuzzle. All types of touch are not created equal.[37]

To understand the meaning of touch communication, consider these dimensions of touch:[38]

A. The intensity or amount of pressure (soft/hard)

B. The duration (brief to prolonged)

C. The location of touch on the body (shoulders, face, hands)

D. The body part delivering the touch (hand, foot, lips, upper torso)

E. The frequency of contact (single or multiple touches)

Box 6.4

Practical Research
Hugging Kids = Happy, Successful Adults?

According to a recent long-term study, children who are hugged and kissed frequently when growing up are much more likely to turn out to be successful professionally and socially.[39] The study, which began in 1951 with 379 kindergartners, has tracked these children for almost 40 years into their adult lives. The study, by Dr. Carol Franz, a psychologist at the University of California, Berkeley, Institute of Human Development, found that adults who had received regular affection (kissing, hugging, affectionate touching/holding) as children were significantly more likely to have happy, enduring marriages; be raising children of their own; be socially happy with friends; and have other satisfying recreational activities. Interviews with the original children in this study 36 years later revealed a direct link between original "parental warmth" scores and the follow-up "social accomplishment" scores. So don't underestimate the power of touch, even in the form of a hug, to communicate powerful and lasting nonverbal messages.

For example, consider the example of the stroke again, this time applying the five dimensions of touch listed above. How does a brief, soft, single, light stroke on the arm (as a greeting or acknowledgment from an acquaintance) communicate something different than multiple, long, and intense stroking of the body (or of many parts of the body)? Each dimension of the same nonverbal behavior (stroking) adds important information about the context of the nonverbal behavior being described. You should consider each of these dimensions as you interpret the meaning of others' touch, and as you use touch in your interpersonal interactions.

Appearance and Artifacts

Think back to the story of Marissa we used to introduce an earlier part of this chapter. On her first day of college, she "sized up" just about everyone she met by their appearance, clothing, and the objects they possessed. Like it or not, our appearance and the artifacts we display are used by others to make judgments of us. Sometimes our appearance provides the *only* information others have about us. **Artifacts** include all the personal objects we use to announce our identities, interests, and backgrounds (our clothing, jewelry, cars, purses, bags, bikes, tools, books, and laptop computer). Our appearance includes everything from our body type to our hairstyle to our skin color to eye color to height. We communicate nonverbally in each of these ways with or without knowing it, and we perceive others in each of these ways. In our appearance-obsessed culture, the way we look counts and we are judged and perceived extensively, sometimes exclusively, on appearance alone.

In the United States, girls as young as 6 years old report dieting. Anorexia has become a national epidemic. People are spending millions of dollars a year on the latest wrinkle-reducing creams and ab-buster machines. Why? The answer might lie in the importance that U.S. culture places on the nonverbal messages that our appearance sends to others. Others attribute how likable, powerful, friendly, intelligent, wealthy, attractive, persuasive, competent, trustworthy, ethical, and fair we are by our appearance. Research shows that we tend to judge attractive people as more successful, happy, sensitive, interesting, competent, and persuasive than their less attractive counterparts.[40] Attractive students are even judged by other students and teachers to be more intelligent and prepared than others. Attractive employees are more likely to be hired and promoted. With these findings, it is no wonder that so many of us are concerned with the way our appearance communicates nonverbally.

Even our height communicates something, possibly power and intelligence. According to research, height plays a role in election results, especially those with male candidates; of the 11 presidential elections since 1952, the taller candidate won nine times. Further, the tallest U.S. presidents were found to have a greater number of leadership qualities.[41] In 1990, for example, the taller candidate won 21 of 31 contested U.S. senate races in which heights could be determined.

The use of artifacts, those personal objects we choose to surround ourselves with, are interesting forms of nonverbal communication. The clothing we select is one of the most common and visual forms of the artifacts we use to communicate our style and personal identity. Think of the judgments we make when we see someone in a long white lab coat with a tongue depressor in the pocket and a prescription pad in hand. We assume that person is a doctor. We purposefully dress our police officers in uniforms with badges, and give them squad cars and sometimes guns, to communicate clearly their role and status. Most of us don't have to dress in a uniform, so our clothing choices say a great deal about who we are and what we like. What do you communicate by your appearance and the way you dress? Do you project a confident, successful look? Do you try to communicate that you are stylish and up-to-date with the latest fashionable looks? Or that you're an individual and won't be taken in by the latest fashion trends? Is your hair long or short? Do you dye it—maybe green, red, or blonde? Do you carry a purse or bag or backpack? What do you think your choice communicates nonverbally? Do you hook a coffee cup on the outside of your bag, communicating your busy life and use of caffeine to get you through your busy day? Do you use a PDA or laptop computer? What kind of vehicle do you drive? A skateboard, old bike, moped, vintage BMW, new Volkswagen Jetta, large sport utility vehicle, minivan, or older rusty Oldsmobile? What does your choice of transportation communicate about you? Practicality? That you're a parent? Safety? Style? That you're environmentally conscious? That you support domestic labor?

Think about all the ways your choices of dress, adornment, artifacts, and appearance communicate about your interests, choices, lifestyle, personality, and moods. Even though you might not want to admit it, and you might not intentionally always try to communicate through your appearance and artifacts, both are significant aspects of your nonverbal communication. The dress and appearance of many teenagers have come under scrutiny lately because of what such choices potentially communicate. Some school officials argue that the way kids dress and the items they carry (beepers and cell phones, for instance) are communicating the wrong messages and have banned them—over resistance from the children and even parents. These issues have even reached the highest court in the nation. The U.S. Supreme Court recently ruled in favor of an Ohio school district who banned a student from wearing a T-shirt that the school defined as "objectionable" (it depicted Marilyn Manson with a three-faced Jesus on the front and the word "BELIEVE" on the back and the letters "L I E" highlighted). The student sued when he was told to either turn the T-shirt inside out or change it.[42]

Chronemics

When you have a 9:00 a.m. class, what time do you generally arrive? Fifteen minutes early? One minute early? Five minutes late? What about a party with good friends that is supposed to start at 8:00 p.m.? Do you arrive at 8:00? Or do you come 15 or 20 minutes, or even an hour or more, late? Your answers to all these questions communicate something about you. The study of the way we use, perceive, interpret, react to, and structure time is called **chronemics**. In North American cultures, for instance, time is sequenced, highly valued, and structured. We live in a time-obsessed culture in which "time is money" and being on time and not "wasting time" are important.

Our use of time communicates in a number of ways. First, it indicates our status. For example, higher status people are allowed to be late when others are not. The amount of time we spend with others tends to communicate our liking for them. Our use of time can also communicate our personalities and backgrounds. For example, are you more aggressive, impatient, and hostile or more reserved, patient, and calm? Our use of time even tells us something about our health. For example, cities with the fastest paces—more watches worn, faster walking pedestrians, quicker service from tellers and clerks—have the highest rates of heart disease.[43] As you think about your own orientation to time, be sure to be aware of how your use, perception, and attitude about time communicates nonverbally to others in your interpersonal interactions.

Coenetics: Nonverbal Codes Across Cultures

As we discussed in Chapter 2 and throughout this book, the dominant values of a culture reveal what is important to members of that culture. Just as language is a reflection of culture, so too is nonverbal behavior. In this final section of the chapter, we will introduce just a few aspects of nonverbal communication across cultures and discuss **coenetics**, the nonverbal codes of a particular cultural or co-cultural group. You should look to some of the summaries of cultural nonverbal communication research if you'd like to learn more about this topic.[44]

Most nonverbal behavior is culturally specific. Because there is such great variation in nonverbal communication across cultures, innocent misunderstandings can easily occur when we are communicating with someone from a culture different from our own. Consider the examples below as a way to begin to think about how nonverbal communication varies greatly between cultures.

Even though most people in U.S. culture share a meaning for this common, positive nonverbal gesture, people from other cultures might be offended if you make this gesture toward them.

Innocent Nonverbal Cultural Misunderstandings

Amidst all the forms of nonverbal cues we have introduced in this chapter (touch, appearance, space, gestures, etc.) arise multiple opportunities for offending unintentionally as we meet and greet others from other cultures. For instance, something as simple as a "yes" or "no" head nod can cause great confusion and is highly cultural. In Turkey, an up-and-down head nod is a negative expression (not "yes"). In India, a "yes" is a sideways movement of the head (which is often interpreted in Western cultures as "no"). In many other cultures, the head movement up and down has no meaning whatsoever.

Vice President Richard Nixon once went on a goodwill trip to Latin America, making a now well-known nonverbal faux pas by holding both hands in the air in the "A-OK" gesture. In many Latin American countries this is an offensive gesture, similar to "giving the finger" in the United States. News photos of Nixon making this nonverbal sign spread throughout the newspapers of Latin American countries, causing irreversible damage to international relationships at the time.

Two well-known intercultural communication researchers explain the importance of understanding the way touch—even the simple act of shaking hands—is highly cultural and has the potential for offending others with a simple handshake. Everett Rogers and Thomas Steinfatt[45] explain how the firm handshake perceived as appropriate in U.S. culture is often offensive and inappropriate in many others. In Kenya and Tanzania, they explain, the Masai generally prefer that the palms barely touch during a handshake. In India, handshaking is not widely practiced, or a very limp handshake is usually preferred. A generally more appropriate greeting in India (especially of a respected individual such as a parent or teacher) is to touch his or her feet. In Korea the right forearm should be touched with the left hand while shaking hands. People in Turkey often shake hands continuously while negotiating a deal, and do so until it is complete.

Japanese usually prefer little touching and greet each other with a bow. The depth of the bow reflects status (the lower the bow, the higher the status of the one being greeted).

Cultures tend to organize time in one of two ways: **monochronic time (M-time)** or **polychronic time (P-time).**[46] M-time is characteristic of the United States, Germany, Austria, and Switzerland. M-time cultures tend to view time as something valuable, fixed, usable, linear, segmented, and manageable. People in these cultures abhor "wasting" or "losing" time. People from a P-time orientation view time quite differently. P-time is characteristic of the cultures of Africans and of many people who are Spanish, Portuguese, Arab, Greek, or Mexican. From a P-time perspective, time is not as tangible and not as "valuable" as M-time people see it. P-time people put great value on the activity, conversation, or meeting that is happening currently, regardless of the time. Schedules are not highly valued, and thus they are often "broken" or rearranged without explanation. The lifestyles of P-time cultures are often more spontaneous and focused on relationships. Table 6.2 illustrates the way time is used nonverbally, and very differently, in these two cultural orientations.

Table 6.2
Cultural Orientations Toward Time

The way in which time is used nonverbally often varies between cultures with a monochronic orientation and those with a polychronic orientation.

Monochronic People	Polychronic People
Do one thing at a time	Do many things at once
Perceive schedules as sacred and extremely important	Believe schedules are useful (not sacred)
Believe you should be on time	Believe you should focus on relationships before time
Believe you should adhere to plans	Change plans frequently and easily
Believe time is money or a precious commodity; time can be spent, wasted, given, or saved	Believe life should direct time, not time directing life
Consider one's job a priority before friends, family, and other relationships	Consider family and interpersonal relationships the priority; tasks are often accomplished because of personal relationships, not in spite of them
Emphasize promptness	Base promptness on the relationship

Some cultures (many cultures in Latin America and Southern Europe, such as France, Greece, Italy, Spain, and Mexico, as well as Israel and Indonesia) are considered *contact cultures*, where people stand closer while talking, prefer more direct eye contact, touch frequently, and speak louder. Other cultures (many countries in Northern Europe, North America, and East Asia, such as China, Hong Kong, Japan, Taiwan, Thailand, Sweden, Finland, and Germany) are classified as *noncontact cultures*, where people prefer more personal space and view casual touch as less desirable and appropriate. Imagine the potential for offense or misunderstanding if you pat someone on the back in Japan, or keep your distance from your friends in Spain. One aspect of making "contact" with others is in eye behavior. For many in the United States, maintaining eye contact is perceived as respectful. In Japanese culture, however, the preferred focus is not often on the other's eyes, but on his or her Adam's apple or on the knot of his tie, particularly if the other person is of higher status.

Appearance, space, and environmental factors are also highly cultural. As you might guess, beauty is not only in the eye of the beholder, but has a cultural basis as well. For instance, although tall and thin is considered attractive in U.S. culture, short is attractive in Japanese culture. When building homes and businesses, cultural rules for what space "means" and communicates are very important. The Navajo always build their hogans (six- or eight-sided one-story structures) to face the east, the direction of the rising sun.[47] Islamic people believe entrances to buildings should face Mecca. This proved an important intercultural dilemma for one group of planners. An intercultural researcher served as a consultant in the planning of the curriculum and facilities for a new school of communication in a Middle Eastern country. A U.S. architectural firm then designed the building. Just prior to building, a major error was detected—the building did not face Mecca. It was subsequently turned 90 degrees to correct the mistake.[48]

Box 6.5 provides further examples of how nonverbal cues can generate various meanings depending on cultural or co-cultural orientation. They are offered here not as generalizations of all members of any particular group, but as information to assist you in recognizing potential sources of miscommunication.

Box 6.5

Cultural Nonverbal Perceptions

Specific Behavior	Possible Interpretations by Members of Various Cultures
Avoidance of direct eye contact	Used to communicate respect or attentiveness by Latinos/as. (Direct eye contact is perceived as respectful to many in the dominant culture in the United States.)
Using finger gesture to beckon others	Appropriate for Asian American adult to use for children, but highly offensive if used to call an adult. (Appropriate gesture in most of U.S. culture to use in any situation.)
Silence	A sign of respect, thoughtfulness, and/or uncertainty or ambiguity among many Native Americans. (Indicates boredom, disagreement, or refusal to participate in most dominant cultures of the United States.)
Touching another person and standing closely in social contact	Normal and appropriate for daily interpersonal interactions among Latinos/as; often viewed in dominant U.S. culture as violation of personal space outside of intimate relationships.
Public displays of intense emotions	Valued and appropriate in most settings for African Americans; deemed inappropriate for most public settings in dominant U.S. culture.

Stereotypical Assumptions of Nonverbal Cues

One of the cautions we should note when comparing cultures (nonverbally, or in any aspect) is not to overgeneralize about groups of people or to form stereotypes based on such conclusions. Although research has been able to uncover a number of interesting and important cultural variations in nonverbal behavior and communication styles, not all individuals in every culture reflect the conclusions of the general cultural orientation. For instance, even though the United States has been found to be a monochronic culture where time schedules are valued, you might have been raised in a family where time was more fluid, where relationships took precedent over schedules, and where the here and now were a priority. Or, for instance, you might be from a high-contact culture where, in general, touch is valued and used frequently in casual interpersonal interactions. However, we should be careful not to make stereotypical assumptions or conclusions about your touching behavior. Your individual experiences in your relationships, work, or home life might have shaped your behaviors and orientation toward touch as a form of nonverbal communication differently more than is common in contact cultures.

Summary

After reading this chapter, you should be more aware of the many ways that nonverbal cues communicate, are similar and different across cultures, are indicative of relationships and power dynamics, play a large role in the communication of meaning in our interpersonal interactions, and can be used to more effectively communicate interpersonally. Most importantly, after reading this chapter you should be more informed and better able to make choices that will allow you to be more effective in your interpersonal interactions.

This chapter opened with a series of myths and truths. After reading this chapter, you likely are easily able to identify each of the following statements as myth or truth:

Myth: You can read a person like a book.

This is a myth. Nonverbal communication takes place in "packages" and works within a large context with verbal communication. It also varies greatly between people. Be careful about concluding that one nonverbal behavior means the same thing for every person.

Truth: Most people are unaware of the extent to which their nonverbal behavior is communicating to others.

Nonverbal messages always communicate; most of the time we don't think about or intend to communicate nonverbally when in fact we are.

Truth: Nonverbal communication often accounts for a majority of the meaning in interpersonal interactions.

Nonverbal communication is dense with meaning; as mentioned, some researchers suggest that 65 to 93 percent of all meaning communicated in an interaction is in the nonverbal cues.[49] Although other current scholars dispute the accuracy of these earlier studies, we should be aware of the potential for our nonverbals to play a significant role in all of our interactions.

Myth: Most of the nonverbals we use (facial expressions like a smile, and hand gestures like a wave) are the same around the world.

This is a myth. Most nonverbal communication is learned behavior and thus varies greatly between people, families, groups, cultures, and co-cultures.

Myth: We can diagnose problems in relationships by specifically observing nonverbal communication.

Nonverbal communication is only one part of the interpersonal context; we have to consider the verbal to have a complete picture of communication in any relationship.

Key Terms

Adaptors	Nonverbal communication
Affect displays	Paralanguage
Artifacts	Personal distance
Chronemics	Polychronic (P-time)
Coenetics	Proxemics
Emblems	Public distance
Haptics	Regulators
Illustrators	Social distance
Intimate distance	Territory
Kinesics	Vocalics
Monochronic (M-time)	

Suggested Contemporary Readings

D. Carbaugh. " 'Just listen': Listening and landscape among the Blackfeet." *Western Journal of Communication* 63 (1999): 250–270.

K. Floyd. "Attributions for nonverbal expressions of liking and disliking: The extended self-serving bias." *Western Journal of Communication* 64 (2000): 385–404.

J. Gorham, S. H. Cohen, and T. L. Morris. "Fashion in the classroom III: Effects of instructor attire and immediacy in natural classroom interactions." *Communication Quarterly* 47 (1999): 281–299.

A. F. Koerner and M. A. Fitzpatrick. "Nonverbal communication and marital adjustment and satisfaction: The role of decoding relationship relevant and relationship irrelevant affect." *Communication Monographs* 69 (2002): 33–51.

J. C. McCroskey, A. Sallinen, J. M. Fayer, V. P. Richmond, and R. A. Barraclough. "Nonverbal immediacy and cognitive learning: A cross-cultural investigation." *Communication Education* 45 (1996): 200–211.

J. Oetzel, S. Ting-Toomey, T. Masumoto, Y. Yokochi, X. Pan, J. Takai, and R. Wilcox. "Face and facework in conflict: A cross-cultural comparison of China, Germany, Japan, and the United States." *Communication Monographs* 68 (2001): 235–258.

P. Paul. "Color in intercultural communication." *Australian Journal of Communication* 18 (1991): 40–51.

K. D. Roach and P. R. Byrne. "A cross-cultural comparison of instructor communication in American and German classrooms." *Communication Education* 50 (2001): 1–14.

Chapter Activities

1. Take some time and reflect on the discussion in this chapter on how artifacts and appearance communicate nonverbally. What do you think your choice of artifacts and your appearance communicates to others? Jot down your ideas. After doing so, get together with a small group of people in your class and have each person share how they perceived you, based solely on your artifacts and appearance, on the first day of class. Continue this activity until everyone in the group has both shared and received information from others in the group. Reflect on how closely their perceptions match your own ideas. What does this tell you about the inevitable nature of communication (as discussed in Chapter 1)?

2. Use an electronic database in your college's library to locate at least one article on *nonverbal* and *culture*. What types of articles did you find using these two key words? How does the information extend what you learned in this chapter on nonverbal communication across cultures? Select one interesting finding and share it with a small group in the class.

3. Try using at least five of the emoticons introduced in this chapter—or others you know of—when sending an e-mail to friends or family members. Try writing the same message without using any emoticons. Were you able to accurately express what you were trying to communicate? Note how the use of emoticons changes the nature of your message, and write a brief paragraph describing your experiment to bring to class the next day.

4. Go on a "nonverbal environment tour" around campus. Here's how: Select three or four places on campus (such as the main administration building, a classroom building, the study center, or a friend's residence hall room). Spend time in each of these spaces taking notes on how the nonverbal environment is communicating. What does the décor, the color of the walls, the artwork, the artifacts, the arrangement of the room, the size of the room, and even the location of the room on campus communicate to people entering, working in, or living in that space? What is the feeling you get in each of these spaces? After compiling your notes, share the results of your nonverbal environment tour with others in the class. Were your analyses of certain environments the same? Different? Discuss as a class.

5. Visit the website *http://members.aol.com/nonverbal2/entries.htm#Entries*, where you will find *The Nonverbal Dictionary of Gestures, Signs, and Body Language: From Adam's-Apple-Jump to Zygomatic Smile*. Browse the dictionary, clicking on any definitions you are not familiar with (for instance, what is "agnosia," "apraxia," and the "Steinzor effect"?). Select at least five terms or ideas that expand your knowledge about nonverbal communication, and be prepared to share them with your class.

6. Select a local community-based agency or organization (such as those we've suggested in previous chapters—schools, faith-based organizations, community centers, food

shelves, job corps), and spend time over the semester serving in a capacity that would be beneficial to that organization. For instance, you might volunteer at a local school or organize meals at a local food shelf. While there, raise your awareness too, by keeping a journal and writing reflections about the way the nonverbal environment (the location; the lighting; the color of walls, décor, and interior; the artifacts such as furniture; the arrangement of furniture and desks; etc.) of this organization communicates to others. Also note how the nonverbal environment actually influences the communication of those using or working at this site (for instance, do certain offices or the arrangement of furniture inhibit open communication?). With the approval of your instructor, share your notes and observations with someone at your community site to help them consider the way their nonverbal environment affects communication and communicates messages to others. ✦

Chapter 7

Listening

Contemporary Issues: Listening in Littleton

Most of us remember the day in April 1999 when we learned that two students at Columbine High School in Littleton, Colorado, opened fire on their classmates, killing 13 of their peers and then taking their own lives. Fifteen lives were lost that afternoon in one Colorado High School; millions of others were affected, either physically or emotionally, for life. What most of us don't know is exactly how the lives of those students who survived the attack, and those in the community of the Denver suburb of Littleton, were affected by the unlikely attack. In a news report shortly after the Columbine shooting, writer Sue Hoye explained how listening was one of the most important things anyone could do for those survivors, relatives, and families of the Columbine shooting during the days, weeks, and months to follow.[1] Dr. Dan Mosley, chair of the Disaster Mental Health Service Team, explained how important it was for counselors not to be intrusive, but to simply be there to listen to the students who survived the attack, and those who lost friends and loved ones. According to Mosley, "It's best to let people know counseling is available and let them decide when and how to talk." Another counselor, Adolth Montana, who works with Denver-area youth, explains the importance of listening without judgment when a trauma sufferer chooses to talk. On all levels, counselors emphasize the importance of listening empathically and actively to those affected by the event.

Although you may not ever become a professional counselor, and you may never know someone who will experience a horrific tragedy like that experienced at Columbine, you will be faced with many opportunities in life where listening to another—empathically, actively, and without judgment—will be essential. Can you identify times, even recently, when you have been asked to listen actively, empathically, or without judgment? Do you feel you had the skills and knowledge to effectively do so? Are there times when you think you could be a better listener? Have you ever considered how learning about listening might improve your interpersonal relationships?

You can apply the listening skills you will learn in this chapter to significantly improve your relationships and the perceptions that others have of you as an interpersonal communicator. By learning to listen mindfully and intentionally, you can find much success and improved satisfaction in your interpersonal interactions.

Myths About Interpersonal Communication

Before you begin this chapter, take a moment to reflect on the following statements, some myths and some true, about listening. Try to identify which you think might be myths (M = myth; T = true):

_____ There are important differences between listening and hearing.

_____ In interpersonal communication, listening is as important as speaking.

_____ Effective communication is primarily the responsibility of the speaker.

_____ Listening is a passive activity that is accomplished pretty easily.

_____ Listening is one aspect of communication that is similar across all cultures.

After reading this chapter, you should be able to not only identify all the truths versus myths, but also explain why each of the above statements is true or not. As you read, look for information related to each of these common myths and assumptions.

We've heard it many times before: "Listening. What can I possibly learn about listening that I don't already know? I've been doing it all my life!" Based on conversations we've had with our own students, and remembering our own days as students, we realize that many people can't imagine what else they might learn that could *really* affect their listening abilities. Will study really change how I listen? Will it *really* make me a better communicator?

If you are thinking these same things, then we have a challenge for you. We would like to challenge you to carefully and thoughtfully read this chapter, and reflect on your own listening skills and behaviors. After doing so, and if you are motivated to apply what you learn about listening to your own interpersonal interactions, we are confident that you can significantly improve your listening skills and your effectiveness as an interpersonal communicator. We expect that you will be surprised by what you can learn and how improving your listening skills can result in greater satisfaction in your interactions and relationships, and might even help you get that promotion you wanted or secure that job you are dreaming about after graduation. Most of us underestimate the power of listening. Unfortunately, we are wrong to do so.

Listening: An Essential Interpersonal Skill

Listening is one of our first communication skills. We listen before we can speak, read, or write, and we use listening for learning language. Listening is such a familiar activity that many of us forget to pay attention to it. Yet it is an essential skill. We use it to develop and maintain relationships, to conduct effective communication in the workplace, to work through decisions that affect every aspect of our lives, and to monitor and safeguard our health, our loved ones, our property, and our future. Much of our education is spent learning to speak, write, and read well, yet we spend approximately 53 percent of our communication time listening. In contrast, we spend about 17 percent of our communication time reading, about 16 percent speaking, and about 14 percent writing (see Figure 7.1). According to writer Marilyn Buckley, we "listen to the equivalent of a book a day; talk the equivalent of a book a week; read the equivalent of a book a month; and write the equivalent of a book a year."[2]

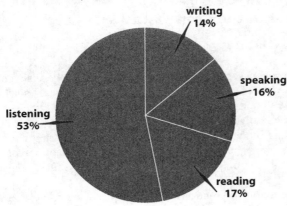

Figure 7.1   Daily Communication Activities

How much of your day is spent listening?
How much is spent on other communication activities?

writing 14%

speaking 16%

reading 17%

listening 53%

Most of us think that *speaking* is the communication skill we use the most and should spend the time improving. However, research shows that we spend over 50 percent our communication time *listening* compared to other communication activities. Since more than half of our day is spent listening, it makes good sense to spend some time improving this important communication skill.

Think about a person in your life who you think is the best listener you've ever known. Jot down a few terms that would describe that person. Now, think of a person in your life who is the worst listener you know. Jot down a few terms that you think best characterize him or her.

Assess your answers by comparing the lists. What are the qualities of communicators who listen well? Why are we drawn to good listeners? Would you be a person someone might list as a great listener, or as the worst listener they know?

Most people are attracted to good listeners because they communicate care and interest in us by listening to us. People who don't listen are sending the message that we are unimportant and that what we have to say is not interesting or important enough to pay attention to. Two experts who study and write about listening summarize in their book *Listening* the findings of dozens of researchers who have studied the effects of poor listening on organizations and in the workplace.[3] They report that listening is:

- the most frequently reported communication deficiency among new employees;

- the communication competency most lacking among organizational members;

- one of the most frequently reported skills managers think they are bad at;

- the second most challenging communication skills for all employees (first is motivation);

- the second most important skill (second to learning to learn) essential to the "upskilling" of workers in the United States;

- the skill at which the majority of high school graduates are most deficient.

If you want to be successful as an employee or in any organization, listening is one of the most important interpersonal skills you can learn. Take a look at Box 7.1 for some perspective on this "hardest of easiest tasks" called listening. The information in the box, and in the remainder of this chapter, will help you recognize your own listening abilities as well as give you ideas about how to improve your current skills and apply new listening skills in a variety of contexts.

Box 7.1

Self-Reflection[4]

Listening Is the Hardest of the "Easy" Tasks

by Harvey Mackay

Ask people if they are good listeners, and usually they'll say yes. And they'll say it's easy to be a good listener. Business publications are full of articles about the sorry state of communication in today's workplace. The chief culprit is always "poor listening skills." If being a good listener is so easy, what's the problem?

To answer that, we must identify the skills that make up good listening.

Many people think that communication means getting others to do what you want them to do. For them, good listening means, "I talk, you listen." Such an approach might work. These folks get their point across by shouting, "Didn't you hear me?" Or by moralizing, "This is the only fair decision we can make." Or by pulling rank: "It's my way or the highway."

Managers who use such tactics might get the staff to follow instructions. But these managers complain that their best staffers always seem to leave. "I had no idea there was a problem until I got the resignation letter," they whine. "After all, we communicated so well!"

These people have forgotten the basic truth about being a good listener: Listening is a two-way process. Yes, you need to be heard. You also need to hear the other person's ideas, questions and objections. If you talk at people instead of with them, they're not buying in, they're caving in.

Believe it or not, being a good listener is more important in sales than being a good talker. Ben Feldman, the first insurance salesman to pass the sales goal of $25 million in one year, had a simple formula for his success. He was New York Life's leading salesman for more than 20 years, operating out of East Liverpool, Ohio, a city of 20,000. His secret? Work hard. Think big. Listen very well.

Good listeners steer conversations toward other people's interests. This is what a good conversationalist is. And remember, you can't learn anything when you are doing the talking.

More than a century ago, a young woman who had dined with both William Gladstone and Benjamin Disraeli explained why she preferred Disraeli: "When I dined with Mr. Gladstone I felt as though he was the smartest man in England. But when I dined with Mr. Disraeli, I felt as though I was the smartest woman in England."

Being a good listener also means paying attention to context as well as content. A listener who can paraphrase what you've said without changing your meaning is a great listener. A listener who merely can repeat your words is a parrot.

It takes skill and determination to be a good listener, but the effort yields terrific results.

Perhaps the biggest reward to being a good listener is that you also become a better talker. You learn the best way to get people to hear what you're saying, and you find that you don't need to force-feed your ideas and opinions to others. You'll know you've attained your goal when you can utter two sentences in an hour-long conversation and the other speaker thanks you for your input and adds, quite earnestly, "You always have so much to say!"

Mackay's Moral: Easy listening is a style of music, not communication.

Reprinted with permission from nationally syndicated columnist Harvey Mackay, author of the *New York Times* bestsellers *Swim With the Sharks Without Being Eaten Alive* and *Pushing the Envelope.*

Effects of Poor Listening

Listening is important in all aspects of our lives, particularly in seeking satisfactory health care. Think about the way you receive information about your health and the role that listening plays in health care. Some researchers have studied listening in the health care context.[5] In one study, doctors were observed interrupting most patients almost immediately after patients began explaining their symptoms.[6] In the study, 51 of the 74 patients were interrupted by the physician within the first 18 seconds of explaining what was wrong. Only one of the patients got to finish her explanation later. Other research found that patients who exerted more control during checkups with physicians, such as being more assertive and being the one to interrupt, showed statistically significant improvements in their medical conditions months later.[7] Listening, it seems, is not only important for our personal relationships and our professional well-being, but plays an intriguing role in taking care of our personal health as well. You can read more about these findings in the Applied Concepts (Box 7.2).

Box 7.2

Applied Concepts
Is Your Doctor Listening?

When your doctor finally enters the room and asks, "What seems to be the problem?" do you find that you feel rushed, you are interrupted before finishing your explanation, or your doctor's response is abrupt or disinterested? If so, you're not alone. According to recent research, many physicians are being criticized for lack of listening and for being too controlling in conversations with patients about their medical concerns. Often, doctors never really find out what a patient's serious medical concern really is.

Poor listening is at the core of most complaints by patients about their doctors. In a study conducted by Dr. Richard Frankel and his colleagues, over 90 percent of complaints in 1,000 letters from dissatisfied patients were about the way doctors and other medical staff communicated with them. Common complaints included the doctor never looking at the patient, humiliating him or her, or using medical jargon. In another study, researchers found that most patients are interrupted during the first 18 seconds of their explanation of what is wrong. Researcher Dr. S. A. Cohen-Cole explains that because most patients, on average, have three problems on their mind when they come into the examining room, not listening fully to patients is a significant problem. Dr. Frankel found that in his studies, the third complaint of a patient is, on average, the most troubling. Frankel's research suggests that most patients will never get to explain their most serious complaint because their doctor is not listening fully and interrupts too quickly. Until medical training for doctors and other medical professionals shifts toward an emphasis on listening, researchers suggest that patients need to be more assertive and controlling in the doctor-patient conversation (ask questions, tell their doctors what they want, ask not to be interrupted). Patients who already do this also tend to actually do better medically.

The Message of Poor Listening

What does poor listening say to others? According to some listening experts, listening is a compliment and a commitment.[8] When we listen poorly, we are saying to others that they aren't important enough to pay attention to. It takes mental commitment to put aside what you want to say in order to really listen to what is important to others or to how someone else is feeling. It means putting aside your own needs, feelings, and biases and really focusing on the other's perspective. When you do so, you are complimenting the other person. You are saying to them, "What you have to say is important and I care about it." We often don't make an effort to listen well unless there is a clear and immediate payoff (a new relationship developing, getting a new job, impressing a boss, or winning a million dollars on a game show!). Unfortunately for those of us who don't listen well or make the effort to do so, the message sent by poor listening is both clear and harmful.

Is Adequate Listening Good Enough?

Effective listening is different from *adequate* listening.[9] You might be able to listen well enough to go to class, take notes, recall enough information to take the midterm exam, maintain your friendships, keep your job, and do fairly well at your daily activities, but you could probably be more effective in each of these areas. Is it enough just to listen adequately? It might be for now, but for most of us to be our best, professionally and personally, we need to learn to be more effective at listening, not just be satisfied with doing it adequately. There are a number of ways you can overcome common barriers and blocks to listening, and learn about the different types of listening and important skills for engaging in each type.

By attentively listening to others, we communicate a clear nonverbal message to them ("You're important to me!"). Have you ever been offended or simply annoyed by someone's unwillingness to listen fully to you?

Listening in the Twenty-First Century

As we move into the twenty-first century, the challenges for us as listeners are different than they were for our ancestors and previous generations. Listening demands, styles, and barriers change as technologies change.[10] For instance, many new and innovative communication technologies are changing the ways we listen and communicate. As we connect with others more often through the use of technology, the proportion of time we spend listening naturally increases, as does the chance that something or someone will interfere with our ability to listen well. Consider the way the following new technologies, over the past decade or so, have changed the way you communicate interpersonally, and thus changed the way you listen: voice mail, call waiting, video résumés, electronic greeting cards, interactive videotapes, cellular and cordless phones, audio books, pagers, interactive voice-response systems, voice-activated telephone cards, voice-powered computers, voice-recognition computer technologies, telephone speech-recognition systems, voice-activated cars, and talking signs, elevators, cameras, TVs, cars, and refrigerators.[11]

In her 2000 article, one listening and technology expert argues that how, when, where, why, and to whom we listen are in a state of change and are significantly different in the twenty-first century.[12] For starters, she suggests that Americans are spending more time than ever simply communicating. The average American worker handles 201 messages (including phone calls, voice mails, e-mails, faxes, postal mail, and others) in a day, similar to many other cultures such as Germans, who encounter 177 messages a day; the British, who have a per-day total of 171 messages; and 169 messages per day for Canadians. Because of this overload in messages, we are changing the ways we listen and the behaviors used to indicate listening.

For instance, as we engage in more **asynchronous listening**, listening to a message delivered at an earlier time (such as voice mail), we cannot always give immediate feedback and ask questions of the other person.[13] The increase in videoconferencing has replaced many face-to-face meetings in the business context and has changed the nature of the listening demands in the business context. The dramatic increase in the use of cellular phones has raised a host of issues related to interpersonal communication and listening: Do we assess what others are saying and not saying based on where they are, whom they are with, or what other types of activities they are doing simultaneously? The increase of Internet use has reduced the amount of time individuals spend listening in other ways: More people get their news from an Internet source versus public radio, more people are sending e-mail instead of calling family and friends long-distance, and more people are ordering products and services online, something they used to do by visiting a store or making a phone call.[14] The very nature of listening itself is indeed changing as technologies allow us to communicate in more diverse ways.

The way we listen is being changed, and challenged, by the development of new communication technologies. Some of these technologies distract us from listening, some give us more opportunities to talk and listen to others, many actually "listen" to us, and some even demand we listen carefully to them. In what ways has technology both enhanced and challenged your listening skills?

Listening experts suggest that listening differs in the twenty-first century in many ways, one of the most important for the interpersonal communicator being to whom we will listen.[15] One leading scholar argues that the biggest challenge for listeners in the twenty-first century is cultural differences in communication styles. As our global world continues to expand, we will need to become increasingly more aware and skilled at the way cultural differences affect listening and communication styles. For example, researchers studying the listening style differences between American, German, and Israeli students found that German students prefer action-oriented listening, approaching communication with an inquisitive and direct style.[16] The German students often employed strategies of negotiation in their interpersonal interactions and expressed directly what they desired. The American students had more of a people-oriented listening style, concerned about the social aspects of their interactions with others. They also had a time-oriented style of listening, concerned about the amount of time interpersonal interactions required. The Israeli students, on the other hand, preferred a content style of listening, where they would frequently and carefully analyze the information that emerged in an interpersonal interaction before seeking action, seeking social interaction, or communicating directly or verbally. As many intercultural researchers point out, cultural differences in communication and listening styles are vast. As our technologies allow for more cross-cultural transactions, our

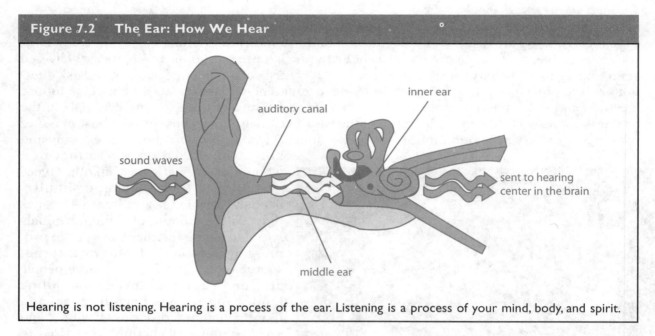

Figure 7.2   The Ear: How We Hear

sound waves

auditory canal

inner ear

sent to hearing center in the brain

middle ear

Hearing is not listening. Hearing is a process of the ear. Listening is a process of your mind, body, and spirit.

ability to communicate effectively in intercultural interactions will be more crucial than ever, and sensitivity to cross-cultural differences in listening will be essential.

Bentley suggests that, similar to business associates from different cultures who must select a language in which to speak and negotiate, parties in intercultural interactions must also be aware of the "listening language" they are using.[17] Doing so will increase understanding of the message being communicated and the success of the relationship between the communicators. Listening is a skill that demands that we adapt to the changing nature of culture and advancing communication technologies.

Hearing Versus Listening

Can you hear if you're not listening? Can you listen if you can't hear? Can you hear and listen at the same time? When you're not listening, are you hearing? Listening and hearing are two separate activities. To become better listeners, let's begin by understanding the difference.

Hearing is a natural, physiological process; listening is not (see Figure 7.2). Listening takes thought, intention, effort, and even some training. Unless you have some damage to your ears, you have been hearing sounds since before you were

Listening is an active process requiring your thoughtful and mindful attention. What are some of the competing stimuli or thoughts that often take your attention away from listening in class or in other situations that demand active listening?

born. Hearing is actually a process of sensing small changes in air pressure, a process that is happening continuously, even when you are sleeping.[18] Hearing is what makes it possible for us to wake to the sound of a loud voice, a ringing alarm clock, or the rumble of thunder. This sensory process is natural and out of our control. Listening, however, is very different.

Listening is a choice. It allows each of us to decide which sounds and messages we hear are meaningful, interesting, and useful to us. We can decide what we want to listen to, and can "tune in" to messages we like or find interesting and "tune out" those we don't want to hear or find boring. In your classes, you probably have many examples of turning to the student next to you to ask, "What did the professor just say? I didn't 'hear' him." In fact, you probably did hear the professor; you just were not listening carefully. You might have been thinking about something else, listening to the conversation of the two people behind you, or glancing out the window while daydreaming.

One misconception about listening is that it is a passive, not an active, process. Because we can't really see anyone listening, we think they must not be doing anything to make listening happen.[19] People who listen for a living (counselors, therapists, doctors, lawyers, consultants) know that much work, effort, training, and thought are involved in effective listening. Listening is a work-intensive task that requires us to receive information, sort and process it, relate it to what we already know, and make connections with other thoughts and ideas. When you're listening, your brain is working hard.

Mindfulness and Listening

Julia Wood is a well-known researcher and author in the area of interpersonal communication. She says that to become a good listener, you must first make a decision to be mindful.[20] **Mindfulness**, as she explains, is a concept from Zen Buddhism that means to be "fully present in the moment." Being mindful is keeping your mind on the present, being fully present in the moment, and paying attention to the here and now. When we are mindful, we are not distracted by our own thoughts or needs, nor do we let our minds wander from the present situation. Think about how it feels to really be present in the moment. You are fully focusing on what another person is saying, what the mood and emotion of the message are, and what the person is trying to share. You aren't thinking about whether you're hungry at the moment, or worrying about an exam you just took, or wondering whether someone across the way is looking in your direction.

According to Wood, being mindful is the first step in becoming an effective listener. If we are not mindful, we aren't able to understand others fully. Instead, we engage in superficial listening, and we are likely to miss important parts of the others' message. Further, mindfulness is not a skill you have to develop. Rather, it is a choice you make. You can make that choice right now. When you choose to be mindful, you make a decision and a commitment to listen carefully and fully to someone.

Think about times when you have not been fully present in a situation, and what potential consequences it had. Make a decision to be mindful in at least one conversation you will have in the next hour. Take note of how it feels and how the other person responds when you are mindful of everything they are saying.

Listening: A Cultural Form of Communication

Like all other aspects of interpersonal communication, listening too is a reflection of one's culture or co-culture. The rules, styles, and importance of listening vary greatly between and among individuals, often based on their cultural or co-cultural membership. We cannot talk about the "effectiveness" of listening skills without taking into consideration how culture mediates definitions of what is right, effective, and competent in communication.

For instance, research suggests that men and women in U.S. culture often develop listening styles based on distinctive masculine and feminine communication styles.[21] Women's speech generally reflects an emphasis on equality and symmetry, resulting in a participatory mode of communication.[22] Women, more often than men, work to invite others into the conversation and show support for the speaker.[23] As listeners, they tend to use more encouraging statements such as "Tell me more . . . " or ask questions such as "What did you say after that happened?" Further, women are more likely than men to respond nonverbally to another person with encouraging eye contact or a nod that is reassuring the speaker of the listener's interest.[24] Women have even been found to interrupt a speaker to show support or encourage further elaboration by the party speaking. Researchers show that men actually interrupt others more often than women do, although they do so with a different purpose: to challenge the speaker or gain a turn at speaking.[25] As these examples reveal, rules in U.S. culture for gendered speech styles naturally extend to gendered listening styles as well. We discuss these gender differences in listening in greater depth in Chapter 10.

The examples above also begin to reveal that listening, as part of the transactional process of communication, is not a single or discrete activity. More often, listening and speaking are simultaneous and fluid. As we discussed in Chapter 1, we think of speakers and listeners as not separate individuals or roles in the process, but jointly as sender-receivers engaging in both processes continuously and simultaneously. As we consider the way that culture influences the speaking-listening process, the transactional nature of the communication process becomes even more apparent.

Some communication researchers have argued that there are different listening response patterns between many African Americans and European Americans.[26] They hold that African Americans often employ an interactive style of verbal response in many communication contexts known as *call and response* (for example, calling out "Amen" or "Tell it like it is!" to support a speaker *as* she or he is speaking); European Americans more often use nonverbals such as eye contact and facial expressions to suggest interest in and provide response to a speaker. Such differences often lead to members of one co-culture believing a communicator from the other co-culture is not really listening or is acting rudely.[27] Hall suggests that many listening problems arise in intercultural settings because individuals fail to recognize the influence of cultural and co-cultural communication rules on definitions of effective listening.[28]

Authors have even critiqued the very assumptions behind an interpersonal approach to listening, suggesting that a monocultural approach to listening falls short of considering the more complex intercultural questions of meaning and the co-creation of such meanings.[29] These scholars, for instance, question how interpersonal scholars have defined where meaning falls during listening. They suggest that the idea of empathic listening—listening with the goal of understanding how another is feeling—falsely dichotomizes the speaker from the listener. Instead, listening and the creation of meaning, they suggest, take place *between* (not within) the speaker and listener. This view more adequately recognizes multiple cultural meaning systems at work when individuals come from a multitude of cultural backgrounds and settings.

Communication researcher Donal Carbaugh has studied a cultural form of listening among a tribal group known as the Blackfeet.[30] The Blackfeet, known to themselves as *nizitapi* ("real people"), are groups of men and women who have lived for centuries in northern Montana. The

Blackfeet use a form of "listening" that is uniquely a part of their culture. "Listening" to a Blackfeet is not at all the same kind of communication act that listening is to someone outside of this cultural group. To Blackfeet, *listening* refers to a form of communication that, when enacted in its special way, serves to connect participants to a specific physical space, and serves as a very unique form of interpersonal communication.

Carbaugh recounts in his ethnographic essay the explanation of Two Bears, a tribal elder: "If you have a problem, or can't find an answer for something, our belief is that you can come out here (the sacred site of the Sun Dance), or to the mountains, or just about anywhere, sit down and listen. If you sit and listen patiently, you'll find an answer."[31] For the Blackfeet, the plea "to listen" is aroused by the place, the physical context of the moment. Carbaugh explains that place invites listening, a cultural action that represent a complex communication practice. Based on cultural rules for communicating, to listen has a very different meaning to a Blackfeet individual than it likely does to you, an American student. When you say to your friend, "Listen carefully to me . . ." or "Listen to what I just heard . . ." you are expressing a cultural belief about what it means to listen; that you request another person to assign meaning or give significance to what you are saying. To Blackfeet, the act of listening is not as simple as assigning meaning to what you are hearing; to Blackfeet, listening requires one to be co-present with the natural and historical place in which, and to which, one listens. Blackfeet listening is based on a cultural belief that the natural world is active and expressive and should be consulted—listened to—as an important source of information and inspiration.

Further, to the Blackfeet, listening does not happen as a result of one's will. One cannot make listening happen like you and I can choose to listen during interpersonal communication. The Blackfeet believe that efforts that force listening will likely fail. Carbaugh explains: "Listening is not a product one makes and wills for oneself; it is a gift from that world in which one lives."[32] To an outsider, the act of listening in Blackfeet style might seem incomprehensible and even unsatisfactory. When you come from a culture that values verbal communication and speaking to increase understanding, you likely will have difficulty understanding a culture where listening is valued and silence is used as a means for increasing understanding.

The Blackfeet example, as well as the earlier gender, African American, and European American examples of listening styles, further emphasize the point we have made at many points in this text: A person's culture affects how they communicate with others. Every aspect of our interpersonal communication takes place within a larger cultural context. Listening is no exception. As you read the remainder of this chapter, keep in mind the way your cultural beliefs, values, and communication rules affect the way you view and engage in the process of listening, and even the way you would define the ways and reasons we each listen. In this next section, we attempt to identify common types of listening that exist in American culture.

Types of Listening

We listen for many reasons. Consider the many different reasons you choose to listen to the people around you today. Take a moment and jot down at least four different reasons you listened today. Did you listen for entertainment? Enjoyment? To comprehend a lecture? For some information? To make a decision? To get perspective on something? To help a friend? To understand someone better? Your list probably includes a number of these, and maybe some others.

We engage in multiple types of listening every day, many of them simultaneously. The five primary types of listening are active listening, appreciative listening, empathic listening, comprehensive/informational listening, and critical listening. A common type of nonlistening is called pseudo-listening. To introduce some of these different types of listening and some of the reasons we listen, look at a day in the life of a young mother and professional named Tyra. Following the scenario, we will define and explore each of the types of listening in depth:

Tyra was getting ready to go to class this morning when her youngest son Michael asked her to come up to his room, where he told her he wasn't going to school today. Tyra asked Michael if he wasn't feeling well. When he said he was feeling fine, but didn't want to face his friend who was mad at him, Tyra listened to Michael tell her about feeling angry, sad, and hurt by his friend's actions. She encouraged him to explain more of how he felt and responded by saying, "It really sounds like you're upset by what he did." When Tyra did so, she was listening to be empathic. *When Tyra finally arrived at work, one of her coworkers, Bill, began telling her about a change in the presentation she was to give later that morning. Bill told Tyra about a small change in the order of the slides, of how Tyra's boss Kris wanted the main message to be altered just a bit, and reminded her to be sure to include some figures on the latest grant their organization had received for her work on a large public awareness campaign. As Bill told Tyra of these developments, Tyra carefully jotted some notes, asked for clarification of some of the information, and indicated she understood some points by nodding, paraphrasing some of the points, and encouraging Bill to continue. As she listened, she also thought about how she would use her boss' suggestions to change and improve her presentation. When Tyra did so, she was listening* actively *and* comprehensively. *Later that morning after Tyra's presentation, her boss called her into her office to discuss the reaction of one of their top clients to Tyra's presentation. She said that after the presentation, the client was so impressed that they would like to hire the organization to take on a huge market research project for them. Tyra's boss shared the details of the offer, and asked her for her opinion on whether she thought it sounded fair and reasonable, and if she thought the company should take the project. When Tyra listened to the details and carefully assessed the information about the proposal, she was engaged in* critical *listening. After a long day, Tyra began the short drive home and tuned her car radio to a local light rock station. They were playing an artist she had recently heard of and noticed she was fond of the lyrics and rhythm. Tyra enjoyed the song as she drove along the highway. When it was over, she listened carefully to hear if the DJ announced the name of the artists and track so she might purchase the CD later that evening. When Tyra was listening for that information and as she listened to the new artist, she was engaged in types of* informational *and* appreciative *listening.*

Like Tyra, most of us engage in each of these types of listening many times in the span of one day. Let's take a closer look at each of these types of listening and explore some of the reasons why we listen in our everyday lives.

Active Listening

Active listening is involved listening. The term *active listening* is actually redundant because, as you've learned, to listen at all means that you need to be actively attending to and processing what you're hearing. We will use the term *active listening* to refer to a particular type of listening. Many of the other types of listening we'll discuss are also kinds of active listening, yet active listening has some distinguishing characteristics. Recall Tyra, in the above scenario, who actively listened to her coworker describe changes that needed to be made in the presentation. Tyra was involved in listening with her mind, by paraphrasing Bill and asking questions, and with her nonverbal feedback of nodding (demonstrating her understanding or need for clarity). Active listening engages both the listener and the speaker, and requires that the listener be present mentally, verbally, and nonverbally in the interaction. Active listening is different from passive listening because it requires explicit effort and participation. See whether you can identify where active listening takes place in the following interaction:

Bob arrives home from work and finds his wife of 16 years and their two children watching the evening news and relaxing together in the living room. After greeting them, he sits down in the rocking chair next to them and asks about their day. Jim, their oldest son, is focused on the television set and responds, without looking away, with "uh-hun" and "yep, dad" when asked if he had a good day at school. Sheila, Bob's 9-year-old daughter, jumps out of her chair to smile and hug her Dad while greeting him with a loud "Hi Dad!" Margy, Bob's wife, turns toward Bob and responds to his inquiry about her day with a story about taking Sheila to the doctor that afternoon. "We waited for almost an hour before even being seen. But Dr. Murry said that Sheila's tests results were normal and that we shouldn't worry about the more frequent asthma attacks, but just treat them as we usually do. She did give us a slightly different inhaler, just in case the other was getting less effective in bringing medicine in her lungs."

Bob leans forward and touches Margy on the arm while looking her in the eyes "What a huge relief. Great news. You seem very relieved. I wish I could have been there today, too. Did the doctor say anything else about her height or growth patterns?" Margy explains a bit more about the doctor's description of what she thinks. Bob nods to indicate he is understanding and says, "When does she want to see her again?"

"In a couple of months," explains Margy.

"That's great news. That must have been a stressful afternoon before finding out," replies Bob. Margy agrees with a sigh. Bob winks at his wife with reassurance and begins to walk toward the kitchen. "I think I'll go start the grill for dinner."

It's obvious that Bob is displaying many behaviors of an active listener. He is mentally processing the information provided, nonverbally indicating that he's listening and involved, and verbally attending to the speaker by asking questions and reflecting her feelings.

What role do you think active listening plays in our interpersonal interactions? People who are actively listening are sending the message that they would like the speaker to continue and that they care about what is being said. Active listening sets the stage for dialogue because it is engaged and encouraging. Bob's active listening encouraged Margy to continue; it told her that he was interested in what she had to say and was engaged in her story and experience. Active listening encourages the speaker to explore his or her feelings and thoughts. Imagine now that Bob had responded to Margy by looking toward the television set while she talked and saying, "Um. Hmmm. Really. That's good. I think I'll go start the grill for dinner." It's clear that Bob's behaviors as an active listener played a large part in the way this interpersonal interaction continued.

You can use a number of strategies for improving your skills as an effective and active listener. You probably already noticed some of them in the above scenario. Here are three:

- *Paraphrase the speaker's thoughts:* **Paraphrasing** is stating in your own words what you heard the speaker say. You can do this by saying, "What you're saying is . . ." or "You mean that . . ." By paraphrasing, you give the other person a chance to elaborate on what he or she is saying and thus encourage an active and engaged interaction. It also lets the speaker know you're being mindful and attentive to his or her words. Paraphrasing is an important technique in empathic listening, which we discuss in detail later in this chapter.

- *Express an understanding of the speaker's feelings:* In addition to paraphrasing the speaker's words, you should try to reflect his or her feelings and check the accuracy of your perceptions. Bob did this by saying, "You seem very relieved," and, "That must have been a stressful afternoon," to check how Margy was really feeling and to acknowledge her feelings. Expressing such understanding is also a sign that you are mindfully attentive to the speaker, and is a way to encourage the speaker to talk more about his or her feelings.

- *Ask questions:* Asking questions is probably the simplest and best way to actively engage with any speaker. It not only ensures your own understanding of the information, feelings, or experiences of the speaker, but also it tells him or her that you want to know more or need clarification or elaboration on certain points. Questions are a simple and effective way to engage your mind as a listener and confirm your interest in the speaker, whether in the classroom, in the family room, or during a meeting.

There are many reasons to listen actively. For instance, when one listens attentively and mindfully, the chances of asserting one's power increases through acquired knowledge, accurate perceptions of the person or group, and the creation of satisfying interpersonal relationships. As we have discussed repeatedly throughout this text, power is present in all interpersonal interactions. Because listening is an often overlooked and underestimated aspect of the communication process, particularly in the dominant cultures of the United States, you are wise to consider how improving your listening skills can enhance the powerfulness of your own communication style.

Appreciative Listening

Much of the listening we do every day is quite passive and purely for enjoyment. We take part in **appreciative listening** when we listen because it gives us pleasure. Take a minute to think about all the things you enjoy and appreciate listening to. Maybe it's the sound of a baby talking to herself in her crib as she wakes in the morning or the voices of your favorite artists each time you play the songs on their latest CD. Maybe it's the words and images evoked by the story your mom or dad used to read to you each night before bed, the comedians onstage at a local comedy event, the wind rustling through the trees, your loved one's voice on the phone after you've had a bad day at work, the story on your local public radio station about a topic that interests you, the conversation among friends at a party or evening out together, or one of the thousands of other things you might enjoy listening to in life.

You can probably think of a number of ways, just today, that you have listened because you simply wanted to. You enjoyed listening. We listen quite often just for the pleasure it brings us. Listening for enjoyment, however, can sometimes interfere with our thought processes and ability to concentrate. The very music we enjoy listening to can serve as a type of "noise" competing for our attention. For more on research related to listening to music while studying, take a moment to read the information in Practical Research (Box 7.3).

Box 7.3

Practical Research
Music and Studying Don't Mix

Do you enjoy having your stereo cranked up while you read your interpersonal communications textbook? Do you like to take along your portable CD player with earphones to the library or computer lab while you research or write a paper? You might recall many arguments with your parents about how music helps you relax and thus study better. According to recent research, you should turn off the music and leave your iPod at home. Listening to music while studying distracts you and results in less efficient and effective writing and studying.[33]

Sarah Randsdell is a researcher at Florida Atlantic University who recently studied the way students wrote essays with or without music playing in the background. Those students who listened to the music while writing wrote 60 words less per hour on average than those who did their writing without music. The type of music made no difference, either; both vocal and instrumental music had the same distracting effect. According to Randsdell, most of us can't listen and write well simultaneously because our brains our distracted by the two competing tasks.

So the next time you're looking to get your studying done in a more efficient manner, turn down the stereo before you turn on the computer. The results will likely be a paper that is written faster and with fewer competing distractions.

Empathic Listening

Your friend finds you sitting in the library and sits down next to you. He looks upset, so you say, "What's up?" He responds with the following:

> Not much. I'm just annoyed with my parents. They're impossible. I called them to tell them the great news about deciding, finally, what I want to do with my life. That I finally picked a major and that I'm really excited about it. I thought they'd be really happy for me. They've been pushing me to get my life in order and to make sure I'm taking classes that matter for something. So when I tell them I've decided to be a communication major, they first were just silent. . . . "Ah, hmm," they finally murmured, and then asked, "What do you do with a communication major?" I tried to tell them about all the things I've been learning in my interpersonal class, and in my communication theory class, but they just didn't get it. After yelling back and forth, my dad ends with the same old question: "What's wrong with being a business major?" They just don't get it! I hate business! . . . Parents can be so annoying! I don't know how to get through to them.

We often use empathic listening when a friend or someone close to us shares a problem or is looking for our support. What do you find is the most challenging aspect of empathic listening?

Many of us are faced with situations where someone comes to us with their problems, complaints, or troubles. You can probably recall being faced with a friend, coworker, or family member who wanted to share a problem, use you as a sounding board, or ask you for help with a troubling situation. One of the choices you can make in this interpersonal situation is to use empathic listening.

Empathic listening is listening to try to understand and feel what another person is feeling. It serves many important functions in interpersonal relationships, such as helping your friend solve a problem, assisting your sister in getting a clearer perspective on a problem at work, or aiding a loved one in sorting out his feelings and emotions. Empathic listening is one of the first and most important skills that trained counselors and psychologists learn, and it is one that all of us can use in our own interactions with others.

There are a number of behaviors for listening empathically, one of the most important of which is paraphrasing, defined earlier as stating in your own words what you heard the speaker say. Paraphrasing is a good way to check your understanding of a message and indicate to the other person that you are listening closely. Paraphrasing can take many forms, such as "You seem to be feeling . . . " "You seem to be describing . . . " "I hear you saying . . . " "You sound like you're feeling . . . " or "What I hear you saying is. . . . " It is one of the first skills any counselor learns in his or her training, because it helps those being counseled feel like they are really being listened to and understood. Paraphrasing also serves to build the trusting relationship between client and counselor; as the speaker hears the counselor accurately paraphrasing and reflecting her feelings, she trusts that the counselor is listening fully and effectively. Doing so sends the following message: "I really care and want to help you." It is a simple technique that anyone can use when faced with the opportunity, or need, to listen empathically. Take a moment to practice the technique of paraphrasing by using the Skill Builder activity in Box 7.4.

Box 7.4

Skill Builder

Paraphrasing: An Empathic Listening Skill

One of the most important behaviors in empathic listening is paraphrasing, or summarizing the content or feeling expressed in a message. Paraphrasing is one of the key ways a listener can indicate that he or she is actively listening; paraphrasing also is a way to check your understanding of a message.

In the spaces below, write how you might paraphrase the following statements to both indicate listening and check comprehension. Remember: Try to summarize the feeling or the idea of the message without responding to it with advice or with questions.

Your friend says: "My mother is driving me crazy! She keeps calling and asking me all sorts of questions about how my schoolwork is going, did I go out last night, and even how late I slept! Can she ever leave me alone?!"

You could paraphrase by saying:

For example: You sound really bugged by her overprotectiveness.

Other paraphrases might be:

_____

_____

_____

☞ *Your brother calls and is upset about something at work. He says:* "I've had a really awful week. We had to lay off 11 more people in my department, people are taking it out on me personally, and I have to make some tough budget decisions that might require even more layoffs. I'm not sure I can face it another day."
Your paraphrase might be:

_____
_____
_____

Your 8-year-old daughter comes home from school and is crying: "All my friends hate me! I told the teacher that Jerome was cheating on the test and they are all calling me a tattletale. I can't go to school ever again!"
You could paraphrase by saying:

_____
_____
_____

Your friend is upset with a grade in her communication class: "I worked so hard on this project and the professor still gave me a B– on it! I can't believe she couldn't see that my group did nothing and I did all the work. It's so unfair."
You could paraphrase with:

_____
_____
_____

Your buddy just returned from a weekend with his family and complains: "I've got the strangest family in the world. My sister is marrying some weirdo, my brother is thinking of using his entire life savings to open a coffee shop, my dad is going through some kind of midlife crisis, and my mom acts like I'm the one to be concerned about, just because I'm not doing great in one of my classes. What a bunch of nuts."
You might paraphrase by stating:

_____
_____
_____

Other strategies for good empathic listening include focusing your attention on the speaker through eye contact and other nonverbal behaviors, listening actively (including asking questions), and creating a supportive and positive communication climate (by confirming the other person's feelings and experiences and offering encouraging and supportive messages).

As you most likely are noticing, active listening and empathic listening are very similar types of listening. In fact, some scholars argue that empathic listening is actually a type of active listening. We don't disagree that empathic listening requires many of the same skills demanded of the active listener. The key difference, however, is that the empathic listener is intentionally attempting to understand what the other person is feeling and expressing, thus creating an interpersonal environment of empathy. In active listening, the goal is not always one of empathy, but rather one of engagement and involvement in a variety of ways with the speaker. Although the similarities between empathic and active listening are many, keep in mind that empathic listening is often regarded as a more specific and directed kind of skillful listening than the more general category of active listening.

Comprehensive/Informational Listening

When you hear your professor say, "Be sure to get this down. It will be on the test," it is your cue to listen very carefully to the information he or she is about to present. Every day we engage in **comprehensive** (or informational) **listening**, or listening to gain knowledge or information. The classroom is one obvious place where we engage in informational listening, but there are many others.

Take a moment and identify at least three occasions today when you listened with the purpose of getting information. Did you listen to the weather report on the radio so you knew what to wear to school? Did you listen to a report on the morning news about calcium supplements because it is a personal health concern of yours? Did you listen to your coworker tell you the name of the new client? Did you listen to the directions your friend gave you to get to her new apartment? You can likely think of dozens of examples where you listened for information or to gain knowledge. It is one of the most common forms of listening. Despite the fact that we need it so often, many of us do informational listening particularly poorly. In fact, most of us will forget the majority of the information we listen to in a lecture, sermon, or speech, remembering only about 50 percent of what we hear a day after, and only 25 percent two days later.[34] Being mindful of the situation, and of the information you want to gather, can dramatically increase your chances of gathering and remembering the information you need. You can also ask questions related to the information you want to remember, take notes if appropriate, relate the new information to what you already know, ask for additional details related to the information, repeat key concepts to yourself, and rephrase the information you just heard in your own words. Each of these strategies is helpful when attempting to improve the amount of information you are receiving. Practice helps, too. For tips on how to remember people's names, for example, check out the information in Applied Concepts (Box 7.5).

Box 7.5

Applied Concepts
Why Can't I Remember Your Name?!

One of the most common complaints concerning listening and memory skills is the difficulty of remembering people's names. If you are like most people, the task of remembering the name of your friend's roommate, your husband's new coworker, your partner's client, or the new neighbor down the block is not an easy one. Even when we listen carefully to the name of someone new, we often forget it shortly after. Why can't we remember names more easily? According to researchers, there are a few simple steps you can take to increase your chances of remembering names.[35,36] Memory experts suggest a series of three steps: learning the name, learning the face, and linking the name and face.

"Eric"—Learning the Name:

When you first meet someone, you need to listen carefully for the correct name. Actively and intentionally listen to it. If you didn't hear it clearly, ask for it to be repeated until you hear it correctly. Discuss the name with the person, if appropriate (Where did the name come from? Is that your original name? Mention other people you know with the same name). Then, rehearse the name silently to yourself, and use the person's name multiple times during the conversation. Later, write the name down or at least repeat it to yourself. ☞

☞ **Learning the Face:**

Next, you need to learn the person's face. Really look at the other person. When doing so, try to identify one prominent feature about that person (very curly hair, a large beard, an interesting mole on the cheek, a small nose, a receding hairline) that might help you remember the face.

Linking the Name and Face:

To link the name and face, you must connect the mental picture and the name somehow. You could come up with a ridiculous connection (the sound of the name is like a cartoon character who has hair like the person you just met), or you might associate the first letter of the person's name with the prominent feature (the person, named Eric, has a round face and bluntly cut bangs; these shapes together remind you of the small letter "e"—the first letter of his name). Or connect the person's name to his or her occupation ("Eric is a person who can't make many errors in his work," because he's an accountant) or make a silly rhyme using the person's name ("Eric likes parrots who eat carrots").

The process of remembering a name is a great example of active listening. Your brain is doing a great deal of work even though it appears to be doing nothing at all. The ability to listen well, and remember details and names, can enhance not only your professional life, but your personal satisfaction as well.

Critical Listening

One step beyond listening for information is **critical listening**, whose purpose is to evaluate a message or information. Critical listening moves a step beyond comprehensive listening, because once you have the information you need, critical listening demands evaluation of the information. We use critical listening in many situations, particularly when we want to separate facts from inferences, identify fallacies in reasoning, or evaluate evidence that is being presented. You are probably a critical listener when you are being persuaded to purchase a stereo, take your doctor's advice, donate money to a worthy cause, take the suggestion of your employer, respond to the request for a loan from a family member, sign a petition, forward an e-mail to people who support a common cause, volunteer your time, or join a group. Critical listening is essential in our world where thousands of messages come our way on a daily basis from multiple sources: television, radio, billboards, e-mails, the Internet, telemarketers, friends, family, public announcements, speakers, lectures, and groups, to name just a few.

The job interview is a great opportunity to use critical listening. Both the interviewer and interviewee are engaged in critical listening because each wants to make the best decision. As an interviewee, you need to listen critically to evaluate whether the job and work environment will be suitable to your needs. As an interviewer, you need to determine whether the applicant is well qualified and suited for the position. Both parties must carefully evaluate information presented by the other to determine whether it is a true representation without distortion or bias.

Pseudo-Listening

There are many times when we want to appear as if we're listening when we're really not. According to researchers, **pseudo-listening**[37] is a masquerade for real listening. When we pseudo-listen, we are not *really* listening; rather, we are meeting some other need (such as making others think we're interested, buying time to prepare for our next comment, looking for someone's vulnerabilities, or checking how others are reacting). We might pretend to listen by nodding occasionally, smiling, or even interjecting "hmmm" or "yeah" to encourage the speaker to continue, but we are not really paying attention to what the speaker is saying. Pseudo-listening is the ultimate form of being mindless in our listening. We are not even trying to be present in the moment, but rather are interested in other goals and thus aren't attempting to attend the speaker. Think of a time when you were pseudo-listening. What were you trying to accomplish instead of listening? How does it feel when someone pseudo-listens to you? When are you most likely to be a pseudo-listener? The next time you are, make a choice to listen actively and mindfully in the situation. As the information in Practical Research (Box 7.6) explains, it might be that we know we're really listening effectively when we get goose bumps, or the *feeling* of listening well. Check out the information in this box for an interesting and different way to approach and think about what it means to be a good listener.

Box 7.6

Practical Research
Listening With Goose Bumps: Is Listening a Feeling?

According to Bob Gunn, if you've ever had goose bumps when you were listening to someone speak, it probably means you were hearing the truth or something special.[38] The feeling of goose bumps, or having the hair stand up on the back of your neck, according to Gunn, "is nature's way of letting you know you're hearing something special." It is your body's physical sign of feeling good or certain. Gunn suggests that instead of listening for words or for meaning, if we are really going to listen well and mindfully, we need to listen for the *feeling*. In his own experience, he found that the more he "thought" while listening and took notes during a conversation, the less insight and understanding he gained. On the contrary, the more he simply listened for the true feeling and beauty of the conversation, the more clarity he had (even days and months later) for the substance of the discussion.

Gunn is the head of a large consulting group that works with Fortune 500 companies, helping them improve communication, value, and productivity among employees. According to Gunn, the art of listening is not about thinking or remembering, but about a kind of feeling. He suggests that "you are listening deeply whenever you become lost in the words and find yourself experiencing deep feelings of joy, gratitude, surprise, curiosity, warmth, closeness, wonder, beauty, or appreciation." He calls this hearing on a more profound level. "The stronger the feeling, the more profound the understanding," Gunn explains.

He encourages you to avoid saying, "This won't work for me!" and really try, for at least a week, to connect with people on a personal level, turn your back on your own thoughts, and notice that when your mind is conducive to deeper listening you are more likely to really feel the peace, quiet, and emotion of a conversation. According to Gunn, listening is a feeling. If you haven't felt it, you're listening the wrong way.

Skills for Better Listening: Avoid Listening Blocks

Now that we've reviewed the importance of listening and the many types of listening, let's explore some of the ways we can recognize and avoid habits that prevent us from listening well. Scholars point out a number of common blocks to skillful listening.[39] All of us have encountered these at times, so our focus here is on ways to improve as listeners.

Comparing

It is natural to relate what others are saying to our own situations or experiences. Yet comparing can serve as a serious block to listening when we focus our attention on ourselves instead of on the speaker and the message. We are not able to really listen to another person when we are thinking; "Geez, I can't believe he doesn't know that," "I can recite all those by heart," "I'm funnier than she is," "Why is she complaining?" "That's nothing compared to what I've been through," or "I'm 10 times busier than he is, so what is he worried about?" Next time you are listening, try to listen fully first, and compare later. You might be surprised at how much of the meaning you are missing when you spend your listening time comparing.

Mind Reading

Do you try to guess what the speaker is thinking, instead of listening mindfully to what he or she is saying? Mind reading can be a block to listening because when you mind read, you are not "trusting" what the other person is saying. Further, you are not paying much attention to it because you are trying to figure out what the person is *really* thinking. Often, the mind reader is not listening as much to the verbal message, but to the nonverbal aspects of the message. As we learned in the last chapter, often the nonverbal cues are more accurate than verbal ones. However, the mind reader is focused almost exclusively on making assumptions and going on intuition, instead of really trying to focus on what is being said and listening to the whole of the message being offered. Instead of mind reading, try listening fully and mindfully to what the person is saying. If you don't understand, use paraphrasing to check your comprehension of what the speaker is thinking.

Rehearsing

We all want to sound good, organized, and effective when we speak. Sometimes that requires a little rehearsing of what we are about to say. However, rehearsing our own messages can be a significant block to really listening to what others are saying. Many of us have become very skilled at looking like we're interested in what someone else is saying (pseudo-listening), when in fact we are busy thinking about our own messages and ideas. Instead of rehearsing, use the skills of active listening. Your message, in turn, might be more informed and effective because you listened completely and accurately to the other person.

Filtering

When we listen to just part of the message and decide another part is not interesting, relevant, worthwhile, important, or significant, we are filtering the message to fit our own needs. Once we hear what we want to know, we might not listen to the rest of the message. Sometimes we filter out the things we don't want to hear (criticism, negative messages, hurtful comments) and pretend we actually didn't hear them. When we listen mindfully and fully, we hear the whole message and thus avoid this common mistake.

Prejudging

As you've learned in other chapters, making prejudgments of others can be dangerous. Because our perceptions guide our behaviors and thoughts, prejudging a person or message as dumb, useless, and uninteresting will likely result in our not listening fully or with an open mind.

On the other hand, if we judge all messages to be important and reliable before we hear them, we are equally likely not to listen critically. Both forms of prejudging can serve as blocks to our listening. "A basic rule of listening is that judgments should only be made *after* you have heard and evaluated the content of the message."[40]

Advising

We don't always recognize giving advice as a block to listening because we usually do it with the intention of being helpful. When you are searching your thoughts for the best advice to offer, you are often limiting your ability to listen effectively. Listening fully to the other person's feelings, experiences, or story often puts us in a better position to help and offer advice if it is desired.

Debating

Debate is often helpful and useful. Yet it can be a block to listening when you are too quick to point out what is wrong with the message or what your own perspective is. Debaters often fall prey to the other listening blocks already mentioned (especially rehearsing, filtering, and judging), and sometimes use harmful "putdowns" that quickly dismiss the other's point of view or experience. For example, when Jenny begins to share her complaint about a coworker and her partner Rob interrupts by saying, "Don't let him push you around. You can be such a wimp around those engineers at work," Rob's putdown is a block to effective listening because he did not allow Jenny to talk and he discouraged further discussion on the topic. Be aware when your good intention to debate might actually be a block to your chance for better listening.

Being Right

When you feel the need to be right by whatever means it takes (yelling, distorting the facts, dominating, making excuses, making accusations, name-calling, putdowns, etc.), you are likely not going to be listening fully or effectively. Using the skills of empathic listening will help you reduce your need to "win" or have the "correct" answer in a conversation. When we listen with empathy, we are truly attempting to understand what the other person is saying and feeling and reduce the focus on ourselves and our own needs.

Derailing

When you derail a speaker, you do so by changing the topic of conversation. You might bring up a related topic, or comment on something irrelevant to distract the speaker from the original point. We often make this listening error because we are uncomfortable with or uninterested in what the speaker is saying. Derailing is a block to listening simply because it doesn't give the other person the chance to finish sharing their story, idea, or experience. Can you think of a time recently when you engaged in derailing? Maybe you weren't even aware of the fact that you were. As with the other blocks to listening, your attitude toward listening will make a big difference in how you approach each listening opportunity. If you approach each conversation as a chance to listen actively and mindfully, the chance that you will derail or not listen fully is minimized.

Placating

We've probably all been the victims of others placating us while they listen: "I know. . . . I know. . . . Right, right. . . . Sure. . . . Sure. . . . I bet, yeah. . . . Of course, yes. . . . " Placating as a block to listening is being nice, supportive, and pleasant while not truly listening to the message. When we placate we want to appear like we're listening, even sound like we're listening, when in fact we aren't. Placating is a prime example of pseudo-listening, because we are usually half-listening, while the other half of us is wandering with our minds.

Blocks to listening can take many forms. They represent the range of personal communication habits that can get in the way of effective listening. They aren't the only issues, however, which affect our abilities to listen well. In the next section we introduce common *barriers* to listening, those aspects of our environment and context of communication that interfere with effective listening.

Barriers to Effective Listening

Barriers to listening are similar to listening blocks in that they both cause problems for listeners. Barriers are slightly different from listening blocks because barriers tend to be found primarily in the context or the environment in which communicators are interacting and/or tend to be those qualities of communicators that are harder to change or control. Blocks to listening are more likely the habits of communicators themselves, whereas barriers tend to be those things more inherently challenging to all communicators (e.g., dealing with information overload in our high-tech world or being motivated to listen well). Being aware of potential barriers to listening should allow you to make choices about reducing the likelihood that they will get in the way of effective listening. Below, we introduce four common listening barriers and some suggestions for reducing them in any interpersonal situation.

Culture can serve as a barrier to listening. Have you ever had a misunderstanding with a person from a culture or co-culture other than your own? Did you ever consider that it might have something to do with a slightly (or dramatically) different approach to listening?

Barrier 1: Noise

As you remember from Chapter 1, though a natural part of the communication process, noise is a barrier to effective listening. We encounter noise in every communication interaction, and in interpersonal interactions the sources of noise are many.

External noise includes anything external to the self that interferes with the communication of messages. When you shut the window, turn down the TV or stereo, purchase a home away from the airport, minimize traffic noise, turn off the vacuum cleaner, or select a location for your conversation that is away from other people talking, you are minimizing the possibility that external noise will interfere with your ability to listen effectively. It's desirable to eliminate as many types of external noise as possible, but of greater concern is the possibility that internal noise will interfere with mindful and attentive listening.

Internal noise includes sources of distraction inside the self, such as feelings, attitudes, your physical state (are you hungry, cold, or tired?), or other preoccupations (is the speaker using an accent, making it more challenging to understand her message?). Although sometimes internal noise is out of your control (you are tired from being up all night, or you have the flu and a headache), many times if you are mindful of the internal noise you are creating (coming to an interaction with a prejudgment or an attitude about the speaker, either positive or negative), you can reduce internal noise and listen more effectively.

For instance, a key difference in listening approach is found in high- and low-context cultures. In **low-context cultures** such as the United States and Germany, most of the meaning in an interaction or relationship is communicated in words and in the explicit verbal message being delivered. Effective communication, therefore, is largely viewed as the responsibility of the speaker. In **high-context cultures** such as Japan and Saudi Arabia, however, most of the meaning in an interaction is assumed to exist in the *context,* or the setting, the environment, and the relationship between communicators.[41] Effective communication, therefore, is largely seen as the responsibility of the listener.

You can imagine the potential for misunderstanding when a person from a high-context culture engages in elaborate verbal explanations during a friendly conversation with a person from a low-context culture, who perceives the overexplaining as patronizing. On the other hand, the business negotiations between a person from a high-context culture, where many things are not viewed as appropriate or necessary to discuss explicitly, might be perceived as deceptive and untrustworthy by the person from the low-context culture who assumed that the parties had discussed all aspects of the deal, only to find out later they had not.

Culture is always a factor we must ask ourselves about when engaging in any kind of interpersonal interaction: Is the cultural orientation or background of the communicators playing a role in the way the interaction is unfolding? Listening is no exception. We should not assume that everyone listens in the same way or for the same reasons. And when someone does employ a different listening or speaking style than we are accustomed to, it can instantly create noise in the interaction, distracting us from the situation or information being shared.

Barrier 2: Information Overload

What is a typical day like for you? For most of us, information and stimuli bombard us simultaneously and constantly throughout the day: the music on the radio, the sitcom on television, the beeping of new mail messages on your computer, the flash of advertisements on the Internet, the ringing of our cellphone, the beep of our pager, the barrage of advertisements in newspapers and magazines, the calls from telemarketers, the conversations with friends, the memos and data from coworkers, the requests of your family, and the lectures and handouts from professors. **Information overload**, the arrival of more information or stimuli than we need or can process, is a common communication barrier in our fast-paced, high-tech society. When too much information is coming at us, we can't focus on it all.

Advances in communication technologies not only give us more and enhanced opportunities for communicating and interacting with others, but also create a greater potential for information overload. When we employ more and varied forms of communication technologies, we are opening ourselves up to the likelihood that we will encounter information overload. Consider the student who attends her communication class for one hour, talks on her cell phone on the way to class and again on her way out of class, and then checks her e-mail using her wireless Web connection on her laptop while at the bus stop. While on the bus, she reads the student newspaper, thinks about how she will respond to an e-mail from her friend, and listens to music with her portable MP3 player. While on the bus, she also notices a voice mail indicator flash on her cell phone. She removes one ear of her headphone to listen to the message from her roommate. This student is probably not unlike you in many ways. She is being bombarded with information and stimuli that, in some instances, will result in a distracting amount of information overload. Was she able to attentively listen to the voice mail from her roommate? Did she mindfully listen during every minute of the one hour she was in class? Did she actively listen to the parties on the cell phone calls?

Regardless of the medium we use to interact interpersonally, we need to be aware of the potential for information overload. We need to work actively to reduce the sources of information around us so we can attentively and selectively listen and attend to the conversation at hand. We can reduce the information around us in many ways: being selective about what we perceive, limiting the sheer volume of information we seek, communicating to one person at a time, doing one thing at a time, and, most importantly, actively and mindfully choosing to focus on the message or speaker at hand. Further, when you want someone else to listen mindfully to you, try asking him or her whether it is a good time for you to speak: "Is this a good time for me to tell you something really important?" or "Can I tell you something now, or would you prefer to wait until later?" Taking these simple steps can enhance the interpersonal experience, and reduce the chance for information overload, for both the speaker and the listener in many situations.

Barrier 3: Speech Rate/Thought Rate Differential

Have you noticed that you are able to make a grocery list or plan an activity for the day during your biology lecture while still paying attention to just about everything your professor says? Do you find yourself thinking about other things while your friend is telling you a story, realizing that you really did listen to the majority of what she was saying? You may not actually be fooling yourself.

One barrier to effective listening is the difference between the speed at which our brain can process information and the speed at which the average person speaks. Most of us have the ability to process between 600 and 800 words per minute. The average person only speaks, however, at a rate of 125 words per minute. The difference between these numbers gives us quite a bit of time to do other things in our heads while we listen: daydream, plan, create, wonder, think, project, list, number, organize, remember, categorize, and so on (see Figure 7.3).

The gap between the speaking and listening rates can be a serious barrier for listeners when they are not being fully present and focusing on the message and speaker. Instead of using the extra thought time to let your mind wander, use that time to actively listen. By doing so, you will be a more effective listener, prepared to ask questions, paraphrase, and engage the speaker with your thoughts and feedback.

Barrier 4: Motivation

When it comes down to it, there is one key barrier to being a more effective listener: *motivation*. Although it is essential that you are aware of the listening skills and strategies we presented

Figure 7.3   Speech-Thought Rate

"the second point is..."

"what should I have for lunch?
...what is that kid drawing in his book?
...I have to remember to get those notes from Michael.
...the second point she said was..."

Our ability to think (600–800 words per minute) much faster than others can speak (125 words per minute) allows a great deal of time for our minds to wander, become distracted, and interfere with our abilities to listen well and mindfully.

in this chapter, none will do you any good if you are not motivated and want to become a better listener. Being a good listener is a little about being skilled and a lot about wanting to be better. Although motivation is a key part of becoming a more competent interpersonal communicator on many levels, it is probably most important in listening. As we discussed in the beginning of this chapter, listening is the largest portion of our communication activity, yet it requires only a little bit of effort to make a big improvement in it.

Summary

After reading this chapter, you should have many ideas of how you can become a more effective listener, and thus a better and more desirable interpersonal communicator. You have learned about the importance of listening in our daily lives, an essential and frequently used communication skill. You also have learned about the potential effects of poor listening on your health, your personal relationships, and even your employment or career. We discussed the key difference between hearing, a physiological process, and listening, a mental process requiring thought, effort, and skill. We also highlighted the similarities and differences between active, empathic, appreciative, and comprehensive/informational listening, as well as described pseudo-listening, a type of nonlistening that we often use to pretend we're actually listening. As we explained, the Zen Buddhist concept of mindfulness is a critical aspect of becoming a better listener; because listening is an active, selective process, when you choose to be mindful, or fully present in the moment, you are taking an important first step toward more effective listening. We discussed throughout how mindfulness is among the most critical of all the skills necessary for becoming better as a listener and as an interpersonal communicator.

There are a number of skills we addressed throughout this chapter toward becoming a more effective listener. For instance, the skill of paraphrasing, or stating in your own words what you heard a speaker say, is useful for improving your aptitude for many different kinds of listening. The skills of questioning and reflecting the speaker's thoughts and ideas are other useful behaviors toward improved listening. Further, we discussed how avoiding a number of bad listening habits, or listening blocks, is an important step toward better listening. Common listening blocks include *comparing* what others are saying to our own situation instead of listening, *mind reading*, *rehearsing* our own message instead of focusing on the speaker, *filtering* the message, *prejudging* the message of the other person, giving *advice* instead of listening fully, *debating* with the speaker before listening completely to the message, needing to *be right*, and *derailing* or *placating* the speaker.

Part of becoming a more effective listener requires that you consider the many barriers in the context of interpersonal communication that get in the way of good listening. We discussed a few such barriers, including the presence of noise, both external and internal, in all listening situations; the reality of information overload in our daily lives; the speech-thought rate differential; and the level of motivation to listen well. Throughout the chapter, we highlighted the need to be aware of cultural differences in listening styles, the effects of culture on our listening, and how new technologies are changing—and sometimes inhibiting—the ways we listen. To conclude, we list the answers to the "myths" and "truths" quiz we used to introduce this chapter:

Truth: *There are important differences between listening and hearing.*

Listening is an active process that takes thought, attention, intention, and some training; hearing is a natural physiological process.

Truth: *In interpersonal communication, listening is as important as speaking.*

Listening is one of the most important interpersonal skills, occupying over 50 percent of our communication time.

Myth: *Effective communication is primarily the responsibility of the speaker.*

As an important part of the communication process, listening is a key element in effective communication.

Myth: *Listening is a passive activity that is accomplished pretty easily.*

Actually, listening is an active activity that requires motivation, mindfulness, and skill. As you learned throughout this chapter, good listening is something that is hard, takes work, and is a very active process.

Myth: *Listening is one aspect of communication that is similar across all cultures.*

As with almost all other aspects of interpersonal communication, culture greatly influences the way one listens, the value placed on listening, and how, when, with whom, and in what form one listens.

Key Terms

Active listening	High-context cultures
Appreciative listening	Information overload
Asynchronous listening	Internal noise
Comprehensive listening	Low-context cultures
Critical listening	Mindfulness
Empathic listening	Paraphrasing
External noise	Pseudo-listening

Suggested Contemporary Readings

C. S. Bentley. "Listening in the 21st century." *International Journal of Listening* 14 (2000): 129–142.

K. R. Dillon and N. J. McKenzie. "The influence of ethnicity on listening, communication competence, approach, and avoidance." *International Journal of Listening* 12 (1998): 106–121.

W. Ford, S. Zabava, A. Wolvin, and S. Chung. "Students' self-perceived listening competencies in the basic speech communication course." *International Journal of Listening* 14 (2000): 1–13.

K. Halone and L Pecchioni. "Relational listening: A grounded theoretical model." *Communication Reports* 14 (2001): 59–71.

W. M. Purdy. "Listening, culture and structures of consciousness: Ways of studying listening." *International Journal of Listening* 14 (2000): 47–68.

A. Wolvin and C. G. Coakley. "Listening education in the 21st century." *International Journal of Listening* 14 (2000): 143–152.

Chapter Activities

1. Using one of the electronic databases in your library, use the keywords *listening* and *culture* or *technology* to locate at least two articles that enhance your learning in this chapter on how listening is changing in our global environment and due to the technological advances of the twenty-first century. Share what you learned from those two articles in a small-group discussion with others in your class. Discuss the ways in which listening as an interpersonal communication skill is different now than it was three decades ago.

2. Over the course of the next day or so, select at least one interpersonal conversation in which you decide you are going to listen mindfully, being fully present in the moment and in what the other person is saying. Then select another conversation in which you intentionally engage in one of the blocks to listening (such as derailing, rehearsing, filtering, or mind reading). Compare the two experiences. How did the other people in these two interactions respond to you? Were their responses similar or different? If they were different, how and why? How often do you find yourself engaging in one or more of the blocks to listening identified in this chapter?

3. Try this activity in class: Have one person in class write down the details of a recent event (for example, an interesting experience of getting through security at the airport,

when you almost had your car stolen, an accident you witnessed, a discussion with your advisor about what classes you need to register for next year, or a family vacation you recently had). That person should read his or her description of the event to one person in your class so that others cannot hear it. After listening, have that person share the story with another person, and then the listener should share it with yet another person. Repeat this activity until the story has been told and retold about five to seven times, each time making sure the next person does not hear the story. The last person who listened to the story should retell the story to the entire class. Compare this version to your original version. Why and how did the story change from your original story? Discuss as a class why, even when we try, we cannot listen to and remember accurately every detail of what we hear. What can we do to improve our listening and comprehension?

4. In a small group, practice your paraphrasing skills. Select a topic that most people in your group believe is interesting and feel strongly about (for instance, pro-life/pro-choice or a campus policy currently under discussion). Discuss this topic for 5–10 minutes. Each person in the group is required to use paraphrasing at least two times during the discussion. After the discussion, talk about how the discussion went when paraphrasing was being used. How might the discussion have been different if people had not been required to paraphrase the statements of others? What functions did paraphrasing serve in this discussion? Discuss the role of paraphrasing and how you might use it in your daily conversations with others.

5. Visit the Web site of the International Listening Association (*http://www.listen.org*). While there, go to the "Quotations" menu and browse the hundreds of quotations related to listening and learning. Select two quotes that you think are most insightful or revealing about how you think about or approach listening. Be ready to share your selection of quotes with the class and explain why you selected them.

6. Take time in your semester to do an important service at a local community organization (such as an elementary school, shelter for those who are homeless, community organization for teens, or assisted-living facility or nursing home). While there, pay careful attention to the role that listening plays in this particular communication environment. You should carefully note the many kinds of listening that are used, and reflect on the way the communication context demands certain listening skills and/or adaptations. For instance, what are the unique challenges or demands when listening interpersonally to people at a nursing home? What makes you an effective listener in this environment versus what might be effective in an elementary school or at a shelter for teens? Write an application paper in which you identify how you put into practice your new listening skills while working in this community organization. While there, also try to practice and model mindful listening to the others at your site. ✦

Chapter 8

Creating Positive Interpersonal Climates

Contemporary Issues:
Gay Students Face Abusive Social Climates

Most high school students feel a bit of trepidation about going to school. They might feel insecure about making friends and fitting in; they might be nervous about the pressures of peers, of being "cool," and of academic achievement. For Michael, however, going to high school was not just about the normal jitters of a teenager trying to fit in; it was about daily verbal and physical harassment. Michael, who is gay, was 14 when he realized how dangerous his high school in New Jersey really was. Being called "faggot," "homo," and "queer" was just the beginning. The climate at Michael's school soon turned violent. According to his story, published at CNN.com, Michael's life was threatened a number of times.[1] One time, he explained, "They pinned me up against the fence . . . and they started taking their shots—punching me, kicking me . . . they were just chanting 'kill the faggot, kill the faggot'."

According to statistics reported in the CNN.com story, nearly half of all gay and lesbian students don't feel safe at school. According to the study, 70 percent of the students polled report being taunted, sexually harassed, shoved, kicked, punched, and even beaten. Most of them were the targets of frequent slurs. Over one-third of the students polled said that many of the slurs came from their teachers.

According to this study and many others like it, today's school climate is one of the scariest places gay students know.[2] It's an environment where experts believe hateful words are paving the way toward violence. Counselors report that kids still think it's cool to attack gay kids. As one African American student in the study explains, "It's OK to say a gay joke . . . everybody sits around and laughs." Because homophobia is among the last prejudices to be acceptable in public, many students—and even teachers—do not realize the hurtful and harmful environment that such verbal threats against gays and lesbians create.

The communication climate of an environment is a key factor in determining what kinds of behaviors are expected and approved of in a particular context. In general, a communication climate is the overall mood or feeling we experience when we enter an environment, or the atmosphere of a particular context or relationship. The idea of a communication climate can be applied to interpersonal relationships, referring to the emotional tone of a relationship, or can be about a social context, such as the climate between friends or, in the case of Michael and other gay students, the social climate at school.

The idea of interpersonal climate has gained a great deal of attention recently as a way to understand interpersonal and relational communication. For instance, think about the different kinds of relationships you have. You probably can identify that each one has a different feeling or pervasive mood. That mood or feeling is the interpersonal climate of the relationship. Although you might have never thought about it in these terms, the climate of a relationship has a lot to do with determining the way people communicate with each other, and explaining why certain reactions and patterns exist between people. As the climate of hate determined the communication assaults waged against Michael and his gay peers, so does the climate of a relationship determine the reactions and behaviors present within a relationship.

In this chapter we will discuss the way in which communication climates develop, particularly in the interpersonal context. We will introduce the idea of communication competence and explore how you can use the idea of competent communication to create the most satisfying communication climates possible. We will also explain how to transform negative interpersonal climates into positive ones. Throughout this chapter, you will be able to apply a number of the interpersonal concepts already discussed in this text. Specifically, you should be able to distinguish between confirming and disconfirming messages and between supportive and unsupportive behaviors, and explain how each of these distinctions relates to creating more positive interpersonal climates. After being introduced to the idea of communication competence, you will also learn how to increase your own competence as a communicator.

As the title indicates, this chapter is about creating positive communication climates. The idea of what is "positive" is a perceptual and cultural variable, as you learned in Chapters 2 and 3 and throughout this text, so you should keep in mind as you read that what is generally defined as positive in U.S. culture may not parallel your definition of positive emotion or communication behaviors. For instance, although some of the communication behaviors that researchers suggest will contribute to a more positive communication climate might not apply to every cultural and co-cultural group, the research does highlight those behaviors that generally contribute to a positive communication climate for many people in the United States in a variety of interpersonal contexts. This chapter is about exploring those behaviors and introducing the idea of communication competence—an idea and framework that should aid you in applying many of the skills and concepts you have been reading about in the previous chapters, and will read about in those yet to come, particularly the next chapter on conflict.

Myths About Interpersonal Communication

One of the common myths held by individuals is that some people are just competent communicators and some are not, and that the "feeling" of a relationship—or the climate, as we call it—is something that is impossible to change. As you should have realized by this point in the book, there is a lot that each of us can learn about being better interpersonal communicators and a lot of choices we can make in our own communication that affects others' communication as well. A number of other myths exist in this area of communication, including some in the following list. As in other chapters, identify those you think are myths (M) and those you think are true (T):

_____ The climate of a relationship is the same thing as the culture of relationship.

_____ It takes only one person to create or change the climate of a relationship.

_____ Being competent as a communicator is a relatively simple concept.

_____ Communicating with certainty is generally an effective way to communicate.

_____ Responding in a defensive way is always bad.

The information in this chapter should assist you in clarifying the nature of these myths and truths as well as others you might have about the nature, or climate, of our interpersonal relationships.

Defining Positive Communication Climates and Increasing Communication Competence

Like the weather, some of your relationships are probably warm and sunny, some cold and stormy, and yet others fair and mild. Some change rapidly, and some have more stable climates. Like the weather on a particular day or in certain seasons, relationships tend to have a particular feeling or a mood about them—what we might call the *temperature* of the relationship. This mood or feeling, as we described in the chapter opener, is the **communication climate** of that relationship. Although similar to the idea of relationship culture—that "unique private world" you share with those in your personal relationships—that we introduced earlier and will elaborate on fully in Chapter 10, climate is the overall feeling in a relationship, often guiding the nature of the relationship culture that develops. Relationship climate is always guided by issues of the larger cultural context, and by the rules developed within the relationship culture.

Although climate was originally a metaphor used by organizational researchers to help them evaluate and examine the work environment of corporations and other organizations,[3] it remains a useful concept for interpersonal communicators because it allows us to look at the patterns and behaviors in a relationship with greater clarity and understanding. For instance, compare the climate or emotional tone of one of your relationships where there is a great deal of satisfaction and loving messages exchanged, and where most comments are perceived as positive and helpful, to a relationship where there is general dissatisfaction, hurtful messages are common, conflict is often heated and unresolved, and even "neutral" comments are responded to defensively. Comparing these two relationships should make clear the difference between the two communication climates of these relationships.

Research repeatedly reveals the connection between climate and relationship success and satisfaction. For instance, as we will discuss in detail in Chapter 11, many researchers have been able to identify those communication patterns that separate happy from unhappily married couples. In satisfying relationships, couples often have communication climates in which confirming, or being positive to each other, is a pattern; in the unhappy couples, however, there are often long series of complain-defend interactions, where one member complains and the other defends him- or herself, often 10 times in a row or more.[4] According to two experts in interpersonal conflict, the key difference in the satisfaction or dissatisfaction of personal relationships is how members manage conflict in those relationships.[5] Not surprisingly, patterns of conflict are reflected in, and affected by, the communication climate of the relationship.

How Does a Communication Climate Develop?

You may be wondering how a communication climate develops. It's an important question given that climate is so closely related to satisfaction and experiences in interpersonal relationships. The climate of a relationship begins to develop immediately as people start to interact. The nature of their verbal and nonverbal messages—either confirming or disconfirming, supportive or unsupportive—is the key to what kind of climate will develop. Although you can't change the weather forecast—whether it will rain, snow, or be sunny tomorrow—you *can* change the communication climate in your interpersonal relationships. The good news is that it doesn't necessarily take two people to change the climate of a relationship. Because our choices as communicators can greatly affect how others respond, even slight changes in our communication tone, approach, and choices can greatly affect the way others choose to communicate and, ultimately, the communication climate of our interactions

Happier couples tend to have more positive communication climates. What is the communication climate like in relationships that you find satisfying? How does it compare to relationships that cause you more grief than good?

and relationships. For instance, if you are at work and one of your coworkers is expressing a concern about some information you included in a report, you can choose to respond in a hostile, defensive, and sarcastic tone ("What was wrong with what I wrote?!"), or you could respond in a more positive and inquisitive way that suggests you are genuinely interested in finding out what is wrong ("What was wrong with what I wrote?"). Just the tone of your voice can greatly affect the entire interaction and the overall climate of the relationships you develop with others.

Most people wish they were highly competent and skilled at interpersonal communication but falsely believe that most highly competent communicators are just naturally savvy as interpersonal communicators. In reality, communication competence is not overly complicated. Below, we explore two basic principles of communication competence and explain how they can be used to develop more positive communication climates.

Communication Competence: A Key in Developing Positive Climates

Think of people you know whom you'd define as competent communicators. What kinds of skills or behaviors do they have? Are they friendly? A good listener? Are they clear and convincing? Do they manage conflict well? Do they respect others' opinions? Are they funny? Other-centered? Easy to talk to? Do they show concern for your moods? Do they ask good questions? Are they interesting? Are they eloquent when they speak? Do they have good ideas and know when to share them? What defines the "competent" communicator in terms of style, skills, and ability is different not only from person to person, but also from culture to culture and between members of co-cultural groups, such as males and females and those of various ethnic groups, those of different ages, and even people from various regions of the country. Further, the standards you use to judge a person's competence vary in different communication contexts. In the public context, such as giving a speech to a large audience, being *competent* is very different from being *competent* in interpersonal communication with friends and family members, and being accurate and concise might be more important than being friendly or a good listener.

There are two ways we can identify communication competence. **Communication competence** is the ability to be judged as both *effective* and *appropriate* in a given communication situation.[7] According to this definition, you are a competent communicator when you can achieve your goals, which demonstrates **effectiveness**, while also taking into account the needs and expectations of other people, which demonstrates **appropriateness**. An easy way to think about it is this: "Effectiveness represents getting your way and appropriateness reflects getting along with others."[8] Competence consists of both these attributes, not just one or the other. So to be competent, you need to exhibit both effective *and* appropriate behaviors.

Let's talk a little more about each of these criteria. If you are trying to persuade a friend to loan you his car so you can travel to see your significant other on the weekend, you are effective if he allows you to take his car. You have achieved your goal. But if you use threats, verbal assaults, and bribery as a way to persuade your friend to say "yes" to your request to borrow his car, are you fulfilling the expectations of your friend and taking into account his goals in the situation? Probably not. In other words, the *appropriateness* of your persuasive strategies was low; in this situation, your behaviors were not only offensive to your friend, but also had negative consequences for him. He might have felt that you broke a trust he had in your friendship by threatening to share private information with others, and might have been hurt by the way you talked to him. He also might have found your behaviors inappropriate because the rules of your friendship call for mutual respect and negotiation, not for verbal assaults and aggressiveness.

Relationships rules, those jointly understood rules that are developed within the context of a relationship and guide what behavior is appropriate and expected in that relationship, often serve as a basis for defining appropriateness of communication. For instance, if there is a rule (which might be implicit or explicit) in your friendship that you celebrate each other's birthdays with small gifts and/or cards, it would be inappropriate and offensive if you were to only acknowledge your friend's birthday with a verbal "Happy birthday." In another friendship, the rule might be that anything more saying, "Happy birthday" is too much, and "overdoing it" with a gift would be inappropriate and embarrassing to the other. The rules of any relationship define what is appropriate and guide how one would judge the behaviors of another in that relationship.

Communication competence is culture specific, so communication that is effective and appropriate in one culture or co-cultural group might be perceived very differently in another. For instance, in Ireland it is not unusual to have extended conversations with others (even strangers); to greet one another using the national greeting, *"Cead mile failte"* ("One hundred thousand welcomes"); and to be invited in for something to drink or eat when just passing by or asking for directions.[9] In another culture, such behaviors would be seen as inappropriate for a stranger. For many women who use a feminine cultural form to communicate, for instance, where communication and mundane talk often serve to form and cement relationships, effective communication would likely be defined very differently than it would for those who use a masculine form of communication. A recent study, for instance, suggests that the way men and women communicate via e-mail is very similar to their styles during in-person conversations. The study found that masculine communicators are more brief, less prompt, and more "functional" than women, who almost never send one-word responses and who respond in more elaborate ways in their e-mails.[10] Even in the world of electronic messaging, perceptions of what is appropriate and effective are important.

Although the criteria of effectiveness and appropriateness might at first seem contradictory, they are actually quite complementary. For instance, achieving your goals (effectiveness) is often the result of getting along with others (appropriateness). Think of a time when you were able to achieve an interpersonal goal, such as persuading your professor to change your grade. If you call your professor and leave an irate voice message stating, "I'm coming to your office to discuss the ridiculous grade you gave me. I can't believe you could be so stupid for a person with your credentials! I'll be there at 4 p.m. and hope you're ready to hear what I have to say!" what are your chances of achieving your goal? Probably not as great as they would be if you would consider the appropriateness of your message, taking into account the needs and expectations of the other person. In this case,

It can sometimes be challenging to be both effective and appropriate at the same time in our interactions, especially in those where there are power differences between us and the person we're communicating with. What are some ways you think different power bases can make either appropriateness or effectiveness more difficult to achieve?

your professor is a person with human feelings and probably expects, given the context of the professor-student relationship, that you will be respectful of the rules that guide appropriate communication in such a relationship. A more appropriate voice message, delivered in a pleasant and friendly tone, might be, "Professor Johansen, this is Gary and I'm wondering if I could make an appointment with you to talk for a minute about my grade? I'd like to run a few things by you and ask you to explain a few items on that last test that I got wrong. I'm free at 4 p.m. today if you happen to be also. I'll try stopping by and I hope you'll be free so we can chat for a minute. Thanks." The odds of achieving your goal (being effective) by using this more respectful (appropriate) tone of voice and message are much greater than if you were inappropriate. Before reading on, try to think about a few of your recent interpersonal interactions where the criteria of appropriateness and effectiveness were both met. Did one aspect of competence seem to enhance the other?

Competence is never an absolute or constant; we might be competent in one situation or in one relationship, but not in another. And we might be competent at one time in a relationship but not at another. In a relationship with a long history of violent outbursts (a turbulent, tornadic climate), for example, you might not expect or attempt to be effective. Instead, you might opt for appropriate behaviors, those you know are least likely to incite the abusive temper of the other. Or, in a relationship with a positive climate like a sibling relationship, you might be willing to divulge a secret to another family member if that secret would end up helping your sibling solve a problem. Your divulging of the secret might be inappropriate in the eyes of your sister, but is a choice you make at the risk of effectively helping her solve a serious problem or issue. As you will see below, the behaviors most commonly associated with positive communication climates are those that take into account both effectiveness and appropriateness in a given communication context. As you read about them next, ask yourself the question, "Is this behavior likely to be judged as both effective and appropriate?" And if you generally keep this question of competence in mind during all of your interpersonal interactions, you are much more likely to be able to create or alter communication climates as you desire.

In Applied Concepts (Box 8.1), we summarize the communication strategies offered in a pamphlet entitled "Talking With Kids About Tough Issues." As you review the strategies presented in the pamphlet, notice how the concept of communication competence is at the core of all of the advice given to parents for creating a positive communication climate when talking with kids. The authors of the pamphlet are basically advising parents to carefully consider the appropriateness and effectiveness of their communication when talking with their children about difficult issues such as violence, drugs, sex, and even terrorism. See for yourself whether you can judge both the effectiveness and appropriateness of the suggestions offered.

Box 8.1

Applied Concepts
'Talking Competently With Kids'

Lynne Dumas, an expert in family communication, has put together a resource for parents entitled "Talking With Kids About Tough Issues."[11] It is designed as a helpful tool for parents to think about how to talk with kids about issues such as drugs, violence, AIDS, and sex. Parents often have a difficult time creating a climate of openness with their children around these and other tough topics. This resource provides tips and strategies for creating a positive communication climate and offers the following 13 "rules of thumb" for talking with children about just about anything, especially difficult or taboo topics. As you read, keep in mind the two criteria for judging communication competence—effectiveness and appropriateness—and determine whether you think a rule meets one or both of the criteria of communication competence. According to Dumas, when talking with kids, parents should:

1. *Create an open environment:* Children will turn to parents when it comes to sensitive subjects—like AIDS or violence—if they feel parents will be receptive to their questions. It's up to parents to create such an environment by being encouraging, being supportive, and offering positive reinforcement for questions asked. Be sure to validate your child's curiosity.

2. *Consider your child's temperament:* Be aware that how you respond to your child and the kind of open environment you create should depend on your child's personality and approach to life.

3. *Respect your child's feelings:* Allowing children to express their feelings openly will increase the chances that they'll come to you whenever they have a problem.

4. *Understand the question:* Be sure you understand exactly what your child is asking so that you avoid talking above the head of your child.

5. *Always be honest:* By answering honestly—always—in response to his or her questions, you increase your child's capacity to trust you.

6. *If you don't know something, admit it:* Children will look up to parents more if they are honest and admit not knowing something than if they lie. Try "I don't know" or "Let's find out" instead of offering false or misleading facts.

7. *Don't leave big gaps:* Although you might not want to share all the details of a particular issue because of your child's developmental stage, you should be careful to not leave too big of a gap in the information. Children often fill in the blanks themselves, which can end up creating a good deal of concern and confusion.

☞

☞
8. *Use age-appropriate language:* Always speak to your child with language and words he or she can understand. For most children, using simple, short words and straightforward explanations is best.

9. *Get feedback:* If you're wondering if your child has understood a certain topic, just ask. Usually allowing a little time in between your discussion and asking her to tell you what she understood is best.

10. *Be patient:* Listen patiently to your child and allow him to finish his sentences before finishing them for him. By doing so, you're communicating that he's worthy of your time.

11. *Say it again and again:* Most children can only take in small bits of information at any given time, so be ready for them to ask again and again about the same topic. Repetition is normal and good, especially when it comes to tough topics.

12. *Give them your undivided attention:* Stop folding the laundry or working on the computer when you want to talk to your child. Try looking him or her right in the eye and giving your child all of your attention. It helps build your child's self-esteem when you give him or her your undivided attention and will give your message added conviction.

13. *Speak separately to kids of different ages:* If your children are of different ages, it's best to talk with them separately. Think carefully about the different kinds of information you will give to a 13 year old versus a 6 year old.

Creating a positive and open communication climate with children can be challenging, especially on topics that are not easy to discuss for many parents and children. After reading the suggestions above, which of the 13 do you think fit the criterion of appropriateness? Effectiveness? Both? Decide for yourself, and then share your ideas with others in your class. Remember that judgments of competence are individual and perceptual, so your answers might be slightly different than others. Overall, these 13 tips seem to be consistent with the ideas for creating positive communication climates that we discuss in this chapter.

Family communication scholars report that openness in communication between parents and children, especially around topics such as sex and other difficult issues, is key in creating satisfying relationships in the family.[12] Openness is also a characteristic of competent communication, which considers the goals of the communicator as well as others, in this case children, in the interactions.

Confirming and Disconfirming Messages

One of the key differences between a positive and negative communication climate in the dominant culture of the United States is the degree to which people feel *valued*.[13] We specify that this is true for communicators in the dominant culture of the United States because, as you have been learning throughout this text, what is perceived as confirming and disconfirming communication—like all communication—is culture specific. The behaviors we will discuss in this section are those that reflect the values and communication style of many people in the United States, although not all cultural or co-cultural groups would define these behaviors in the same way. The validation of another's self-image and self-definition is **confirming communication**. It sends the message "To me, you exist and are significant." **Disconfirming communication** refers to those messages that negate another's self-image. A disconfirming message essentially says, "You do not exist and are not significant to me."[14]

You can probably think of many ways in which you communicate to others that they are important and that their existence is significant to you. As you might have guessed, disconfirming messages tend to create negative communication climates and confirming messages tend to do the opposite. Let's take a look first at what kinds of confirming messages you might choose to use if you want to develop a more positive communication climate.

Types of Confirming Messages. Confirming messages come in three forms. Using these types of messages won't automatically result in a positive communication climate, but they are most likely to help you create the positive communication climate you desire:[15]

- *Recognizing* the other: By saying hello to people as they walk by you on campus, sending an e-mail to your aunt, or making eye contact with your spouse or partner in the morning, you are recognizing that person on a most basic level. You probably have all had the experience of someone not recognizing you; they might have failed to return your e-mail, forgotten to send a message on a very special day, or avoided looking at you when you were in the same room. Even the most simple lack of recognition creates a tense, undesirable, and negative climate. So when you're thinking about how to create a positive communication climate, be aware of the many ways that you can communicate your recognition of another person.

- *Acknowledging* the other: Acknowledging another takes recognition to the next level. When you acknowledge another, you don't just recognize they exist; you actually respond to their communication in a direct and relevant way. For instance, if your friend is upset about something that you have done, you might acknowledge her by saying, "I see that you're really upset with me. I don't fully understand why my talking with your mother would make you so mad, but I am truly sorry. Can we talk more about it?" When you acknowledge someone, you engage in one of the most valued forms of confirmation because your direct response encourages the other person to continue discussion and further communicate his or her ideas and/or feelings. Imagine the above conflict interaction if you failed to acknowledge the other person's point of view; instead, you ignored her feelings and did not invite further discussion about the conflict. Lack of acknowledgment often comes in the form of not listening or engaging in a type of pseudo-listening. Lack of acknowledgment also sends a disconfirming message and assists in developing negative communication climates.

- *Endorsing* the other: While recognizing and acknowledging the other do *not* require that you agree with his or her opinions or ideas, endorsing is a form of confirmation that means you do agree that what they have to say is, in whole or in part, *true, accurate*, and *okay*. Recall that to confirm someone is to communicate that they have *value*. When you endorse someone, you are communicating the ultimate form of valuing because you are saying, in essence, you think the other person is right. Endorsement often can take a nonverbal form, such as positive reinforcement of ideas through head nods, smiling, and eye contact. In the example used above, endorsing is reflected in the statement: "You have every right to be mad at me for talking with your mother without your permission. I'm very sorry about that. It wasn't the right thing to do."

Like all forms of communication, confirming messages are a matter of perception. What you perceive as an endorsing behavior might be perceived differently by your sister, friend, or coworker. Further, you might unintentionally communicate lack of recognition or acknowledgment to a friend or colleague because you are busy and haven't been able to return an e-mail they sent to you. Although unintentional, such perceived messages can have an impact on the communication climate because, as we learned in Chapter 3, our perception is our reality. A recent study conducted in England reflects this idea precisely. The study, conducted by a leading marriage guidance organization, suggests that the Internet is one of the latest threats to marriage because obsessive use of the medium by one spouse leaves the other spouse as an "Internet widow."[16] Although to one spouse, Internet use is perceived as necessary or warranted, the other spouse often perceives it differently. In the study, 1 in 10 couples report the Internet as a problem in their marriage. They cite behaviors that reflect a lack of recognition of one spouse, the most basic form of confirmation. Some of the couples report a lack of acknowledgment from their spouses when the spouse spends hours downloading software or surfing the Web and spends less time engaging in meaningful discussions with them.

We need to be aware of all the ways we are communicating in confirming and disconfirming ways if we want to build more positive communication climates. As we do so, we should also keep in mind the criteria of communication competence—is my behavior effective *and* appropriate?—as we select those behaviors that contribute to a more positive interpersonal communication climate.

Types of Disconfirming Messages. The opposite of confirming messages, disconfirming messages, tends to cause another person to question his or her self-worth or communicates in some way that they are *not valued*. Like confirming messages, disconfirming messages are dependent upon the perceptions of the communicator. We can identify some ways that you can disconfirm someone in an interaction.[17] As you read, think of ways and times you witnessed each type of communication or engaged in these kinds of disconfirming messages yourself.

You can disconfirm someone by:

- Offering *no* response: When you ignore the other person or what the other person said, you are disconfirming them. Ignoring is obvious when we simply don't answer a question, do not respond to the comments of another, do not wave to or make eye contact with someone who is looking or waving at us, or do not return a phone call or e-mail.

- Offering an *interrupting* response: We all have probably experienced the feeling of being interrupted. It sends the message "What I have to say is more important than what you are saying." Interrupting is disconfirming for this very reason.

- Offering an *irrelevant* response: When you respond to another person in an irrelevant way, you are saying something that has little or nothing to do with what the other person is expressing. When your father says, "How did your communication class turn out this semester?" your irrelevant response "We really should think about how I'm going to get back to school in the fall" would disconfirm your father and his interest in your work at school.

- Offering a *tangential* response: A tangential response is one where we acknowledge what the other person is saying, yet quickly shift the topic to something different. When we do so, we "take the rug out from under" the other person; in other words, we use what the other person has said to take over the conversation. When your partner says, "Honey, we've got a lot of bills to pay this month. I think we should sit down this weekend and figure out how to make it all work," a tangential response to your partner would be "Bills are important; we should make a plan for those. That reminds me: I was thinking about what I might do after graduation." Tangential responses are not as disconfirming as some of the others because they involve some recognition of the other.

- Offering an *impersonal* response: Impersonal responses are those where the response is not interpersonal, but feels like it is meant for anyone who wants to listen. An impersonal response is disconfirming because it sends the message that the person talking is not necessarily interested in us or our opinions per se, but in the response of anyone. An impersonal response to your friend who is sharing her news of her new job might be "A new job? The state of the economy is an issue worth exploring. We should all be concerned about the rate of new jobs in our country."

- Offering an *incoherent* response: An incoherent response is one that, on the surface, might appear to be a reasonable reaction but actually does not make much sense at all. If your coworker says, "Do you have a sense of what that client was asking for in terms of a deadline?" an incoherent response would be something like "It seems like a lot to ask, ya know. I was thinking, like, maybe a few more weeks would be good." Incoherent responses often include clichés and verbal fillers like "ya know" and "like." They are disconfirming because they simply do not acknowledge the actual message or question with a relevant and sensible response.

- Offering an *incongruous* response: An incongruous response is an example of a disconfirming message because incongruous messages often are self-contradicting. For instance, when our verbal and nonverbal messages contradict one another (smiling while saying, "I'm really upset with you," or laughing while saying, "I'm taking your complaint seriously"), we are sending an incongruous response.

Disconfirming messages of all kinds send the message "You do not exist and are not important to me." In dominant cultures of the United States, where clear messages and direct communication are often valued, communicating in disconfirming ways often creates negative feelings and sets up a negative communication climate.

Within the framework of communication competence, most of the disconfirming messages cited above would not meet the criterion of appropriateness, as they don't take into account the needs and self-worth of the other. Many of them might also be ineffective, depending on the context and the goal of the communicator. The disconfirming responses cited above are not only inappropriate and ineffective, but also might likely lead to divorce. Studies of thousands of couples reveal that showing contempt (such as rolling the eyes when the other is talking) is one of the most destructive behaviors in a marriage.[18] Contempt is a kind of disconfirming response that basically says to the other person, "You're an idiot."

In the world of business, being a competent interpersonal communicator has recently become more important than ever. With rising unemployment rates, the failure or downsizing of many dot-com companies, corporate hiring freezes, and the slowing of the economy after the September 11, 2001, terrorist attacks, many people are looking for employment in a very tight and highly competitive job market. In the first half of 2001 alone, 80,000 employees of dot-com companies were laid off; over 65 percent of those laid off reported still looking for work six months to one year later.[19] The most important skills you can develop to increase your chance of landing a job during tough times are those related to confirming behaviors and interpersonal competence. "People skills," including recognizing, acknowledging, and endorsing, may be more important than technical expertise when employers are deciding whom to hire.[20] One manager at a company in California counts how many times the prospective hire interrupts him during an interview. Confirming behaviors, in the context of appropriateness and effectiveness, will help not only your personal relationships, but your professional prospects as well.

For another look at how confirming and disconfirming communication plays out in real life, Self-Reflection (Box 8.2) summarizes the experiences of one woman communicating with her friends, mostly African American women. Take a moment to see how principles of developing positive communication climates are applied in the context of women who get together and share what they call "girlfriend power."

Box 8.2

Self-Reflection

'Girlfriend Power'

A writer named Laura Randolph Lancaster recently wrote an article in *Ebony* magazine based on her experience of "girls' night out." An excerpt of that article is below.[21] As you read, reflect on the principles and types of disconfirming and confirming messages. As you will see, this woman has identified, based on her experience, what she believes is important in creating a positive communication climate among her friends:

> After more than 20 years of organizing, hosting, and attending all kinds of "girls' nights out," I know one thing for sure: When Sisters get together for this time honored event, something magical happens. When Black women gather for a few days or a few hours of Sisterhood and Sisterspeak, nerves have a way of calming, problems have a way of solving, anxiety has a way of dissolving. It's called "Girlfriend Power."
>
> No matter what kind of stress we may be facing—a funky job, a failing marriage, a future breakup or breakdown—there's something about the company of women that gets us through it. The type or size of our get-together matters not. Whether it's two Sisters huddling over hamburgers or 20 sisters conversing over caviar, there's something at the core of the experience that helps us cope with the crisis, handle the heartache, deal with the devastation and the damage and the drama.
>
> I am convinced that a large part of that something is the way women communicate with each other. The way that, in our reflections and in our responses, we separate sorrow from the solutions, the feelings from the fixes, the anguish from the answers to it. . . . Women's conversations aren't about solutions—at least not exclusively, although they have their value. They're about comfort and consolation, support and solace, empathy and emotional relief.

Lancaster is suggesting that to her, a positive communication climate has developed among her African American women friends. She calls this "climate" something *magical,* and believes it is based on how her friends, all a part of the African American co-cultural group, communicate with one another when they are together: with empathy, support, and affirmation. In essence, she is describing many of the confirming behaviors summarized in this chapter. Notice how what she does not describe are *impersonal* responses, *impervious* responses, or *interrupting* or *irrelevant* responses. Instead, she describes responses that *recognize, acknowledge,* and *endorse.* In essence, she is describing how friends communicate to each other that they are *valued.* Based on her description of her experience with girls' night out, what else do you think she would include in a list of behaviors essential to developing positive communication climates?

Communication climates, although often magical in how they feel, do not happen by magic or accident. Instead, we create them in our communication choices. As you think about your own experiences that might be similar to those that Lancaster describes above, reflect on what choices you make in your communication that lend to the climate that you have been a part of developing.

Disconfirming Messages and Power

Disconfirming messages often comment on the power differences between communicators. Those who respond in disconfirming ways are suggesting that they have the right—the power—to respond in such a manner.

According to the synergistic perspective on power, the one that is consistent with ideas of communication competence, power is generated and shared by all those involved in an interaction. From a synergistic perspective, individuals should be aware of their own resources and work to generate power for self and others. The use of disconfirming messages—those messages that say, "You are not valued"—tends to undermine synergy, or the power of collaboration, in interpersonal communication. Because disconfirming messages function to put another person down, they are messages that attempt to suppress the power that another individual either has or is perceived to have. For instance, consider the interrupting response, a common type of disconfirming message. If you are excited to share some news with your friend about the purchase of your new car and she interrupts what you are saying to share her news about her recent trip, you might perceive her response as a clear message that her news is more important than your news. Who has control in this conversation? Unless you express your desire to not be interrupted, your friend is exerting control of the conversational topics. Does your friend interrupt all the time in your interactions? Over time, use of these disconfirming messages actually can reveal the power structure of your relationship.

How do you use confirming communication messages to create positive communication climates? What other kinds of messages—either verbal or nonverbal—do you think are crucial in developing positive relationship climates with others?

When another individual, be it a boss, coworker, mother, brother, or intimate partner, uses disconfirming responses consistently over time, what does it reveal about your relationship? What power bases is each person drawing from in the relationship? The person using disconfirming messages is likely drawing on many power bases—expert power, legitimate power, reward power, or others; the cumulative result of using disconfirming messages in your relationships is not synergy and teamwork, but control and self-centeredness. If you recognize that you are often responding to others in one or many of the disconfirming ways we described above, you might want to consider whether your behavior is assisting you in developing the kind of interpersonal relationship—and interpersonal climate—you desire.

Supportive and Defensive Behaviors

Communication researcher Jack Gibb believes that an important part of creating positive relationships and communication climates is the way we handle defensiveness.[22] Gibb has identified six specific behaviors he believes arouse defensiveness in others, and six corresponding supportive behaviors that he says reduce defensiveness. Gibb's typology of these behaviors and the communication climates they create are listed in Table 8.1 and explained more fully below.

Table 8.1 Gibb's Typology of Defensive and Supportive Climates	
Defensive (Negative) Climates	**Supportive (Positive) Climates**
1. Evaluation	1. Description
2. Control	2. Problem orientation
3. Strategy	3. Spontaneity
4. Neutrality	4. Empathy
5. Superiority	5. Equality
6. Certainty	6. Provisionalism

Supportive and defensive behaviors are culturally specific, which means that people from different cultures may perceive them differently. For instance, traditional African beliefs of inter-connectedness and a worldview of interrelatedness are often reflected in the communication patterns of African Americans.[23] A communication practice of some African American individuals is the call-and-response pattern where a speaker (such as a teacher) gives a speech and the listeners (in this case, the students) respond verbally during the speech offering encouragement ("You tell it," or "Right on!"). Individuals from co-cultural groups where the values are different from those in the African culture may see such verbal participation as rude and disruptive or, in terms of communication competence, as inappropriate.

Some of the behaviors listed as creating defensiveness in Table 8.1 might not generate defensiveness in you. As always, behaviors may be perceived differently by those who have certain kinds of power in particular contexts and those who do not. The perception of each participant is often the most important factor in understanding the role of power in the interaction. For instance, violence in family relationships is frequently the result of the abuser perceiving him- or herself as powerless, even though those being abused would argue that the abuser is clearly the one with a variety of power resources. As a result of feeling threatened by a lack of perceived power, the abuser uses violence as a defensive response to the perceived threat, even when that "threat" is a small child. See Practical Research (Box 8.3) for more on how the perception of power plays a key role in violence against children.

Box 8.3
Practical Research
Violence Against Powerless Others

When many people think of violence against women, children, and others in intimate and family relationships, they often think of the abuser as the one with *power*. Research, however, has revealed the importance of looking at how individuals attribute or give power to others in understanding communication and other behavior in violent families. For instance, abusive individuals who engage in violence against others actually tend to attribute more power to the person being abused than they perceive themselves as having.[24] Daphne Blunt Bugental believes that ☞

☞ physically abusive parents often engage in role-reversed relationships with their children. Usually parents have legitimate and/or coercive power over children. However, in the role-reversed relationships, parents tend to attribute high levels of power—possibly legitimate power, coercive power, reward power, and other types—to children. When this happens in families where there is a pattern of violence, Bugental argues, children become highly threatening in the mind of the parent and the parent feels vulnerable, typically putting up his or her defenses against that child and becoming physically abusive toward the child. Abusive parents have reported feeling at risk in the situation, even when the child was only 3 years old.

The nature of our perceptions is very important to consider in all interactions, especially as it related to power. As this research reveals, perceptions of power are often more important than actual power structures.

Evaluation or Description? If you want to create a less defensive and more supportive climate, do you think evaluation or description would be a more appropriate and effective choice? Let's compare the two. When you evaluate, you pass judgment; when you describe, you are inviting another person's interpretations, perceptions, or thoughts without implying blame. According to Gibb, **evaluation** is most often a defense-arousing behavior because when we evaluate ("You are always late"), the person you are talking to is likely to go on guard. Instead, Gibb suggests that **description** is less likely to elicit a defensive response because with description you are not implying that the other person must change behavior. For instance, you could use description by saying, "You must have been busy at work; I noticed you're about an hour late." What do you think the communication climate would be like in a relationship where there were more descriptive statements than evaluative statements? Take a look at some different ways of saying the same thing, and imagine their impact on climate:

Instead of *Evaluation:*	*Try Description:*
"You're crazy!"	"I'm having a hard time understanding what you mean."
"Your crying is really irritating."	"You must be really upset."
"I can't believe you said that."	"When you say things like that, my feelings are really hurt."
"You're so self-centered."	"I feel really unimportant when you say those things."

It is easy to see that by shifting from evaluation communication to description communication, you can quickly change the tone of a communication climate. Skill Building (Box 8.4) gives you a chance to practice transforming messages of evaluation to messages of description.

Box 8.4

Skill Building

Reducing Defensiveness: Practice Description Versus Evaluation

As you just read, one of the ways that we increase defensiveness in a communication climate is by using evaluative communication instead of descriptive communication. In the spaces below, practice rewriting the following evaluative messages in a more descriptive way.

Sample Evaluation: "You can't be serious. That is the stupidest thing I've ever heard!"

Sample Description: *"Your idea is interesting. Could you tell me more about it?"*

Evaluation: "This office is very disorganized."

Description: _____ ☞

☞
> **Evaluation:** "Your family is so weird. I don't think I can visit you next month."
>
> **Description:**_____
>
> **Evaluation:** "What were you thinking? I can't believe you broke the window!"
>
> **Description:**_____
>
> **Evaluation:** "Your report is late. When will you ever get caught up?"
>
> **Description:**_____

Control or Problem Orientation? What does it feel like when someone is trying to control you? According to Gibb, **controlling communication** is a second kind of defense-arousing message because it sends the message "You are inadequate." Implicit attempts to control other people in verbal statements or through nonverbals tell those people that they are ignorant, unable to make their own decisions, uninformed, unwise, or in need of changing their views or attitudes. You can start to see why controlling communication tends to elicit defensiveness in others.

Often, our controlling messages come in the form of subtle nonverbal cues. For instance, when you take the best seat in the room, you are exerting control. When you speak first and most, you are controlling a conversation. When you persuade someone to do it your way, you are controlling the outcome of a situation. When you interrupt, raise your voice, or insist on sharing your opinions even when others have not, you are using controlling communication. Each of these behaviors is likely to contribute to a defensive communication climate.

According to Gibb, a **problem orientation** is much less likely to provoke defensiveness in others. When we take a problem orientation in our communication, we are looking for a way not to persuade another that our way is best, but to work together to find a mutual solution to a problem or issue. A problem orientation sends a very different message than does controlling communication; it says to the other, "You are important," or, "You have good ideas." Can you think of times when you used controlling communication and other times when you used a problem orientation? When you compare the different kinds of communication in these two approaches, you can easily see how control lends to negative climates and a problem orientation to a more positive climate.

Strategy or Spontaneity? Gibb suggests that yet another way we can arouse the defensiveness of others is by strategically planning how we will interact with them, deceive them, manipulate them, and/or persuade them. By **strategy**, Gibb means our ulterior and hidden motives. When others realize that we have a strategy for interacting with them, they are likely to feel like a victim or a guinea pig, or that we used them in a kind of human drama. Think of a time when you used a communication strategy for communicating with another person and he or she realized what you were doing. Or have you ever received a call from a telemarketer? When we realize the strategy behind their persuasive attempts, Gibb suggests that we are likely to get defensive because we feel manipulated. Even when we are not persuading others, we might be using strategy. It is not always bad to have an idea of what and how you are communicating, although Gibb's research has found that when a communicator is perceived as too strategic, a defensive reaction is likely.

Although the term might be misleading, Gibb suggests using **spontaneity** in your communication. Spontaneity is not just communicating "off the cuff" or saying whatever comes blurting out of your mouth, but when others perceive us as spontaneous, straightforward, and honest, the climate of communication is more likely to be positive and open. Contrast the above example of the strategic persuasive moves to the spontaneous conversation you might have with a friend about the deadly effects of cigarette smoking. During a mundane conversation, the topic of smoking comes up. You ask your friend, "Have you ever smoked?" Your friends responds that he will never smoke and explains that not only did his aunt recently die of lung cancer, but his father died when he was very young from lung cancer as well. Your friend tells you of the horror of watching someone you love die of cancer, and growing up not really knowing his father. Your friend has strong, reasoned opinions about the antitobacco campaigns and shares them with you during this conversation. As a result of this honest and spontaneous conversation with your friend, you have changed your opinion about smoking as well. The spirit of such honesty and spontaneity in communication gets at the heart of Gibb's idea of nondefensive climates.

Neutrality or Empathy? See if you can notice the differences in the following conversations between two friends:

Conversation One

Jasmine: "That test was so hard. I can't believe it. I know I didn't do well at all. My grade in this class is going to keep me out of grad school, I just know it."

Regina: "Yeah. Tough one. Hey, what'cha wanna do tonight? Should we go out?"

Jasmine: "I'm completely depressed about this exam. My parents are going to kill me when they see my grades this semester. Ugh. I'm so depressed."

Regina: "Let's get moving. Sitting around here isn't going to help."

Jasmine: "Why are you being so selfish? Can't you see that I'm down here? What kind of friend are you?"

Conversation Two

Jasmine: "That test was so hard. I can't believe it. I know I didn't do well at all. My grade in this class is going to keep me out of grad school, I just know it."

Regina: "You sound really upset. That test is really important to you, eh? Is there anything you can do extra in class to boost your grade?"

Jasmine: "Yeah, I am really depressed about it. I guess I could talk to my professor. I do still have a big paper due in there, so I can focus on that. It might push me up a grade."

Regina: "It's really stressful when you don't know what grade you're getting. That's a good idea, though. You should call you professor first thing tomorrow."

Jasmine: "You're right. I will. Thanks for listening. Hey, wanna go grab a bite to eat and go out tonight? I could use some company."

Regina: "You bet."

How would you explain the key differences in these conversations? In the first conversation, Regina's communication is neutral, or uncaring and unsupportive. According to Gibb, **neutrality** can provoke defensiveness because neutrality communicates a lack of concern for or indifference toward the other person. When Regina seems not to care for the feelings of her friend Jasmine, the defensiveness in the interaction quickly heightens. By contrast, the second conversation depicts a more supportive and less defensive communication approach called **empathy**. As we discussed in the last chapter, empathy and empathic listening demonstrate concern and understanding of what the other person is feeling and expressing. When Regina uses empathy instead of neutrality, it sends the message to Jasmine that what she is saying is important and that her friend cares about her feelings. The difference in the communication climates being developed here is obvious. Can you think of times when you have used neutrality with a similar outcome? How about the use of empathy? For many people in the United States, neutrality is a clear message that one perceives him- or herself as having the power to remain uninvolved or indifferent.

Empathy, expressed either verbally or nonverbally, is a kind of communication approach that demonstrates concern and care for another's feelings. Have you ever tried using empathy to enhance the climate of one of your relationships? If not, give it a try! You might be surprised just how effective (and appropriate) it can be.

Superiority or Equality? You can probably guess that communicating **superiority** is likely to create defensiveness in others, while communicating equality is more likely to reduce defensiveness. When we communicate to another person that we are *superior* in status, wealth, intelligence, power, physical attractiveness, or even communicative style, we are saying to the other person, "I am better. You are inadequate." You have probably had the opportunity in your life to encounter another person who communicated their superiority to you. How did you feel? Contrast that feeling to a recent interaction where another person communicated that you were equal, maybe in intelligence, power, status, or your interests or abilities. **Equality**, according to Gibb, is a better kind of communication for creating positive communication climates because even though differences might indeed exist in your power, status, or abilities, when you communicate in a way that does not highlight such differences, the message is, "I respect and trust you. Let's work together."

The way people communicate with persons with disabilities reflects a kind of superiority.[25] When we *assume* persons with disabilities cannot speak for themselves, *force* our help on persons with disabilities, *avoid* communicating with persons with disabilities, or *assume* that a disability defines a person, we are communicating a kind of superiority. Instead, we should treat persons with disabilities as persons first. For instance, using the term *persons with disabilities* instead of *disabled people* puts the person before the disability. Although we should avoid assuming that every person with a disability feels the same way, we should consider carefully our language choices. In making these small, but significant, differences in the way we communicate, we send a message of equality and are on our way toward a more positive communication climate in this cultural context, as well as others.

Certainty or Provisionalism? The last behavior that Gibb identifies as having great potential to increase defensiveness in others is called certainty. **Certainty** includes behaviors suggesting that you know all the answers, require no input from others, or believe that your way is right or best. It increases the defensiveness of others because the message you send is, "I am right."

Although some people might mistake certainty for confidence, certainty is the tendency to control others. With confidence, you might feel good about your ideas or opinions, yet still be willing to hear the ideas and perspectives of others and work together.

When you communicate with **provisionalism**, you can reduce defensiveness in others and avoid the pitfall of certainty. Provisionalism includes behaviors that suggest that you do not necessarily have all the right answers and are willing to explore others' input. Certainty might be reflected in the statement said to a colleague, "I have finished this report and it is ready to go. There is no need to change it." In contrast, provisionalism might sound more like, "The report is done, and although I think it is pretty good, there might be some ways to improve it a bit more." There is a high potential for a negative communication climate to develop in a climate of high certainty and low provisionalism.

Of course, none of these behaviors guarantees that a positive communication climate will develop. A great many variables play a role in the way each of these behaviors will be perceived and the many other contextual factors at work in every interaction, such as culture, power, and the perception and preferences of the participants. However, because defensiveness tends to interfere with communication and because the development of positive communication climates and supportive behaviors tend to do the opposite, it is worth exploring the potential impact of these six sets of behavior in your own interpersonal interactions.

There is also a connection here to communication competence. If your goal is to be both effective and appropriate—to be regarded as competent—then your choice for certain behaviors might be different than if your primary goal is just appropriateness, or only effectiveness. For instance, although the likelihood of increasing defensiveness is greater when you use certainty and strategy, if achieving your goal in the interaction is most important, you might consider ways that these can be used effectively by compromising some appropriateness. Your choices for communication should be based on a number of factors, including those related to climate and competence.

Summary

This chapter has explored the ways we can develop more positive communication climates in our interpersonal communication. Specifically, we learned that positive communication climates often develop through the use of confirming behaviors, such as communication that recognizes, acknowledges, and endorses another. We also develop positive communication climates by choosing supportive as opposed to defensive behaviors. Supportive behaviors include using description instead of evaluation, taking a problem orientation instead of being controlling, using spontaneity rather than strategy, displaying empathy instead of neutrality, communicating equality rather than superiority, and employing provisionalism as opposed to certainty in our interpersonal interactions. In addition, the competent communicator—the person whose communication is judged as both appropriate and effective by others—is more likely to build positive communication climates as well as use confirming and nondefensive communication. We conclude by listing the following answers and explanations to the myths and truths quiz that we gave at the beginning of the chapter.

Myth: The climate of a relationship is the same thing as the culture of relationship. Why is this a myth?

The climate of a relationship reflects the general mood or feeling between communicators, just one part of a how a relationship culture develops.

Truth: *It takes only one person to create or change the climate of a relationship.*

Although each person in a relationship plays a role in the communication climate that develops, changes in the behavior of just one person can greatly affect the nature of the overall communication climate.

Truth: *Being competent as a communicator is a relatively simple concept.*

Although learning about interpersonal communication is a complex and ongoing process, the idea of communication competence is the judgment of just two qualities: the *effectiveness* and *appropriateness* of our communication. So it is actually a relatively simple and helpful concept that is easy to understand and apply in all of our interactions.

Myth: *Communicating with certainty is generally an effective way to communicate.*

Although there are times when the communication context calls for certainty, often communicating with certainty can arouse defensiveness in others when it sends the message "My way is the right way."

Myth: *Responding in a defensive way is always bad.* Why is this not true?

Members of different cultural and co-cultural groups perceive defensiveness, like all communication behaviors, differently. It is not always a bad or negative way to communicate, although it is generally associated with negative communication climates in the dominant culture of the United States.

Key Terms

Appropriateness	Empathy
Certainty	Equality
Communication climate	Evaluation
Communication competence	Neutrality
Confirming communication	Problem orientation
Controlling communication	Provisionalism
Description	Spontaneity
Disconfirming communication	Strategy
Effectiveness	Superiority

Suggested Contemporary Readings

D. J. Canary, W. R. Cupach, and R. T. Serpe. "A competence-based approach to examining interpersonal conflict." *Communication Research* 28 (2001): 79–104.

E. Kerem, N. Fishman, and R. Josselson. "The experience of empathy in everyday relationships: Cognitive and affective elements." *Journal of Social and Personal Relationships* 18 (2001): 709–729.

Y. Y. Kim. "Mapping the domain of intercultural communication: An overview." *Communication Year-book* 24 (2001): 139–157.

R. J. Koper and M. A. Jaasma. "Interpersonal style: Are human social orientations guided by general-ized interpersonal needs?" *Communication Reports* 14 (2001): 117–129.

K. S. McNeilis. "Analyzing communication competence in medical consultations." *Health Communi-cation* 13 (2001): 5–18.

M. Morgan and M. L. Hummert. "Perceptions of communicative control strategies in mother-daughter dyads across the life span." *Journal of Communication* 50 (2000): 48–64.

S. A. Myers and K. A. Rocca. "Perceived instructor argumentativeness and verbal aggressiveness in the college classroom: Effects on student perceptions of climate, apprehension, and state motivation." *Western Journal of Communication* 65 (2001): 113–137.

Chapter Activities

1. Identify at least five confirming communication responses you have experienced in the last 24 hours. After doing so, get into a small group in class and share your responses with each other. Are they similar or different from one another? Discuss why there might be differences in your perceptions of confirming behaviors. Also, discuss as a group what it is about confirming behaviors that serves to create more positive communication climates. Are there any other behaviors that you would add to the list of confirming communication?

2. Volunteer at a community-based organization some time during the semester. While working at that organization, assess the communication climate of the people who work at, live at, spend time at, attend, and/or use the resources of this organization in some way. For instance, if you spend time reading books to children at a local center for teen mothers, note the kinds of confirming and disconfirming messages that are used by the mothers, children, staff, and/or volunteers. You can do the same at any organiza-tion: serving meals, helping develop community-action plans, or working with at-risk youth or young adults. Keep a journal in which you provide examples of the various kinds of messages that you believe are contributing to a positive or negative climate (or something in between). Apply your newly developed understanding of communication competence, and note in your journal when you and/or others are being both appropri-ate and effective.

3. Watch a short sitcom or segment from a popular movie, and apply the judgment of communication competence to the characters in the show. When did you see them communicating in effective but not appropriate ways? When did you see them acting appropriately but not effectively? Were any of the characters displaying communica-tion competence, using both appropriate and effective communication behaviors? It is interesting to watch the same show as your peers and discuss if you and your peers have different assessments of the effectiveness and appropriateness of the actors.

4. Using one of the electronic databases in your library, use the keywords *defensiveness*, *climate*, and *power* to find articles related to those topics discussed in this chapter. Select at least one article that extends your learning in this chapter, and share a sum-mary of it with your class.

5. Ask five of your friends and/or family members to share, in writing, their perceptions of you as a communicator and person. Instruct them to be as honest as possible and to be sure they not only describe what you are like but also include examples that support their descriptions. For instance, tell them they might write, "She's thoughtful. For example, she always remembers my birthday." When you get your responses back, use the concepts of communication competence and the Gibb model of defensive and supportive communication to analyze what kinds of behaviors your friends have identified in you. Of the behaviors discussed in this chapter, what matches did you find among the lists you were given? Did any of the perceptions surprise you?

6. Using any common search engine, surf the Web for scales that assess organizational climate. Using the keywords *organizational climate* should provide you with multiple scales to choose from. We found a great one, developed for the educational context, at *http://www.mllc.org/surveys/OCDQ_instrument.htm*. Either use this one or select one of your own, and review the test thoroughly. Determine how many of the questions are related to the principles of building positive communication climates that we discussed in this chapter. Did the scale address issues of confirmation, disconfirmation, defensiveness, and supportiveness in the organizational setting? Were there other ideas in the tests about organizational climate that might be helpful when thinking about interpersonal communication climates? Share you findings in a small group in class. ✦

Chapter 9

Managing Conflict

Contemporary Issues: Mismanaging Emotions During Conflict

When she was 17, Lauren McEntire went to the movies with her best friend, something that she had done many times before. However, this time her best friend brought his new girlfriend with him. As she watched the movie, Lauren began to feel different emotions: "I was jealous. I was scared he wouldn't be my friend anymore. . . . But I didn't know how to tell him how I felt." So Lauren found herself fidgeting nervously in the movie, trying to control her emotions. Without really thinking about it, she yanked the tab off of a can and pressed it into her thumb. Her thumb started to bleed, but with the pain came a greater feeling of control, as well as feelings of anger that she couldn't automatically place. Over the next month, Lauren continued to inflict self-injuries that became progressively more serious until she was carving deep grooves into her skin by using a razor blade.[1]

Lauren's case was highlighted in a 2000 news story that included the following statistic: More than 2 million people in the United States will engage in some form of self-injury during their lives. These individuals represent a cross-section of the general public; however, over 70 percent are women, mostly between the ages of 11 and 26. The most common form of self-injury is cutting, but other variations include burning, hitting, hair-pulling, and not allowing wounds to heal properly. According to Dr. Wendy Lader, people who engage in self-injury "would rather feel the physical pain than the emotional pain." Dr. Lader is a leading expert in self-injury and co-director of Self-Abuse Finally Ends (SAFE) Alternatives, the only in-patient center for self-injurers in the United States.

What makes this case study relevant to a chapter on managing conflict and interpersonal communication? Experts have found that as many as 90 percent of individuals who engage in self-injury share one common element: They grew up in homes where communication between parents and child(ren) was lacking and where conflicts were avoided or completely ignored. Steven Levenkron, author of Cutting: Understanding and Overcoming Self-Mutilation, *believes that inflicting self-injury can be best understood as a nonverbal expression of anger and frustration used when individuals lack the communication skills to express their emotions effectively. In fact, two years after the incident at the movies, Lauren McEntire understands that "self-injury was [her] way of telling people that something was wrong." One of many SAFE program "graduates," Lauren now has learned how to use her voice to express her emotions to others.*

As the title indicates, this chapter focuses on managing conflict. You might be aware of individuals who deal with conflict in self-destructive ways including self-injury. All of us, if we are honest with ourselves, realize that we communicate in both productive and unproductive ways during conflict. Within this chapter, we focus on understanding both productive and unproductive conflict, as well as the nature of conflict as it is understood in different cultures. We also discuss the role that emotions can play during conflict as a means to promote effective conflict management. Last, we offer specific frameworks to help you learn particular strategies that will achieve greater productivity during conflict.

Myths About Interpersonal Communication

One of the myths about self-injury is that individuals who harm themselves are suicidal. While writing this book, we learned that most self-injurers are very careful and controlled when cutting or burning themselves. Their goal is not to inflict serious injuries, only to gain control of the situation by attracting the attention of parents, friends, and others.[2] Similarly, a number of popular myths exist in the area of conflict. See if you can differentiate which statements below are myths (M) and which are truths (T).

_____ Conflict is destructive and should be avoided at all costs.

_____ Conflict is a natural part of all relationships.

_____ Compromise is generally the ideal strategy for conflicts because it results in a win-win situation.

_____ The closer you get to someone, the more opportunities for conflict increase, not decrease.

_____ The source of all conflict is ineffective communication.

_____ Emotions should be ignored when trying to make rational decisions during conflict.

This chapter will help you to dispel some of the myths listed above, as well as others that you might have regarding conflict, emotions, and other topics.

Defining Conflict

When people think of conflict, they typically think of disagreements between individuals who are connected in some regard. Interpersonal conflicts might occur between best friends who find themselves disagreeing about who is the better student, or between strangers who are vying for the last parking space on campus. The connection between the individuals can be fleeting (like those in the parking lot) or more substantial (friends, family members, coworkers, and so on).

No universal definition of conflict exists, but most have a great deal of similarity.[3] We draw something from several of these definitions, and define **conflict** as *interpersonal situations in which two or more individuals perceive their needs or ideas to be at odds with, or opposed to, the needs or ideas of someone else.* Central to this definition is the role that perception plays during conflict. Think back to Chapter 3, where we discussed how perception affects interpersonal communication. Remember that actual disagreements are not necessary for conflict to occur. In fact, many conflicts occur when people have similar needs, ideas, or goals; problems arise when individuals *perceive* these to be different.

For example, consider the case of Felipe and Maria. Both work full-time and attend classes at the local community college a couple of nights a week. Recently they have become engaged and are planning for their upcoming wedding. The closer the wedding date gets, the more conflict they seem to be experiencing, especially when it comes to Maria's mother. Both Felipe and Maria agree that she should be involved in the wedding; however, their perceptions about her involvement are quite different. Felipe feels as if he is being left out of several decisions, while Maria believes that she and her mom are doing Felipe a favor by not including him in all the last-minute details. What Maria and Felipe have yet to understand is that the conflict is not necessarily about the role that Maria's mom is playing. It is more about how each of them perceives her role as it relates to their own needs and ideas.

We can understand conflict as stemming from four basic sources. In the case of Maria and Felipe, the source of conflict was the *perceived interference* of a third party (Maria's mom). Interference occurs when the presence or behavior of one person hinders another's ability to achieve certain goals. One of the things that makes this source of conflict especially volatile is that people often assume that others are aware they are interfering, when this is not always the case. Another widespread source of conflict is *competition over limited resources*. For many of us, conflicts are specifically linked to a shortage of time, money, space, or opportunities. At times, we find that conflicts result when we compete with others for limited resources (e.g., scholarships or the best shifts at work). Other times, the conflict comes when individuals (professors, family, loved ones, employers) want more of a limited resource (like our time and attention) than we can give.

The final two sources of conflicts are *individual differences* and *cultural differences*. Individual differences are probably one of the most common, but least discussed, sources of conflict. Many times, the cause for interpersonal conflict is simple: Two individuals—because of their different personalities, experiences, and desires—disagree. For instance, all human beings have similar basic needs like food, shelter, security, and a sense of belonging. However, they may have vastly different ideas about what each of these means and how each should be achieved.

Differences can also reflect variations in culture (broadly defined to include all those identity markers discussed in Chapter 2). Across cultures there are variations in the ways people understand, value, and engage in conflict. At times, these cultural assumptions (to be described in detail later on in this chapter) themselves can represent the primary source of conflict.

When defining conflict, we must also recognize that intensity levels can vary greatly. *Conflict* is a general term used to describe all types of disagreements between individuals. However, scholars like J. W. Keltner[4] remind us that conflict can range from mild differences and disagreements to fights and wars. Interpersonal communication plays a key role in managing conflict effectively; this can include resolving mild disagreements, for example, before they escalate into full-fledged fights. Ideally, our hypothetical couple, Maria and Felipe, would be able to talk

Conflict is an inevitable part of all relationships.

with one another and work through the emerging conflict about Maria's mom. Yet without a clear understanding of the nature of conflict and without the interpersonal skills to use productive conflict strategies, a satisfactory resolution is less likely.

Thinking About Conflict

Our ability to handle conflict can have both positive and negative effects on the way we see ourselves, how well we are able to manage our personal health, and how effective we are in our personal, social, and professional relationships. That is why it is important to manage conflict effectively. The first step toward this goal is understanding the process by which we can increase our ability to productively engage in conflict. Within this chapter, we focus on two related tasks: (1) becoming more aware of our personal approaches to conflict, and (2) increasing our knowledge of conflict strategies. We hope to empower you with the knowledge you need to make the best choices in managing interpersonal conflict in your life.

Increased Self-Awareness

Many of us have never invested the time to "take inventory" of how we engage in conflict. The times we are most likely to be aware of our approach to conflict occur when we are least likely able to do anything about it. Think about it for a minute: When are we most likely to receive information, from both self and others, about how we manage conflict? For most of us, the answer is during, or immediately following, some sort of conflict. The information we receive is usually critical evaluations of our effectiveness and includes "coulda/shoulda/woulda" (I could have/I should have/I would have) judgments. What we do not usually take time to think about are some of the underlying issues that have fueled the conflict.

Take a moment now to complete the brief self-reflection exercise in Box 9.1. Remember to be as honest with yourself as possible, and attempt to "dig deep" in order to foster the best insights. In Chapter 3, we discussed that each of us has a number of "selves" at work when responding to questions such as these. We may answer the questions according to our actual self, perceived self, or ideal self. Given that tendency, it might be helpful for you to approach family members, friends, or others and have them respond to the same questions about your conflict tendencies. We have found that this is an excellent strategy to receive information about how others view you. It also helps you to focus on your actual behaviors during conflict and not necessarily on those that are ideal or perceived.

Once you have completed the self-reflection exercise, think about your responses. For instance, you may want to take note of any patterns that emerge across the three conflict scenarios. Do they revolve around one issue, or a couple of similar issues? Do they involve the same person, or different people who have a similar relationship with you? How did you respond in each situation? Did you record having similar verbal and nonverbal behaviors across situations? Or did your communication change depending on who the conflict was with, where it occurred, or what it was about? The answers to all these questions, as well as additional ones that we will pose throughout the chapter, represent an important step toward becoming more effective at managing conflict.

BOX 9.1

Self-Reflection

In order to help you understand how conflict happens in specific contexts, please take a few moments and think about your three most recent conflicts. Then complete the information for each.

Conflict #1: _____

Who was involved? _____

What was it about? _____

What were some of your behaviors during the conflict?

Verbal: _____

Nonverbal: _____

How, if at all, was it resolved? _____

_____

Conflict #2: _____

Who was involved? _____

What was it about? _____

What were some of your behaviors during the conflict?

Verbal: _____

Nonverbal: _____

How, if at all, was it resolved? _____

_____

Conflict #3: _____

Who was involved? _____

What was it about? _____

What were some of your behaviors during the conflict?

Verbal: _____

Nonverbal: _____

How, if at all, was it resolved? _____

_____

Power of Socialization

Like all aspects of our communication, what we learned about conflict was gained through the socialization process. Some contemporary communication scholars[5] still point to evolutionary explanations for how we communicate, but our focus here is on the socializing messages that we received about conflict and communication. For instance, we do not dispute that individuals might have been born with a natural tendency toward conflict (aggression, avoidance, compromise, and so on). Still, each of us has been socialized to think about, describe, value, and manage conflict in particular ways. In other words, what did you learn about conflict and how to deal with it?

In many ways, your first communication teachers were your family members and others with whom you spent considerable time early in life. Think about specific instructions that you received from family members about conflict while you were growing up.

"Don't fight with your brother."

"I've had a rough day at work and don't want to hear about any problems."

"Grandma doesn't want you to be mean, so go apologize right now."

"If you can't watch TV without arguing about what channel to watch, then the TV goes off."

"Don't talk back—just do what you're told."

"Don't tell me about what your sister did; go work it out with her."

"Do you have something to say? If so, you better keep it to yourself."

"Tell me why you did what you did and how you think I should handle it."

"You are the oldest; it is your job to see that your younger brothers and sisters get along."

"Let's talk about what the problem is and what options we have to solve it."

Sometimes these messages might be confusing. For instance, you might have been spanked while one of your parents said, "Don't ever do that again; it's not right to hit others!"

The point here is that all of us were given direct and indirect, and likely quite different, messages about conflict and how it should be handled. In addition to receiving specific instructions, we also have been socialized through our observations of others. For instance, how did the adults in your family handle conflict? Was it something that occurred in open, meaningful ways, or behind closed doors with a great deal of arguing? How did you see others deal with conflict? Were particular problems settled through family meetings where everyone had an opportunity to voice their opinions? Or did one person make a decision that everyone else had to adhere to regardless of how they felt about it?

Our family members represent one source of our socialization, but others also exist. The media, for example, can play a significant role in how we come to understand conflict. The books we read, television shows and movies we watch, music we listen to, and games we play all contain messages about dealing with conflict. Sometimes the television shows we watch feature characters doing whatever is necessary to win in their conflicts with others. Some lie, cheat, manipulate, or even use violence when engaged in conflict. However, we might also observe productive ways that conflict is handled on television. These can include open communication with family and friends, using compromise and collaboration, or enlisting the help of a third party to resolve conflict. Yet, trying to model your personal conflict strategies based on how conflict is managed on television can be problematic. The story line of most 22-minute sitcoms, for example, hinges on the emergence of a problem that is solved by the end of the program. Solving problems this quickly is obviously not very realistic. Some viewers of *The Cosby Show*, for example, reported modeling their own family communication after it by having family meetings to address particular areas of conflict. While this might be a productive practice in general, it can be unproductive when individuals expect a quick, neat solution to complex problems that are unlikely to be resolved as easily as it appears on TV.

Our participation in different organizations in our communities also socializes us to deal with conflict. Some of us might have been, or might be currently, involved in school peer-mediation or conflict-resolution programs. In some of these programs, students—as early as the first grade—are taught the value of using "I-messages" in disagreements with classmates ("I am angry that you tore my book" as opposed to "You tore my book on purpose to make me angry"). As the students get older, they can be trained as peer mediators and used to facilitate effective conflict resolution throughout the school. Other individuals might learn about conflict through their religious training. For instance, some people have been taught the value of "turning the other cheek." Others might have learned "never to go to sleep while angry with someone you love."

These examples highlight the fact that all of us are, to a certain degree, a product of our socialization. Early in life we were socialized to approach conflict in fairly specific ways. That is not to say that it is possible, or even desirable, to relearn ideas and values that were a part of our past. Rather, we must increase our awareness of how our early socialization influences our communication as adults. Changing our current approaches to conflict is not always easy. We can learn about new conflict strategies, but unlearning old ones can be difficult. We often fall back on what we know, especially when we are stressed or feel under pressure. However, learning to use new strategies is necessary if we are ever going to maximize the positive outcomes of conflict.

Table 9.1
Conflict Metaphors

Conflict is a war:	Conflict involves a series of battles, strategic moves, and countermoves; at each stage of the war, there are winners and losers.
Conflict is an explosion:	Conflict is the result of lots of quiet anticipation; it's like hearing the time bomb ticking and then watching someone blow up.
Conflict is a trial:	Decisions in conflict depend on which side argues his or her case best; it typically involves evidence, witnesses, and judgments of truth.
Conflict is a struggle:	Conflict is a difficult, ongoing element of a person's life; struggles may be over small issues or larger ones like getting the upper hand.
Conflict is an act of nature:	Conflict, either anticipated or unanticipated, happens to people; while powerful and potentially destructive, it can not be controlled.
Conflict is animal behavior:	Conflict is a natural part of the lives of all creatures; through aggression and violence, only the strong will survive.
Conflict is a mess:	Conflict is filled with low blows, personal attacks, and trash talk; it often is difficult to deal with because it is messy and spills over to other things in our lives.
Conflict is miscommunication:	Conflict is the result of communication breakdown; it can involve one-way communication, the silent treatment, or unproductive talk.
Conflict is a game:	Conflict is a fun activity where those with a competitive spirit can test their skills against others; the goal of conflict is to win.
Conflict is a heroic adventure:	Conflict involves exploring new territory, taking risks, and conquering the unknown; it can also involve "saving" one another or the relationship itself.
Conflict is a balancing act:	Conflict is a delicate practice where one false move may prove fatal; it requires precise skills like those of a tightrope walker or a juggler.

☞

Table 9.1 **Conflict Metaphors (*Continued*)**	
Conflict is a bargaining table:	Conflict involves people coming together for a common purpose; the schedule and procedure depend on how the table is arranged.
Conflict is a tide:	Conflict comes and goes; based on past observations and good recordkeeping, we should be able to effectively predict when it is coming.
Conflict is a dance: ✓	Individuals must learn how to move through conflict—how and when to move, and when to start and end. This takes lots of practice with your partner.
Conflict is a garden: /	Conflict episodes represent the seeds for our future; if they occur in a carefully cultivated environment, they will result in a great harvest.

Source: Hocker and Wilmot, 1995.

Conflict Metaphors

When people compare conflict to other things in the world, they often use figurative language (analogies or metaphors) to help describe their perceptions. For instance, some individuals think that "conflict is a game." If you were asked to use a metaphor to describe how you view conflict, what would it be? Some conflict scholars, like Joyce Hocker and William Wilmot, have identified common conflict metaphors.[6] As you read through Table 9.1, think about how each one can limit, or expand, the possibility of productive conflict. We saw in Chapter 4 that the language people use to describe conflict is important because it indicates their underlying values and assumptions. In fact, scholars have reported that the conflict metaphors that people use can provide significant insight to their expectations of what will occur during conflict.[7]

The Nature of Conflict

In the Chinese language, the character for conflict is made up of two different symbols. One reflects danger and the other opportunity. We like to refer to this when discussing conflict with students because it emphasizes the fact that managing conflict effectively means recognizing it in terms of both potential danger and opportunity for growth. Many times, what stands out during conflict episodes is the inherent danger—the danger of offending someone else, having things get out of control, or having the relationship go bad or completely dissolve. These dangers should make us take conflict seriously. Yet it is equally important to understand the potential good that can come out of conflict.

Positive and Negative Effects of Conflict

By its very nature, conflict can have positive and negative effects on the way people relate to one another. It all depends on how each person handles the conflict. Take a few moments to think back to the conflict episodes you listed in Box 9.1. Now think about what effect(s) each conflict had on the relationship in which the conflict occurred. How would you describe these effects: mostly positive, negative, or a combination of both? Most individuals recall negative experiences because these stand out in our minds more than positive ones. Did you? If so, can you recall other conflicts that had positive outcomes?

Depending on how it is managed, conflict can have both positive and negative effects. Most often, it is easier to identify the negative effects that conflict can have on our interpersonal relationships. Conflict disrupts the natural, enjoyable nature of relationships. Conflict over relatively small issues can distract individuals from more important matters. It can also reveal, and ultimately increase, the negative feelings that individuals have for one another. If not managed effectively, conflict episodes can trigger unhealthy, abusive verbal and nonverbal attacks. Engaging in conflict can deplete a person's energy and willingness to invest in others. Ultimately, conflict can lead to greater distrust between individuals, closed communication channels, and the end of a relationship.

Conflict can also have a number of positive effects. Through it, individuals can gain a better understanding of themselves, others, and the relationship itself. Sometimes conflict can clarify what is important to us and what is not (see Box 9.2). It can force individuals to examine a problem, understand its importance to both individuals, and work for a potential solution. Conflict can draw our attention to issues before they become larger and more difficult to manage. Other effects include a sense of accomplishment when conflicts are resolved, a stronger sense of commitment to the relationship, and greater satisfaction in the relationship.

Box 9.2

Practical Research

Scholars have studied interpersonal conflict in a variety of contexts, including romantic relationships. Over time, research has revealed that a relatively small number of issues are at the core of most conflicts that couples experience. The vast majority of the research in this area has focused on heterosexual couples, and some studies indicate that the prevalent conflict issues may differ for gay and lesbian couples. However, Lawrence Kurdeck studied gay, lesbian, and heterosexual couples and found significant consistency about the topics of conflict among couples.

According to Kurdeck's 1994 article,[8] all couples experience six areas of conflict. In order of the most cited to the least cited, these were:

1. Intimacy issues (including sex, affection, and self-disclosures)
2. Power issues (including lack of equality in relationship, power struggles over control, and excessive demands)
3. Personal issues (including criticisms over personal habits)
4. Distance issues (including time together, presence at home, and balancing of other commitments)
5. Social issues (including disagreements related to politics, values, and other beliefs)
6. Trust issues (including those arising from previous relationships, honesty, and commitment)

Consider these research findings in the context of your own romantic relationships. Do these six issues reflect those that are the source for conflict in your current or past relationships? Do different ones exist? How might particular aspects of your culture (age, gender, national origin, spirituality, and so on) affect your response to these questions?

Productive and Unproductive Conflict

Thinking back to your responses for the earlier self-reflection exercise in Box 9.1, can you imagine how each of these conflict episodes could have had either negative or positive effects, or a combination of both? The way you communicate during conflict episodes has a significant impact on the conflict itself, as well as on the relationship as a whole. An example can help illustrate this important idea. Latosha and Mercedes are college seniors who have developed a close friendship. While different in age (Latosha is 30 and Mercedes is 22), they have much in common, including close relationships with their mothers. As graduation approaches, the two women discuss their plans to each pursue graduate degrees, despite their mothers' disapproval. For both Latosha and Mercedes, the topic of graduate school creates a great deal of conflict in their homes, largely because both their mothers think it is time, as they put it, "to get a real job." Both women are experiencing similar conflict. But the way they manage it can lead to very different outcomes.

Latosha's relationship with her mother has always been fairly good, with the exception of a couple of years when she rebelled against authority during her late teens. As an adult, Latosha has continued to increase her respect for her mother's strength and support, despite disagreeing with some of her traditional values. Through a series of conversations, Latosha has come to understand that her mother's opinions about graduate school are rooted in her perceptions that a 30-year-old woman should be focusing on family, not education or career. Although Latosha doesn't agree, she avoids communicating with her mother in a way that might suggest her ideas are wrong or that Latosha disagrees with the value she places on family. When discussions begin to get heated, Latosha tries to take a break in order to avoid saying things that might be hurtful. She also attempts to explain to her mother, through a variety of ways, the important role that education will play in her family's future. The bottom line for Latosha is that she loves her mother and wants her relationship with her to grow. She recognizes that this conflict should not dominate all their interactions. With time, Latosha expects that her mother will come to understand and support her decision. Both recognize that the conflict is natural to the ongoing development of their relationship as mother and daughter.

Mercedes is not as optimistic as Latosha. She sees her mother as a "control freak" who refuses to let her adult children make their own decisions. While her mother shares many of the traditional values that Latosha's mom has, Mercedes refuses to acknowledge that they have any relevance in the twenty-first century. Her mission is to break free of her mother's influences and establish herself as an independent professional woman, something that is highly likely given her fiery spirit and never-give-up attitude. The problem is that she has inherited these very characteristics from her mother, who is unwilling to let Mercedes keep making "mistakes." Recently, both women have avoided talking about the issue, but they find themselves arguing over little things (like the condition of Mercedes' room, or her eating habits). More and more often, simple discussions spiral out of control with emotional outbursts and personal attacks. Neither woman is willing to budge from her position, and each waits for the other person to admit that she is wrong. Mercedes finds herself spending more and more time at school or with friends; her mother sees this as an indication of her growing independence and asks Mercedes to move out of the house.

As you can see from the examples of Latosha and Mercedes, similar conflicts can have drastically different outcomes depending on how the conflict is managed. Interpersonal conflicts are typically not as extreme as those described in this example. Most reflect both productive and unproductive characteristics. Our ultimate goal, however, is to maximize the positive outcomes of conflict, while minimizing the negative ones, however those might be defined. The most effective way to accomplish this goal is by fostering productive conflict management. Figure 9.1 summarizes different communication characteristics associated with productive and unproductive approaches to conflict. Take a moment to look at these characteristics. How would your approach to conflict be characterized?

Figure 9.1	Characteristics of Productive and Unproductive Conflict	

Conflict That Is *Unproductive* Is Typically Characterized By:	Conflict That Is *Productive* Is Typically Characterized By:
A lack of focus on issues	A focus on a specific issue or issues
Escalated feelings of anger, fear, disgust, and frustration	More controlled feelings ranging from anger and fear to hope and love
Prolonged silence and long-term avoidance	Purposeful silence and breaks to regain focus
Inflexibility and unwillingness to change	Flexibility and willingness to change
Competition and a focus on winning	Cooperation and collaboration with a focus on protecting the relationship
Communication that intensifies and spirals out of control	Communication that is managed and maintains productive levels of interaction
Personal attacks and retaliation	Constructive comments and focus on issues
Attempts to ensure understanding through constant reiterations of key points	Attempts to ensure understanding through diverse strategies geared toward the other person

Different Cultural Perspectives

Much of the traditional literature on communication and conflict has reflected a Western bias in which conflict is accepted as something that should be managed directly in order to be effective. Thus, communication scholars have defined avoidance styles as those styles in which there is a lack of concern for self and other. In 2000, communication scholars Min-Sun Kim and Truman Leung described how this perception reflects a cultural bias against collectivistic approaches to conflict that use more subtle forms of conflict resolution.[9] In this section, we look at intercultural research that focuses on two specific cultural dimensions—individualism/collectivism and high-context/low-context cultures—to help us see the relationship between culture and conflict.

Being an effective communicator includes having an awareness of how culture influences how people manage conflict.

Individualism/Collectivism

One central concept within traditional cross-cultural research focuses on how cultures regard individual and group identity. As you will recall from earlier discussions of culture, **individualism** refers to the cultural values that emphasize the identity, rights, and needs of the individual over the collective identity, rights, and needs of the larger group. Communication in individualistic cultures is generally more self-focused, ego-based, and self-expressive. High individualistic values have been found in the United States, Australia, Canada, Great Britain, the Netherlands, and New

Zealand.[10] In the United States, individualism is recognized in laws that protect an individual's right to free speech, to privacy, and to bear arms. These rights exist, for the most part, regardless of the impact they might have on the larger society.

Collectivism describes cultural values that emphasize a group identity over an individual identity. Group obligations and needs take precedence over individual wishes and desires. In other words, collectivistic cultures emphasize a "we-identity" more than an "I-identity." Communication typically adheres to group norms and is evaluated in the context of others' behaviors. China, Taiwan, Korea, Japan, and Mexico have been described as cultures with high collectivism. In China, for example, a proverb states, "The first person to raise his voice loses the argument." This reflects a cultural value that privileges group harmony over an individual's right to self-expression.

High-Context/Low-Context Cultures

Earlier communication scholars, like Edward T. Hall, have looked at the role that context serves in different cultures.[11] As presented earlier, in high-context cultures differences can exist between what is meant and what is actually said. In order to communicate effectively, people must rely on inferred meaning. In other words, they must "read between the lines" and have a keen sense of who is saying what, how it is being said, as well as what is *not* being said. Communication in high-context cultures, like Japan, features many subtle nonverbal nuances and forms of indirect negotiation. Collectivistic cultures are highly sensitive to the effect of their words on others, and members weigh what they say very carefully.[12]

The role that context plays in low-context cultures is different. In low-context cultures, a person is expected to say what he or she means. The norm is not to rely on contextual clues for communicating meaning but to strive for literal meaning. As you might imagine, effective communication includes direct statements, linear speaking patterns, and overt forms of expression. Generally low-context cultures have been associated with individualism. Confrontations, regardless of the impact they have on others, are valued. Not communicating honestly and openly, for example, is viewed negatively in individualistic, low-context cultures like the United States.

As you will see in the next section, these two cultural dimensions serve as anchoring points for the way we view ourselves and others during times of conflict. By combining these dimensions, we can gain additional insight into how conflict is managed in different cultures.

Contrasting Cultural Perspectives

Figure 9.2 highlights some of the core differences in the ways different cultures regard conflict. As you read through these descriptions, think about what might occur when a person from an individualistic, low-context culture interacts with someone from a culture that is collectivistic and high context. Can you see how this situation presents unique challenges in negotiating conflict in productive ways? For the most part, we communicate in ways that are grounded in our cultural values. Many times, we do so unconsciously and without realizing that others might enter the interaction with different values, expectations, and communication norms. Assuming that everyone approaches conflict in similar ways can be a major roadblock to effective communication.

Two points of caution as you read through the comparison between individualistic/high-context and collectivistic/low-context cultures. First, these insights reflect generalizations and are

Figure 9.2   Core Cultural Differences in Conflict

Individualistic/Low-Context Cultures	Collectivistic/High-Context Cultures
Issue Orientation • Conflict is necessary to work out major differences and problems. • Conflict is functional when it provides a way to address problems. • Focus should be on specific issues; relational issues should be handled separately.	**Relational/Face Orientation** • Conflict is damaging to social status and relational harmony. • Conflict reflects emotional immaturity and a lack of self-discipline. • Topical issues and relational issues are intertwined and must be dealt with together.
Goal Orientation • Focus is on achieving specific goals with an eye on the future. • Conflict episodes must be isolated and addressed accordingly. • Conflict management should follow a preset schedule with clear agenda items.	**Process Orientation** • Focus is on the process and how it relates to the past, present, and future. • Conflict management has no clear beginning and end. • Conflict management is a delicate, subtle process that has no predetermined schedule.
Use of Formal Mediator • Preference is for formally trained mediator. • Mediator should be impartial and not known to any parties involved. • Mediator should only focus on the issue(s) at hand.	**Use of Informal Mediator** • Preference is for informal mediator, usually a well-respected elder. • Mediator should know all parties involved. • Mediator should attend to past events to help understand current conflict.
Tangible Power Resources • Power is reflected in the ability to reward and/or punish others. • Struggles to gain more power happen both overtly and covertly. • Power is asserted through threats, direct requests, and aggressive defense strategies.	**Intangible Power Resources** • Power is reflected in gains or losses in reputation, prestige, or status. • Fewer struggles to gain more power exist; if they do, they happen covertly. • Power is displayed subtly through indirect requests, tag questions, and inferences.
Direct/Competitive Communication • Communicators have a responsibility to be open, direct, and clear. • Emphasis on verbal offense and defense to justify one's position. • Uses communication strategies that reflect a win-lose competition between parties.	**Indirect/Integrating Communication** • Communicators have a responsibility to pick up on the hidden meanings and intentions of others. • Relies on ambiguous, indirect verbal and nonverbal messages. • Uses communication strategies that reflect a win-win negotiation between parties.

not meant to reveal "truths" about all members of any given cultural group. Many textbooks include cultural generalizations in their descriptions: French people find confrontations stimulating. Middle Easterners take great delight in haggling and arguing with others. People from Japan find overt displays of conflict distasteful and potentially damaging. We opt to shy away from such vast generalizations for a couple of reasons. One reason is that we recognize that all cultural groups are highly diverse and members of these groups may or may not embrace traditional culture values in similar ways. We believe that communicating with another person based on your perceptions of how you think they will communicate—and not how they actually communicate—is ineffective.

In addition, as we saw in Chapter 2, all individuals have multiple cultural selves. Not only do we have a national origin, but we also have a specific age, gender, socioeconomic status, and citizenship status—all of which can influence our conflict strategies. For instance, some researchers have pointed to how age and immigrant status affect how closely individuals adhere to traditional cultural values.[13] Others have reported differences in the ways women and men manage conflict.[14] Keeping these findings in mind, you can see how dangerous it is to assume that all members of a country share a common approach to conflict. So, while it is useful to recognize general culture trends for conflict management, it is equally important to understand the diversity within each cultural group that renders each point not universally true.

A second caution has to do with ethnocentrism. **Ethnocentrism** is an orientation toward a person's own cultural group. Individuals are ethnocentric when they use their cultural norms as a standard by which to evaluate others' cultures. When individuals think in highly ethnocentric ways, they can refuse to recognize the value in other conflict approaches, to change their own conflict approaches, or even to consider that alternative orientations exist. You may see yourself in one or the other columns of Figure 9.2, or sometimes both. Instead of falling into the trap of ethnocentrism, exercise **ethnorelativism** by recognizing that various cultures have different norms, values, and practices. And instead of viewing these differences as deviant or inferior, realize that different simply means different. In other words, no value is placed on the differences, and one is not seen as superior to the other. The key to increasing your communication effectiveness during conflict is to remain open to others who might approach the situation differently. Later in this chapter, we also discuss the importance of having some flexibility in your conflict strategies so that you might adapt your style to match others' when necessary.

Conflict Strategies

Communication scholars have traditionally identified five basic strategies that reflect core approaches to managing conflict. Different names for these basic strategies exist, but most often they are known as avoiding, accommodating, compromising, forcing, and collaborating.[15] In this section, we describe each strategy and explain in which situations it is most appropriate.

Most of us may have a "natural" approach to conflict that is situated in one basic strategy. For instance, two individuals may find themselves typically in "fight" mode with a clear focus on "winning" arguments regardless of the impact it may have on their relationship. However, a closer look probably reveals that they—as well as all persons—use different strategies in different conflict episodes, depending on the particulars of the situation.

As a conflict unfolds, each individual must be aware of the importance of (1) achieving his or her own individual goals and (2) maintaining the relationship with the other person. For instance, in any given conflict, you should ask yourself a number of questions: Is resolving the conflict to my satisfaction top priority? Or is making sure that the relationship remains intact the priority? Are both equally important? Is there a way I can address the conflict without damaging the relationship? If you are to manage conflict effectively, the strategy you choose should reflect your answer to these questions.

To illustrate how the process of effective conflict management can work, consider five students, Vernon, Willis, Xavier, Yusef, and Zack. They knew one another casually, but had limited experience living with roommates. Once they discovered that they were all going to work at the same resort for the summer, however, they decided to become roommates in order to share living expenses. At first everything went smoothly. After a couple of weeks, however, the five men found themselves constantly in conflict over the cleanliness of the apartment they shared. Let's use this scenario, and the way Vernon, Willis, Xavier, Yusef, and Zack respond to it, to illustrate the appropriateness of each of the five basic conflict strategies.

Avoiding

By definition, **avoiding** occurs when an individual withdraws, either physically or psychologically, from a conflict situation. As illustrated in Figure 9.3, avoidance is an appropriate strategy when an individual sees the conflict and maintaining the relationship(s) as unimportant. Sometimes avoiding can be easy, especially if others adopt a similar strategy. However, when someone else is attempting to force an issue, avoiding can be counterproductive. Yet people who are practicing avoidance believe that dealing with the conflict has more potential disadvantages than advantages.

Vernon has had a couple of different interactions with roommates who were either upset that the apartment was a mess or frustrated with others for trying to force them to be superclean. He can feel the tension in the house, but he isn't interested in getting involved. Personally, he doesn't really care about how clean the house is, and doesn't expect to see any of his roommates after the summer. So how does he manage the conflict? By leaving when discussions begin to occur and by ignoring attempts by other roommates to get him involved.

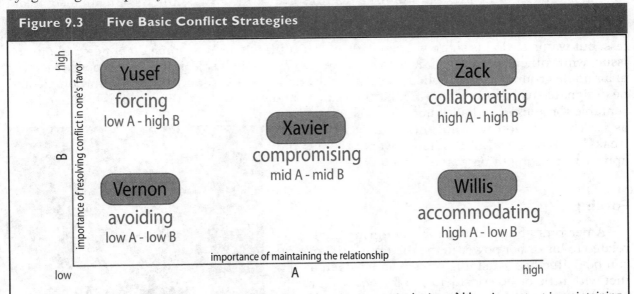

Figure 9.3   Five Basic Conflict Strategies

Two basic considerations are present in every conflict: How important is the issue? How important is maintaining the relationship? Five basic conflict strategies exist; each may be appropriate depending on how an individual weighs these two basic considerations. Based on the example of Vernon, Willis, Xavier, Yusef, and Zack, can you see how their individual strategies reflected their feelings about the conflict and one another?

Accommodating

Accommodating, also known as obliging, is a conflict strategy that seeks to satisfy the other person's need to settle the conflict while neglecting our own. People are likely to accommodate in order to maintain what they perceive as a valuable relationship. This strategy may suit some conflicts, especially if the source of conflict is unimportant to you but of great importance to someone you care about. Over time, however, it can also produce a situation where one person can take advantage of another's commitment to the relationship.

Willis has used the accommodating strategy as his primary conflict strategy. Growing up, he was an only child who got accustomed to living in a neat and orderly environment. This is still his preference, and his current living conditions are far from ideal. Yet he has developed a brotherly relationship with a couple of his roommates—something that means the world to him. Accordingly, he is willing to tolerate the mess because a clean home is not as important as maintaining the great relationships that he has formed. Willis plans to address the issue if it ever gets out of hand, but for now he is content with not making a big deal of it.

Compromising

When two people attempt to resolve a conflict situation by giving up something so that each person ultimately gets at least some satisfaction from the outcome, they are compromising. **Compromising** is a sharing strategy designed to address each person's concerns, at least to some extent. *Bargaining, trading off,* and *negotiating* are terms that sometimes are used interchangeably with compromising. When two or more individuals perceive the conflict as having some importance, and are also moderately committed to maintaining existing relationships, compromising is a likely strategy. Compromising can resolve short-term conflicts, but can also create additional problems if neither party is totally satisfied with the solution.

Xavier has attempted to compromise. He doesn't have the time to keep the apartment spotless, but wants to do his share to keep it clean. The difficulty is that some do not care about the issue, while others expect the house to be clean "24–7." Xavier's solution was to propose meeting at a middle ground: Some public spaces, like the kitchen, living room, and one bathroom, would be designated as "clean places." Each roommate would work to keep these rooms clean and presentable for guests, and all other rooms could remain as is. This solution was not totally what the "clean freaks" or the "slobs" of the house wanted, but it did appear to be something that all could accept.

Forcing

A person's ability to use forcing during conflict is related to his or her power in the relationship. **Forcing** can be defined as satisfying one's own needs in a conflict with little or no consideration for how that might affect the relationship. As shown in Figure 9.3, forcing is a common conflict strategy when people feel that resolving the conflict to their satisfaction is of greater importance than maintaining a good relationship.

Emotions, regardless of how they are expressed, are a basic part of being human.

Practicing dominance during conflict episodes might be necessary during times of emergency or when someone needs to take control, but in the long run it typically leaves others with feelings of resentment, hostility, and a desire for revenge. This, however, is of little concern since the relationship itself is not viewed as important.

If you were to ask the roommates, most would probably point to Yusef as the instigator of the conflict about the apartment's cleanliness. He seems to be the one who is most determined to make sure the house is clean, and is not afraid to confront others when it is not. Like Vernon, Yusef sees his roommates as friends, but their relationship is not overly important. It doesn't matter if he loses any friendships over this issue; he believes that if they were all friends, then the others would take better care of the apartment. As the person who originally found the apartment, he feels that he should have some say about how others treat it.

Collaborating

You might have been taught that compromising was the ideal way to handle conflicts. Compromising can provide some satisfaction for all parties. Yet collaborating, if done properly, can result in greater overall satisfaction. **Collaborating** occurs when individuals involved in the conflict try to fully address the needs and issues of each person and arrive at a solution that is mutually satisfying. As you might imagine, this strategy takes a significant amount of time, energy, commitment, flexibility, and creatively. But if both the issue and the relationship are important, then it is the only strategy that does not prioritize one party over the other and still simultaneously focuses on long-term success. Remember that compromise means "giving something to get something." Collaborating, on the other hand, means creating a solution where no one feels as if they are giving up anything that is important to them.

Zack, the communication major of the bunch (of course!), has watched each of his roommates engage in conflict with different priorities. Although seemingly impossible, his goal is to have all the roommates work through the conflict toward a solution with which all can be 100 percent happy. The compromise suggested by Xavier worked okay, but Yusef was still not completely satisfied because the smell from certain rooms seemed to spread all over the apartment. After talking more with Yusef, Zack learned that he was working overtime in order to send money home. His frustration stemmed from his not being able to relax in the mess and the lack of effort by others who were putting less hours in at work. Zack knew that Yusef was referring mostly to Vernon and Xavier. Through a series of conversations with them, he learned that they too would prefer a clean house. But their focus was on enjoying the summer. They worked, not because they had to, but because it put extra spending money in their pockets.

Based on this information, Zack felt as if he understood everyone's concerns well enough to propose a solution. After talking with all parties individually, he called a house meeting. At that meeting, he announced the master plan: Yusef had agreed to take primary responsibility to make sure that certain public areas (kitchen, living room, and one bathroom) were cleaned daily. For his efforts, each roommate would chip in so that they would cover one-fourth of his rent each month. All the other roommates would be responsible for keeping their own rooms clean. The collaborative solution worked brilliantly! Yusef, with less rent to pay, was able to cut some of his hours at work and relax much more comfortably at home (in an apartment cleaned just the way he liked). Vernon and Xavier didn't mind paying Yusef for his efforts, as long as they could enjoy the rest of their summer.

The Role of Emotions During Conflict

Conflict is often accompanied by strong emotions such as anger, frustration, and disgust. This section will help you (1) understand how emotions affect conflict management and (2) identify ways to communicate emotions that are healthy and productive.

Emotions are a basic part of being human. The verbal and nonverbal expressions of emotions like joy, happiness, sadness, and fear represent the core of many close relationships. Effectively communicating our emotions to others, and accurately interpreting others' emotions, are also crucial to effective interpersonal communication. Yet we do not always share our emotions with others, and sometimes the cost of not doing so is high. Individuals can experience a range of negative consequences when they repress their emotions including headaches, high blood pressure, ulcers, eating disorders, as well as several forms of destructive behavior.[17]

We might not share our emotions with others because we have great difficulty in identifying exactly *what* we are feeling. Or we might lack the necessary interpersonal skills to communicate *how* we feel. Perhaps we were socialized to believe that certain emotions are not appropriate to express, or appropriate only in specific situations. Can you think back to a recent conflict when you didn't express the emotions that you were feeling? Why was this the case? Within this section, we discuss the important role that productive emotional expression plays in effective conflict management. Specifically, we share some basic information about emotions and outline particular guidelines to shape how to maximize the outcomes for communicating your emotions to others.

Basic Emotions

Emotions are feelings that consist of distinctive thoughts, physical and psychological reactions, and a range of motivations to act.[18] Researchers agree that emotions are universal to the human experience, but the acceptance (and value) of expressing emotions varies greatly. We also know that emotions are different from moods,[19] which are typically less intense and longer lasting than emotions. We usually experience emotions with greater clarity than moods. Emotions have specific identifiable consequences. Yet, with all we know about emotions, researchers still debate the role perception plays in emotions, and even whether emotions should be considered instinctual or learned.

Scholars also continue to argue over precisely which emotions are primary and which are secondary (secondary emotions are combinations of primary emotions); others question whether any emotions are primary at all. In recent years, Daniel Goleman's book *Emotional Intelligence*[20] has shifted attention from these debates and focused on the important role that emotions serve in humans' ability to be successful in their personal, social, and professional lives. Goleman identifies eight primary emotions: anger, sadness, fear, enjoyment, love, surprise, disgust, and shame. Table 9.2 lists these eight primary emotions, as well as others that are closely associated with each. The most recent research available, which was published in 2000, indicates that certain emotions—joy, sadness, fear, and anger—develop within the first three or four years of life. Others that are more self-conscious, like shame and disgust, appear to emerge later.[21]

Table 9.2 Eight Primary Emotions	
Anger:	Fury, outrage, resentment, wrath, indignation, animosity, annoyance, irritability, hostility
Sadness:	Grief, sorrow, cheerlessness, gloom, self-pity, loneliness, dejection, despair, depression
Fear:	Anxiety, apprehension, nervousness, concern, misgiving, wariness, edginess, dread, fright, terror, pain
Enjoyment:	Happiness, joy, relief, contentment, bliss, delight, amusement, pride, sensual pleasure, thrill, satisfaction, euphoria, ecstasy
Love:	Acceptance, friendliness, trust, kindness, affinity, devotion, adoration, infatuation
Surprise:	Shock, astonishment, amazement, wonder
Disgust:	Contempt, disdain, scorn, distaste, revulsion
Shame:	Guilt, embarrassment, chagrin, remorse, humiliation, regret, mortification

Communicating Your Emotions During Conflict

One of the most important, yet sometimes most difficult, parts of managing conflict is communicating your emotions in productive ways. In order to help you maximize your efforts in this area, we outline five steps.

Identify and Understand Your Emotions

In order to be effective at communicating your emotions to others, you must first identify them and their sources. This might take some time and require significant self-reflection (like writing in a journal, talking to friends, or working with a counselor).

Decide How You Want to Act on Your Emotions

One of the most dangerous things to do during conflict is to communicate without thinking about the impact of your actions. Remember that all communication includes some degree of risk. In some situations, and in some cultures as discussed earlier, expressing your emotions directly is not appropriate. In others it is more acceptable, but it still might result in unwanted outcomes. Consider all these points when deciding whether to express your emotions or not. If you decide it is not the appropriate time to currently express your emotions, identify indirect outlets that you can use in the short term (e.g., writing in a journal, doing physical exercise, or talking with a friend).

Think Through Your Communication Strategies

Even when you've decided that communicating your emotions is the right thing to do, you must consider how to maximize your communication efforts. This includes anticipating how the other person will perceive and react to your messages. Maximizing your effectiveness includes considering *when, where,* and *how* you should communicate your emotions.

Present Your Message

Present your message in ways that are most appropriate given your cultural values, your relationship with the other person, and the particulars of the situation. Have a plan, but maintain some flexibility in your communication. Typically, "I-messages" ("I am angry") are more effective than "you-messages" ("You made me angry"). It may be helpful to let the other person know exactly what you would like them to do with the information you are sharing. For instance, do you want them to simply listen, affirm your feelings, explain their actions, apologize, or change their behavior?

Take Time to Evaluate Your Communication Effectiveness

Learning how to communicate your emotions effectively is a lifelong process. Taking the necessary time to reflect on your past experiences is crucial to your future success. The goal here is to highlight those things you did that were effective and determine how you might use similar strategies in the future. Along the same lines, it is helpful to identify any "mistakes" you might have made and try to avoid repeating them.

Assessing Others' Emotions During Conflict

Thus far, we have focused on how individuals can effectively communicate their emotions to others. Another important aspect to consider is the skills necessary to interact with others expressing their emotions to us during times of conflict. The way we receive messages with emotional content will have a direct impact on the ultimate success of our conflict management with others. In other words, if we are effective in respecting the expressions of emotions of others, then we are much more likely to create a productive climate where conflict resolution will be most productive.

So, what guidelines exist for interacting with others' expressions of emotions during conflict? We could spend a significant time outlining these here, but instead point to the information covered in Part I of the textbook. Within these chapters, we presented a lot of basic ideas related to the foundations of effective interpersonal communication—all of which are applicable to various communication contexts. In addition, you may want to review some of the key concepts in Chapters 6 (nonverbal communication), 7 (listening), and especially 8, where we discussed communication competence. These chapters can serve as especially helpful reminders of key principles and effective skills that are applicable to managing emotions during times of conflict.

Cyberspace Conflict

More and more of us are finding that conflicts emerge while we are communicating online—with friends, family, coworkers, acquaintances, and strangers. Recently, researchers[22] studied which communication channels were most effective in communicating different needs (inclusion, relaxation, control, affection, pleasure, and escape). Six communication channels were tested: face-to-face, telephone, voice mail, electronic mail, letter, and fax. The study overwhelmingly found that needs were most effectively addressed through face-to-face interaction and telephone calls. These findings are troublesome given that more and more of us rely on communicating online with friends, family members, and coworkers. In this section, we focus specifically on conflict that occurs while communicating in cyberspace.

Just about all the information we have presented in this chapter is applicable to communication in all contexts, including the computer-mediated context. But one of the things that makes conflict online different from face-to-face conflict is the lack of contextual clues. When we engage in conflict via the computer, all we have are the words on the screen in front of us (and maybe a few "emoticons" thrown in). Conflict can arise when we are communicating with a friend or with a stranger whose identity is represented only by their online name. This makes understanding the source, as well as the dynamics, of the conflict more challenging. Online conflicts are thus often the result of innocent misunderstandings.

Some forms of cyberspace conflict are specific to the nature of computer-mediated communication. For instance, conflict can arise when an individual violates the norms of a particular chatroom, or interrupts existing conversations with irrelevant or unwelcome information. Guidelines for communicating online, known as netiquette, have developed along with our use of technology. Netiquette rules, like those that exist for face-to-face social interactions, provide guidance for those unfamiliar with the accepted norms of computer-mediated communication. Specifically, they advise against **spamming** (sending someone unsolicited e-mail or repeatedly sending the same mail), **flaming** (sending messages that personally attack others), and **trolling** (sending false information and extreme viewpoints for the purpose of watching others' reactions). As you well might imagine—or have experienced yourself—these behaviors often result in cyberspace conflict.

However, conflict can also arise about the use of the computer itself. Have you ever disagreed with a loved one about whether it is appropriate to send an e-mail greeting instead of a traditional card? In 2001, Ann Landers responded to a reader who questioned the appropriateness of an obituary that stated "condolences may be sent to the family via e-mail at XXX@e-mailaddress.com."[23] Effective communicators are well aware of the impact our choice of medium has on our interactions with others. (For those who were wondering, Ann Landers advised that "e-mail is better than no mail at all," but called e-mail condolences "tacky, no matter what the century.")

Using technology to handle conflict has both advantages and disadvantages.

Guidelines for Managing Conflict Effectively

You might be wondering how practical the information in this chapter is in the "real world," which doesn't always seem so logical or orderly. For instance, are the five steps we presented for communicating emotions effectively unrealistic to follow in the midst of conflict?

Certainly it's not possible to apply *all* the new things you've learned about conflict in every situation. Our objective is not to make an instant transformation in your communication strategies. We do hope, however, that your increased awareness will lead to changes—even small ones—that increase your ability to manage conflict effectively. Apply at least some of what you've learned in this chapter and see how it helps in your personal, social, and professional lives.

Here are some general guidelines that provide practical strategies for you. Read through each guideline and think about past experiences when you might have followed (or not followed) it during conflict. This bit of self-reflection will help you identify specific areas that you can work on in terms of handling conflict more productively in the future.

Be Mindful About Your Approaches to Conflict

When people engage in conflict mindlessly, they rely on old ways of communicating without considering how new ones could enhance their personal effectiveness. As we highlighted in Chapter 7 regarding listening, individuals who practice **mindfulness** think about how they are communicating to others and remain open to new information. They are also aware that there are many perspectives and approaches possible for each conflict situation.[24] Part of maintaining a state of mindfulness is recognizing the effects that our cultural assumptions can have during conflict. Self-reflection helps us recognize both productive and unproductive conflict patterns in their interactions with others.

Develop Clear Expectations and Rules for Conflict

Those who are most effective at handling interpersonal conflict work together with others to discuss a common set of guidelines. Based on past experiences, discuss your personal expectations for when conflict arises, and determine ahead of time the "rules" to follow. For instance, a couple might decide not to initiate conflict when they do not have enough time to handle it appropriately. Or they might agree that all distractions (phone, television, music, other people) should be eliminated during times of conflict and that personal attacks are off-limits. The logic here is not to create a universal set of rules; instead, each couple should work together to set guidelines that work for them.

Communicate With Appropriate Levels of Specificity

Be as specific and clear as possible and appropriate for the situation. Use language that accurately captures what and how you are feeling. For instance, avoid generalities like "I feel terrible" because they don't provide enough clarity to the other person. Avoid mixed messages where your verbal and nonverbal behaviors give off contrasting signals. Instead, use language that accurately describes the source(s) of the conflict and the intensity of your feelings.

Use Perception Checks to Understand Yourself and Others

Individuals should assume some responsibility for receiving others' messages effectively. **Perception checks** are statements by which you verify that your understanding of a problem or someone's position is accurate. Some common forms of perception checks are direct requests for confirmation, paraphrasing, and the use of third parties to help clarify meaning.

Be Aware of the Advantages of Style-Flexing

Style-flexing occurs when individuals adapt their conflict strategies to match the specific needs of each situation. For instance, Samantha may typically prefer avoidance when in conflict with her mother, but adopt a forcing approach when dealing with issues that are important to her. Style-flexing has three steps: (1) Determine the relative importance of the issue and the relationship, (2) identify the most appropriate strategy for the situation, and (3) adopt the most appropriate strategy. Style-flexing can also mean changing strategies within any given situation.

Remain Focused on Solvable Issues

Understanding the cause(s) of interpersonal conflict is crucial to approaching the situation productively. Once you understand the issue, remain focused on it even if it becomes increasingly difficult when the discussion gets off track or when individuals purposely bring in unrelated issues as a means to gain advantage. Have each party involved in the conflict constantly ask themselves the following question: Is this information helpful in addressing the conflict, or does it take our focus away to another issue? Be careful, however, because some information that initially might seem irrelevant could actually provide information that is central to resolving the conflict.

At times, conflicts over certain issues might be irresolvable. This may be true, for instance, in situations where both individuals have long-standing values and beliefs about the same issue. The best that we might do in these situations is recognize that it is okay to "agree to disagree." While complete resolution might not be possible, the very fact that the issue has been identified as central to each person's belief system can be an important part of their relationship.

Summary

This chapter has focused on effective conflict management. Specifically, we have discussed various cultural approaches to conflict and outlined various strategies to enhance your ability to maximize the productive outcomes of conflict. Emotions also play a central role in many conflict situations, so we also discussed the importance of communicating emotions clearly. We close by explaining each of the myths or truths listed at the beginning of this chapter.

Myth: Conflict is destructive and should be avoided at all costs.

Conflict can be productive and/or unproductive depending on how both individuals manage it collectively; sometimes avoiding conflict can lead to greater relational destruction.

Truth: Conflict is a natural part of all relationships.

Conflict is a normal occurrence in all relationships, and doesn't necessarily indicate that the relationship is in trouble.

Myth: Compromise is generally the ideal strategy for conflicts because it results in a win-win situation. Why is this a myth?

No one ideal strategy exists; much depends on the specific needs and desires of the individuals. However, generally speaking, collaboration, not compromise, is more likely to result in a win-win situation.

Truth: The closer you get to someone, the more opportunities for conflict increase, not decrease.

The more time you spend with others, the more opportunities for potential conflict exist.

Myth: The source of all conflict is ineffective communication. Why is this a myth?

In some instances, conflict is the result of ineffective communication or miscommunication. However, conflict may still exist when both individuals have communicated effectively.

Myth: Emotions should be ignored when trying to make rational decisions during conflict. Why is this not true?

In order to make the best possible decisions during conflict, it is important to recognize and understand the emotional states of all those involved. Ignoring emotions works against effectively managing conflict.

Key Terms

Accommodating

Avoiding

Collaborating

Collectivism

Compromising

Conflict

Emotions

Ethnocentrism

Ethnorelativism

Flaming

Forcing

Individualism

Mindfulness

Perception checks

Spamming

Style-flexing

Trolling

Suggested Contemporary Readings

B. Broome. "Responding to the challenges of third-party facilitation: Reflections of a scholar-practitioner in the Cyprus conflict." *Journal of Intergroup Relations* 29 (2002): 24–43.

F. Delgado. "Mass-mediated communication and intercultural conflict." In *Readings in intercultural communication,* edited by J. N. Martin, T. K. Nakayama, and L. Flores. New York: McGraw-Hill, 2002.

R. Dumalo and R. Botta. "Family communication patterns and the conflict styles young adults use with their fathers." *Communication Quarterly* 48 (2000): 174–189.

M. Hojjat. "Sex differences and perceptions of conflict in romantic relationships." *Journal of Social and Personal Relationships* 17 (2000): 598–617.

R. C. A. Klein and R. M. Milardo. "The social context of couple conflict: Support and criticism from informal third parties." *Journal of Social and Personal Relationships* 17 (2000): 618–637.

S. T. Mortenson. "Sex, communication values, and cultural values: Individualism-collectivism as a mediator of sex differences in communication values in two cultures." *Communication Reports* 15 (2002): 57–70.

J. Oetzel, S. Ting-Toomey, M. Idalia Chew-Sanchez, R. Harris, R. Wilcox, and S. Stumpf. "Face and facework in conflicts with parents and siblings: A cross-cultural comparison of Germans, Japanese, Mexicans, and U.S. Americans." *Journal of Family Communication* 3 (2003): 67–93.

L. Pecchioni and J. Nussbaum. "Mother-adult daughter discussions of caregiving prior to dependency: Exploring conflicts among European-American women." *Journal of Family Communication* 1 (2001): 133–150.

M. C. Toale and J. C. McCroskey. "Ethnocentrism and trait communication apprehension as predicators of interethnic communication apprehension and use of relational maintenance strategies in interethnic communication." *Communication Quarterly* 49 (2001): 70–83.

S. S. Vrooman. "The art of invective: Performing identity in cyberspace." *New Media & Society* 4 (2002): 51–70.

Chapter Activities

1. Within your classroom, break up into groups of four or five. Have each person select a recent conflict situation that they listed in their self-reflection exercise (Box 9.1) with the group. Then have the group discuss similarities and differences between how each person communicated during these conflict episodes. The following questions can guide the discussion: What are some of the similarities and differences that were noticed? Can you identify any particular patterns across different conflict situations or types of people? How has this exercise helped students to become aware of their own conflict behaviors?

2. Emotions Anonymous is a 12-step program (similar to Alcoholics Anonymous) created for the purpose of working toward recovery from emotional difficulties like depression, anger, grief, anxiety, jealousy, and despair. Founded in St. Paul, Minnesota, in 1971, the program has grown to over 1,200 chapters in 39 countries. Go to their Web site (*http://www.emotionsanonymous.org/*) and see how the principles of the program relate to the concepts and guidelines included in the chapter. One productive place to start is to read through "The Twelve Promises of Emotions Anonymous."

3. Use a database, like InfoTrac, in your campus library to locate articles that discuss both compromise and collaboration (use both as keywords). Did the articles use both of these terms interchangeably, or did they differentiate between them like we did in this chapter? What were some examples of how these conflict strategies appeared in everyday life?

4. Anonymously describe recent conflict situations on note cards. Select several that are most interesting and/or thought provoking, and divide the class into groups of four to five students and have them discuss the situations. Ask them to brainstorm the various ways that someone might respond to each conflict, and identify specific examples of how someone might practice avoiding, accommodating, compromising, forcing, and collaborating. What would each student do in the particular situation that has been posed to his or her group?

5. The Association for Conflict Resolution is the largest national organization designed to promote peaceful, effective conflict resolution. Visit their Web site at *http://www.acrnet.org/* and learn about some of the conflict resolution efforts across the world. Click on "Topical Sections" to select a specific area of interest. Then pick one of the many stories and see how the different concepts discussed in this chapter apply to real-world situations.

6. Locate a local school or community organization that has a conflict-resolution program. Review the program materials, observe different sessions, and interview

teachers and students regarding their experiences. Then volunteer to offer training that utilizes some of what is covered in this chapter to enhance the program's effectiveness.

7. *http://eqi.org/* is a valuable online resource for information on emotions and emotional intelligence. Visit the site and read current research and findings on the topic or locate additional references to read. You can even measure your own emotional intelligence via an online test at this site. ✦

Part III

Communication Contexts

Chapter 10

Communicating in Personal Relationships

Contemporary Issues: E-Romance

It is Valentine's Day, 2001. Steve and Robbie, longtime partners, will not see each other today. Steve is an investment banker who lives in Philadelphia; his partner Robbie lives in Minneapolis. They spend most of their weekends together, but live and work in separate cities during the week. Although they would prefer to live in the same city, their professional lives keep them at a distance most week-days. Like many couples, however, their long-distance relationship is easier and more convenient than ever, largely thanks to e-mail and the Internet. Robbie and Steve will connect today online and share Valentine messages using the Web. According to a recent news headline on February 14, 2001, "An estimated 33.5 million Internet users in the United States will e-mail their sweetheart today."[1] They cite the ever-increasing role of the Internet in many relationships, especially long-distance and "last-minute" couples who like the convenience and ease of connecting online. Regardless, if it's Valentine's Day and you send your special someone love ballads from MusicGrams.Sonymusic.com, personalize a Web browser with custom graphics for your sweetheart at Hotbar.com, or simply send an e-card at BlueMountain.com, you are part of a growing trend: Couples seem to be logging on in record numbers with their sweethearts, as well as connecting on a daily basis the other 364 days of the year. Although experts agree that the computer won't be replacing "Cupid" anytime soon, the Internet and e-mail are allowing many couples the opportunity to not only keep in daily contact through e-mail messages, but also manage long-distance relationships like never before.

Like Steve and Robbie, thousands of couples are able to stay connected, develop rituals, keep in close contact, and "interact" in each others' daily lives through the use of new technologies like e-mail, digital photography and imaging, and the Internet. Although technology is changing some of the ways that we communicate in our personal relationships, one thing remains the same: Communication, in any form, is the foundation of our personal relationships. Our relationships are created and sustained through communication. As we will discuss in this chapter, the process of communicating interpersonally has special significance in our personal relationships.

Myths About Interpersonal Communication

Below are statements about communicating in personal relationships. Can you identify which are myths and which are actually true?

_____ Personal relationships are simple.

_____ Changing your communication will change your personal relationships.

_____ Most good, satisfying personal relationships remain the same over time.

_____ Wanting independence in a relationship is healthy and normal.

_____ Most personal relationships are relatively the same.

_____ The answer to most problems in relationships is communication.

_____ Friendships and relationships are either good or bad; individuals can do little to change them.

If you aren't sure which of the above statements are myths or true statements, you're probably not alone. Many of the myths (answers will be revealed at the end of the chapter!) are commonly held beliefs in the U.S. culture about relationships among friends, family members, and others. As you read, you will learn which of the above statements are true and which are not.

Communication and the Development of Personal Relationships

Think about all the relationships you have experienced in your life: friendships, romantic partnerships, relationships with coworkers, relationships with family members. Some we would probably describe as very satisfying and some less so. Some have probably lasted the span of your entire life, while others lasted only a short duration. Regardless of their length or your experience of them, communication is central to the creation of all personal relationships.

Although communication is often promoted as the answer to all relationship problems, not all problems are communication problems, and communication is not the answer to all challenges in relationships. However, communication is such a central part of our relationships and everyday relational processes that learning about communication issues, perspectives, and skills can lead to us making better and more informed choices in our relationships. Most scholars who study long-term relationships like marriage, for instance, agree that it is communication that will make or break that relationship, and has everything to do with the satisfaction experienced in relationships. And since most of us strive for happiness in our relationships, learning about communication and how it can lead to more satisfying relationships is important.

Many scholars regard communication as the primary process that creates intimacy in relationships.[2] Communication is a process of creating and sharing meaning between people. Whether you are making decisions, working to solve problems, expressing your desires, or deciding when you would like your in-laws to come, communicating forms much of the content of our relationships.

In this chapter we will examine a number of ways to think about the role of communication in your personal relationships and how communication is used to develop, maintain, and even end our relationships. We will also examine the role that gender plays in our intimate relationships and the misunderstandings that often result when masculine and feminine communication styles meet. To begin, we introduce some popular theories that explain why and how we actually develop the friendships and romantic relationships that are central in most of our lives.

How and Why We Form Personal Relationships

The way our friendships and our romantic relationships develop is not necessarily random or beyond our comprehension. Although sometimes you might feel that your relationships are beyond your control or have developed amid strange or unusual circumstances, we actually have a number of theories that help us understand the process of how and why we develop and dissolve personal relationships. As you recall, theories help us predict and explain how and why something happens. All theories aren't equally useful and good, but some have stood the test of time and of scrutiny by others who study similar topics. The theories you are about to learn are like all theories—some are better at explaining relationship development than others, some have been heavily criticized by others in our field of study, and some simply make more sense to us than others. We encourage you to decide as you read which theories *you* think are most useful to help *you* understand and explain the development of your relationship. As you read, ask yourself these questions: Which of these theories is most similar to my experiences? Which help me explain how and why certain of my friendships have not been successful in the past? Which help me explain why I am attracted to certain people and not others? Your own experiences can be very important as you consider the value of the ideas and explanations offered in each of the following theories.

Attraction Theory

One of the primary reasons why we develop relationships with others is because we are attracted to them in some way. We might find them physically attractive or attractive socially, or find their ideas and values attractive. Researchers tell us not only that attraction is one of the primary reasons we develop relationships with certain people and not others, but also that there are a host of different ways that we find others attractive. We most often base our judgments of others' attractiveness on one or more of the following four dimensions:

1. *Similarity:* Is this person similar to me?

2. *Proximity:* Do I usually develop an attraction to people with whom I interact frequently or who are in close proximity to me in my work, school, or home life?

3. *Physical and social attractiveness:* Do I find this person to be physically attractive and/or have an attractive personality or style in social situations?

4. *Reinforcement and reciprocity of attraction:* Does the other person reward me in some way? Is this person attracted to me as well?

Let's examine each of these dimensions of attractiveness more thoroughly.

Similarity and Attraction. Most research points to one striking conclusion: In most cases, we like people who are similar to us.[3] Your friends are probably people who share similar viewpoints, likes, dislikes, interests, experiences, and upbringing. Why do we like people who are similar? Because they reinforce our own beliefs, values, and ideas; they validate our very existence. Interacting with someone who confirms and validates you and your interests and ideas, as we learned in Chapter 8, makes for a positive communication climate and simply feels good.

We often seek others who are similar to us through common or shared activities. For instance, if you have an interest in organic foods, you might join your local co-op and attend classes on organic gardening. During those classes or as you work and shop at the co-op, you might develop a particular attraction to certain individuals who not only share your interest in organic foods, but also are similar to you in other ways as well, maybe in age, communication style, family type, and/or work experiences. We generally like people who are similar to us in ethnicity, age, physical characteristics, intelligence, attitude, and communication style. We also tend to develop relationships and be attracted to those people who live by us and work near us, or with whom we have frequent contact, as we discuss in the next section.

Are the people you tend to be attracted to similar to you in some ways? Do they tend to live near you or have similar interests or hobbies?

Some researchers have argued for a slightly different understanding of the similarity-attraction model. They advance the repulsion hypothesis, which states that rather than being attracted to those people we perceive as similar, we are actually repulsed by those people we perceive are dissimilar.[4] They believe that when we encounter others who do not share our beliefs, interests, or values, we disregard them as potential friends and relational partners. What we have left, as a result, is a group of potential friends and acquaintances who are similar to us. One recent study testing the repulsion hypothesis found that when individuals were judging others on their *social attractiveness*, or how much they liked others and enjoyed their company, they were more repulsed by dissimilarities than they were attracted by similarities.[5] This finding would support the repulsion hypothesis. However, the same researchers realized that when individuals were judging others on the basis of *intellectual attractiveness*—how intelligent they were and how much general knowledge they had—both dissimilarity and similarity played an equal role in determining repulsion or attraction. In other words, where intellect was concerned, dissimilar levels of intelligence did not repulse people as much as dissimilar levels of social attraction had. Based on this study, it appears that similarity in social behaviors is more important than it might be on other dimensions of attractiveness when it comes to relationship development. It further suggests that the repulsion idea remains an interesting hypothesis to consider as we attempt to understand the how and why of relationship development. It is also interesting to consider which might come first: attraction or repulsion?

Proximity. **Proximity** is the physical distance between people. According to research, the people in close proximity to you and the people you tend to interact with most often are also those people with whom you are most likely to develop friendships and close relationships. For example, your friends are most likely people you work with, go to school with, or live near. If you have a spouse or significant other, it is most likely a person with whom you crossed paths frequently and developed an attraction to after interacting several times. Although it isn't always the case, most people find themselves developing an attraction to those people who they see and talk to frequently, especially in the early stages of a relationship. For instance, if you went away to a college where you didn't know anyone, you most likely developed your first friendships with the people who lived in your residence hall or were in your classes.

Even in those classes and that residence hall, you are most likely to form a relationship with the people who sat on either side of you in class, and with your roommate or the person living next door. Similar is the fact that we are more likely to develop a friendship with our next-door neighbor than we are with the person two blocks down. When we are physically close to others, the chances that we will find them attractive is much greater. Although proximity always plays a role in the relationships we form, it becomes less important as we develop longer term relationships and have the chance to interact with people who don't live or work near us. The advent of the Internet and e-mail has further changed the way we think about proximity as well. We can interact with people who live on the other side of the globe on a daily basis and "feel" physically close to that person because we "chat" with them on a daily basis. In these cases, proximity—as well as similarity—play an important role in why and how we are attracted to certain people. Communication

We often develop relationships with others in close proximity to us—people who live or work nearby, or even just sit next to us in class. How many of your current friendships developed as a result of close proximity?

technologies have allowed us to be in closer virtual proximity, even though we are more distant in physical proximity, and develop relationships with others we might not have otherwise.

Physical and Social Attractiveness. What does it mean when you say, "That person is really attractive"? You might be referring to that person's **physical attractiveness**, the extent to which that person's physical characteristics are appealing to you. Or you might be referring to that person's **social attractiveness**, the kind of attraction based on personality and behaviors. Let's examine each.

The first information we often perceive about another is about his or her physical appearance. Most of us use that information to make judgments about others, including how attractive we find the person. Generally we seek others whom we perceive to have the same level of physical attractiveness as ourselves. You probably have noticed that people in long-term relationships, such as your grandparents or parents, often not only have similar physical characteristics, but also are similar in their levels of attractiveness. It is not unusual for others in our culture to make note of a couple who seems to have very different levels of physical attractiveness—one is strikingly beautiful, whereas the other might be rather plain or unattractive. In part, it is because beauty is in the eye of the beholder. In part, it is because for the most part research has confirmed that we tend to mate with others we believe are similarly physically attractive. In fact, physical characteristics help us in narrowing our pool of potential relationship partners. You can probably identify the kinds of physical features you find attractive in another person: Do you prefer thin and muscular, or bulky and soft? Do you prefer darker skin and brown eyes, or lighter skin and blue eyes? Someone who dresses casually and modestly, or someone who is fashion-forward and flashy? Someone with short or long hair, curly or straight? Your answers to these questions are based on not only your personal preferences, but your culture as well.

Culture plays a very significant role in what we define as physically attractive. Author and researcher Regina Spellers writes in her article "Happy to Be Nappy!" that for women of color in the United States, mainstream standards of beauty (light skin, blue eyes, thin, and blonde and straight hair) have created great dissatisfaction for women who do not meet such beauty ideals.[6] She tells a story from her childhood of having *blonde ambition*. "You desire hair that is longer, bouncier, straighter, and shinier than your own. You invest in potions and lotions and gels and pomades that hold the unspoken promise of good hair; pretty hair; Indian-looking hair, baby hair, kinda curly/kinda straight hair, hair like a White person's hair; hair that is anything but nappy. . . . You are not convinced that Black is beautiful." Although in dominant U.S. culture, beauty is often equated with being White, blonde, young, thin, and blue-eyed, the same is not true in all cultures and co-cultures.

Although physical features often play a role, at least initially, in determining why we are attracted to others, we often make early judgments of others' social attractiveness as well. As we introduced above, social attractiveness is attraction based on personality and behaviors. Do I like being around that person and his or her behaviors? Do we get along well? Our friends are usually people we enjoy hanging around with because they have personalities we like. Most likely they use communication behaviors that we admire and enjoy, or that are simply similar to our own. Again, culture always plays a role in what we find attractive in how others behave socially. If you are raised in a high-context/collectivist culture, for instance, such as Korea, you will probably be attracted to others who have less of a compulsion to talk unless there is information to be transferred, listen more, and are highly sensitive to the context of the communication interaction. Someone from the United States, for instance, which is a generally low-context/individualistic culture where verbal communication is valued and silence is considered abnormal, would most likely find another low-context communicator more attractive socially. The two are more likely to have a similar view of the nature and function of talk in social situations. How you define social attractiveness might also be based on your family experiences. The following example, explained by noted cultural anthropologist and researcher Geert Hofstede, is revealing of the role of culture (and family) in defining what we find socially attractive and appropriate. In his article "I, We, They," he recounts a story about social life he heard told in a speech by Raden Mas Hadjiwibowo, an Indonesian businessman from Java:

Visits from Javanese family members needed no previous appointment. . . . It never occurred to one that a visit would not suit the other party. It was always convenient. Unexpected visitors did not exist. The door was (and still is) always open.

The visitors were welcomed with joyful courtesy and would be asked to take a seat. The host and hostess hurriedly withdrew to change into more suitable attire than their workaday clothes. Without asking, a servant brought in coffee or tea. Cookies were offered, while in the meantime the host and hostess had joined the party.

There we sat, but nobody spoke. We were not embarrassed by this silence; nobody felt nervous about it. Every now and then, thoughts and news were exchanged. But this was not really necessary. We enjoyed being together, seeing each other again. After the first exchange of news, any other communication was utterly redundant. If one did not have anything to say, there was no need to recite platitudes. After an hour or so, the guests would ask permission to leave. With mutual feelings of satisfaction, we parted. In smaller towns on the island of Java life is still like this.[7]

Culture, including our experiences, is always important to consider when we evaluate our social attraction (or repulsion) to others.

Reinforcement and Reciprocity of Attraction. There are two other common reasons that we are attracted to others. We usually like others who reinforce or reward us in some way, as well as like others who also like us. Often, reciprocity of liking is a reward in itself. When we are attracted to someone and discover that he or she is similarly attracted to us, it feels good. It validates our wishes and desires. We also often find others attractive when they give us rewards such as compliments and praise or gifts and favors.

Communication researcher Charles Wilkinson has identified the importance of developing a vocabulary of loving messages in longer term relationships so that relationship members recognize what the other person in the relationship perceives as rewarding and not.[8] **Relational currencies**, those verbal and nonverbal behaviors that express care and love in relationships, are shared between members of a relationship. Often, what would be defined by one person as rewarding and as an expression of love (such as washing the car) would be defined as a simple task by the other. Wilkinson suggests that couples develop a common understanding of all the possible relational currencies in their relationship to avoid misunderstanding and optimize continued attractiveness of the relationship. Some of the most painful experiences in families, he suggests, occur when members value different ways of sharing affection. A list of common relational currencies can be found in Box 10.1. As you read, consider which might be rewarding to you and thus heighten the attractiveness of another person, and which would not. It's interesting to consider the many different ways that people define rewards, and thus the different definitions of what makes another attractive.

Box 10.1

Common Relational Currencies in Personal Relationships

Direct relational statements are oral or written messages that directly indicate love or caring—for example, saying, "I love you," or writing a card that expresses love or affection.

Positive verbal statements are also oral or written messages, but these directly or indirectly indicate support, praise, or liking. For example: Compliments, encouragement, and praise (saying, "Nice job!" or a note that says, "Glad you could make it today") all convey liking and affection.

Self-disclosure includes statements you make about yourself that the other is unlikely to discover in other ways. Self-disclosure usually deepens understanding and trust between people.

Listening, although frequently underestimated, can send the message of involvement and interest in the other.

☞ *Nonverbal expressiveness* is spontaneous displays of affection that communicate excitement, interest, or care for another. Examples include smiles, wide eyes, outstretched arms, or general nonverbal excitement about the presence of the other.

Touch can communicate physical intimacy and care in a number of ways, from a pat on the shoulder to the warm embrace between friends.

Sexuality, for adults, provides a special opportunity to express care and affection in a romantic relationship.

Aggression, at first glance, might not seem compatible with affection. However, in many families and other relationships, people who do not know how to appropriately express intimacy might use verbal or physical aggression as a sign of caring. Some conflictual couples maintain their conflict through bickering and arguments.

Gifts are symbols of affection and often signal a person's investment in a relationship.

Money given or loaned to someone you care about can express affection and caring when it is done freely and without obligation.

Food is a common symbol of nurturing in many cultures, relationships, and families.

Favors are those helpful acts that are performed willingly. Doing favors, such as washing another's car or cleaning up another's room, can be messages of affection and care.

Service is a kind of favor that has evolved into a habitual behavior, such as picking up children from school every day, making the beds every morning, or balancing the checkbook regularly. Providing services in a relationship or family, although often overlooked, can be a sign of one's involvement and care for the relationship.

Time together is a special expression of affection and love, indicating to the other person, "I want to be with you."

Access rights are those permissions you give to others to use or borrow things you value, such as your car, your lipstick, or the key to your apartment.

Social Exchange Theory

Although theories of attraction provide some initial clues about why we develop relationships with some people and not others, there is more to relationship development than just attraction. **Social exchange theories**, which represent not just one theory but a group of theories, suggest that we engage in a process of weighing rewards and costs in determining whether a relationship is worth pursuing or, for relationships that already exist, whether or not they are worth continuing.[9] In essence, social exchange theories suggest that relationships develop when they are more rewarding than costly or are more rewarding than alternatives, and are terminated when they cost too much. People often do a cost-benefit analysis to determine if what they are investing into a relationship is enough given what they are getting out of it. It is similar to the basic economic principle many of us use when purchasing a certain kind of car, camera, or computer. We might ask ourselves: Is this product (relationship) worth it? How much will this product (relationship) cost? What features does it offer relative to cost? Is there another alternative that would provide more benefits for less cost? Is this a smart investment?

Costs are those features of a relationship that have negative value to an individual; **rewards** are those relationship features that have positive value to an individual. When we subtract our costs from our rewards, we end up with the overall worth, or outcome, of a relationship.

Rewards – Cost = Worth/Outcome of the Relationship

Consider the relationship of two friends, Maria and Rosa. Maria finds many aspects of her friendship with Rosa rewarding: She has someone to talk to when she feels stressed about school, a failing romantic relationship, or problems in her family. She also finds Rosa funny, someone who gives her good advice, and someone who has introduced her to many of her other friends and even provided a family contact that got her a great internship. Maria and Rosa also have a long history as friends, and value the depth at which they know each other's feelings, thoughts, and dreams. These factors are all part of what Maria might consider when she thinks about the positive value of her friendship with Rosa. When considering the costs of being friends, Maria might consider the time she spends with Rosa when Rosa needs someone to listen to her talk about her abusive family, her failing romantic relationship, and her insecurities about finding a good job after graduation. Time spent listening actively and empathically to Rosa is an obvious cost, because it is time not spent on other activities or work. However, this is one of the only perceived costs of her friendship with Maria, and is something that Maria considers a necessary investment in a friendship she values. Overall, Maria considers her friendship with Rosa very valuable; the relative worth or outcome is high. According to social exchange theories, this is a relationship Maria would most likely work to continue.

Social exchange theorists also suggest that we enter relationships with a **comparison level** (CL)—an idea of the kinds of rewards and costs we expect to have in a typical relationship. Maria, for instance, has a general subjective idea of what she should give and receive in her friendship with Rosa. Her CL, like anyone's, has been developed and shaped by her experiences in past and current relationships, by observing others in relationships, and by messages about friendships and relationships she has received from television, books, and movies about what she should expect from certain kinds of relationships. Because they are personal evaluations, comparison levels vary greatly among people. If you have experienced wonderful and fulfilling friendships in the past, you likely have a high comparison level when evaluating potential or current friends. If you have had negative experiences in your past relationships, then you likely have lower standards (a lower CL) of what you expect from a friend.

Social exchange theorists also suggest that we evaluate the worth of relationships using our **comparison level of alternatives** (Clalt). Simply, we compare the rewards we are receiving from a current relationship with those that we predict we might receive from an alternative relationship. Accordingly, if Maria has just met a new friend, Karla, she will consider the kinds of benefits she might receive from Karla as an alternative to those she is receiving in her friendship with Rosa. According to this theory, if we predict that rewards from a potential new relationship might be more profitable than those we are getting from a current relationship, we might leave the current relationship to pursue this new, more satisfying and rewarding relationship.

Social Penetration Theory

Now that you have some idea of *why* people develop relationships, let's explore in more depth *how* relationships develop, and what happens to the communication in a developing relationship. Social penetration is one of those theories that offers interesting insights into the way communication represents and changes as a relationship develops. We briefly introduced this theory in Chapter 3 as it related to self-disclosure. Here, we extend that discussion by examining the process of social penetration as part of the process of communicating in a developing relationship.

Researchers Irwin Altman and Dalmas Taylor developed **social penetration theory** many years ago to characterize the way that bonding occurs between individuals.[10] Updated somewhat over the years in response to criticism,[11] it remains a popular theory for explaining communication in the developing relationship. They suggest that a process of social penetration occurs when communication between people moves from more superficial topics (such as your names, occupations, and interests) to more intimate topics (your fears, desires, and worldviews). The *depth* of a relationship is reflected in the degree to which topics discussed are more intimate or get at the core of one's personality. They also suggest that relationships are reflected by the number, or *breadth*, of topics individuals talk about.

Describing people as onions, Altman and Taylor explain that most people have multiple layers of information about themselves. Each layer on the onion (like Figure 3.4 on page 64) represents the depth of a person's personality, or the depth at which someone is willing to reveal certain kinds of information. Relationships develop when people penetrate through the outside layer of topics that are light or superficial (What's your favorite food? What do you like to do on the weekends?) to a middle layer of topics (What are your political beliefs? What are some of the social causes you believe in?) and finally to the inner core, where topics are deeply intimate and personal (Do you believe in a God? What are your greatest fears? What personal insecurities do you have?).

Further, the onion can be cut into wedges, representing different topic areas that can be explored at various depths. Your relationships with your friends, for example, might reflect a high level of breadth *and* depth of topics (you talk about many topics at both superficial and highly intimate levels—school, love, pressures, feelings, jobs, careers, other friends, and your fears, hopes, and dreams). A relationship with your teacher might reflect great depth, but little breadth (you talk in great depth about your fears of test taking and about your future career plans, but you do not discuss many non-school-related topics). Some students tell us about how their relationships with their parents reflected little depth but great breadth at times during their adolescence (they were unwilling to share their innermost feelings on any topic with their parents, but discussed a great range of topics—schoolwork, home responsibilities, jobs, friends, and extracurricular activities—on a superficial level). Can you identify different kinds of relationships you have as reflected in the depth and breadth of information you share with those individuals?

Keep in mind that this theory was developed at a time when relationship researchers believed that openness was the single best pathway to a close relationship. Models like this often represent relationships in an overly simplistic and linear way, not accounting for the complex way that individuals relate in long-term or less traditional relationships. More recent research, discussed later in this chapter, suggests that more openness is not always better in relationships, and that relationships are much more complex than this simple model of intimate communication advances.[12] Further, we should always consider carefully the ways that different cultures define and evaluate disclosures and openness in relationships.

Relational Maintenance: What Keeps Relationships Going?

Two of the major criticisms of all the models of relational development we have presented so far are that they are (1) too simple and (2) too linear. To many scholars, understanding **relationship maintenance**—the work that it takes to keep a relationship going—is actually the most important information that relationship members need.

We agree that understanding the communication behaviors and strategies people use for dealing with the often messy, and usually complex, long haul of relationship work is extremely important. The remainder of this chapter is dedicated to understanding relationship maintenance from the cultural and dialectical perspectives.

Relationship Cultures

Over two decades ago, researcher Julia Wood introduced a new way of thinking about relationships and the communication that creates them.[13] Although we've long known that two people come together to form intimate bonds, Wood's idea was to look at relationships as **relational cultures**, or as "mini-cultures of two." Your relationship is a culture, influencing how you behave, think, and act. You and the other people in your personal relationships share your own "unique private world." It is a jointly constructed way of knowing, influencing what you believe and value.

How do you define *culture*? Reflect on what you read in Chapter 2, and then take a minute and jot down what you think culture is. Most people would agree that our culture is the worldviews, language, customs, rituals, and values we share. We might think of it as our "logic," or what seems logical. When we go to another country, for instance, the way people talk, touch, smell, drive, eat, and/or run their lives may seem strange, or illogical. We live and breathe our culture. We don't question it because it's "logical" to us.

Culture is a useful metaphor to help us better understand how our relationships work. Our relationships are mini-cultures because in them members jointly develop their own language, rituals, worldviews, customs, values, and systems of meaning unique to that relationship. These "cultures of two" are created through and by communication. And they are logical to relationship members, because they have been jointly constructed to make sense in the context of that relationship. For example, you may have encountered a friend or other relational partner who came from a family where talking about sex or money, or openly engaging in conflict, was common, expected, and encouraged. In your family, talk about sex or money, or engaging in conflict, was taboo. The two of you come from two relational cultures that developed different (equally logical) relationship cultures, with different sets of rules. Neither is better or worse, just different. In relational cultures, the key is that they are constructed by relationship members, and that they make sense to all members. When a relational culture isn't working, it is the job of all members to co-construct and/or negotiate a shift in the relationship culture. Such shifts occur through communication.

Take a moment to think about one of your personal relationships. How would you characterize that relationship? Make a list of all the things that make that relationship unique. Do you have special rituals that you share? Have you developed words that have meaning only between the two of you? Do you share a special song? Do you enjoy doing certain things together? What rules have you developed (either stated or unstated) that guide your relationship? Do you have shared ideas about your future together? What memories of your past stick out in your mind? How have each of your networks of other relationships begun to interact? What private jokes do you share? Are there objects (such as a ring, a necklace, a card, or a poem) that have special meaning or that represent your relationship or a certain aspect of your past? What qualities do you think make your relationship special? The list you just created and your answers to the above questions describe your relationship culture. Each of your answers reflects important communication processes in relationships.

Manifestations of Relationship Cultures. There is no one way to be successful in relationships. The basic idea of relationship culture is that no two relationships are exactly alike because each is unique to the people involved and is a result of what each person brings to create a new relational culture. There *are* a number of common ways that we develop strong relational cultures, such as through developing a private language, sharing symbols in a relationship, playing together, and developing rituals. We will discuss two of these—rituals and private language—as types of communication dynamic central to our personal relationships.

Private Language. One of the most revealing aspects of any culture is the language developed and used by members of that culture. It is well known that people who live in Arctic climates have multiple words for snow, because snow is central to the daily life and basic survival of members of that cultural region.[14] They need to know if they can travel, build, hunt, and engage in other activities. The language of that culture reveals what is valuable to members of that culture.

What is valuable and important to many traditional-aged college students? Coffee? Beer? Time? Dating? Sleep? We know that many college students share similar experiences and, because of such, also share an extensive language reflective of their common experiences. You could probably list a dozen words for coffee, hundreds of words for the state of drunkenness, a half-dozen terms to talk about time, and even more labels for sexual behavior. Each of these "concepts" reflects important issues for many college students; many represent issues that the media communicate as important to young adults. Students in our interpersonal communication class can provide the following lists of words in less than five minutes. As you read, think about why some of these lists are long and contain many euphemisms and slang for a concept, and other lists contain only a few words or phrases. In all, the words in Table 10.1 reflect the language of a culture, that of many young adults in the United States.

Table 10.1
Words in College Culture

Coffee

Java	Starbuck
Cup	Cappuccino
Booster	Latte
Caffeine-jolt	Dunn
Caf	

☞

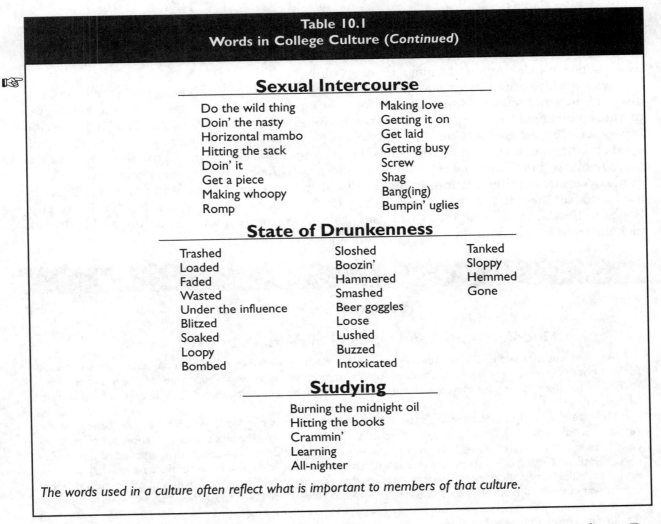

Table 10.1
Words in College Culture (*Continued*)

Sexual Intercourse

Do the wild thing	Making love
Doin' the nasty	Getting it on
Horizontal mambo	Get laid
Hitting the sack	Getting busy
Doin' it	Screw
Get a piece	Shag
Making whoopy	Bang(ing)
Romp	Bumpin' uglies

State of Drunkenness

Trashed	Sloshed	Tanked
Loaded	Boozin'	Sloppy
Faded	Hammered	Hemmed
Wasted	Smashed	Gone
Under the influence	Beer goggles	
Blitzed	Loose	
Soaked	Lushed	
Loopy	Buzzed	
Bombed	Intoxicated	

Studying

Burning the midnight oil
Hitting the books
Crammin'
Learning
All-nighter

The words used in a culture often reflect what is important to members of that culture.

In a similar vein, the Japanese language reflects the nature of the Japanese culture. For instance, the Japanese place great emphasis on the hierarchy of relationships. Being a high-context culture founded in Confucianism, their culture respects people and objects of higher status (such as elders). Even the use of verbs in Japanese language reflects this cultural value and hierarchical structure. The verb *to give* would be used in all of the following sentences in U.S. culture:

I need *to give* my plant some water.

I want *to give* my friend a present.

I need *to give* my teacher the assignment due today.

In Japanese, however, an entirely different verb would be used for each instance of *to give* depending on the status of the object being given something.[15] *Yaru* is the word for giving something to a lower status person or inanimate object, like your plant or the cat. The verb is *ageru* when giving something to a similar-status person, or someone in your inner circle, such as a peer or family member who is not an elder. The verb *sashiageru* is the most polite form of the verb, used only when giving something to a person in your "outer circle" who is of higher status, such as a teacher or elder. Again, language reflects culture.

Relationships are cultures, and the language of relationships is revealing of their culture. It is also an important feature of maintaining long-term relationships. For instance, research on the private language of friends and married couples reveals that many friends and partners develop **idiosyncratic communication**, the unique or "personalized" communication behavior developed and maintained within relationships. For example, one couple might use the term *elephant shoes* to mean "I love you" or refer to their children as "little us." Nicknames also represent kinds of idiosyncratic communication. In one study the most frequent kind of idiom was nicknames for a spouse, including names like Puddin', Peeper, Poochy, Patty Pooh, Bootie, Buttercup, Boobala, Buddy, Sweet Pea, Pussy Cat, and others.[16] For more about the nature and history of nicknames, take a look at the information in Box 10.2.

Box 10.2

Practical Research

'Cuddle Bumps' and 'Munchkin': What's in a Nickname?

Are you embarrassed to admit your own nickname? Maybe your father or brother has a nickname he's used for you since you were a toddler? Maybe your intimate partner has developed a nickname for you based on a trait that he or she likes about you? Maybe your friends refer to you by a name that sounds similar to your unique last or first name?

Most people are hesitant to share their nicknames with others outside their personal relationship circles. And that is not surprising. According to researcher William Betcher, nicknames are often a shorthand way, especially between intimates, of saying, "I know you in a way no one else does."[17] Nicknames, in most relationships, are very private. And many of us, according to Betcher, are embarrassed by our nicknames because we're hesitant to act in "childlike" ways. Nicknames reveal parts of us that are often childlike—the playful, fun, and creative part of us that wants to change our friend's name from Amelia to "Mealy" or Bernard to "Nardo." As researchers point out, most nicknames are spur-of-the-moment creations. And many originate from a partner's feature or trait (Lardo, Fuzz-head, Pumpkin-breath).

The 10 Most Common Nicknames
1. Honey
2. Baby
3. Bear
4. Sweety
5. Pumpkin
6. "___" butt
7. "___" lips
8. Snuggle "___"
9. Bunny
10. Peanut

☞

> **Creative Couple Nicknames**
>
> Ever know a couple who used the following nicknames? Betcher calls these some of the "most outrageous" he's come across in his research:
>
> Fussy Pants and Petty Spaghetti
>
> Printout and Abacus
>
> Honeypoopoo and Lickedysplit
>
> Honeydew and Melonhead
>
> Whimpina and Towelhead
>
> Toe Crusher and Ninetoes
>
> Sheepwoman and Midnight Shepherd
>
> As Betcher points out, nicknames given to men tend to refer to status or accomplishment ("Superman," "Top Enchilada," "Big Guy"). Nicknames for women tend to comment on their passive behavior or physical appearance ("Sweet Pea," "Sweety Pie," "Beef Cake"). Does your nickname fit this pattern of gendered naming?
>
> Nicknames are one kind of idiosyncratic communication. Like other kinds of idioms, they are expressions of relational culture. And using nicknames contributes to that special feeling between people. Whether you're friends, partners, or family members, it seems that nicknames are a good thing to develop and use. And even though we may not want to share our special title (my little "Poopy-Loopy" or "Doobie-Doo") with others, we can take comfort in the fact that according to researchers, nicknames are generally good for our personal relationships.

Researchers have identified eight different kinds of idioms, including:[18]

- Partner nicknames, terms of address used exclusively by the couple, such as "Moo" or "Pumpkin Breath."

- Expressions of affection, idioms that express love or affection; examples include using a double wink to say, "I love you," or the term *noodle* to express liking and affection.

- Confrontations, idioms that show displeasure for a partner's behavior, like the word *edge* to say, "You're on the edge of driving me crazy!"

- Labels for outsiders, nicknames for specific individuals or categories of people outside the relationships, such as *funkmaster* referring to the neighbor and his loud music.

- Request and routines, idioms requesting some form of action, such as "Let's take a bobo" meaning "Let's go take a nap," or "Need to nest" as a request for a hug.

- Teasing insults, idioms that put down the partner in the spirit of play, like the couple that refers to the husband as "fat daddy," a playful acknowledgment of the husband's extra pounds gained since marriage.

- Sexual invitations, idioms proposing sexual intercourse, such as "I'm really hungry" or "Let's make a sandwich."

- Sexual references and euphemisms, idioms referencing body parts or sexual behavior, such as *puffing* or *flo* referring to menstruation, or terms for male and female genitalia such as *chickie, wonder cave*, and *little sausage*.

Idiosyncratic communication is an important part of relationship cultures because it not only is revealing of the core but also builds the strength and character of the culture. For instance, idioms can aid in developing intimacy between partners and in building cohesion. They also can be used in the spirit of fun, adding playfulness and humor to the relationship. Many idioms serve to aid relational partners in resolving conflict, avoiding conflict, talking about taboo topics, and ensuring the privacy of aspects of the relationship. In a study done by Carol Bruess and Judy Pearson of 116 married couples, the more idioms couples reported, the higher the marital satisfaction of the couple.[19] They also found that couples who were married fewer years (newlywed couples) reported using more idioms than couples in later years of marriage (retired and "empty nest" couples). Other researchers suggest that intimacy is probably both a manifestation and a cause of idiosyncratic communication.

Idiosyncratic communication isn't only used within intimate relationships. Friends often develop their own private language, although possibly not as extensively as intimate pairs. One group of roommates developed a saying: "Pigs of the world unite—don't be afraid to eat at night!" which they sang together happily during late-night study sessions while indulging in ice cream and cookie dough. Another group of friends developed nicknames for each other (Soup, Ronts, and Hotts), which had meaning only within the friendship circle and which emerged from events they experienced together. In all relationships, an idiomatic system of communicating facilitates a "shared reality" in the relationship and builds the uniqueness of the relationship culture.

Relationship Rituals. Another way researchers have found that couples and friends build and maintain a strong relational culture is through the enactment of rituals. Rituals were originally studied by anthropologists who were interested in religious rituals. We know from their research that rituals serve essential functions of group cohesion and a sense of predictability for group members.

Rituals are common in our personal relationships, too, and are important for similar reasons. They are forms of communication that reveal what is important to relationship members and provide a host of important benefits. **Rituals** are defined as repetitive communicative enactments that pay homage to a person or object that is sacred.[20] This definition is useful in thinking about rituals as parts of relational cultures, because understanding what is "symbolically significant" between relational members is revealing of their culture. To one group of friends, a playful ritual of exchanging flamingo lawn art or going on an annual "Tough Guys' Night" is an important ritual in their friendship. Rituals such as putting toothpaste on the others' toothbrush, calling each other every day at 3:30 in the afternoon, e-mailing each other at work using a privately developed e-language, developing games such as competing to say "Happy Anniversary" on the thirteenth of each month, or "checking each others' belly buttons at night for fuzz" are all examples of relationship rituals that provide rhythm and predictability for members of any relationship. Many think that rituals need to be highly planned or ceremonial—like an annual holiday gathering—but in fact, most of our rituals are everyday, mundane occurrences (like those mentioned above).

Are you starting to think of the rituals you have developed in your friendships or personal relationships? Maybe you can think of some that you had in the past but have since faded or disappeared altogether. Take a moment and list a few of the rituals you share with friends or significant others. Now list a few of the ways that rituals function in those relationships. You might be surprised how important and common rituals really are.

In all relationships, rituals serve important functions for the relational culture such as providing fun and playfulness, serving as a means for communicating, symbolizing important aspects of the relationship bond, creating strong bonds and cohesion, and transmitting relationship values. The importance of daily, mundane rituals in our personal relationships is significant. Two researchers who have studied rituals in families for decades said it best: "Just as those religions with the most elaborate and pervasive rituals best retain the allegiance of their members, so families that do things together prove to be the most stable ones."[21] Rituals are relational cultural enactments important in all personal relationships. Recognizing where and how they exist in your own personal relationships might allow you to preserve and appreciate those you currently have, and knowing about their importance will encourage you to develop new ones.

Dialectical Theory: Understanding How Relationships Work

Leslie Baxter is known not only for her research in relational symbols and other aspects of relationship cultures, but also has introduced a new way (through dialectical theory) for us to think about our personal relationships. Baxter explains that **Dialectical tensions** are those contradictory pulls or needs that exist in all relationships, and that pull us in opposite directions at the same time.[22] For instance, most of us want both a sense of togetherness with another person as well as a degree of independence. Togetherness and independence are dialectical tensions— they exist at the same time but are opposing needs. Another example of a dialectical tension you have likely experienced is the contradictory needs for both revealing your private thoughts and feelings to your partner, as well as keeping some of your thoughts or ideas to yourself, secret from that person. Maintaining a relationship, according to dialectical thinking, means that we need to learn how to deal with the inherent dialectical tensions that will exist in all of our relationships, at all times. Take a moment to read Applied Concepts (Box 10.3) because it will help introduce even further the core idea of dialectical tensions.

Box 10.3

Applied Concepts
The Porcupine Dilemma

A writer named Leopold Bellak wrote a book in 1970 called *The Porcupine Dilemma*.[23] He begins his book with the story of two porcupines:

One wintry day, a couple of chilled porcupines huddled together for warmth. They found that they pricked each other with their quills; they moved apart and were again cold. After much experimentation, the porcupines found the distance at which they gave each other some warmth without too much sting. (p. 3)

Bellak's story of the porcupines is a beautiful illustration of a key dialectical tension in all personal relationships: How can we find the right closeness with one another, while at the same time find the right distance? This is the tension we talk about in this chapter between autonomy and connection (or the "me" versus "we").

All dialectical tensions exist in a similar manner in our personal relationships; there is a constant struggle to find the right balance between opposing tensions. Although the porcupines in this story seemed to find a suitable distance from each other, dialectical struggles aren't so easy to resolve. As you read more, you'll learn that

☞ dialectical tensions are ever-present in our relationships and have no absolute or easy resolutions. However, knowing what they are and how you can manage them will lead you to choices that will reduce the "sting" as much as possible in your relationships.

Dialectical tensions take a number of forms and exist in all relationships. For instance, in every relationship we have a need for being close, intimate, and together ("we-ness"), while at the same time we have a need for a certain amount of being apart or independence ("me-ness"). This is a great example of a dialectical tension, because one side of the "tension" wouldn't exist if there wasn't a tension pulling us in exactly the opposite direction. One side of a tension often fuels the other. For instance, relationships are generally founded on the notion of togetherness; we come together because of a desire and need to be close to another person. At some point in any relationship, however, many of us experience the feeling of "suffocating" (too much closeness); this feeling often gives rise to the need for some "breathing room" (a little distance) in that relationship. Often, our needs in relationships feel at odds with each other.

Relational dialectical processes give shape to our relationships cultures. They don't exist apart from our relational cultures; rather, they reflect the unique relational structures developed between and among members. All relational members must constantly deal with dialectical pulls if they are going to find satisfaction in the relational culture.

One of the key principles of relational dialectics is that they are present and normal in all relationships. No matter what kind of personal relationship you're in (parent-child, friend-friend, sister-brother), you will experience the surfacing of dialectical tensions. Some researchers like to think of "relationships-as-contradictions."[24] If you are in a relationship, you will be constantly challenged to work on balancing the inherent contradictions. It is important to also understand that there is no way to ever completely balance the opposing needs of a dialectical tension. The only way to deal with dialectics is to manage them over time, giving attention to them as they continue to arise at various points in our relationships.

For instance, you and your sister might currently live in separate parts of the country. You might have trouble staying close because of your distance. Although you send weekly e-mails, you feel a little disconnected from the core of her daily life. When you feel like this, you might send a few extra e-messages, scan some pictures of your children and send them as an attachment, call her more frequently, or send her something you know she enjoys (like a pair of wooly mittens or a two-pound bag of peanut M&Ms). Your response to feeling "disconnected" (one side of the dialectic) is to make efforts toward more intimacy (the other side of the dialectic). A few years from now, you might need to manage the dialectic in the other way as you find yourself living a few blocks away from one another and feel a little bit "suffocated" by your close proximity and the closeness in the relationship. Dialectical tensions are ongoing and nonresolvable. How you manage them is an important part of maintaining your relational culture.

There are three dialectical tensions that are most common in almost all relationships[25] (see Figure 10.1). Although others do exist, these three are reported most often by people in relationships, and cause the most relational trouble when not dealt with effectively.

Autonomy—Connection. As in our example of the two sisters and the porcupine dilemma, the dialectic of *autonomy versus connection* represents simultaneous needs for both independence and intimacy in relationships. The most central concern in most relationships is balancing these needs of closeness and distance in a relationship. This is especially true in long-term, enduring relationships. Our good friends Laura and Todd have experienced this in their long-

Figure 10.1 Three Most Common Dialectical Tensions in Relationships

Autonomy (Me)	vs.	Connection (We)
Predictability (Old)	vs.	Novelty (New)
Openness (Reveal)	vs.	Closedness (Conceal)

term, romantic relationship. After their two boys were born, Laura and Todd experienced a greater need for developing systems and strategies to stay connected as a couple. Having two children to feed, bathe, play with, and care for every day created a disconnect between them as a couple, as is common for many parents with young children. Their needs for intimacy and connection were greater at this point in their lives than they had been when they were first married because of the many demands of having young children and the little time and energy left over for focusing on a relational partner. As their boys grew and moved out of the house, giving Todd and Laura much more time to be together, reignite common activities and interests, and spend a great deal more time as a couple again, it is likely that Laura and Todd will then experience greater needs for independence yet again, giving necessary attention to the other aspect of this common dialectical tension.

Take a moment to think about when *you* have experienced this kind of simultaneous, opposing pull in a relationship. Did it occur when you wanted some independence from your parents, despite the fact that you still needed and loved them? Did it occur when you found yourself needing to have a little "cooling off" in your romantic relationship because you felt things were getting too serious, too fast? Or maybe when you and a friend felt you needed to spend more time together because you had drifted a little apart over summer vacation? Each of these represents some aspect of the dialectic of independence versus autonomy. Your experiences with this dialectic are probably as varied as your relationships.

Novelty—Predictability. The second most common dialectical tension in relationships is *novelty versus predictability*. This tension represents the ongoing needs of wanting sameness, consistency, and familiarity on the one hand, and wanting newness, change, and novelty on the other. Most people in relationships enjoy the comfort of their friends, families, and romantic partners. It's nice to know a person, their needs, their likes, their dislikes, and so on. The predictability of routines, rituals, and roles is desirable for most people in relationships, at least for the most part. It is comforting and makes life seem easier when you can predict what your friend will do when you purchase her a gift from her favorite store, when you know that Friday night is "sandwich night" at home, and when you know how your partner will respond when you bring up a recurring conflict. The predictability of such interactions is pleasing, most of the time.

Most people also have needs for change within a relationship. When life is too predictable, we might become bored. The monotony of our relationships, including the predictable nature of interactions, rituals, and roles, can create feelings of lack of interest, boredom, and even unhappiness with the relationship. When this happens, we need change, newness, and novelty. We might decide to plan a big surprise for our friend's birthday, spontaneously take the family out to dinner on sandwich night, or encourage a new perspective on a recurring conflict. Each is a way to infuse novelty into a relationship that is experiencing too much predictability.

On the other hand, many people can start to feel out of control or overwhelmed with too much novelty. As with all dialectics, the key is finding the right balance within the confines of your relational culture, satisfying the current needs of each member. Take a moment to think of times when you have experienced this dialectic in one of your personal relationships.

Openness—Closedness. Finally, the last common dialectical tension is experienced in opposing needs for both *openness* and *closedness*. In all relationships, we have to share a certain amount of ourselves within a relationship. Relationships are created and sustained through the communication of members. Being open about certain topics and expressing yourself are essential and desirable for developing and maintaining a relationship. In the past decade or so, researchers have also begun to recognize the importance of having a certain part of our selves remain private in relationships. "Telling all" is not necessarily healthy for an individual or the relationship, since certain disclosures might hurt the relationship or relational members. For instance, if your partner insists that you talk openly about an issue that in your family of origin was taboo (such as sex or money), or wants you to reveal a family secret that he insists he must know, you might feel attacked or uncomfortable because you believe that this information is part of your hidden, private self. A certain amount of discretion in self-disclosure is not only desirable, but also important in most healthy relationships. As with all the dialectics, finding the right balance is key.

Researchers have discovered a number of strategies people use to deal with the ongoing management of dialectical tensions. They include responding to one dialectic at a time, such as the one that is most important at the time (for example, Joe and Tina decide to focus on developing their intimacy for now, and agree to work on their separate interests later); attempting to meet the needs of both sides of the tension by separating them into different contexts in their lives (for example, Bill and Jordan agree to talk completely openly about their family and relationship, but to have privacy about some aspects of their professional lives); trying to neutralize the tension through managing both needs somewhat, but neither fully (Chris and Sarah agree to make a ritual out of being spontaneous on Friday nights); or "reframing" the dialectic as not existing in its entirety (Alex and Natasha no longer view the need to have separate friends as an important part of their relationship). As you thought about your own examples, were you able to recognize how you dealt with these opposing tensions? It is important that you give attention to understanding the nature of dialectical tensions in your personal relationships. They are present in all relationships, and by working to acknowledge their presence and manage them in an ongoing way, you are realizing the centrality of communication and change in your daily life.

The Power of Gendered Styles: Women and Men in Relationships

Finding satisfaction and making more informed choices about your communication behavior are not always simple matters, and there are no easy answers. Further complicating the picture, most of us think that there must be a difference in the way men and women communicate. Every time we ask a group of college students, a group of middle-aged working people, a group of preschoolers, or a group of new parents to describe the difference between men and women (or boys and girls), without hesitation they provide very similar comments about the "way boys are," "what girls do," "the tendency of men," or "how women are." In our own interpersonal communication classes, we begin a discussion of gendered styles of communicating by asking students to describe all the ways they think women and men each tend to communicate. They immediately and consistently fill entire blackboards with their thoughts, descriptions, stereotypes, prototypes, experiences, and perspectives on men and women. A sample from our most recent class includes statements such as, "Men are physical, sexual, tough, like to be successful, don't like to talk about relationships. . . . Women are kind, smell good, pretty, caring, emotional, like to talk about things, and are empathic." What would your list look like? Our guess is that it would have many similarities and share common themes with the lists above.

We learn a great deal about communication through the games we played as children, often in same-sex groups. What kinds of games did you play as a child?

Most of us come to relationships with a great deal of personal experience, and personal opinion, about what we think to be true about those relationships and how they work. We are theorizers in our everyday lives, making predictions, trying to understand behaviors, and explaining why things happen. And when it comes to gender issues, most of us have a lot to say, and even more that we want to know. That is why this section of the chapter is meant to provide you with some of what communication scholars have learned in their studies of gender and communication and of the nature and impact of gendered styles of communicating in personal relationships. It might leave you wanting to know more, as well as give you some concrete insight into gender as an important issue in our interpersonal relationships and communication interactions.

Gender affects just about everything we do. It influences how we dress, the roles we assume or are assigned, the way we view ourselves, and the expectations we have of others. Although there has been great debate on the issue of gender, and on how much sex and gender influence our communication and relationships, many scholars now believe that women and men do differ significantly in the ways they approach and communicate in their personal relationships. Julia Wood is one such person. She is a researcher, professor, and writer from the University of North Carolina, Chapel Hill, who has researched, taught, and studied the role of gender in our communication and personal relationships probably more than anyone else. According to Julia Wood, "Obviously, what happens between intimate friends and romantic partners is not determined by sex or gender alone; yet, among the many influences on relationships, sex and gender are important ones."[26]

It might be helpful to begin by refreshing your memory about what we mean when we use the terms *gender* and *sex*. As we pointed out in earlier chapters, they are two different, yet interrelated, terms. **Sex** is a simple category; it refers to the genetic or biological characteristics of males and females, determined by the number and type of chromosomes you have. **Gender**, however, is not so simple. Gender is the socially prescribed meanings for each sex. It is not innate but something you learn beginning the day you are born. For instance, your gender is what your culture tells you to be if you're a woman or a man: the way you should walk, talk, dress, act, and think, and even the careers that are more appropriate for you. Gender expectations for men in

U.S. culture include being assertive, independent, successful, and competitive; gender expectations for women include being expressive, caring, emotionally sensitive, and cooperative.[27]

We are encouraged, in subtle and explicit ways, to conform to the gender that society prescribes for us. Think back to Chapter 2, when we discussed how power dynamics exist at the microlevel and macrolevel. Gender socialization occurs at both levels. For example, boys and girls are socialized regarding masculinity and femininity in many ways: The media, peers, family, and teachers all send messages about the appropriate gender expectations. We say to our boys, "Don't cry," "Shake it off," "You can do it," and "Don't settle for less than what you really want." We encourage them to be independent, successful, strong, and competitive. We say to our girls things like "Take it easy—you don't want to get hurt," "Be nice—don't hurt others' feelings," "Make sure you include everyone," and "You look so pretty." In so many ways, we begin the process of gender socialization the first day of life. The minute we wrap a baby girl in a pink blanket and put a stuffed football in the crib of our infant boy, we begin the process of fusing our expectations of sex with gender. We teach our boys to be masculine; we teach our girls to be feminine. Those lessons are ones that are carried into adulthood and into our personal relationships. Many parents today are resisting the use of rigid sex roles in raising their children, instead encouraging boys and girls to engage in chores, activities, sports, or other behaviors not traditionally viewed as most appropriate for their sex.

"Talking about the relationship" can be challenging for people socialized into different gender speech communities. What do you feel when a relational partner says to you: "Let's talk about our relationship"?

One of the primary lessons we learn through our socialization into masculinity or femininity is the way communication functions and the ways we use communication. Much of how we learn to communicate in gender-specific ways comes from the games we played as children.[28] What kinds of games did you play when you were a 5 year old? Did you typically play "house," "school," or "Barbies" with a group of your friends? Was one of you the teacher, husband, or mother, while others played the children? Did one of you have "Ken" who married "Barbie," and then created a pretend house under the kitchen table or in the corner of your room? Games like these, which typically are played by girls, tend to include everyone in the play, involve talking as part of the game, and don't involve elaborate "rules" or have winners or losers.

Maybe you remember most often playing games like "kick the can," baseball, or kickball. These kinds of games tend to be played more by boys, have clear rules and goals, include multiple players, and have winners and losers. Girls and boys begin to learn the nature, function, and use of "talk" beginning in their often distinct arenas of play. The following are the communication rules that boys and girls learn from their distinct kinds of play:[29]

Feminine Communication Rules

1. Use talk to build and maintain relationships. Talk should be collaborative and cooperative.

2. Avoid outdoing, criticizing, or putting down others. Include everyone.

3. Pay attention to others' feelings and emotions. Be sensitive and attentive to your relationships with others.

Masculine Communication Rules

1. Communication should be used to assert yourself. Be sure to make your ideas known and clear, and use communication to achieve your goals.

2. Attract and maintain an audience with your communication.

3. Use talk to achieve status. Learn to take the focus off others and onto yourself.

You quickly notice that many boys are learning communication rules that have underlying themes of independence and status. Many girls are learning that communication should be used in an almost opposite way: to reduce independence and instead foster relationship building and inclusion. When girls and boys grow up, they bring these different rules and ideas about how to use communication and the rules for communicating to their personal relationships. For years, girls and boys who did not embrace traditional expectations of gendered behavior experienced negative consequences within their relationships. Sometimes this was because their communication did not meet the expectations of others. Other times, it was primarily because others viewed their nontraditional behaviors as inappropriate. You can start to understand why misunderstandings, based in gendered styles, can be a real issue and problem in our personal relationships.

There are a number of ways that differences in gender styles manifest themselves in our personal relationships.[30] Based on the lists above, what misunderstandings have you experienced in your personal relationships that you think have something to do with the gendered rules you learned as a child and now bring to your adult relationships? Take a moment and think about the rules you learned. How are they different from the gendered rules for communicating used by those around you? We're guessing that you can probably identify at least a few instances where these differences in gender rules and styles have had an impact (or even caused serious conflict) in your personal relationships.

Expressing Care and Closeness. To many men, talk is a primary way to solve problems and achieve goals. To many women, talk is a primary way to create and express closeness. Although this isn't true for *all* men or *all* women, many men and women in our culture have been socialized along these lines. Depending on our socialization processes, however, we do know that men can learn feminine rules and women can learn masculine rules. Most typically, however, the socialization of boys and girls and men and women follows gendered lines.

Masculine rules for communicating suggest that many men express their closeness and care through more instrumental activities, like "doing" things with or for others instead of talking. This difference in the use and function of talk makes it likely that men and women might not even recognize that each is communicating care. Janet, for instance, feels that her boyfriend John doesn't want to talk about their relationship enough. She defines a close relationship as one in which the two of them share intimate disclosures, talk about the daily aspects of their lives, and have meaningful conversations about the future of their relationship. Janet wants John to want to talk more about "them," not just save talking about the relationship for when it's not going well or they are in conflict. John, like many men socialized to the masculine way of communicating, views talk about a relationship as something only necessary when something *is* wrong. He would argue that he *does* communicate how much he cares about Janet, but he does so in ways that are less obvious to her like washing her car, folding the laundry without being asked, and running out to the drug store on a cold winter night to get her some better tasting cough drops. Janet, because she defines closeness and caring in a relationship by how much two people talk about their feelings and express their thoughts verbally, finds these instrumental expressions of care confusing. John is frustrated because Janet doesn't interpret all he "does" for her as expressing his love. Janet and John are easily frustrated because they are each socialized to define the function of talk in different ways, and count different things as evidence that the other cares. And because of their different definitions, each is often unaware how and when the other person is trying to show they care and show interest in the relationship.

Talking About the Relationship. Another potential for misunderstanding and frustration between men and women socialized to use talk in distinct masculine and feminine ways is in the idea of "talking about us." When Beth says to Allen, "Let's talk about our relationship," the first thing that Allen thinks is, "Oh no. Something is wrong now!" But Beth's invitation to talk about their relationship was meant to simply enhance their intimacy and build closeness. As you recall from the rules that boys and girls learn when they are young, feminine communication rules suggest using talk to build and maintain a relationship. The rule that boys learn as a part of the masculine speech culture is to use talk to accomplish a goal. Allen does not see the need to talk about their relationship unless there is some need—a particular goal—they are working toward.

According to Allen: "If it ain't broke, don't fix it." According to Beth, however, talk in and of itself is useful. According to Beth: "If we talk about it, it *is* good." Allen would probably suggest developing joint hobbies or interests—doing things together—to enhance their closeness and build cohesion in their relationship.

Listening Styles. Finally, as we suggested in Chapter 7, men and women are often socialized to listen differently and engage in listening with different styles and motives. As we saw above with Beth, many people socialized into femininity view relationships as built upon talk and expressing care verbally for others. When it comes to listening, women like Beth are taught to be responsive when others are talking and to express their responsiveness by using listening noises like "Oh, yeah," "Mmmm," and "Um-hmm," and by offering verbal affirmation and encouragement for what the other is saying, such as "I totally know what you mean" and "Exactly, yes, you're right." They might even use *talk-over*, a way of offering verbal encouragement for someone by speaking at the same time the other person is speaking. This is distinctly different from interrupting, which is using talk to change the mode or topic of discussion to one's own.

For Allen and others socialized into masculinity, communicating responsiveness or care is not a primary goal in talking. When listening, men might often not respond with the same encouragement and responsiveness as women do. They might listen to their partner in complete silence, and wait until she is finished to offer a comment or question. Because of their socialization, they might view a talk-over as a form of dominating the conversation, or as a type of interruption. Many women, however, interpret the lack of listening noises and encouragement while they are talking as lack of interest, concluding that he is not involved or doesn't care about what she is saying. The key here is not who listens better, but the realization that people use different styles of listening. The information in Applied Concepts (Box 10.4) further suggests that some of our listening style differences might actually have to do with how our brains are designed.

Regardless of your style of talk or the way you use communication, you should become more aware that not everyone with whom you have a personal relationship would necessarily have the same style as you. And when you are frustrated with a listener who seems to be insensitive,

Box 10.4

Applied Concepts
Men and Women Listen Differently: Is It All in Our Heads?

The observation has often been made that men and women have different styles of listening. As you read in this chapter, men and women are often socialized into different speech communities, resulting in different styles of talking and listening. Recent research on the human brain suggests that differences in listening style might not be all in our heads, but rather in our brains. Dr. Michael Phillips, a neuroradiologist at the Indiana University School of Medicine, has found that men listen with only one side of their brain, while women use both.[31]

The study of men and women found that men typically use the left sides of their brains while listening to language, while women appear to use both sides. The researcher does *not* suggest that men do not listen as well as women, but simply that men and women appear to do it differently. Dr. Phillips concludes that it would be dangerous and unfair to suggest that one sex listens more effectively than the other does. However, the research is intriguing, suggesting that more needs to be understood concerning the connection between our biology and our interaction styles.

overbearing, nonresponsive, uncaring, or just plain rude—ask yourself whether your perception might have something to do with the differences in gender communication styles we explained above. Not every misunderstanding or frustration occurs because of someone's gender (that would be too easy!). However, if you reflect on some of what you know now about these style differences, you just might find yourself thinking a little differently about those frustrating conversations or recurring misunderstandings.

Finally, take a moment to read Practical Research (Box 10.5). It presents an alternative viewpoint on the gender debate, suggesting that gender differences in communication might not be as significant and clear-cut as some researchers suggest. One thing is clear, however: There are no easy or definitive answers when it comes to understanding the influence of our gender and sex on our communication in personal relationships.

Box 10.5

Practical Research
Men and Women Communicating: Is There Really a Difference Worth *Talking* About?

A number of people don't like the research on gender differences. Beyond the fact that it can perpetuate stereotypes and limit our perceptions of others, many people wonder why we spend so much time focusing on how we're different, instead of figuring out how we're the same.

Two communication researchers decided to do just that: figure out if men and women are actually more similar than they are different as communicators. Dan Canary and Kimberley Hause wrote an article titled, "Is There Any Reason to Research Sex Differences in Communication?"[32] For all the studies that suggest that there is such a thing as a "gender gap" or "gendered styles" of communication, they believed, based on intuition, their own experience, and reading a lot of communication research, that the gender differences in communicating are small and insignificant. As they say, "Fifty years of research on the topic of sex differences in communication have provided no clear findings" (p. 129).

To find out just how clear (or unclear) the findings are on sex differences, they took a close look at hundreds of previous research studies on the topic of sex differences and analyzed the set of findings as a whole. What they found was that small differences in communication often seem to be due to sex, but often there are a number of other factors (such as communication styles, the nature of the interaction—competitive versus cooperative—and whether the researcher in the study was male or female, to name just a few) that influence the results. According to Canary and Hause, although we might enjoy reading the latest studies on how men listen differently or how women talk differently, they believe that such reports are not "good science." The researchers *do* say, however, that they believe there *are* sex differences in communication, but such differences are eluding us in the research at the moment. Their hope is for better and more conclusive findings . . . in the next 50 years.

The "jury is still out" on whether there are substantial differences (or even small but important differences) in the way men and women communicate. Until we know, we believe it is important to consider all the information that is available so that you can make better, more informed choices in your own personal relationships. After reading this chapter and the above findings, what do you think? Does your experience suggest that there are sex differences in communication? Or do you think that such differences are not significant? Talk about this with people in your class and your life. It should make for interesting conversation (regardless of your gender!).

Summary

This chapter focused on the nature of communication in our personal relationships. Specifically, communication is central to the creation and maintenance of all of our personal relationships. Relationships develop for a number of reasons and in a variety of ways, and contradictory theories exist to explain that development. You read about attraction theory, for instance, which suggested that we develop relationships with those who we are similar to, who we work or live in close proximity with, who we find physically and/or socially attractive, who like us too, and/or who provide us with rewards. Social exchange theories suggested that we weigh the potential outcomes of being in a relationship. Accordingly, we tend to develop and maintain those relationships that are more rewarding than they are costly. Social exchange theorists further suggested that we compare our relationships with our expectations (comparison level) and compare our relationships with any viable alternatives (comparison level of alternatives) when considering our satisfaction and willingness to continue in a relationship. Social penetration theory was introduced to explain the way that the breadth and depth of communication change in a developing relationship.

We also discussed the way relationships are maintained. As a relational culture develops, that culture is maintained through relationships rituals, private language, symbols, and intimate play, as well as through managing common dialectical tensions of autonomy/connection, predictability/novelty, and openness/closedness. Finally, we discussed differences between gender and sex, and the ways in which culture socializes us to develop gendered ways of communicating and viewing talk in relationships. We hope that you can use the information in this chapter to make better, more informed choices about your own communication behaviors that affect your personal relationships. We also hope you are now better prepared to identify which of the statements in the beginning of this chapter were myths and which were truths. Following are the answers and explanations:

Myth: *Personal relationships are simple.*

In actuality, personal relationships are very complex; this chapter introduced just a few of the many existing theories that attempt to explain how communication is the foundation of relationship development, maintenance, and termination.

Myth: *Changing your communication will change your personal relationships.*

Although communication is indeed the foundation of all personal relationships, changing your own communication will not necessarily change your relationship completely. Both parties in a relationship play a role in the outcome and experience of that relationship.

Myth: *Most good, satisfying personal relationships remain the same over time.*

Actually, most good, satisfying personal relationships are constantly changing and responding to the various pressures, dialectical tensions, and changes that all relationships naturally face.

Truth: *Wanting independence in a relationship is healthy and normal.*

This is true. People in healthy, satisfying relationships have needs for *both* independence and intimacy; it is one of the most common dialectical tensions experienced in relationships.

Myth: *Most personal relationships are relatively the same.*

As you should realize after reading about relational cultures in this chapter, this statement is a myth because each relationship represents a unique relational culture with its own private language, worldview, and shared history.

Myth: *The answer to most problems in relationships is communication.*

You can learn a great deal about your relationships by understanding the communication in them, but communication is never a panacea for solving all problems.

Myth: *Friendships and relationships are either good or bad; individuals can do little to change them.*

Relationships are the products of our interactions; making more informed choices in our relationships can often create positive relationship change.

Key Terms

Comparison level (CL)

Comparison level of alternatives (Clalt)

Costs

Dialectical tensions

Gender

Idiosyncratic communication

Intimate play

Physical attractiveness

Proximity

Relational cultures

Relational currencies

Relationship maintenance

Rewards

Rituals

Sex

Social attractiveness

Social exchange theory

Social penetration theory

Suggested Contemporary Readings

J. Fitzpatrick and D. Sollie. "Unrealistic gendered and relationship-specific beliefs: Contributions to investments and commitment in dating relationships." *Journal of Social and Personal Relationships* 16 (1999): 852–867.

J. Flora and C. Segrin. "Relationship development in dating couples: Implications for relational satisfaction and loneliness." *Journal of Social and Personal Relationships* 17 (2000): 811–825.

D. Holmberg and S. MacKenzie. "So far, so good: Scripts for romantic relationship development as predictors of relational well-being." *Journal of Social and Personal Relationships* 19 (2002): 777–796.

A. Hoppe-Nagao and S. Ting-Toomey. "Relational dialectics and management strategies in marital couples." *Southern Communication Journal* 67 (2002): 142–159.

S. Planalp. "The unacknowledged role of emotion in theories of close relationships: How do theories feel?" *Communication Theory* 13 (2003): 78–99.

J. R. Vittengl and C. S. Holt. "Getting acquainted: The relationship of self-disclosure and social attraction to positive affect." *Journal of Social and Personal Relationships* 17 (2000): 53–66.

Chapter Activities

1. Reflect on all the relationships (other than with your family) you have currently or have had in the past. Select at least three of those relationships and make a list of the various ways that you were "attracted" to each of the people both early in the relationship and as the relationship progressed. Take a look at your list and ask yourself the following questions: Were these people physically attractive to you? Socially attractive? Were they similar to you in many ways? Did you live or work near them? Did they reinforce you in some way? Did they indicate they were similarly attracted to you as well? In all, how does your experience in your developing relationships reflect or contradict what attraction theory says about how and why we develop relationships with others?

2. Using an electronic database in your library (e.g., CommAbstracts or something similar), utilize key words such as *culture, ethnicity, relationships, attraction,* and/or other terms we have used throughout this chapter when discussing relationships to find at least one article that extends your learning in this chapter about how culture and ethnicity influence the way we develop relationships. After locating and reading the article, share a brief summary of the key points with the class. As a class, discuss the importance of considering culture in all aspects of interpersonal communication, particularly the area of personal relationships.

3. Select one of your closest relationships (maybe it is with your best friend from childhood, your sister, your mother, or your significant other), and try to describe what kind of relational culture you have developed with that person. How have you developed this "mini-culture of two"? Describing a relational culture can be a difficult task (because it is often "taken for granted"), so you might answer the following questions: What kinds of private language do you share (nicknames or other idiosyncratic language)? What rituals have you developed? Have you developed a similar set of values, beliefs, or outlooks on the world? Can you think of ways that you have developed an intimate game or type of play that makes sense only to the two of you? Are there other

activities or behaviors that make your relationship unique and special, unlike any other relationship in the world? Discuss with others in the class how important you think a strong relationship culture is for maintaining long-term relationships. Also discuss the following question: Can you change a relationship culture that isn't what you want it to be?

4. In writing, identify specific examples of when you have experienced each of the three common dialectical tensions in your relationships (autonomy versus connection, predictability versus novelty, and openness versus closedness). After doing so, compare your examples with others in the class. Are your experiences with each of these dialectical tensions similar or very different? Did you find that certain kinds of dialectics tend to occur more frequently within certain types of relationships (e.g., parent-child, friendship, or romantic)? What did you do to manage the dialectical tensions in your relationships?

5. Spend time during each week of the course to volunteer your time at a local community-based organization (such as a girls/boys club, elementary school, English as a Second Language school, or community center). While there, take note of the ways that dialectical tensions are at work in all types of the relationships and interactions you observe and experience. Where do you see, experience, or hear others express contradictory needs for autonomy and connection, predictability and novelty, and openness and closedness? Monitor your own interpersonal relationships that develop within the organization, and write an application journal reflecting on if and/or how your relationships develop as the theories presented in this chapter suggest they would (attraction/proximity, social exchange, social penetration, dialectical oppositions, and so on). ✦

Chapter 11

Communicating in the Family

Contemporary Issues: A Different Kind of Family

The Shuetzes aren't your typical family. Lynette and D. J. Shuetze of Southern California have 92 children. As D. J. says; "If someone had told me 10 years ago that I would be living in Mexico with 92 kids, I would have told them they were absolutely crazy." But, according to a recent news release, the Shuetzes have decided to turn a love of children and family into their life by running the Door of Faith orphanage in northern Mexico.[1] In doing so, they have given dozens of children a home, food, a lot of love, and a family.

Families aren't only those that consist of a mother, father, and two children. Families come in all shapes and sizes, as do friendships and other personal relationships. The children living at the Shuetzes' orphanage learn this very quickly. Because many of the children dropped off at the orphanage know no one else and have no family that come and visit, they develop relationships with other children, often like brothers and sisters, says D. J. One of the things that the Shuetzes try to do for the children, beyond giving them shelter and other basic needs, is to help them build new relationships. A number of these children have very little experience in developing positive, caring personal relationships. At the orphanage, the couple works to model for the children what a family can be, and what it means to care for a sibling, a friend, or someone you love. Much of this teaching involves communication basics.

In many ways, the Shuetzes' "family" of 94 probably isn't all that different from yours. As D. J. says, like any other family they are busy "giving haircuts, making birthday cakes, putting on Band-Aids." This family may appear very different from your own based on things like size, ethnicity, regionality, family type, and socioeconomics. Yet the thing every family has in common is that communication is central to all personal relationships. Like your family, the members of this family are developing relationships based on the communication among its members. Like the relationships you maintain with your friends and significant others, the relationships among the children at the orphanage are developing in the same exact ways: through the creating and sharing of meaning. As we will discuss in this chapter, the process of communication in the family has a direct effect on our happiness, health and well-being, identities and self-concepts, and who we believe we are and can become.

Since we all have been raised in some type of "family," we often believe we know quite a bit about what families are and how to communicate in them. However, you may be surprised at how much you can learn about family communication that can help you, currently or in the future, to create healthier and more satisfying family relationships.

Myths About Interpersonal Communication

The following list contains some truths and some myths about communication in the family. See if you can correctly identify, before reading the chapter, which are myths (M) and which are true (T).

_____ Members of families can act independently of the family.

_____ Family happiness is only somewhat related to family communication.

_____ Family is defined as the people who are related to you by blood, adoption, or marriage.

_____ The divorce rate is increasing dramatically year by year.

_____ The most *typical* family in the United States is the nuclear family (two parents and their biological children).

_____ Despite the 50 percent divorce rate, most young adults still plan on getting married some day.

_____ Family interactions are generally predictable, organized, and patterned.

The information in this chapter will explain why the above statements are either true or not, as well as introduce much more information related to all aspects of communicating interpersonally in families. To begin, we introduce a framework for understanding family communication.

The Twenty-First–Century Family

Not all families are alike. Your classmates might talk about their own families: one that consists of two mothers, one with a grandparent or aunt who is living in the home, one who has experienced homelessness, one in which the parents reside in a far corner of the country, or one with 92 children like the Shuetzes. Families are rich with diversity, and the communication in them is diverse as well. As you will see in this chapter, there is really no "typical" family in the United States today. There are, however, a number of concepts and issues about communication in families that are relevant to all types of families. We will address all these issues—the uniqueness and diversity among and within families—as well as the way members use communication to develop and create the relationships in their families. We'll also talk about the way culture is influencing our perceptions about family and our interactions with family members, and the way technology affects both.

Defining Family Through Communication

Who would you include in a list of people you consider family? Some of us would include our family pet, some of us our extended family of relatives; some of us might have a dozen or more siblings and two parents, and some of us might just include one other person, maybe a parent or a sibling. How *you* define family is a very important part of how *we* define family. Although scholars from many disciplines offer definitions of family, we agree with the broad and inclusive definition offered by two family communication scholars, Rich West and Lynn Turner. Accordingly, we define family as follows:

> A family is a self-defined group of intimates who create and maintain themselves through their own interactions and their interactions with others; a family may include both voluntary and involuntary relationships; it creates both literal and symbolic internal and external boundaries; and it evolves through time: it has a history, a present, and a future.[2]

Notice the central role of communication in this definition of family, as well as the role of self-definition. We believe that families, as special kinds of interpersonal relationships, are formed through the communication of members. We also believe that less inclusive definitions of family exclude those families who have, for decades, been invisible in our culture because of the restrictive definitions of what counts as family. For instance, our definition allows for a more inclusive picture of family that might include grandparents living in the home, gay and lesbian parents raising their children, and the extended network of intimate others who are committed to as family. We also believe that families create, through their interpersonal communication and interaction, verbal and nonverbal boundaries for members of their families, and that families exist and evolve through their communication with members over time.

Think about how our communication often sends messages about what we believe is a family. For example, one of the authors has two friends, Linda and Terry. After about 10 years of marriage, Linda and Terry realized they weren't able to have biological children of their own. They soon adopted twin girls, Heather and Hanna, and began to develop their lives as a family of four. Linda and Terry do things that many parents do with their children: take them to parks, go shopping for groceries, and attend church on Sunday mornings. Often, however, their outings are interrupted by others who stare and even ask questions such as, "Are those your *real* children?" They have even had people ask if they are "babysitting" and friends ask, "Is it hard for you to think of them as your *own* children?" As you might have guessed, Linda and Terry's girls are a different ethnicity than they are. Such comments from strangers send a very clear message about how we, as a culture and as individuals,

Families come in all shapes, sizes, and forms and are defined in various ways by different people. Who would you consider part of your "family"?

define family. Although Linda and Terry's children are not their biological offspring, the girls are very much their family. As we proceed, consider carefully how your definitions of family affect the ways you perceive others and their families, and how you communicate interpersonally in and about families.

The Nature of Family Communication: A Systems Approach

Communication is a useful lens through which to examine family because it plays a significant, if not the most important, role in determining the quality and satisfaction of family life. According to much contemporary research, communication is often the difference between healthy, happy, and long-lasting families, and those that are not.[3] Communication not only shapes family life and reflects family relationships, but it is also instrumental in family functioning. As we discussed in Chapter 10, communication is also central in establishing the relational culture within family.

One the most widely accepted approaches to studying communication in the family is a systems approach. The **systems approach** proposes that all family members are connected to all other members, or are **interdependent**, and that together they form a whole. **Wholeness**, the most fundamental concept in systems theory, suggests that we can not view individual parts separately from the whole they create together. According to this concept, the whole is different from the sum of its parts. If you look on your kitchen table and see two eggs, a bucket of flour, a bowl of sugar, a stick of butter, and a bag of chocolate chips, you recognize that each item has a different taste and texture. Once you mix all these ingredients together in certain amounts and bake them in the oven at a given temperature, together they would be called a "cookie," something more than—different from—each ingredient alone. If you add a bit of peanut butter to the mix, the entire flavor of the cookie changes. Now imagine adding some hot chili pepper seasoning to the batter! Even a small amount will change the entire outcome of the "whole."

The idea of *wholeness* is similar in families; although each individual is a part of the whole, together they create something larger than, and much different from, any of the individuals in isolation. Every new part or change to one part (new member, new experience, new idea, new life stage, new perspective) adds to the whole in ways that affect the entire family.

If we view the family as a system, then to examine the communication within the family we can not isolate any part of the system. In other words, we can not understand the communication of any one member of the family in isolation from communication among other family members. For instance, Joe's family consists of his three older siblings and his two parents, Mark and Francine. Joe has been seeing a counselor because he has been involved in a number of fights at his high school and has become verbally abusive to his mother and siblings. From a systems perspective, we cannot understand Joe's behaviors and communication patterns completely without examining the family communication system within which he belongs. Every member of the family not only is affected by Joe's behaviors, but also affects his behaviors in some way. Even though Joe's sister Jill says that she ignores Joe's behaviors and tries not to take offense at his verbal outbursts, she is indeed affected by his behavior. By shutting her door or pretending she has to leave the room when he arrives, she is responding to his behaviors. Further, she has recently had a number of fights with her boyfriend about his use of language, and she has not been doing as well in school since Joe started having problems. Within a system, the parts and the relationship between them form a whole so that changes in one part result in changes to the others. As part of the system, Jill is affected by the other parts, in this case by Joe.

As you think about the systems view of family, it might be helpful to picture your family as a mobile suspended in the air.[4] The objects on the mobile are not fish or birds, but the people in your family. If you've ever bumped, even slightly, into a mobile, you know that all the parts reverberate in response to even the slightest movement of one part. In the family, if one member of the family gets a new job, quits school, is voted homecoming queen, is arrested for selling drugs, is on the honor roll, is laid off from work, or has a new baby, all members of the family are affected. Marriage researcher John Gottman reveals how in marriage, the behaviors of one spouse can greatly affect the behaviors—even the health—of the other spouse. For example, in his research on couple communication he found that by counting the number of times a husband uses facial expressions of contempt (e.g., rolling his eyes, or other nonverbal behaviors that put down the other person), his research team could accurately predict how many infectious diseases that man's wife would have over the next four years.[5] As a part of a system, the behaviors of one part clearly affect the other (see Figure 11.1). Think about the way that your family is connected as a system and how the communication of one member affects others in the system.

Figure 11.1 Family System

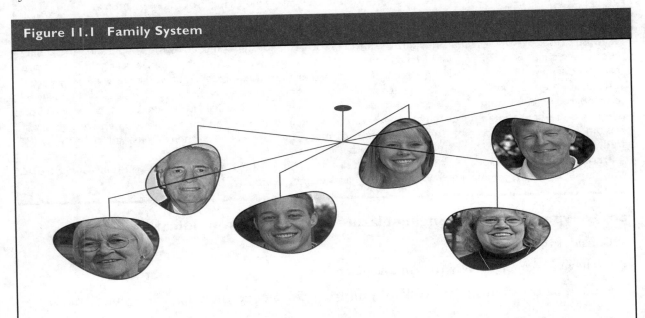

Like parts in a mobile, viewing the family from a system approach recognizes that family members are interconnected and affect each other in everything they do. Even the slightest movement of one member sends ripples throughout the entire family.

In the case of Joe, even though his sister doesn't want to admit it, Joe's verbal abusiveness has resulted in some change in her behaviors and in her own life. Her perceptions of the appropriate use of language in her own relationships and her inability to concentrate on her homework when she hears her mother and father screaming and yelling with Joe are just a few of the obvious ways she is affected as part of the system. In any system, each part is interdependent. Taking a systems perspective on family communication means that you will always consider the family relationships together, and not look only at any one individual. Take a minute to read the study reported in Practical Research (Box 11.1) for another example of interdependence in family systems.

Family systems come in all shapes and sizes. Let's examine some common family types in our culture and the way family is changing in the twenty-first century.

Box 11.1

Practical Research

In long-term relationships like marriage, interdependence among couples is a natural result of building an intimate and close relationship. A recent study, however, points out one of the potential drawbacks to the kind of interdependence experienced by members of dual-career couples. The study, reported as a recent news feature,[6] reports that when wives work more than 40 hours a week outside of the home, the health of their husbands declines significantly. The research, conducted by Professor Ross Stolzenberg at the University of Chicago, found that when a wife works up to 40 hours a week, there seem to be no negative effects on a husband's health. When a wife works more than 40 hours—as in 45 or 50 hours a week—the chances of the husband maintaining good health were found to decline more than 25 percent.

According to the research, gender roles are at work here. In the marriages studied, wives report being responsible for developing and maintaining the interpersonal relationships enjoyed by the couple and for planning much of the couple's socializing with friends and extended family networks. When a wife works significantly more than 40 hours a week, such socializing is more limited. Further, the study suggests that women are generally better at nurturing and encouraging their spouses to take care of themselves, such as through exercise and scheduling to see a doctor when needed. With more time spent at work, less time is available to encourage healthy habits on the part of husbands. In an unrelated study,[7] researchers found that divorced and separated men are two and a half times more likely to commit suicide than married men. They cite as one of the reasons, similar to the work study, the different ways that men and women often form social bonds.

From a systems perspective, these results are not surprising. After reading this, can you think of ways that your family is interdependent in ways you might have not noticed before?

Family Types and the Changing Nature of Family Communication

Consider these statistics:[8]

- The average length of a first marriage ending in divorce is about eight years.

- Each year, about 25 percent of children experience their parents separating or divorcing.

- Approximately 50 percent of all marriages will end in divorce, 75 percent of divorced individuals will remarry, and 60 percent of all remarriages will end in divorce.

- Childless women under 30 are the most likely to remarry following divorce.

- The median age for first marriage is increasing. In 2000, census data show that the age of first marriage is about 25 for women and about 27 for men (compared to age 20 and 23 in 1970).

- The number of young women (age 20–24) who have never been married has doubled since 1970 (currently, 73 percent of women in that age group have never been married).

- Although census figures on gay and lesbian families are not available because the government does not recognize this family form, estimates suggests that there are between 1.5 and 2 million lesbian mothers and gay fathers in this country. There are an estimated 5 million children who have a lesbian mother or gay father.[9]

- Currently, there are about 12 million single-parent families in the United States; 10 million of those families have single mothers, and 2 million are headed by a single father.

- Census statistics reveal that in the year 2000, approximately 4 million cohabiting couples existed in households in the United States, although experts estimate that the actual number is much higher.

- The number of young adults (age 18–24) living at home with their parents has increased dramatically; in 2000, 56 percent of men and 43 percent of women in this age group lived at home with at least one of their parents.

- Children living in female-headed families, Native American children living on reservations, African American children, and Hispanic children are most likely to live in poverty in the United States.[10]

- In the United States, 12 percent of wives are two or more years older than their husbands. Further, 15 percent of wives earn at least $5,000 more than their husbands annually.

- In the year 2000, unmarried partners were about twice as likely to be of different races than married couples.

Are you surprised by any of these statistics? Even if you are, you probably are *not* surprised that the nature of the family in the United States is changing. Your own family experience might be reflected in a number of the above statistics, or your experience might be different than the trends reflected in these data. Overall, demographic data indicate later ages of marriage, different compositions of family households, increases in family diversity of all kinds, and a larger variety of family forms. What kind of impact do you think such changes have on communication in the family? Then imagine the way that technologies are changing the nature of family interactions. For instance, a recent study found that 64 million people in the United States use e-mail regularly to communicate with family members.[11] According to another recent report, over two-thirds of adults in the United States own a cell phone.[12] The daughter in one family reports that her family members don't have names, just numbers on her cell phone: memory one, memory two, memory three.[13] Her family relies on their cell phones to keep in touch with each other and for more conveniently managing the family's everyday activities. More than ever, families are signing up for family plans that allow for shared minutes and free calls among family members.

Families in the twenty-first century clearly face different challenges than did family members in the past, and they respond to them with different communication strategies and patterns. Family communication plays a very important role in how families function regardless of the cultural landscape around them. As mini-relational cultures, families use communication to develop and sustain themselves as a system. Before examining some common communication patterns and issues in families, let's look at the variety of family types we will talk about. Although researchers categorize them in a variety of ways, we identify six family types.[14]

Nuclear Families. The **nuclear family** is what many people think of as the "traditional" family—a married couple living with their biological children. The nuclear family typically has a husband who works outside the home and a wife who works at home as a full-time homemaker and mother. More contemporary variations of the nuclear family include dual-career or dual-worker couples and families with stay-at-home-dads. Census statistics reveal that nuclear families are anything but the norm anymore. Experts cite many reasons for the decrease in nuclear families, including changing technologies, the state of the economy, more women in the workplace, and overall increasing mobility in a global world. Communication challenges for the nuclear family are many in a world where sex roles are less traditional than prevailed even a century ago. Further, there are fewer role models for mothers, fathers, and even children in the nuclear family type, so the negotiation of roles in the family is more common and conflict about such changing roles is more likely.

Gay and Lesbian Families. **Gay and lesbian families** consist of two people of the same sex in an intimate relationship, sharing a household and often parenting responsibilities for one or more children. Gay and lesbian families face a number of societal challenges because of homophobia (the fear of homosexuals or homosexuality), a lack of legal recognition as "real" families, and often a lack of social and economic support. In the year 2000, 33 states had adopted laws that prohibit same-sex marriage. In April 2000, Vermont passed the first law in the United States that would allow same-sex couples to enter into a legally recognized union.[15] In 2004, Massachusetts became the only state to allow same-sex marriage. Although most states don't legally recognize gay and lesbian families, many organizations *have* begun to offer domestic-partner benefits. According to a recent report,[16] in the year 2000 there was a one-year increase of 25 percent in the number of employers offering domestic partner health benefits in the United States. Fifty-one percent of Fortune 500 corporations offer domestic-partner health benefits. The benefits are not just for gay and lesbian families who marry, but for same-sex families who choose not to marry as well. To many, these benefits send a message of recognition and support for a diversity of family forms in this country.

Communication in gay and lesbian families is just beginning to be studied. One study found that because they face homophobic attitudes and even threats, these families are often more honest and open in their communication, particularly with children and with other members of the family.[17] Overall, though little research has yet been done examining communication in this family form, no studies have found that children living with two heterosexual parents are better off than children raised by gay or lesbian parents in terms of their personal, academic, or social development. In fact, studies suggest no significant difference between children reared by heterosexual parents and those reared by gay or lesbian parents in well-being, gender identity, self-concept, intelligence, personality characteristics, emotional adjustment, behavioral problems, peer relations, or likelihood of being sexually abused.[18] Researchers are now beginning to turn their research agendas toward family communication in gay and lesbian families.

Extended Families. The **extended family** is characterized as a family where relatives—such as grandparents, aunts, uncles, or cousins—live within the family unit of one or more parents and children. As more families embrace their ethnic traditions and as a result of a changing world economy, the presence of extended families is on the rise in our country. Recent research suggests that one in five African American families is extended, compared with one in 10 European American families.[19] Reasons for this difference include a history and tradition of strong villages in Africa and the desire for African American families to provide social and personal support for family members by sharing housing and parenting responsibilities.[20] According to one researcher, in the period between first grade and adolescence, African American children's living arrangements are diverse and fluid in family structure. The author cites, for example, the Woodlawn community in Chicago, where there exist 86 different combinations of adults living in households with first graders, and 35 different extended-family configurations.[21] Not all extended families are the result of cultural preferences and traditions, however. Many families live together with extended members out of economic necessity and a reduction in independence due to aging.

The communication issues central to extended families are similar to those in other family systems—conflict, role negotiation, rule development—but are often complicated by what is usually a larger and more diverse family system. Extended-family homes can be more stressful, according to researchers, but can also offer a source of strength and support. According to recent research, teenagers brought up by single mothers and at least one grandparent are more likely to go to college than those who live with only their mothers.[22] Teenagers in these families are at least as likely and sometimes even more likely to engage in positive social behaviors (like going to college, avoiding drugs and alcohol, and resisting sexual activity) than teens in married families.

Rapidly advancing communication technologies might soon change the way extended families live together. For instance, researchers are beginning to develop "smart" homes that allow families to interact and keep in touch with elderly family members while keeping their distance and allowing for autonomy. See the Applied Concepts (Box 11.2) for more on "Technology: Changing the Idea of Extended Family."

Box 11.2

Applied Concepts
Technology: Changing the Idea of Extended Family

Although many families live in an extended family situation either by tradition or choice, a number of individuals are able to live independently from their family members when traditionally, because of failing health, they might have moved in together to receive necessary assistance. With the help of new technologies, seniors are more readily able to live independently. For instance, a recent report on research being done at MIT and Georgia Tech[23] paints the portrait of an elderly woman baking bread. The woman, who has just kneaded in her secret ingredient, hears the doorbell ring. After attending to the door, she returns to the kitchen but can't remember whether she had kneaded the bread a second time or not. Not to worry, because new technology soon to be available in what researchers call the Aware Home will allow her to press a button on the wall-panel video screen and see herself preparing dinner before the bell rang. "Yep, bread kneaded."

New technologies may allow seniors to live in their homes longer and allow extended family members to interact and keep in touch without interfering too much. For instance, Georgia Tech is developing the Digital Family Portrait, an oversized data display that would be placed in the home of the person caring for the senior. The screen would relay a continuous stream of data showing the movement of the elderly person in 15-minute increments throughout the day. Also being developed is a weight-sensing floor, sending data about movement or lack thereof. Another idea is a giant movie screen that might be put on the wall in grandma's dining room and another in the house of her caregiver, most often a child, possibly thousands of miles away. The screen would be interactive to allow grandma to "have dinner" with her children and grandchildren by teleconferencing.

What do you think are some of the significant ways in which families and family communication might change in light of these new technologies? As some critics say, there is no substitute for actual human contact. Does this also raise concerns about privacy? High-tech houses might be the things of the future, but are they the right thing for families?

Step (or Blended) Families. The **stepfamily**, also referred to as the **blended family**, is a family with at least two adults who care for a child or children, at least one of whom is from a previous relationship. As the statistics presented earlier suggest, the presence of the step/blended family is increasing dramatically. Blended families face the task of bringing together two already established sets of family relationships, rules, roles, and communication patterns. Further, they also often face negative cultural connotations of the "stepparent" or "stepchildren" roles.

In a recent study on how blended families develop their "new" families, a group of communication researchers found that blended families face an ongoing dialectical tension between the "old family" and the "new family."[24] As you recall, dialectical tensions are those simultaneously opposing forces in relationships that are constantly present, such as the desires for both independence and connection, and the mutual desires for both stability and newness. In blended families, one of the key dialectical tensions is between new and old. The researchers found that family rituals were an important communication activity that allowed members to embrace their new family while valuing what was important in the old. The ability to adapt an old ritual to fit the newly blended family signals an important transition. For instance, one stepdaughter in the study explained how her mother instituted a new ritual of big birthday parties. Even though they had birthday parties in her original family, the new ritual is a bigger deal because it includes her stepfather and stepsisters as well as is a positive sign that they are a new family. Researchers argue that rituals are particularly important communicative enactments in families because they serve a variety of functions. As we discussed in the previous chapter, rituals are a way that people can build and maintain strong relational cultures. The same is true for families.

Single-Parent Families. The **single-parent family** includes one adult and one or more dependent children. As census data show, about 27 percent of households in the United States (12 million total homes) have one parent. The number of women as single parents has increased to about 10 million, but the most dramatic increase is in the number of single dads, a 25 percent increase in less than a decade.[25]

The single-parent family has been the target of much scrutiny and controversy. Can the single parent adequately provide for his or her children? Are children in single-parent homes as well-adjusted, educated, and behaved as children in two-parent homes? Research is contradictory. The communication challenges in the single-parent family can be great. Some single-parent families experience stress because they have fewer economic resources and one person trying to accomplish a large number of tasks. Thus, quality communication is often not a priority goal in a single-parent family.[26] Yet despite this, or perhaps because of it, researchers suggest that many single-parent families are strong, resilient, and adaptable. The communication in these families often reflects their adaptability.

Rituals are important communication activities, especially for blended families.

Couples. We recognize that partners in gay and lesbian relationships represent couples. However, in this section we will discuss two other kinds of couples, both having relationships without children involved. **Married couples** are those who live together, are legally recognized, and have publicly declared their love through the bond of matrimony. **Cohabiting couples** are those who live together and share a romantic interest. A 2000 census report suggests there are about 4 million cohabiting couples in the United States, although some estimates put that number at 5.5 million; about 55 percent of those couples will eventually marry. Cohabitation is still often viewed in our culture as a deviant phenomenon, although increasingly is being accepted as an appropriate form of "trial marriage" and/or an option that makes economic sense for many couples.

Census data show that over 90 percent of adults in the United States will eventually marry, although, as mentioned earlier, the average age of marriage is getting later than it has been at any other point in documented history (25 for women and 27 for men). The divorce rate in the United States is at about 50 percent and has been stable at that percentage for over a decade. For many, however, the fact that one in two first marriages will end in divorce is frightening. Many states, in fact, have started to play a role in combating divorce with what many criticize as controversial programs. Florida, for instance, has a marriage-education curriculum, teaching communication and relationship enhancement, for public high-school students.[27] Arizona and Louisiana have approved covenant marriages, in which couples voluntarily impose limits on their ability to divorce. When a couple signs a covenant marriage contract in these states, they are signing a binding contract that requires premarital counseling (much of which is about effective communication strategies and patterns in marriage) and permits divorce only in cases of abuse and other excessive circumstances like the imprisonment of a spouse. Currently, only about 5 percent of Louisiana couples are choosing covenant marriage.[28]

Consider, in Box 11.3, a controversial $10 million Oklahoma program that uses welfare money to teach communication and conflict resolution with the hopes of reducing the state's high divorce rate.

Box 11.3

Self-Reflection

Can Oklahoma Reduce the Divorce Rate?[29]

With the second-highest divorce rate in the nation, Oklahoma has been looking for some help in boosting marriage survival rates in the state. The answer, Oklahoma legislators believe, might be in their newly developed Oklahoma Marriage Initiative. Meichelle Jackson, age 41, is currently enrolled in one of the communication and conflict-resolution courses offered as part of the state's Marriage Initiative. The program is designed to teach participants techniques in relationship enhancement, including a variety of productive communication and conflict-resolution techniques. After divorcing four times, Meichelle is determined to learn some new communication skills to help her in future relationships. A single mother on welfare, Meichelle states, "I won't give up on love."

Oklahoma doesn't want to give up either, and thus has instituted the controversial $10 million Marriage Initiative, which uses welfare money to teach relationship enhancement and divorce prevention. According to some, it is a kind of driver's ed program for those who want to get and stay married and a thoughtful and interesting approach to supporting marriage. To others, it is an inappropriate attempt of the government to intervene in the business of a husband and wife. Even some marriage experts are critical of the program. Marriage researcher John Gottman has called it a poor substitute for meaningful couples therapy and believes that because many couples are dealing with violence, trauma, and depression, one 12-hour group session run by the state is not appropriate or adequate.

Meichelle, sitting in the course, listens to the instructor review patterns in relationships such as escalation, avoidance, and invalidation. She is attentive and interested, even though many others in the class seem to be doodling or giggling. One married couple in the class, after the session is over, declares it "informative." Meichelle, however, is skeptical. Meichelle's four husbands have all been physically abusive. She says that conflict-resolution techniques are fine but "don't stand a chance when your boyfriend is holding a 12-gauge under your chin."

☞   Although research shows conclusively that the quality of communication in a relationship is related to the quality and eventual success of that relationship, many people are not sure of the best way to get those skills to the people that need them. Do you think such a program is at least worth a try? Or should money be spent in other ways to help couples develop better communication skills for marriage?

Communication Behaviors That Predict Divorce and Relationship Breakdown

Finding happiness and success in a marriage, long-term partnership, or family is not simple. However, decades of research all points to a very similar conclusion: The primary predictor of family and marital satisfaction is the kind of communication that occurs between members. Hence, if you want a happy family, you have to consider its communication patterns.

Gottman found that a simple ratio of positive to negative behaviors is one of the key differences between those relationships that survive and those that do not.[30] Happy couples were those that maintained a five-to-one ratio of positive to negative moments in their relationship. It didn't matter if couples fought a lot or very little, or had great passion or very little; what did matter was the overall *balance* of positive to negative. While some couples seem to fight all the time and throw insults at each other on an hourly basis, their marriages are fine as long as they offer five times as many positive comments or behaviors. And while long ago, marital therapists would have thought that conflict-avoiding couples were doomed to failure, Gottman's research has found that as long as these couples share the interactive ratio of five positive moments to one negative one, their fewer negative interactions are simply offset by fewer needed positive moments.

The second striking conclusion of Gottman's research has been that not all forms of negativity are equal. Gottman points out that certain negative communication behaviors are more toxic than others and should, as he says, be outlawed from marital interaction. He has identified four particularly corrosive kinds of behaviors, which he calls the "four horsemen of the apocalypse." He explains how these behaviors work like a cancer in a marriage, ultimately destroying it. These four behaviors are:

Researchers have identified which communication behaviors are most likely to lead to happiness in marriage or partnerships. What communication behaviors would you guess are the best predictors of divorce or relationship breakdown? Are they the same ones that researchers identified (summarized in this chapter)?

- *Criticism:* evaluating and judging the other person in an interaction.

- *Defensiveness:* responding in a resisting manner that does not acknowledge the other person's ideas or opinions.

- *Contempt:* the act of despising or communicating a lack of respect for another person. Gottman suggests that a simple nonverbal behavior such as the "roll of the eyes" can communicate contempt in a relationship.

- *Stonewalling:* removing oneself physically or emotionally from an interaction, like putting up a stone wall. Eighty-five percent of stonewallers in Gottman's research were male.

Gottman cautions that there are often subtle differences between these four behaviors and other forms of negativity, such as anger and disagreement. He says that anger is perfectly fine in a relationship as long as the anger is not expressed with insult or criticism. He also says that all couples probably engage in these four behaviors from time to time, but they should be aware of their destructive nature when such behaviors begin to occupy the majority of their interactions.

Another researcher, Judy C. Pearson, conducted a study called "Lasting Love" in which she interviewed couples married 40 or more years who had what they and others described as the very best marriages they knew of.[31] Her interviews revealed five conclusions about what makes for long-lasting, happy marriages. First, there was *no single model* for a happy couple. The happily married couples in her study were from different religious and ethnic backgrounds, were of different ages, and often had different worldviews. Second, she found that couples who had *lowered expectations* were much more likely to find satisfaction in their relationships and lives. Couples who expected less were happier and less often disappointed with their partner or the events in their marriage. Third, couples with the most satisfying marriages were those who displayed *unconditional acceptance* of the other person. Fourth, happy couples tended to use *positive distortion* when evaluating the behaviors and even the appearance of their spouses or partners. Seeing the marriage and the partner as better than they really are was common among the happy, long-term married couples. And fifth, couples who had the longest and happiest marriages were *stubborn;* they weren't going to let anything come in the way of having a happy marriage. Different from the idea of commitment, Pearson found these couples to have a stubbornness about being happily married.

The link between communication and relationship success and happiness is very strong, although it is complicated. Next we introduce a number of the communication issues that are important for members of any kind of family, including the development of family meanings and the function of communication rules and stories in the family.

Communicating for Family Satisfaction: Family Rules, Rituals, Images, Stories, and Power

In the last chapter, we explained how two or more people come together to develop as a *relationship culture*, or "unique private world" created through the sharing of rituals, language, worldviews, and a history together. Families develop relationship cultures, or a **family identity**, and jointly create meanings just like members of other relationships. In families, a relationship culture is often even more important because as the number of members increases, so does the complexity of the system. As two family communication researchers explain: "Every family creates its own identity . . . and an overall experience of family life that cannot be re-created by any other family."[32] It is through communication that such an identity is created and through daily interaction patterns that a family comes to be "a family."

Communication Rules in the Family

One of the primary ways that families develop their sense of identity is through shared rules for interaction, although often family rules are **implicit rules,** or unstated. For instance, think of some of the rules guiding what you are *not* allowed to talk about in your family. Common taboo topics in families include discussion of family finances or sexual activity. Where and when did you learn such rules? Most of us learn them over time by observing other family members (how did Dad respond when Nate brought up mom's income?) or even by breaking the rule (Dad was not happy when he found out I was watching the "adult" movie).

Still other rules in the family are **explicit rules,** or those stated clearly and intentionally: "Do not talk back to your mother!" "When I'm speaking, you will look at me." "We do not lie in this family."

All families, regardless of the proportion or number of explicit or implicit rules, are rule-governed systems, meaning they interact with each other in an organized, repetitive fashion. Over time, such repetition creates the communication patterns that direct family life. Often, however, it's difficult to recognize the patterns of our own families because we take them for granted and view them as normal. How you would describe your family in a few sentences to someone you had never met before? What kinds of things would you say? You would likely describe the members in your family, things you like to do, how you get along, and what your family is like. Your description would most likely reflect the kind of rule-governed system you are. "My dad is really strict. He likes to be sure we're home on time. My mom is really great; she's cool and my friends like to hang out after school and talk to her." Or "My partner is strong and independent. She is very successful and we have a great relationship. We like to do a lot of outdoor activities and spend a great deal of our free time in the national forest camping and biking. We like to keep ourselves connected through these activities, but we also have a great deal of individual interests and we respect each other's needs to pursue other things." Notice how in both these descriptions, the rules that govern each of these family systems emerge. In the first, the rules reflect who enforces curfews and who communicates about topics "like a friend would." In the second family, the rules about autonomy and independence are clearly revealed. What does your description of family reveal about the rules that govern your family? Can you start to recognize communication patterns based on those shared rules?

In certain types of families, rules play an even more salient role. For instance, in alcoholic families, rule structures are particularly important and reveal a unique picture of what a rule-governed system looks like. Take a moment to read the Practical Research (Box 11.4). As you read, consider the power of family systems to regulate themselves through repeated interaction patterns.

Box 11.4

Practical Research
Don't Talk: Communication Rules in the Alcoholic Family

Claudia Black, a communication researcher, has studied the communication rules in alcoholic families and found a common rule, "Don't talk," shared by many children in alcoholic families.[33] She found that for children in alcoholic families, the rule of "Don't talk" is common and pervasive, and most often implicit. Children living with an alcoholic grow up sharing very similar family systems where not talking about what's happening is the *metarule*—the rule that guides all other rules—in the family system. Children in alcoholic families quickly learn: "Don't talk" about the fact that mom is drinking again, "Don't talk" about dad's problem, "Don't talk" about why dad didn't come home last night, "Don't talk" about why mom seems sick all the time, "Don't talk" about the way dad comes into our rooms late each night, and "Don't talk" about why I had to walk home from school yesterday. ☞

☞ The comments of Steve, the child of an alcoholic father, were common of the participants that Black interviewed: "I thought I was going crazy. I thought I was the only one in my house who knew dad was an alcoholic. I didn't know anyone else knew . . . because no one else ever said anything." At one point in Steve's life, he and his sisters and mother all found his dad lying passed out on the living room floor with vomit near him and his head bleeding after hitting his head on the coffee table. Without saying a word, they picked up their father and carried him off to the bedroom. Steve describes how no one spoke about it. The "Don't talk" rule in this family, like so many others Black interviewed, was pervasive and prevalent. The mother and sisters in this family system explained: "We didn't talk [about the incident] because he hadn't said anything, and we hoped he hadn't noticed."

Black notes that the implications for the thousands of children being, or who have been, raised in an alcoholic home are many, even though many of these children seem to grow up and suffer no ill effects. According to Black, as children of alcoholics grow up and begin to make career and family decisions, the effects of their family system and the "Don't talk" metarule start to emerge. According to her research, many children from these families experience depression and loneliness, and are fearful and anxious. They also have problems maintaining intimate relationships and often experience a lack of meaningfulness in their lives and relationships with others. Commonly, these adult children of alcoholics begin drinking more, or find themselves in a relationship with someone who is, or is becoming, an alcoholic.

You can see, through the research on this particular kind of family, how the family functions as a communication system guided by rules. You should also be able to recognize how each member of the system is affected by (and interdependent with) the other parts of the system. Even when a member of a family tried to leave or get distance from the system—for example, moves out and begins his or her own family—that system, and the rules that govern it, often come along too.

Communication rules in all families are important because they function to provide definition in the family, aid in the development of relationships among members, and contribute to a sense of family satisfaction. Most typically, communication rules come in three forms:

What can we talk about?

How can we talk about it?

To whom can we talk?

As Kathleen Galvin and Bernard Brommel, two family communication researchers, explain, these three types of communication rules provide a framework for looking at the communication rules in any family system.[34] Can you talk about money, death, sex, politics, religion, and drug use in your family? Do you have rules about what topics can be discussed face to face and those that are okay to discuss via e-mail or on the family listserv? Can you use vulgar language, technical terms, or slang when talking about any of these topics? Are there certain people in your family you are allowed to talk with about certain topics, or is everyone an available conversational partner on all topics? You might never have thought about how rules govern these aspects of the way your family communicates before. This is common, because often such rules are implicit in the family. As you consider your family's communication rules, also consider when and how the rules are enforced and in what context. Usually, figuring out how to navigate the rule structure of a family is an ongoing process, very much related to creating and maintaining an identity in the family. In Applied Concepts (Box 11.5), read about one married couple who created an elaborate set of rules in a prenuptial pact so that many of the rules that are often implicit and developed over time in families and marriages (like what time you have to go to sleep) wouldn't be left to chance.

Box 11.5

Applied Concepts
Rules for Marriage

Rules are important aspects guiding relationships. In most families and long-term relationships, rules are developed over the course of a relationship, often in response to current issues, conflicts, or demands. One couple, Rex and Teresa LaGalley of Albuquerque, New Mexico, however, decided to spell out the rules of their upcoming marriage.[35] As reported in a local newspaper, two days before their marriage the couple wrote an extraordinary 16-page prenuptial agreement and filed it as a public record with the local county clerk. In it, Rex and Teresa articulated many of the rules they jointly wished to guide their new married lives together, including:

* "To engage in healthy sex three to five times per week."

* "To retire for the night at 11:30 p.m. and awake at 6:30 a.m."

* "To assign Rex full responsibility for family leadership and decision making."

* "To live within a budget and pay cash for everything unless agreed to otherwise."

* "To leave nothing . . . on the floor overnight, unless packing for a trip."

The couple explained that the list began as a way of getting to know each other and spelling out their goals. They developed it as a prenuptial agreement because they believe that by writing down the rules for living together, they would give their marriage a better chance of surviving. Both Rex and Teresa have been married at least once before.

According to communication researchers, they are on the right track. Shared rules are an important part of a healthy and satisfying relationship. What is unique about Rex and Teresa's approach, however, is that most often relationship rules are emergent and implicit, or made explicit when someone breaks a rule implicitly held by at least one member of the family. Are there rules in your family that are made clear and explicit like those in this prenuptial pact? Do you think it is a good idea to write down a set of rules that will guide a future relationship? Do rules limit flexibility, or set clear expectations? Or both?

You might be wondering how the rules in a family affect children. A study reported in 2001 confirms decades of research that says that rules are good for individuals, family satisfaction, and healthy relationships among members. The study, conducted by the National Center on Addiction and Substance Abuse, found that in households where parents have established clear rules, teens have better relationships with their parents and a substantially lower risk of smoking, drinking, and using illegal drugs than teens in houses with few rules.[36] The study distinguished between a "hands-off" approach to parenting and a "hands-on" approach and found that only one in four teens live with hands-on parents. The parents who take a hands-on approach consistently do at least 10 or more of the following 12 things:

* Monitor what their teens watch on TV.

* Monitor what their teens do on the Internet.

* Put restrictions on the CDs they buy.

* Know where their teens are after school and on weekends.

* Are told the truth by their teens about where they really are going.

* Are "very aware" of their teens' academic performance.

- Impose a curfew.
- Make clear they would be "extremely upset" if their teen used pot.
- Eat dinner with their teens six or seven nights a week.
- Turn off the TV during dinner.
- Assign their teen regular chores.
- Have an adult present when the teens return home from school.

In the study, 47 percent of teens living in the hands-on households reported having an excellent relationship with their fathers; 57 percent reported an excellent relationship with their mothers. Compare those numbers with only 13 percent of the teens in hands-off families reporting an excellent relationship with their dads and 24 percent an excellent relationship with their moms. This study reinforces the importance of rules and the many ways that rules function in developing and maintaining family identity and satisfaction.

Technology has changed the nature of rules in the family, demanding a whole new set of rules as family members are increasingly communicating using e-mail to communicate. For instance, researchers in one study in the year 2000 found:[37]

- 59 percent of people report being more in touch with relatives through the use of e-mail.
- 40 percent of people agreed that e-mail made them closer with their family.
- 38 percent of participants agreed e-mail improved family relationships.
- 25 percent agreed e-mail helped them learn more about their family.
- Only 5 percent of people said e-mail added extra stress to family relationships.
- 31 percent of respondents said e-mail was an easier way to say unpleasant things or bring up difficult topics with family members.

Teenagers who live in households with hands-on parents are teens who report having better and more satisfying relationships with their parents. What kind of parent(s) did you have? Does your experience match that of the research on hands-on versus hands-off parents?

The researchers also found that more children than parents thought e-mail was an easier way for communicating about tough issues, and that what goes on in e-mail and other online forms of communication is similar to the kind of interactions that the parents and children have in their relationships in general. Another report found that family members need to develop rules for effective family e-mailing, such as "no flaming" and "no forwarding chain letters."[38] As noted family author Virginia Satir emphasizes, rules are "a vital, dynamic, and extremely influential force in your family life."[39] Even as technology changes the ways in which we communicate in families, the nature and importance of rules for guiding such family communication and the family system remain.

Family Rituals

We discussed the importance of rituals for relationship satisfaction and the development of relationship cultures in the last chapter. As you recall, rituals are repetitive, symbolic behaviors or practices shared by members of a relationship. They are communication behaviors that pay homage to a person, object, or relationship that is sacred. For example, the evening dinner ritual maintained in many families pays homage to the very idea of being a family and being together at least once every day.

Family rituals serve a variety of functions in strengthening families and are often cited by experts as one of the most important activities you can do for your family. For instance, they bond family members together and provide a sense of meaning. They transmit family values, attitudes, and beliefs, and a sense of belonging. Family rituals also help families create and maintain a shared identity. As we discussed in the last chapter, "Just as those religions with the most elaborate and pervasive rituals best retain the allegiance of their members, so families that do things together prove to be the most stable ones."[40]

With the widespread use of e-mail, the Internet, and digital photography for communicating between family members, family rituals have naturally started to become more high-tech.[41] According to Ron Huxley, author and family expert, rituals in families help form our collective identity and make statements about who we are as a family. In the twenty-first-century family, Huxley argues, new technologies such as computers and digital photography need to be a part of that ritual making because of the way technology is already changing the nature of family.[42] Family members who might live in the far corners of the world are using e-mail newsletters, creating online genealogical projects, and setting up family listservs; these activities are taking shape as a new form of twenty-first–century family ritual. Instead of resisting technology, Huxley says, parents and other family members might want to begin embracing technology as a new forum for creating family rituals.

Although rituals are often an invisible aspect of family dynamics that we take for granted, experts suggest that working to create and protect rituals in the family is particularly important. Recognizing the many functions that ritual serves in creating family identity is an important step in protecting the place and activity of ritual in the family.

Family Images

Another way in which a family develops a common identity is through the creation of a shared image of themselves. A **family image** is a metaphor that reflects what the family is like, what is expected in the family, how important it is, and what patterns of communication exist in the family.[43] Often, images and metaphors of the family are shared among members, although sometimes each member's understanding of the image is different from the rest. What image do you have of your family? Do you see your family as a football team, a concert band, the members of a corporation, the characters in a comedy skit, the waves in an ocean, or the components of a salad? Below are samples of two family images written by our students. As you read them, reflect on what they convey about the identities and cultures of these families and the communication patterns in them.

Family as a Team

I feel my family is like the USA Olympic Team because we all have our individual strengths that we are encouraged to use, yet we all work together as a team for one common goal: to strengthen our family ties. Like in the Olympics, we each strive to be the best that we can regarding school, work, and our personal lives (like our own athletic events). But if someone needs help, comfort, support, or just a hug, we all come together as one team. When it's all said and done, there will be no medals conferred, but something much stronger that will last a lifetime.

My Family: A Fruit Salad

To me, my family is like a fruit salad. My father is like a banana; he is tough on the outside but soft on the inside. He is a stern enforcer with a temper while other times he is a quiet observer. On the interior, he is a deeply emotional man who feels things intensely and who has a great respect and love for his family. My mother is like a strawberry. She is bright, beautiful, and colorful, with a wonderful appreciation for life. She is a favorite among her friends and is the one that everyone gravitates toward. My sister is also hard on the outside but very deep in the inside. I would compare her to a watermelon. She is tough and strong, a natural athlete. She is quiet and sometimes seems shy. On the inside, she is full of seeds of information and intelligence. She has a beautiful exterior, but her true beauty lies within. I think that I am like an orange. I wear my emotions on my sleeve and contain a lot of "juice." I am colorful and bright but can sometimes be a bit sour when I am moody. I have many sections inside of myself. All together, we mix to form a beautiful, colorful mixture of different tastes and textures, but complement each other and work well together.

The image that a family has of itself is an important reflection of that family's relationship culture and shared sense of identity. Often, alliances are formed in the family along the lines of shared images. The daughter who sees her father as "tough as nails" might align with her mother, who also views Dad as "strict as a warden." The father, who sees his family as a place to be "run like a business," where order is a priority and rules are meant to be followed, might align himself with the son who expresses respect for the rules and guidelines of the family and enjoys how the family "runs like a well-oiled machine."

Family Stories

Is there a story that you recall being told in your family? Many of us recall being told the same stories over and over again. Elizabeth Stone, a communication scholar who has written extensively about the way family stories shape our families, suggests that family's stories serve many important functions in families.[44] They delineate rules, teach members about the idea of family, identify family values, give families a sense of history, tell us what is expected of us as family members, and give us identity. They can also serve to simply remember family memories or members, to socialize new members to families, and to connect generations in families. Read the following story, "Life on a Farm," written by one of our students, and identify possible functions served by the telling and retelling of this family story.

Life on the Farm

I had just gotten home from college when my father called and told me to change clothes quickly and come to the upper farm. A new heifer had been calving for at least four hours and was in distress. When I got there, I found the inevitable. The calf was presenting with only one front leg and half the head was coming out. This meant that the other leg was twisted back, preventing delivery.

My father and brother had attempted unsuccessfully for the past three hours to capture her so they could help with delivery. But catching a 1,000-pound laboring cow is not an easy accomplishment. By this time, the animal had run over much of 60 acres and the hope for delivering a live calf was not even a consideration. The effort now was to save the mother from certain death if the calf was not delivered. I was given a rope, as well as the hope that one of us could lasso her while the others narrowed her escape.

What ensued was another hour or more of near misses and chasing a pregnant cow through fences, cornfields, and woods. By this time, we were all exhausted and soaked from sweat and crossing multiple streams that were waist deep. With nightfall approaching and the feeling that we had tried our best, the only option was to put her out of her misery with a gun. None of us wanted it to come to this, but it was the only humane option left. We could not allow her to suffer any longer.

My father and brother went to get the gun. I started out again, this time without a rope. She had crossed another stream and lost us, so I struck out again.

When I located her, she was lying down, attempting again to deliver. This time she was unaware of my presence. I slowly stalked to within 20 feet before she noticed me. With all the strength that was in me, I made one last attempt even though I had no rope. I ran up to her just as she was standing. Jumping across her neck, I grabbed her head and tried to twist her down, but she took off running again, this time with me across her neck and shoulders. I held on with all my strength for the next 300 yards down into another stream, yelling for help all the way. By now she was too exhausted and stopped in the knee-deep water. My cries were heard, and my brother and father drove up. With the weight of the three of us, we were able to knock her off her feet onto one of the banks.

While I held her down, my brother turned the calf and pulled its other leg out. Up to this point, I had only hoped to save the mother. But when my brother was moving the calf, it stuck its tongue out and mouthed his hand. We could hardly contain our joy. It was alive! Through all the running and labor, it was still alive. Quickly my father placed a rope around its leg and they began to pull. It was a big calf and it took both of them to pull it out. It looked like a tug-of-war before we finally won and it came flying out, landing on top of my brother.

We quickly began drying the calf, but now the mother lay motionless. We feared that she was dead. But it was only sheer exhaustion. We placed the calf beside its mother and backed away. We stood watching from a distance in silence, reflecting over all the events of the day that had finally resulted in this miracle. The emotions ranged from frustration to despair to unexpected joy. None of us could speak.

Only the tears in our eyes could express how we felt at that moment. We stood side by side watching as the mother slowly accepted her newborn calf and it began to nurse at her side. The bonding that we were watching reflected that which we felt toward each other.

Slowly we walked back to the truck to return to our lives, somehow changed in our feelings toward each other and the world around us. We had all experienced the most incredible event of life on the farm.

What functions do you think this story might serve as it is told among members of this family? Now reflect on the kinds of family stories told in your family and the functions they serve, and take a moment and complete the Skill-Building activity in Box 11.6.

Box 11.6

Skill Building
Your Family Story

In the space below or using your computer, write the details of a story you have been told in your family, or one that you wish to tell to others in your family. The story might be about a significant family member, event, or experience of a family member. It might be a historical or current event. After recording this family story, answer the questions below and discuss with others members of your class.

Title: _____

_____

_____

_____

_____

_____

1. What does this story reveal about the values, beliefs, and rules in your family?
2. What does this story communicate about your family identity?
3. Does this story reveal a common family image?
4. If this story is one that has been told to you in the past, reflect on and discuss how, if at all, the story has influenced the way you live.
5. What do you think about storytelling as a communication activity? Do you think it is important? What functions do you think it can serve in different types of families and for different family members?

Family stories are powerful ways to gain understanding in families because stories are not "right" or "wrong." Stories are also memorable in ways that other forms of communicating, such as data or statistics, are not. Further, family stories are important ways for members to develop a sense of not only family, but also a sense of self that comes from what the family believes and values. Communication scholar Navita Cummings James writes about how the family stories she heard about race as a child growing up as a "colored girl in the 1950s" greatly influenced her racial and cultural identity.[45] As she says, the telling of family stories not only educates children about their past, but also "passes on family values and helps prepare them for the world beyond the family." Stories told in James's family were a primary way that she learned beliefs and stereotypes about Blacks and Whites. Messages such as "Black people are just as good as White people" and "Black people are just as smart as White people" were common themes in the stories told to her. She explains how she used those stories—and the values communicated in them—combined with her own life experiences to develop a sense of who she was as a young Black woman in the United States.

Stories in all families serve a multitude of functions for individuals in that family and for the family as a whole. Stories are just one of the many ways a family creates an identity and shares meaning.

Power in the Family

In the family, power is often related to a member's capacity to influence the goals, rules, roles, or patterns of communication among family members and in the family system. *Macrolevel power structures* in our culture greatly influence the structure of power in many families. For instance, men have traditionally had more power in the family than women, as in the larger social structures where women remain less powerful than men. In the traditional nuclear family, for instance, dad was the one most often in charge of making decisions in the family. The macrolevel power structure in the United States also privileges adult power over child power. In most families, mom, dad, and grandparents have *legitimate power* over children and grandchildren.

Power is often manifest in the family around the task of decision making. Each family system has a slightly different process of making decisions in the family, although in each of these systems power inevitably plays a role. For instance, in the Johanna family, Marcus wants to get a skateboard because "all his friends have one." His father believes that skateboards are a symbol of a troubled youth culture and does not like the idea of his son "rolling down the street with his pants hanging half way down to his ankles." His mother, although a little worried about the potential for injury, agrees to let Marcus purchase a skateboard. In this family, the mother would be viewed as the one with power in the family in this particular situation. In another decision-making episode, however, it might be the father who prevails. Marcus, who has a close relationship with his mother and knows that she feels good about their relationship when Marcus tells her things about his life and his friends, is exercising his *reward power* by giving his mother the kind of information she likes to have about her son. His mother is exercising *her* reward power by allowing Marcus to purchase an item that he wants. Power structures and bases in the family are very complex. In just this simple example, multiple kinds of power are at work. Imagine the complex way that power would play a role in a multigenerational family conflict that has been going on for over a decade.

Researchers study power in the family from a variety of perspectives—as it takes shape in different family types, as it relates to decision making, as it plays a role in family conflict, as it is exercised according to roles in the family, and as it is related to violence in the family. Researchers have looked at power from a communication systems perspective to see how it is manifest in conversations.

A research team led by Edna Rogers and her colleagues identified a way to look at communication between couples and determine the power distributions that the couple creates together as a system.[46] They believe that power is not the property of one person in a conversation, but emerges in the interaction between individuals. For instance, if Martha says to Tony, "You have been very inconsiderate! You come home late, I have to clean up after you, and you don't even seem to notice that I'm angry." Tony's response to Martha might take a number of forms: (1) "I'm so sorry. You're right"; (2) "That is outrageous! I'm working late and you should be more helpful about cleaning up!"; or (3) "I understand that you're mad, but I'm not sure why sometimes. Let's talk about what we can do."

Researchers, based on a series of conversations between people like Martha and Tony, are able to identify patterns of relational control in the couple and determine the way power is created in their relational system. Each "move" in a conversation can be defined as a move for control (one-up move), a move for neutrality (one-across move), or a move to allow the other person to control the conversation (one-down move). For instance, Tony's #1 response might be labeled a **one-down move**, because he accepts Martha's right to be more powerful. His #2 response might be labeled a **one-up move** because he is trying to gain power over Martha by defending himself and adding his own criticism. Tony's #3 response might be labeled a **one-across move** because the power between the couple seems to be equal. Rogers explains that examining patterns of one-up, one-down, and one-across in conversations can reveal the kinds of relational control in the relational or family system. In a **complementary relationship**, the partners are opposite in their conversational power moves (one is assertive and the other not). In complementary relationships, we often see a number of one-up moves followed by one-down moves. In **symmetrical relationships**, patterns of conversational power moves are similar to one another and power might be the source of an ongoing struggle in the family or relationship. For instance, each person in the family system might be assertive and demand that their wishes be heard; often in symmetrical relationships, one-up moves are followed by other one-up moves.

Power in the family is complex. It requires that individuals are aware of the way that communication works as a system and the nature of power structures in the larger culture influences those present in the family. In all ways, power is yet another aspect of the way a family creates and sustains a family identity and unique family culture.

Summary

Interpersonal communication in the family is complex and offers an exciting context for applying a number of the concepts you have been learning throughout this text. In this chapter, we highlighted the fact that although every family creates its own culture and maintains a unique family system, it is through communication that such family relationships develop. We noted throughout the chapter many current studies emphasizing the central role that communication plays in determining the quality and satisfaction of family life, noting that communication is often the key difference between those families that are happy, healthy, and long-lasting, and those that are not.

We defined families broadly in this chapter, suggesting that a family consists of a self-defined group of intimates who create and maintain themselves through their communication within and outside the family. Our definition of family also suggests that families can contain voluntary and involuntary relationships, create boundaries for family members and their interactions, and develop a shared history over a period of time. To fully explain our definition, we introduced the systems approach to understanding families, using the mobile suspended in the air as an analogy. The systems approach proposes that all family members are interdependent and form a whole, each suspended as part of the mobile, and each connected to and affected by the movement or changes of all others in the system. In a family system, the whole is always different from the sum of its parts.

Throughout this chapter, we offered information on the way family systems are adapting to changes in the twenty-first century. We introduced and discussed six common types of families—nuclear families, gay and lesbian families, extended families, step- or blended families, single-parent families, and couples—and discussed some of the primary communication issues faced by each of these rapidly changing family forms. As people marry later, family households change, and there exists a larger variety of family types, family communication changes as a result. Research on communication behaviors that predict divorce and relationship breakdown suggests that if you want a happy family, you have to consider communication patterns in the family, particularly patterns that include what researchers believe are four of the most destructive communication behaviors in the family: criticism, defensiveness, contempt, and stonewalling. We highlighted the findings of other family communication scholars as well, who suggest that the development of a strong relationship culture and family identity lends to family happiness. Developing a strong culture and identity can be accomplished in a variety of ways, including nurturing family rules, creating and maintaining family rituals, sharing a common family image, developing and sharing family stories, and recognizing the way that power plays a role in all family relationships.

We end this chapter with answers to our myths/truths statements from the chapter opener. Look back at your answers as you read these here and see how you did. The explanations should also serve to further summarize key points about communication in the context of family:

Myth: Members of families can act independently of the family. Why is this not true?

Family members are connected to all other members in a system interdependently, and together form a whole. Although a member might "act" on his or her own, those actions do impact the family in some way.

Myth: Family happiness is only somewhat related to family communication.

This statement is a myth because, as most research shows, the number one predictor of family satisfaction is the communication in the family.

Myth: Family is defined as the people who are related to you by blood, adoption, or marriage.

Actually, what counts as family needs to be self-defined by family members themselves; many traditional definitions of family exclude certain family types or are too restrictive for changing and emerging family forms.

Myth: The divorce rate is increasing dramatically year by year.

The truth is that the rate of divorce is about 50 percent and has remained stable for over the past decade.

Myth: The most typical family is the United States is the nuclear family (two parents and their biological children).

In actuality, the nuclear family is no longer the "typical" family in the United States with the increase in single-parent families, blended families, and a variety of other family forms.

Truth: Despite the 50 percent divorce rate, most young adults still plan on getting married some day.

Census data show that more than 90 percent of adults in the United States will eventually marry, even though the average age of first marriage is getting later.

Truth: Family interactions are generally predictable, organized, and patterned.

Families are rule-governed systems, generally interacting in organized, repetitive ways. Such repetition creates family communication patterns.

Key Terms

Blended family

Cohabiting couple

Complementary relationship

Explicit rules

Extended family

Family identity

Family image

Family rituals

Gay and lesbian families

Implicit rules

Interdependence

Married couple

Nuclear family

One-across move

One-down move

One-up move

Single-parent family

Stepfamily

Symmetrical relationships

Systems approach

Wholeness

Suggested Contemporary Readings

L. Baxter and D. O. Braithwaite. "Performing marriage: Marriage renewal rituals as cultural performance." *Southern Communication Journal* 67 (2002): 94–109.

D. O. Braithwaite, L. N. Olson, T. D. Golish, C. Soukup, and P. Turman. " 'Becoming a family': Developmental processes represented in blended family discourse." *Journal of Applied Communication Research* 29 (2001): 221–247.

J. P. Caughlin, T. D. Golish, L. N. Olson, J. E. Sargent, J. S. Cook, and S. Petronio. "Intrafamily secrets in various family configurations: A communication boundary management perspective." *Communication Studies* 51 (2000): 116–134.

L. A. Kurdek. "Differences between gay and lesbian cohabiting couples." *Journal of Social and Personal Relationships* 20 (2003): 411–436.

M. P. McAdoo. *Ethnicity in families: Strength in diversity*. Thousand Oaks, CA: Sage, 1999.

E. L. Rogers. "Relational communication in the context of family." *Journal of Family Communication* 1 (2001): 25–35.

T. Stephen. "Concept analysis of the communication literature on marriage and family." *Journal of Family Communication* 1 (2001): 91–110.

E. Wartella and N. Jennings. "New members of the family: The digital revolution in the home." *Journal of Family Communication* 1 (2001): 59–69.

G. Witchurch. "Not just alliteration: Communication and committed couples." *Southern Communication Journal* 67 (2002): 89–93.

Chapter Activities

1. Think about your family as a system. On a blank piece of paper, draw what you think the system "looks" like. Who are all the members? How are they positioned in relationship to each other? How are they connected? After drawing your family system, in a paragraph or two describe your family as a system using the key concepts of interdependence and wholeness. Identify at least one example of a family situation where

something that initially just affected one person in the family eventually affected the whole family system in some way.

2. With other members of your class, discuss who you would include in your definition of *family.* Does your family include others who would not traditionally be included in definitions of family, such as friends, extended family members, or significant others? How do you think family is most typically defined by people in our culture? Discuss what implications you think such definitions have for a variety of the family types introduced in this chapter.

3. Find a local assisted-living facility or nursing home at which you can volunteer time with some of the elderly residents this term. Spend time listening to the stories of a resident's family life growing up and/or currently. Document these stories either by tape recording them or taking careful notes. Write your notes into a family history, and then give that written history to the resident at the end of the semester. Reflect on the kinds of family stories the person told you and how such stories serve as an important communication event in his or her family.

4. Using the key words *family communication, power,* and *culture,* find at least one article using your library's database that extends your learning about family communication as it relates to these issues. Summarize what you learn by reading this article, and share it with your class. Also, discuss as a class what kinds of topics and articles came up with these key words.

5. Visit the Web site *http://faculty-web.at.nwu.edu/commstud/galvin/genograms/* to learn about how to create a family *genogram.* A genogram is a family diagram that provides a way of mapping family communication patterns and relationships across at least three generations. This Web site will give you a complete history of the genogram, walk you step by step through the creation of your own genogram, explain how to understand and interpret your genogram, and also provide links to help you understand the communication patterns in your own family.

6. Do you have any rituals in your family, either currently or in the past? What are they? Do you have a shared image or a metaphor that represents your family? What would it be? Are there rules in your family that specify what you can talk about, how, and with whom? What are some of those rules, and how did you learn them? Discuss each of these aspects of creating family identity with others in your class.

7. What is your family image? Create a metaphor for your family and illustrate that image in words and/or images. What does your image reveal about the patterns of communication and relationships in your family? Would other members of your family likely create a similar family image? Share your family image with others in your class. ✦

Chapter 12

Communicating at Work

Contemporary Issues: A Dream Job Goes Bad

In 1985, Beth Ann Faragher was a 19-year-old college student in Florida when she got what seemed like the perfect job: an ocean lifeguard in Boca Raton, Florida, just north of Fort Lauderdale. "Basically, you're getting paid to work out for an hour in the morning, you get an hour paid lunch, and you're sitting on the beach in South Florida," she remembers thinking. But there was just one drawback: sexual harassment. One of Beth's supervisors would constantly try to touch her inappropriately, and another would often make sexual innuendos.

She recalls that one of the supervisors "made comments about me almost immediately. . . . He would make comments about the size of my breasts. He would make comments about my legs. He would invite me to shower with him after a morning workout." Her initial strategy was to try to defuse the situation and avoid both men. "Basically I'd wrap up in a towel and wear an old-smelling t-shirt. I thought maybe if I covered up, I could avoid this type of thing. I'd back myself in a corner at the morning meetings to avoid him being able to get around the back of me."

Although she thought about quitting, she decided otherwise. "Other than these two men, it was a great job. I didn't think I should let these two people control my life to the extent that I would quit." Eventually, she would sue them, and the city, in a landmark case that went all the way to the U.S. Supreme Court. In 1998, Faragher v. Boca Raton was settled and the Court found that employers are potentially liable for supervisors' sexual misconduct toward an employee—even if they were unaware of it. To find out more about Beth Ann Faragher, Faragher v. Boca Raton, the most recent sexual harassment legal decisions, as well as corporate responses to court cases, go to http://www.cnn.com/2000/CAREER/trends/10/03/harassment/index.html. This Web site also has interactive message boards, survey results, self-tests, and information on another growing trend: sexual harassment allegations by men.

Certainly, sexual harassment is not an issue for all individuals in all workplaces. A number of other communication-related issues exist, many of which we will discuss in this chapter. Most adults spend approximately half of their waking hours at work. Because of this, many of the relationships—professional, social, and personal—that we have are connected to the organizations in which we work. Some of these relationships, like friendships and romances, have been addressed in Chapter 10 and throughout other chapters. However, relationships that occur in the context of a workplace are different. Professional relationships are largely not voluntary like other personal relationships.

Anyone who has ever worked, whether in a long-time professional position, summer job, internship, or part-time position on campus, recognizes that a number of interpersonal communication challenges exist in the workplace. Sexual harassment is just one of the challenges we will discuss in this chapter. Many of the general interpersonal communication principles that we covered in Sections I and II obviously apply to communicating at work. In this chapter, we extend these ideas to the unique dynamics of the workplace. Consistent with other chapters, we also highlight the role of culture, power, and technology.

Myths About Interpersonal Communication

Below are six statements that represent beliefs or ideas about interpersonal communication in the workplace. Read each statement and then decide if you think it is a myth (M) or a truth (T).

_____ The use of advanced technology in organizations has been a win-win situation for everyone involved.

_____ Employers always choose the job applicant who has the greatest amount of experience and expertise.

_____ Job satisfaction is a complex concept that includes both task and social dimensions.

_____ Romantic relationships in the workplace can have both positive and negative influences on organizational effectiveness.

_____ In organizations, those with the highest positions always hold the most power.

_____ Sexual harassment is rooted in basic physical attraction.

As in any other context, the interpersonal communication that occurs in the workplace is clouded by different myths. Often, our communication misunderstandings can be traced to these very mistruths. One of the goals of this chapter is to debunk existing myths and help you understand how they can be detrimental to your communication effectiveness.

The Twenty-First–Century Workplace

Several defining characteristics differentiate today's workplace from that of the past, including increased diversity, global competitiveness, greater productivity, and widespread and advancing technology. The impact that these changes have had on organizations specifically, and society in general, is undeniable. Furthermore, we would suggest that the role that they play will only increase. As you read each description below, identify how each affects workplace dynamics.

Increased Diversity

Many predictions made in the 1980s and 1990s are unfolding right before our eyes. Our society is becoming increasingly diverse in terms of race and ethnicity. Some states, like California, have become "minority-majority states," where the number of people of color outnumber

European Americans. This diversity is reflected in the workplace. However, organizational diversity is not limited to different racial and ethnic groups. Women have been entering the workforce in large numbers and now outnumber men. According to the 2000 U.S. Census, the average age of workers continues to rise. In short, our society continues to become increasingly diverse in terms of race/ethnicity, gender, age, spirituality, disability, and sexual orientation. This diversity is reflected in the makeup of our organizations, and how organizations serve the public.

Global Competitiveness

As we are drawn into one big global village, businesses have struggled to position themselves to accommodate international markets. The traditional local small business is being replaced by the multinational company whose products and services are as diverse as their various sites around the world. Many of you probably notice that the small family-owned stores in many neighborhoods are finding it difficult to compete with larger chains that are able to stock a wider variety of items and sell them at lower prices. However, some specialty stores have managed to survive by using the Internet to reach potential customers with few limitations of space and time. For example, a local company with 10 employees can now provide services, regardless of location, to people around the clock. However, it must be able to compete with larger companies whose resources often allow them to generate products and services cheaper and faster. One thing is certain: The competition among companies is fierce and affects each level of the workplace (e.g., how well different units must work together).

Technology has allowed many organizations to interact with others around the world.

Greater Productivity

In order to compete in the midst of local, national, and international competitors, organizations have had to become more and more effective. They are rethinking traditional ways of doing business including business philosophy, operations, organizational hierarchy, and individual and collective expectations. The basic goal of these efforts is to eliminate the duplication of efforts and create the most effective production of services and products possible. In some cases, firms have eliminated worksites, divisions, or departments that were less efficient than others. Sometimes two or more jobs have been collapsed into one, resulting in savings on salaries. These changes simultaneously helped organizations stay competitive in different markets and make their stockholders happy. But they have also had an irreversible effect on employee-employer relations.

Technology

Many of the characteristics described here are interrelated. This is especially true for technology, which has facilitated a global competitiveness that requires greater organizational effectiveness. Advances in technology have transformed the way organizations function. Think, for a moment, about how different technologies have become crucial for communicating at work. The impact of the Internet, for example, is mind-boggling. Yet, a 2000 study[1] found that a substantial percentage of people (over 50 percent) were afraid of or resistant to new technology. Although the vast majority of white-collar workers surveyed recognized that the information superhighway would help their companies, many had concerns about losing their privacy (56 percent), spending less time communicating face to face with colleagues (38 percent), or being required to constantly learn new skills (35 percent). Despite these concerns, technological advances continue to define our communication. For instance, organizational use of the Internet in 2000 surpassed telephone use with over 3 billion e-mail messages being sent each day.[2] Many of us believe we might as well "call it a day" if our computers are down!

Box 12.1

Practical Research

People are becoming increasingly concerned about privacy at work. It's well known, for instance, that e-mail messages are less private than messages written on a postcard. But e-mail isn't the only form of workplace communication about which people worry. A 2000 study conducted by the American Management Association[3] provides some insight into these concerns. According to the findings, of the large companies that were included in their sample:

- 6.8 percent monitored voice mail messages.
- 11.5 percent monitored phone conversations.
- 14.6 percent used video recordings of job performance.
- 30.8 percent monitored computer files.
- 38.1 percent monitored e-mail messages.
- 44 percent monitored telephone use.
- 54.1 percent monitored Internet connections.

After reading these findings, what are your thoughts? Do you think that these numbers would increase or decrease if the survey was done today?

Fear of (or resistance to) technology is only one of the many challenges that face organizations in the twenty-first century. The characteristics described here also generate a host of related issues, several of which are related to interpersonal communication. The Practical Research summarized in Box 12.1 points to one of these issues. However, many other potential problems exist, including:

- Communication-based misunderstandings that are rooted in the lack of interpersonal contact.

- Information overload and technological connectedness that produce an inability to enjoy personal time.

- Greater distractions caused by the opportunity to use the Internet for personal entertainment or enjoyment while working.

- Increased job responsibilities that require more time and energy and result in a longer work week.

- Deemphasis on creativity, the result of organizations focusing more on increased technological access and productivity.

- Strains on interpersonal relationships at home, which can often take a back seat to organizational commitments.

One potential outcome to these challenges is employee burnout, something that is a concern for many professionals. Given the challenges discussed here, how can individuals succeed in the twenty-first–century organization? The next section, which describes how to be an effective communicator at work, provides information for those interested in addressing these—and other important issues—at work.

Being an Effective Communicator at Work

You may have very limited work experience, or you might be returning to college after many years of professional work experience. Whichever is the case, *being an effective communicator is universally recognized as a key element for workplace success.*

For example, read the different job descriptions in your local newspaper, career placement center, or on the Web. The vast majority of positions that college students and/or college graduates are looking for will list specific prerequisites as well as some general skills. If you haven't already, you will quickly discover that "communication skills" are among the most frequently listed requirements for new employees. Many job descriptions will even list specific skills such as public presentations, working in small groups, listening, problem solving, leadership qualities, or interacting with diverse types of people. In fact, two recent surveys found that interpersonal communication skills (often referred to as "soft skills" or "people skills") were regarded as more important than any other type of skills among new employees.[4]

If you look at the top positions in different organizations, you will probably also recognize that the higher the position is, the more likely it is to require that applicants have "strong communication skills." That's because advanced positions require individuals to use their oral, written, and interpersonal communication skills more frequently than other positions. Being able to do a job will secure you a paycheck, but being able to motivate others is what makes a career. At the heart of this type of organizational success is being an effective communicator.

Some people in organizations are managers, while others are managed. Most people play both roles—they supervise others, but also have their own supervisors. One way for us to discuss the different types of communication in the workplace is to differentiate between the interaction that occurs between members of an organization both in their structured roles and in the interactions they have outside of their identified roles.

Work-Related Relationships

We identify four common work-related relationship scenarios as a framework for discussing the importance of being an effective communicator at work: (1) communicating with your supervisor, (2) communicating with your subordinates, (3) communicating with coworkers, and (4) communicating with others outside the organization.

Communicating With Your Supervisor

Communicating with your immediate supervisor is the most common form of upward communication. **Upward communication** involves interactions subordinates have with their supervisors or others in positions of higher authority in an organization. Because supervisors have great influence over their subordinates' daily assignments, their future in the organization, and the way they are perceived by others, most employees take upward communication seriously. Interactions with your supervisor (or manager, depending on the level of your position) typically include asking questions about current projects, providing feedback about job-related activities, passing along job-related problems from the people you supervise, and making suggestions for improvement.

Upward communication plays a key role in the success of an organization. Top managers are removed from the daily happenings in an organization and rely on upward communication to help inform their decision making. Without clear and productive communication channels, they cannot make informed decisions. In other words, organizations with little upward communication are in a precarious situation because crucial information is not able to flow smoothly from the bottom to the top of the organization.

Depending on his or her style—as well as the culture of the organization—talking with your supervisor can take many different forms. Some might set up daily or weekly meetings. Others might prefer written memos. Some supervisors practice an "open-door policy," whereby employees are encouraged to communicate openly and freely. Others might use an administrative assistant as a gatekeeper; trying to meet with this kind of manager can be quite difficult.

Keep in mind that we are focusing on formal relationships in organizations where power differences are the key marker. As discussed in Chapter 2, a number of power bases exist (see Applied Concepts, Box 12.2). While supervisors have greater legitimate power than subordinates, subordinates are not powerless. Think about those employees who perform above and beyond expectations and make invaluable contributions to the organization (a reward to supervisors). Over time, they are likely to establish a greater power base from which they have

---

Box 12.2

Applied Concepts

What power does a supervisor have in the workplace? Think about a current or past supervisor you have worked for, and respond to each statement below.[5] Based on your responses, what types of power bases were used? Did the supervisor draw from one, two, or all the power bases? How might this insight assist in how you understand a particular supervisor-subordinate relationship?

Reward Power

1. My supervisor decided that I got a pay raise.

☞

2. My supervisor provided me with special benefits.
3. My supervisor was influential in a promotion I got.

Coercive Power

4. My supervisor gave me undesirable job assignments.
5. My supervisor made my work difficult for me.
6. My supervisor played a role in making the workplace unpleasant.

Legitimate Power

7. My supervisor made me recognize that I had tasks to accomplish.
8. My supervisor gave me the feeling that I needed to be committed to my work.
9. My supervisor used her or his authority to make sure that I completed tasks on time.

Expert Power

10. My supervisor shared his or her professional expertise with me.
11. My supervisor provided me with needed technical directions.
12. My supervisor gave me sound job-related advice.

Referent Power

13. My supervisor made me feel like a valued part of the organization.
14. My supervisor was someone whom I admire and respect.
15. My supervisor approved of me and my work.

influence with their supervisors and other leaders. For instance, they will be admired by others who will have great respect for their opinions (referent power). They also are likely to gain overt rewards—promotions, bonuses, and raises, for example.

Communicating With Your Subordinates

Generally speaking, supervisors have the responsibility to make sure that their subordinates are doing their jobs. In order to do this, supervisors have to communicate clear and concise instructions, provide necessary feedback—both positive and negative—when appropriate, and motivate workers to do their best work. Effective supervisors also inform workers about policy changes that affect them, help to negotiate conflicts that arise, and help them achieve personal and professional goals. All of these activities represent **downward communication** in an organization, interaction that flows from those higher in the organizational hierarchy to those in lower positions.

Obviously, in real-life interactions, you can't separate talking with your supervisor from talking with your subordinates because you are often doing both simultaneously and continuously (remember the transactional model discussed in Chapter 1). However, it is helpful to understand the different perspectives that are inherent to communicating as a supervisor and as a subordinate.

What is the best way for a manager to communicate with those who are under his or her supervision? Should communication be firm, direct, and definitive? Or should supervisors be flexible in their communication with subordinates, providing opportunities for subordinates to question policy, negotiate expectations, and have input on decisions? There is not one set of answers that works for all supervisors in all situations. The most effective supervisors develop a leadership style that has some degree of both firmness and flexibility depending on the particulars of any given situation. Employees who report having satisfying communication with their managers are more likely also to report greater overall job satisfaction, which is key to retaining valued employees in today's competitive global market.

Effective organizational communication involves being able to communicate with people at all levels of the organization.

Communicating With Your Coworkers

For our purposes, "coworkers" are individuals who function at the same level within an organization. Communication between them is **horizontal communication** (or lateral communication). The goals of horizontal communication are usually coordinating tasks, sharing feedback, solving problems, and providing personal and professional support. Two managers might discuss policy, for instance, and how it affects their departments, or two administrative assistants might create a strategy to approach their boss for a raise. As illustrated in Box 12.3, the language that coworkers use is an important consideration when communicating in the workplace.

Box 12.3

Self-Reflection

In Chapter 5, you learned that language is a tool used to communicate, a lens through which we view the world, and an exhibition of our internal thoughts.

Different employees in the same organization can have different perspectives about their role, and how that role relates to others with whom they work. Many times, these perspectives are not verbalized directly. But effective communicators can look at the language they use as an indicator of the unspoken views of others.

For instance, have you ever noticed the differences between people who talk about "going to the *job*" versus "going to the *office*"? Or a manager who introduces one of her assistant managers as "someone who works *with* me," and one who refers to the assistant manager as "someone who works *for* me"? What about the supervisor who insists that workers use his or her title and last name (e.g., supervisor Jones)? How is this person viewed, compared to others who encourage workers to use their first names?

Some might argue that these differences are small and inconsequential. However, knowing the covert power of language, we would disagree. While a person's choice of language may not be intentional, it may communicate more about their internal thoughts than they wish. Can you think about specific language you use about or at your job that may be sending messages to others?

In today's multinational companies, talking with your coworkers can mean communication with someone else with a similar position in your department, division, or unit. But it can also include interactions with others across company units that may span the globe. Thus, horizontal communication plays a crucial role in the coordination of various activities within a single organization. For instance, take the example of a music company. Making successful CDs requires many different tasks: locating, signing, and developing talent; assisting in the composition, arrangement, and editing of different songs; marketing the music to the general public; promoting the artist to various media outlets; coordinating public appearances; and carrying out other marketing and promotional strategies. One of the challenges for any company is the coordination of activities—something that is impossible without individuals across department units communicating in effective ways.

Another added dimension relates to the increased use of specialized firms. Whereas in the past companies tended to do everything "in-house," more and more companies are now relying on outside firms to perform duties that would cost too much to do themselves. As such, being an effective communicator in an organization includes skillfully negotiating interactions with others outside the organization.

Communicating With Others Outside the Organization

Organizations do not exist in isolation; their ultimate success is tied to others outside the organization. A key form of formalized communication, **outward communication**, occurs with others outside the organization such as customers, the public, and other organizations.[6]

Customer-service communication has gained increased attention in recent years.[6] Salespersons, clerks, cashiers, and customer-service representatives typically have the largest amount of contact with customers. Unfortunately, most people who deal with the public have little training to do so. They are also those who typically earn the least amount of money in organizations. But making sure that customers are satisfied, both with the products and services they purchase and with their interaction with company employees, is crucial to maintaining a solid client base. All of these points were discussed in recent research by customer-service expert Wendy Ford.[7] She has demonstrated that people will shop at a store farther away—and recommend it to others—if they rate customer service positively.

Companies also hope to shape the public's perceptions of their organization. Most large organizations have teams of public-relations professionals whose primary job is to create the most favorable possible public image for the organization by keeping the public abreast of organizational events via press releases, as well as maintaining community-outreach programs and organizing philanthropic events. While *public relations* means communicating with individuals outside the organization, it also includes interacting with different types of media, something that takes additional and often specialized communication skills. One of the most challenging tasks is "crisis management," when organizations attempt to downplay the effects of negative publicity.

Personal Relationships at Work

Anyone who has worked in any organization understands that not all interactions on the job are about work-related issues. Given the amount of time most adults spend at work, personal relationships naturally form in the workplace. In fact, the quality of relationships at work is a key component of job satisfaction.

What would your perfect job entail? First, think about a certain occupation. If you had the choice, would you be an elementary-school teacher, communication specialist in a training and development department, director of human resources at a Fortune 500 company, top sports agent, case manager at a not-for-profit community agency, head of marketing at a new record label, or student-affairs professional at a small Midwestern college? After identifying your perfect job, now list the things this job would entail, focusing on those things that make it appealing to you. Now, imagine that you had this position but in your work you had no close, meaningful relationships with any of the people with whom you work. Would this "perfect job" still be satisfying? Would you continue to work at it? Most of us would answer, "No." We may be able to tolerate, and ultimately survive in, this type of workplace, but it definitely would not be the ideal work environment for most people.

Job satisfaction has two dimensions: task and social. The **task dimension** measures how we feel about the specific duties and responsibilities of our job. How important is our contribution to the overall service or product? How good are we at our job? How challenging is it? Is there room for growth? Do we feel that we are being fairly compensated for our work?

The **social dimension** of job satisfaction measures how we feel about the relationships we have with others with whom we work. Do we feel connected to others on the job? Have our professional relationships developed into more meaningful personal relationships? Do we like our colleagues? Do we feel liked by them? Do they act as a support system for us, both personally and professionally?

You might feel that the social dimensions of the workplace are more important than the task dimensions. For example, many individuals are able to tolerate work they might otherwise despise because of the connection they feel with others on the job. However, is the opposite also true? Do individuals keep jobs they love if they despise (or are despised by) others they work with? Obviously, the answers to these questions depend on any number of related issues, like salary, benefits, and the existence of other opportunities. Yet posing these questions helps us acknowledge that personal relationships in the workplace are important.

Communication via the Grapevine

Personal relationships play a central role in a person's job satisfaction. However, they are also important because they provide individuals with a personal network that functions alongside more formal communication channels. In order to be effective, all organizational members should be aware that they glean information about job-related issues from both formal and informal networks.

Information that spreads through informal networks within an organization is referred to as **grapevine communication**. Grapevine messages don't follow formal communication channels. Instead, they seem to have a life and pathway of their own. Sometimes, identifying how information flows via the grapevine is relatively easy, especially if we understand the personal relationships that exist in the workplace (see Figure 12.1). However, at other times trying to trace the flow of information can be quite difficult because grapevine communication is based on relationships and associations that are constantly expanding. One way to understand how complex this can be is to visualize an actual grapevine. When standing by itself, one grapevine is easy to trace from beginning to end. However, growing alongside, or within, other grapevines makes it almost impossible to figure out where one starts and the others end. Additionally, grapevines are dynamic. They continue to grow, constantly sprouting off in all directions and dying off in others.

Figure 12.1 Formal and Informal Communication Networks

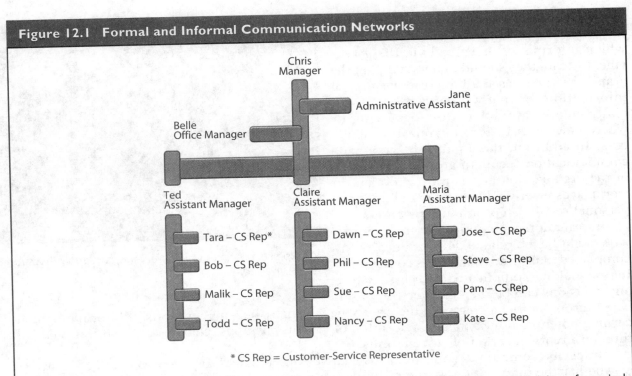

* CS Rep = Customer-Service Representative

Consider the simple organizational hierarchy illustrated above. The colors highlight the organization of a typical department (i.e., who reports to whom). For instance, along these channels, Claire would communicate upward to Chris, horizontally to Ted and Maria, and downward to Dawn, Phil, Sue, and Nancy.

Now consider the personal relationships that exist in the department, as illustrated below. Can you anticipate how these informal communication channels may function in relation to more formal ones?

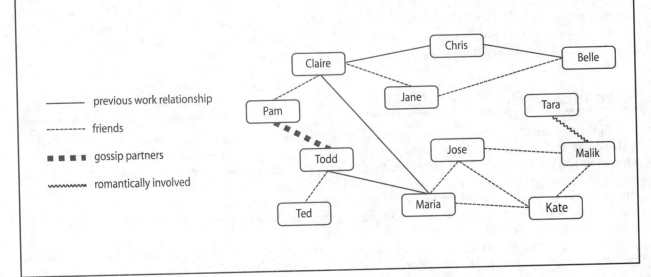

The key for organizational members is not to try to understand the exact process by which information is spread via the grapevine. Instead, they should understand that the grapevine functions as an important source of information for many organizations, especially where rapid change is occurring or where news is critical to organizational success. In addition, the amount of grapevine communication seems to grow with the size of the organization and is most prevalent in workplaces where individuals maintain interpersonal relationships among coworkers.

Information communicated via the grapevine might be job related. For instance, many companies today find themselves contemplating or making complicated mergers. Before any decisions can be made and/or communicated through official channels, the grapevine is usually buzzing with bits of information concerning potential downsizing or relocation of certain positions, changes in organizational culture, or a reorganization of current units.

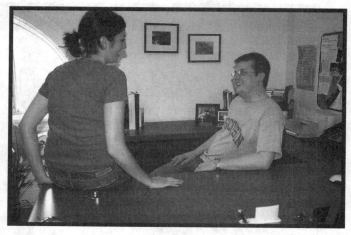

Workplace romances affect everyone, not simply those romantically involved.

Grapevine communication can have negative consequences for the organization regardless of whether the information is true or false. You might be surprised to learn that two different studies suggest that information communicated via the grapevine is between 75 and 90 percent accurate.[8] However, we suggest that you take this research finding with a grain of salt. Remember our discussion of the perception process in Chapter 4. Even with *some* accurate facts, grapevine information might be missing key details, or individuals might be passing along false assumptions and conclusions about it.

Not all grapevine messages are about work-related issues. Organizational grapevines are also the primary source of messages about various personal and social issues that, while not directly related to the job, do have clear effects on how individuals do their jobs. One of the most controversial topics for organizations—and a "hot" topic for many organizational grapevines—is romance in the workplace.

Romance in the Workplace

Personal relationships in the workplace are inevitable. Some may have been established before the individuals arrived at the organization. Others will develop with individuals' professional lives. While workplace friendships are expected and even encouraged, romantic relationships are another issue altogether. Given the heightened awareness of sexual harassment, many organizations have explicit rules forbidding romantic relationships between employees. Some blanket policies exist, but most often romantic relationships are prohibited for individuals who are in supervisor-subordinate roles.

It is not realistic for organizations to think that their members can avoid or eliminate all types of physical and psychological attraction to one another. After all, people are spending a great deal of time together working closely on various assignments. Think about this type of interaction in a context where people share common professional interests, educational backgrounds, socioeconomic status, and the like. Some would argue that the workplace is the best place to meet and get to know potential romantic partners, as the research on proximity and attraction suggests (highlighted in Chapter 10). In fact, romantic relationships that develop in the workplace do not have to be awkward or dangerous. Instead, they can help nurture employees to be more highly motivated and enthusiastic about their jobs. Some argue that attraction between coworkers might even generate an energy resulting in greater creativity, commitment, and productivity. Seen in this light, romantic relationships can have several positive effects in the organization.

Yet, even when the relationship is fulfilling for both individuals, it might have negative effects as well. Let's take the simplest scenario. Isaiah and Megan are both single and new to the company. Both are managers in different departments positioned in close proximity to one another, yet neither is in a supervisory relationship with the other. Their romantic relationship, which developed over the past six months, is public knowledge on the job, but they have made a conscious decision to avoid public displays of affection or other signs of their relationship while at work. Given these circumstances, what possible negative effects might their relationship have?

First, their relationship could possibly create discomfort among coworkers, affecting the chemistry of the organization. For instance, some might question whether Isaiah and Megan can have any sense of objectivity when dealing with issues that concern one another's departments. For others, the relationship might generate questions about confidentiality, loyalty, and trust. When push came to shove, would Isaiah and Megan have greater allegiance to one another or to the organization?

All workplace romances, whether they involve casual dating or even marriage, also invoke questions of what might happen should the relationship be terminated. Will the two people be able to continue working together? If so, how? What impacts will their breakup have on others in the organization? Because of the serious nature of this topic, organizations have developed a variety of ways to manage romantic relationships in the workplace. Some forbid office romances and consequently force them underground, generating a whole host of additional issues. Others deny their existence and ignore signs of potential problems. However, these two types of responses represent extreme reactions to romantic relationships in the workplace.

The most productive way to deal with the potential advantages and disadvantages of romantic relationships in the workplace is through open communication. Discussions about the potential dangers of allowing personal relationships to interfere with work between supervisors and subordinates are one example of open communication. Requiring employees who are romantically involved to report potential conflicts of interest to their supervisors also fosters productive communication. Written policies that address romantic relationships in the workplace can clarify the rules and responsibilities of employees. Policies do not necessarily have to offer specific processes and procedures, but instead can offer general principles to guide interactions at work. While these types of policies will never solve all the potential problems associated with romantic attraction in the workplace, they can go a long way toward clarifying expectations at the start of an employee's tenure with the organization.

Box 12.4 is designed to get you thinking about romance on the job. For those who find themselves romantically attracted to others on the job, we offer several guidelines. These are designed for those who want to benefit from the opportunities of romantic attraction in the workplace but

---

Box 12.4

Skill Builder

Chris has recently been hired by a large multinational company for an entry-level position. Based on his interview and initial orientation, he has been led to believe that he can have a great future with the company. He feels fulfilled with the type of work he's doing and likes the people that he works with. At this point in his life, he can't imagine a better place to work.

Lately he's been assisting Michele, one of the departmental managers, in an important project that has required a great deal of overtime. From the start, Chris has found Michele attractive. However, the more he has gotten to know her, the more his attraction has increased. Chris is sure that Michele is also attracted to him but thinks that she is unsure about how he feels about her.

Chris hasn't dated anyone seriously for the past few years, but realizes that he is ready to settle down in a meaningful long-term relationship. In his mind, Michele seems to be exactly the type of person who would make an ideal life partner. However, he's hesitant because he's not sure about how the company would view their relationship. What would you do if you were Chris? How would you draw from some of the communication guidelines offered in this chapter? In order to build your communication skills, create a role play with Michele and Chris where both individuals seek to foster open, productive communication.

---

minimize the negative effects they may have on themselves and others. The ultimate goal is to maintain a "consciously managed relationship."[9] Guidelines for effectively managing romance on the job include:

- Discussing expectations for the relationship.

- Setting boundaries that help guide professional and personal behaviors.

- Developing a conscious management of your relationship at work.

- Maintaining an openness about the relationship that allows you to reduce the chance for misunderstandings.

- Monitoring each others' actions at work.

- Allowing for cooling-off periods on and off the job.

- Thinking about what you value most in the relationship and on the job.

Power and Leadership in Organizations

In Chapter 2, we discussed three different perspectives of power: those associated with dominance, empowerment, and synergy. In any organization, formal leaders can easily be identified by their titles: CEO, vice president, district manager, and so on. However, their power does not come from their titles alone. As described in Chapter 2, there are six different stages of personal power at which organizational members function.[10] While an individual might move from one stage to another depending on the specific context of the interaction, each of us has a primary stage that represents our power in the organization. See whether you can match people you know to the characteristics of each of the stages described next.

Stage 1: Powerlessness

At the **powerlessness** stage, people feel like they are pawns, trapped in a system without power. They might be the lowest on the organizational hierarchy, but they might also be midlevel managers. They typically are uninformed about organizational decisions, dependent on others to accomplish things, and fearful of the unknown. A fear of physical abuse, punishment, or peer disapproval keeps people at this stage from increasing their personal power.

Stage 2: Power by Association

People at Stage 2, **power by association**, believe that certain other people in the organization have power and that they will gain power if they "learn the ropes" from them. In other words, they act as apprentices to those who have gained power. People at Stage 2 do not have much power, so they must rely on others to lead, nurture, and reward them. Because they are less dependent on others than those at Stage 1, they are also able to engage in greater self-exploration, which typically allows them to gain higher levels of personal power.

Stage 3: Power by Symbols

We can describe **power by symbols** as the "dynamo stage" because it is exciting, grueling, and challenging. People at this stage are focused on getting as much power as possible; therefore, they practice high levels of self-promotion and adopt a competitive orientation to winning. Being powerful, according to those at Stage 3, results in tangible rewards such as promotions, increased salaries, plush offices, and nice homes and cars. Most people at this stage are ambitious, charismatic, and experts in their field. However, by adopting such a limiting perspective of power, they are not able to reach higher levels of personal power like those reflected in the next three stages. Individuals at Stage 3 are only able to function at higher levels by reflecting on their roles in organizations.

Mentoring others in the organization is a key component for some leadership philosophies.

Stage 4: Power by Reflection

In Stage 4, **power by reflection**, people see power as the ability to influence others, unlike those in Stage 3 who see it as being able to control others. Characteristics of people at this stage include being competent, comfortable with their own personal style, skilled at mentoring, fair and honest, and unwilling to practice self-promotion. While those at Stage 4 appear very polished and competent to others, they are typically humble and tentative about themselves. Yet this type of humility is exactly why they are highly respected by others in the organization, regardless of what position they hold. People at Stage 4 are the ones who leaders go to when they want good advice.

Stage 5: Power by Purpose

In Stage 5, **power by purpose**, power is defined as vision. People at this stage do not attempt to gain or accumulate power because they believe that power multiplies infinitely. In other words, the more power you can give away, the more you and others ultimately possess. Individuals who advance to this level of personal power are motivated by internal goals like self-satisfaction, the ability to mentor others, and an appreciation for relationships with others. Others describe them as self-accepting, caring, confident, and spiritual. In many organizations, it might be difficult to identify people at this stage because they attempt to avoid public recognition for their efforts. In addition, they might be misunderstood by others who can not comprehend why they do what they do.

Stage 6: Power by Gestalt

Many individuals have some of the characteristics attributed to Stage 6, **power by gestalt**, but relatively few can claim it as their primary stage. Power is generated from an inner origin and communicated through wisdom at this stage. People at Stage 6 see the larger picture. They often ask questions that seem to be on a higher level and call into question long-accepted assumptions. In addition, they don't attempt to compete with others but instead share their vision and insight whenever appropriate. People at this stage possess unique characteristics that positively affect others; in fact, others are drawn to them. In many cases, Stage 6 leaders are quiet in their service to others and reject outward symbols that others in earlier stages of personal power seek.

Every organization, regardless of its size, complexity, or mission, includes people at each of these stages of personal power. Hagberg does not see the characteristics attributed to the first three stages as bad, nor does she believe that we should try to eliminate them. But she does suggest that effective organizations must have some leaders whose perspectives move beyond these three levels of personal power. Personal power at the higher stages includes the power that comes from external sources like high-ranking titles, expertise, advanced degrees, and organizational responsibility and authority. However, leaders enhance this power by that which they derive from within.

Traditionally, organizations have recognized power in terms of the first three stages. Stage 3—which requires a strong knowledge base, mature ego, as well as hard work and political savvy—is probably the most rewarded stage in organizations. People who adopt a "how-to-get-ahead" philosophy are often rewarded. However, the most effective leaders also recognize that different types of personal power perspectives exist at all levels of the organization.

Sexual Harassment

In recent years, the topic of sexual harassment has gained national attention. We include a section on sexual harassment in this chapter because it represents an important issue for anyone who works in an organization, including CEOs, managers, workers, and volunteers. Yet it also gives us a specific context to discuss the direct and indirect ways that culture, power, and technology influence our communication at work. Before reading any further, take the Sexual Harassment Quiz contained in Skill Builder (Box 12.5).

Box 12.5

Skill Builder

Read each of the brief scenarios below. Then, based on your understanding of sexual harassment laws, describe each as (a) definitely sexual harassment, (b) definitely not sexual harassment, or (c) possibly sexual harassment.

1. Tom's coworker recently asked him out on a date. He politely refused, but since then she continues to ask if he's changed his mind. This morning while walking past him, she winked at him and blew him a kiss. _____

2. Chris's supervisor frequently tells jokes at staff meetings; some of these jokes involve men's and women's body parts. _____

3. This morning Beverly was using the restroom when one of her colleagues, Pat, walked right in without knocking. Throughout the rest of the day, she noticed him looking at her. At the afternoon staff meeting, he kept touching her while talking about a recent report. _____

4. Two of Matt's colleagues have recently begun dating. At first their romance was kept a secret, but more recently he has seen them become more and more intimate with one another. _____

5. Keisha recently began working for a grants and contracts office. Part of the culture of the group is to forward amusing e-mails to one another. During her first week at work, she received several forwarded e-mails that had sexist jokes and cartoons in them. _____

Answers: It may come as a surprise to learn that each of these scenarios *could be considered* sexual harassment if the behavior is unwelcome, is persistent, and has an effect on a person's job performance.

In today's society, most people are familiar with the term *sexual harassment*. This, however, was not the case as recently as 25 years ago. As women have entered the workplace in greater numbers and challenged traditional organizational cultures, laws have been enacted making sexually harassing behaviors illegal. These laws are relatively new and are constantly being redefined through various legal battles and court cases. A good example of one such case is *Faragher v. Boca Raton,* which served as our opening case study for this chapter. We believe that in order to be an effective communicator in the workplace, each and every person should understand what constitutes sexual harassment. This knowledge will allow all employees to reduce their uncertainty and anxiety about the topic and communicate in responsible ways.

According to the Equal Employment Opportunity Commission, **sexual harassment** is verbal or physical conduct of a sexual nature when (1) submission to or rejection of such conduct is used as a basis for employment-related decisions or (2) such conduct unreasonably interferes with an individual's work performance or creates an intimidating, hostile, or offensive working environment. The first part of this definition is fairly easy to understand. However, the second part is often more difficult. In order to decide whether a work environment "unreasonably interferes" with someone's job performance, courts must look at a number of factors including the frequency and severity of behaviors, the direct and indirect effects of the behaviors, and whether the behaviors were welcomed or not.

Contemporary Issues and Sexual Harassment

Sexual harassment, by its very nature, is a communicative act. It can be verbal, nonverbal, or both. But how does sexual harassment relate to issues of power, technology, and culture? At the root of its existence, sexual harassment is about power. Contrary to some popular thinking, sexual harassment is not simply a case of one person being attracted to someone else. It is one person exerting his or her personal power in an organizational context by using sexually charged behavior to intimidate and control others. While a small number of sexual harassment cases might reflect innocent behaviors by naïve offenders, the vast majority do not.

Culture in general, and gender more specifically, play a central role in perceptions of sexual harassment. Women, on average, are more likely to perceive certain behaviors as sexually harassing than are men.[11] In one study this was found to be true when women and men were asked about deliberate touching, letters and calls, pressure for dates, suggestive looks, and sexual remarks. A common pattern emerged when comparing male and female responses. Men report being flattered by these behaviors—things that they might take as compliments even if unwanted. Women, on the other hand, report being offended much more frequently.[12] It is important to recognize that these findings are based on "average" responses of women and men. The recent rise in men filing sexual harassment charges might indicate that male and female perceptions are becoming more similar.

Yet culture continues to play a role in sexual harassment cases. Those with less societal power are more frequently targets of sexually harassing behavior. For instance, women of color report more instances of sexual harassment than do European American women.[13] The same is true for blue-collar workers (when compared to their white-collar counterparts).[14] These trends point back to the fact that sexual harassment is more about power than romantic attraction.

In some situations, certain employees might avoid hostile work environments through the increased use of computer-mediated communication. For instance, telecommuters are able to fulfill their job responsibilities off-site, thereby reducing face-to-face interactions with other coworkers. But we should recognize that telecommuting is typically an option only for a small number of people, most often those in more powerful positions in organizations. And while increased technology has decreased the need for frequent face-to-face inter-

Sexual harassment creates a hostile environment that negatively affects productivity.

actions, it has also opened the door to new forms of sexually harassing communication. These include private e-mail messages, public posts in chat rooms, links to offensive Web sites, as well as other communication that might be so technologically advanced that it hides the source of the message.

Our purpose in highlighting the role that power, culture, and technology play in terms of sexual harassment in the workplace is simple: We want to increase your awareness so that you can feel more empowered when communicating at work. Learning more about sexual harassment provides potential victims with information about their rights. It also can empower all organizational members to better understand how their behaviors might unintentionally be contributing to a hostile work environment. From all accounts, an increased awareness of the power plays associated with sexual harassment in organizations is highly beneficial. Creating work environments where certain individuals are no longer feeling demeaned, oppressed, or harassed can only lead to greater job satisfaction and individual and corporate productivity. As demonstrated throughout this text, effective communication is at the core of creating a supportive organizational climate.

The workplace of a generation ago no longer exists. Instead, the typical workplace has been transformed in times of greater cultural diversity, intense competition in global markets, and an increasing dependence on advanced technologies. It may be true that some smaller, local companies are less affected by these things than others. Yet these companies do not function in a vacuum and continue to feel the impact of larger societal shifts.

Summary

In this chapter, we have identified the tensions between maintaining organizational success and high-quality personal relationships. These tensions have been fueled by advanced technologies and an intensified work schedule. In many ways, our work lives have forever been changed. Communicating in the workplace promises to become more challenging for those who lack an awareness of shifts in organizational culture or the abilities to communicate effectively in a world that is increasingly diverse and technologically savvy. We close this chapter by returning to the statements offered earlier regarding several key points related to communicating at work. Review your answers from the opener and see how you did.

Myth: The use of advanced technology in organizations has been a win-win situation for everyone involved.

This is a myth; the increased use of advanced technology in organizations has several advantages and disadvantages that need to be weighed carefully.

Myth: Employers always choose the job applicant who has the greatest amount of experience and expertise. Why is this not true?

In addition to experience and expertise, employers use the application and interview process to search for a good fit between potential employees and their organizations.

Truth: Job satisfaction is a complex concept that includes both task (how we feel about what we do) and social dimensions (how we feel about those with whom we work).

As we highlighted in this chapter, work life is often about more than just the work.

Truth: Romantic relationships in the workplace can have both positive and negative effects on organizational effectiveness.

As you read in this chapter, romantic relationships at work are complex, resulting in a complex set of potential consequences for individuals and organizations.

Myth: In organizations, those with the highest positions always hold the most power.

Actually, one source of power in organizations is legitimate power, that which is related to position; however, other bases of power (e.g., expert and information) also simultaneously exist. Therefore, those with the highest positions do not always hold the most power.

Myth: Sexual harassment is rooted in basic physical attraction.

Not true. Sexual harassment is related to power and intimidation, not physical attraction.

Key Terms

Downward communication

Grapevine communication

Horizontal communication

Outward communication

Power by association

Power by gestalt

Power by purpose

Power by reflection

Power by symbols

Powerlessness

Sexual harassment

Social dimension

Task dimension

Upward communication

Suggested Contemporary Readings

D. S. Dougherty. "Sexual harassment as [dys]functional process: A feminist standpoint analysis." *Journal of Applied Communication Research* 29 (2001): 372–402.

P. P. Edley. "Discursive essentializing in a woman-owned business: Gendered stereotypes and strategic subordination." *Management Communication Quarterly* 14 (2000): 271–306.

J. A. English-Lueck, C. N. Darrah, and A. Saveri. "Trusting strangers: Worker relationships in four high-tech communities." *Information, Communication & Society* 5 (2002): 90–108.

B. S. Farley-Lucas. "Communicating the (in)visibility of motherhood: Family talk and the ties to motherhood with/in the workplace." *Electronic Journal of Communication* 10 (2000).

W. S. Z. Ford and O. J. Snyder. "Customer service in dental offices: Analyses of service orientations and waiting time in telephone interactions with a potential new customer." *Health Communication* 12 (2000): 149–172.

D. S. Grimes. "Challenging the status quo? Whiteness of the diversity management literature." *Management Communication Quarterly* 15 (2002): 381–409.

K. M. Hopkins. "Manager intervention with troubled supervisors: Help and support start at the top." *Management Communication Quarterly* 15 (2001): 83–99.

S. R. A. Hovick, R. A. Meyers, and C. E. Timmerman. "E-mail communication in workplace romantic relationships." *Communication Studies* 54 (2003): 468–482.

J. Jorgenson. "Interpreting the intersections of work and family: Frame conflicts in women's work." *Electronic Journal of Communication* 10 (2000).

K. L. Mallia and S. Pixy Ferris. "Telework: A consideration of its impact on individuals and organizations." *Electronic Journal of Communication* 10 (2000).

P. S. Parker. "African American women executives' leadership communication with dominant-culture organization: (Re)conceptualizing notions of collaboration and instrumentality." *Management Communication Quarterly* 15 (2001): 42–82.

S. M. Ralston and A. E. Kinser. "Intersections of gender and employment interviewing." In *Women and Men Communicating: Challenges and Changes*, edited by L. P. Arliss and D. J. Borisoff. Prospect Heights, IL: Waveland Press, 2001.

P. M. Sias, G. Smith, and T. Avdeyeva. "Sex and sex-composition differences and similarities in peer workplace friendship development." *Communication Studies* 54 (2003): 322–340.

Chapter Activities

1. Research the sexual harassment policy at your school or place of employment. After gaining an understanding of the policy and procedures, assess the effectiveness of the existing policy. What, if any, improvements would you recommend? How might the process of effective communication with particular procedures be made more clear?

2. What exactly is mentoring, and how important is it to a person's professional success? Use a library database to locate articles that provide insight to these questions. Use the keywords *mentoring* and *relationships* to find relevant articles.

3. Select a campus or community organization and secure a copy of their organizational structure/hierarchy. Then interview the organization's primary leaders and ask them about how the information flows within the organization. Once you have obtained enough information, diagram both the formal and informal communication networks (as illustrated in Figure 12.1). What, if any, differences exist between these two diagrams?

4. Utilize what you've learned in this chapter to create a two-hour workshop for community teenagers that teaches them how to successfully find, apply for, and maintain a summer job. Think about what you would include in the workshop (training curriculum) as well as the most effective strategies for delivery (i.e., location, times, presentational aids, and format). If you've been working with a community-based organization this semester, implement the workshop and then evaluate its effectiveness.

5. Visit RHI Management Resources' Web site (*http://www.rhimr.com/MR/Dispatcher?file=/MR/EO_Vol3_No2*). Read through the management resources that are included in the Executive Outlook section, and select one topic that is of particular interest to you. Summarize the article and share with the class how you might use this information in your professional lives.

6. Your library is a great resource to find articles that talk about the problems that are created by workplace gossip (use the keywords *workplace* and *gossip* to search different business-related magazines). What specific problems have resulted from this form of organizational communication? What, if any, articles could you find that discussed any positive aspects of workplace gossip?

7. Go to *http://jobsearch.monster.com* or another Web site where job postings are listed. Then conduct a search for jobs that include the keyword(s) *interpersonal communication skills* (you might want to limit your search to items posted on the same day). How many hits did you find? Were you surprised by the diversity of jobs that included this qualification as part of their job description? What do the results of your search tell you about how employers value interpersonal communication skills? ✦

Glossary

A

Accommodating One person neglecting his or her own needs and instead focusing on satisfying the needs of others.

Active listening A type of listening where the listener is actively involved in the listening process, intentionally attending to and processing what the speaker is saying.

Adaptors Automatic or habitual nonverbal behaviors most often expressed by someone who is nervous or upset, helping that person adjust to the environment or comfort oneself.

Affect displays Types of nonverbal cues that express emotion or affection.

Age The period of life when a person exists; a cultural marker that marks the life experiences of a person.

Appreciative listening Any type of listening done for pleasure and enjoyment.

Appropriateness One of the two criteria for judging communication competence; taking into account the expectations and needs of others in a communication interaction.

Arbitrary nature of words The idea that words have no inherent meaning.

Artifacts All of the personal objects that communicate nonverbally.

Asynchronous listening Listening to a message delivered at an earlier time.

Attribution theory A set of ideas that explains the process by which individuals create a cause and effect for human behavior.

Avoiding One person withdrawing, either physically and/or psychologically, from a conflict situation.

B

Blended family Another name for what is traditionally known as the stepfamily, which recognizes the *blending* of two families together.

Blind self Information that is known to others but not to you.

Breadth The range of subjects included in your self-disclosures to others.

Bypassing When a person incorrectly assumes that words have inherent meaning.

C

Certainty A defense-arousing communication behavior that sends the message "I am right."

Channel The path through which a message travels.

Chronemics The study of the way we use, perceive, interpret, react to, and structure time as an aspect of nonverbal communication.

Closure A tendency to fill in the gaps so that stimuli make sense.

Co-culture A group of people who share a common identity marker and are bonded through a system of shared values, beliefs, and behaviors.

Coenetics The nonverbal codes of a particular culture or co-culture.

Coercive power The ability to influence based on a person's ability to punish others.

Cohabiting couple A couple who lives together and shares a romantic interest.

Collaborating One person trying to address the needs of each person so that a mutually satisfying solution can be obtained.

Collectivism Cultural values that emphasize group identities, concerns, and needs over individual identities, concerns, and needs.

Collectivistic self-concept Cultural values that see the self as embedded within different social identities.

Communicare Latin root word meaning "to make common."

Communication accommodation theory A theory stating that individuals adapt their communication styles to others with whom they are communicating.

Communication as action model A model of communication that views communication as a one-way process of sending messages.

Communication as interaction model The model of communication that views communication as a two-way process, where one person sends a message and then, after receiving it, the other person provides feedback based on the message.

Communication as transaction model The model of communication advanced in this text. This model views people in a communication interaction as simultaneously sending and receiving multiple messages.

Communication climate The overall mood or feeling of a relationship developed between communicators.

Communication competence The judgment of the effectiveness and appropriateness of communication in a given context.

Comparison level (CL) The kinds of reward and costs we expect to have in a relationship.

Comparison level of alternatives (Clalt) A comparison of the rewards we are receiving from a current relationship with those that we predict we might receive from an alternative relationship.

Complementary relationship A relationship that reflects a balance in needs for, or the exercise of, power in conversations.

Comprehensive listening Also known as informational listening, a type of listening to gain knowledge or information.

Compromising Two or more people trying to resolve a situation by giving up something so that each person gains some satisfaction.

Confirming communication Communication behaviors that tell others that they are valued; messages that validate another's self-image and self-definition.

Conflict Times when two or more people perceive their needs or ideas to be at odds with one another.

Connotative meaning The less formal, subjective meaning of a word.

Constructivism A theory that suggests that we make sense of the world through a system of mental blueprints (schemata).

Content meaning The literal meaning, based on common symbols, of what is communicated.

Context All elements of the environment in which communication takes place; can be physical, cultural, social-psychological, or temporal.

Controlling communication A kind of defense-arousing communication that sends the message "You are inadequate."

Convergence Adapting one's communication to match that of others.

Core identity markers Group memberships that are central to a person's self-concept.

Costs Those features of a relationship that have negative value to an individual.

Critical listening Listening with the purpose of evaluating a message.

Cultural context The way the norms, rules, or beliefs of a culture influence communication.

Cultural-level knowledge Information about others based on aspects of their cultural identities (including, for instance, age, race, ethnicity, and gender).

Culture The learned and shared values, beliefs, and behaviors common to a particular group of people.

D

Decoding Interpreting the encoded message.

Denotative meaning The explicit, formal meaning of a word.

Depth The amount of intimacy reflected in one's self-disclosures to others.

Description communication A kind of communication that invites another's interpretations or opinions, generally suggested for creating a positive communication climate.

Dialectical tensions Those contradictory pulls or needs that exist in all relationships, and that pull us in opposite directions at the same time.

Disability Physical and/or mental conditions that influence, both directly and indirectly, a person's communication.

Disconfirming communication Communication behaviors that negate another's self-image or self-definition.

Divergence Making a conscious effort to distinguish your communication from that of others.

Dominance A perspective that views power as a finite quality.

Downward communication Workplace interactions initiated by supervisors with those people whom they supervise.

E

Effectiveness One of the two criteria for judging communication competence, referring to the ability to reach one's goals in a communication interaction.

Electronic age A time when technological advances transformed how we live.

Emblems A type of nonverbal gesture that can take the place of a word or phrase, which often has a direct verbal translation.

Emotions Feelings that consist of distinctive thoughts that trigger physical and psychological reactions and motivations to act.

Empathic listening Listening to try to understand what another person is feeling.

Empathy The opposite of neutrality; a kind of communication that sends the message of understanding regarding another's feelings and experiences.

Empowerment A perspective that sees power as something to be shared.

Encoding Creating a message based on a feeling, idea, or thought using verbal symbols or nonverbal behavior.

Equality The opposite of superiority; a kind of communication that minimizes differences between people and lends to a more positive communication climate.

Ethnicity Cultural markers that indicate shared traditions, heritage, and ancestral origins.

Ethnocentrism An orientation toward thinking that one's own cultural norms are superior to others.

Ethnorelativism An orientation that recognizes that various cultures have different norms, values, and practices that are equally appropriate and/or effective.

Euphemisms Terms that are substituted for offensive words.

Evaluation communication A type of defense-arousing communication that passes judgment on another person and that tends to lend to a negative communication climate.

Expert power The ability to influence based on one's knowledge or experience.

Explicit rules Those rules that are stated clearly and intentionally.

Extended family A type of family characterized by relatives—such as grandparents, aunts, uncles, or cousins—living with the family unit of one or more parents and children.

External noise Anything external to the self that interferes with the communication of messages.

F

Face-inference confusion When an individual does not distinguish between things that are true and those that are assumed.

Family identity The private world and sense of self created in a family through the sharing of meanings, rituals, language, worldviews, and a history together.

Family image A metaphor or idea of a family reflecting what the family is like, what is expected in the family, how important it is, and what patterns of communication exist in the family.

Family rituals Repetitive, symbolic behaviors or practices shared by members of a family.

Feedback Any response to a message.

Feedforward Any information given about messages before they are sent.

Flaming When someone sends messages that personally attack others.

Forcing One person satisfying his or her own needs with little, or no, consideration for the relationship.

G

Gay and lesbian families Families that consist of two people of the same sex in an intimate relationship sharing a household and often parenting responsibilities for one or more children.

Gender The psychological identity, or socially prescribed meanings, of males and females learned through socialization.

Generalized other Our perceptions of how others generally view us.

Global village The concept that all people are linked, directly or indirectly, through technology.

Grapevine communication Information that travels through informal networks within an organization.

H

Halo effect Assuming that a person with one positive characteristic will exhibit other similar positive characteristics.

Haptics The study of the way touch is used to communicate nonverbally.

Hegemony The predominant influence of one state over others; domination.

Hidden self Information one is aware of but decide not to share with others.

High-context cultures Cultures in which information and meaning are more often assumed to be in the context, setting, environment, or people who are part of the interaction; a culture where people rely on inferred meanings, and where differences may exist between what is said and what is meant.

Homophily Common cultural experiences shared by two or more people.

Horizontal communication The communication that occurs between individuals who function at the same level within an organization.

Human communication The process of creating and sharing meaning.

I, J

Idiosyncratic communication The unique or "personalized" communication behavior developed and maintained within relationships.

Illustrators A type of nonverbal gesture that usually accompanies, but does not have meaning apart from, the verbal message.

Implicit personality theory A body of work that suggests that an individual's perceptions of others are likely to be consistent with initial perceptions.

Implicit rules Unstated rules in the family.

Impression management The idea that we use self-disclosures strategically as a way to communicate favorable images to others.

Individualism Cultural values that emphasize individual identity, rights, and needs over those of the larger group.

Individualistic self-concept Cultural values that see the self as a separate entity that is loosely connected to several social identities.

Information overload The arrival of more information or stimuli than we need or can process.

Intensional orientation The practice of relying on labels for our perceptions.

Interdependence A property of a family system recognizing that each family member is connected to each other and has an influence on all parts of the system.

Internal noise Anything within the self that interferes with the communication of messages, such as feelings, attitudes, physical state, and/or other preoccupations.

Interpersonal communication The creating and sharing of meaning between people who have knowledge of each other on a personal level, and interact on the basis of that knowledge.

Intimate distance The personal space between people generally reserved for intimate contact or for comforting others, ranging from touching (0 inches) up to 18 inches.

Intimate play A private system of play or games that is developed in the context of a personal relationship and is revealing of that relationship's relational culture.

K, L

Kinesics The study of the way that body motions and movements communicate.

Legitimate power The ability to influence based on societal position.

Low-context cultures Cultures in which most of the information and meaning are assumed to be communicated through the verbal message, not embedded in the context or participants; individuals are expected to say what they mean through direct communication.

M

Man-linked terminology Words and phrases that are used generically to refer to both men and women, but place men as the norm.

Married couple A couple who lives together, is legally recognized, and has publicly declared their love through the bond of matrimony.

Meaning The message or idea that one person is sharing with another as well as the interpretation of that message by the others.

Message The idea and meaning that are being encoded and decoded by the sender/receivers.

Metastereotypes Perceptions that one group has of the stereotypes that other groups attach to them.

Mindfulness A concept from Zen Buddhism that means *fully present in the moment*; the process of mentally weighing the advantages and disadvantages of communicating in different ways.

Monochronic time (M-time) A cultural orientation to time in which time is viewed as valuable, fixed, usable, linear, segmented, and manageable.

Myth An idea that people generally believe to be true but which is not.

N

National origin The country in which a person was born.

Netiquette Rules used to guide online communication.

Neutrality A kind of defense-arousing communication that communicates a lack of concern for others.

Noise Any element in the environment that might interfere with the accurate sending or receiving of a message (physical, psychological, or semantic).

Nonverbal communication Any type of communication that does not rely on words or other linguistic systems.

Nuclear family Commonly thought of as the "traditional" family form—a married couple living with their biological children. More contemporary versions include a variety of work arrangements for the parents in this family type.

O

One-across move A kind of conversational power move where power is equal.

One-down move A kind of conversational power move where one person accepts the other person's right to be more powerful.

One-up move A kind of conversational power move where one person tries to gain power over the other.

Open self Information that is known by both you and others.

Outward communication Communication between the organization and others outside the organization.

P

Paralanguage The vocal, but nonverbal, dimensions of our speech.

Paraphrasing Summarizing the content or feeling of a message by stating in your own words what you heard the speaker say.

Perception The mental process through which we come to understand the world.

Perception checks Statements that help to establish shared meaning between individuals.

Perceptual accentuation The likelihood that individuals will focus on those things that meet their expectations.

Perceptual constancy The tendency for perceptions to remain consistent over time.

Personal distance The personal space preferred between casual friends and acquaintances, generally ranging from 18 inches to 4 feet.

Personal-level knowledge Information about a person based on personal interaction with, and knowledge of, that person beyond social or cultural roles and identities.

Physical attractiveness The extent to which a person's physical characteristics are appealing to another person.

Physical context Everything in the physical environment where communication takes place, including the number of people in an interaction.

Polarization When a person uses language that describes things in "either-or" terms.

Polychronic time (P-time) A cultural orientation to time in which time is viewed as more flexible and less tangible; emphasis in P-time cultures is placed on what is happening currently regardless of time.

Power by association The second stage of personal power where individuals rely on others who are more powerful to gain some level of influence.

Power by gestalt The sixth stage of personal power where an individual's power is generated from an inner origin and not captured by outward symbols (like in earlier stages).

Power by purpose The fifth stage of personal power where individuals avoid public recognition but work collaboratively with others to gain self-satisfaction for a job well done.

Power by reflection The fourth stage of personal power where individuals use their own competence level, personal styles, and mentoring skills to influence others in unselfish ways.

Power by symbols The third stage of personal power where individuals use high levels of ambition, charisma, and expertise to gain as much power as possible.

Powerlessness The first stage of personal power where individuals feel as if they are trapped in a system without any power.

Pragmatic rules Guidelines that reduce ambiguity by highlighting how relationships affect meaning.

Problem orientation The opposite of controlling; a kind of communication that invites others to work together and find a mutual solution.

Prototypes A type of schema that represents an ideal form.

Provisionalism The opposite of certainty; a kind of communication behavior that reduces defensiveness in others by suggesting that your way is not the only way and thus invites others to share their ideas and opinions.

Proxemics The study of the way people use space to communicate.

Proximity The physical distance between people.

Pseudo-listening Listening not to listen, but to meet some other need.

Public distance The personal space most preferred between people in a public context, ranging generally from 12 feet to 25 feet or more.

Q, R

Race Social and political categories that divide persons into four primary classifications: African American/Black, Caucasian/White, American Indian/Alaskan Native, and Asian/Pacific Islander.

Reappropriating language Embracing terms, which traditionally have been used to demean, in ways that alter their original meaning.

Receiver Those who interpret messages.

Reciprocity The tendency for self-disclosures to mirror the self-disclosures of others.

Referent power The ability to influence based on one person's desire to be like another person.

Regional origin The specific geographical part of a country in which a person was born.

Regulators Types of nonverbal gestures or facial expressions that are used to control or regulate the flow of a conversation.

Relational cultures The unique, private world developed and maintained by people in the context of their personal relationship, which influences how those people behave and act.

Relational currencies The verbal and nonverbal behaviors that express care and love between members of a relationship.

Relationship maintenance Behaviors and strategies people use to keep relationships working over time.

Relationship meaning The emotional meaning, or the meaning that reveals how to interpret the content meaning and the nature of the relationship between communicators.

Relationship status A term used to describe the type and quality of association between two people.

Reward power The ability to influence based on a person's capacity to provide things that are sought after by others.

Rewards Those relationship features that have positive value to an individual.

Rituals Repetitive communicative enactments that pay homage to a person or object that is sacred.

S

Schemata Mental blueprints that help individuals organize and interpret the things around them.

Script A type of schema that contains guidance for communication behaviors.

Selective distortion A process where individuals alter their perceptions so that existing ideas remain intact.

Selective exposure The tendency for people to expose themselves to those things that support their current belief system and avoid stimuli that challenge or contradict them.

Selective perception The tendency to focus on messages that are personally meaningful.

Self-attribution bias The tendency that individuals possess to judge their own intentions, but others' actions.

Self-clarification A function of self-disclosure whereby information is shared in order to help define a person's self-concept.

Self-concept The mental image one has of oneself, including traits, character, abilities, skills, knowledge, and personality.

Self-disclosure The act of giving others information about oneself.

Self-esteem A measure of how one feels about oneself; one aspect of self-concept.

Self-fulfilling prophecy A prediction one accepts about oneself in such a way that it becomes more likely to be true.

Self-image The way one sees oneself, including various roles; one aspect of self-concept.

Self-perceptions The ideas that are formed through our attempts to understand why we behave the way we do.

Self-validation A function of self-disclosure whereby information is shared in order to gain support for a person's self-concept.

Semantic rules Guidelines that help us understand the meaning of individual words.

Semantics of prejudice The idea that language choices can subtly reflect bias against others.

Senders The participants in the communication process who function simultaneously as encoders and decoders of multiple messages.

Sex The genetic or biological characteristics of males and females, determined by the number and type of chromosomes.

Sexual harassment Unsolicited and unwanted verbal and/or nonverbal messages of a sexual nature that interfere with one's ability to perform necessary tasks.

Sexual orientation The direction of one's sexual interest toward members of the same, opposite, or both sexes.

Significant other A broad term used to describe a person (family, friend, teacher, and so on) who provides messages about how he or she see you.

Single-parent family Includes one adult and one or more children.

Situational identity markers Group memberships that are generally not central to how we see ourselves; aspects of our identity that are only important in certain situations.

Social attractiveness The extent to which one finds another person appealing based on his or her personality and behaviors.

Social comparison The process whereby we measure ourselves against others.

Social dimension One aspect of job satisfaction that involves how workers feel about the relationships that they have with others with whom they work.

Social distance The personal distance generally preferred and used for professional and impersonal business conversations, ranging from about 4 feet to 12 feet.

Social exchange theory A group of theories suggesting that individuals in relationships weigh rewards and costs when determining the future of a relationship.

Social identity The way we define who we are through the groups to which we belong.

Social-level knowledge Information about others based on the social roles they play.

Social penetration theory A theory that characterizes the way that bonding occurs between individuals as the breadth and depth of communication increases in a relationship.

Social-psychological context The way that elements such as the relationship between communicators and their thought processes influence communication.

Socioeconomic status (SES, or class) Social standing that reflects a particular cultural mindset, rather than simply current levels of income.

Spamming Sending unsolicited e-mail or sending the same e-mail repeatedly.

Speech community A group of individuals who share a common language system, complete with collective styles, norms, and goals.

Spirituality Belief in a higher power or other supernatural forms that provide order for the world.

Spontaneity The opposite of *strategy*, a kind of communication that is straightforward, honest, and genuine and reduces defensiveness in a communication climate.

Standpoint theory A body of theories that suggest that different perceptions exist for people in different social groups.

Static evaluation When a person uses language that is fixed, rigid, and not open for change.

Stepfamily Also referred to as the blended family, this is a type of family with at least two adults who care for a child or children, at least one of whom is from a previous relationship.

Stereotypes A type of schema that represents generalizations assumed to be true for all people or things in one general category.

Strategy A kind of defense-arousing communication involving manipulation, deception, or ulterior motives.

Style-flexing Adapting communication strategies to match the specific needs of a situation.

Superiority A kind of defense-arousing communication that sends the message "I am better than you."

Symbolic interactionism The idea that we gain an understanding of who we are through our interactions with others.

Symbols Those things that represent other things.

Symmetrical relationships Relationships that reflect opposite needs for, or the exercise of, power in conversations.

Synergy A perspective that views power as something shared, generated, and owned by all.

Syntax rules Guidelines that explain how words should be used relationally.

Systems approach An approach to studying family that views all family members as interdependent.

T

Task dimension One aspect of job satisfaction that relates to how a worker feels about his or her specific duties and responsibilities.

Temporal context How the sequence of events and the timing of an interaction influence communication.

Territory The space we tend to claim ownership of even when we are not present in that space.

Triggering behavior Verbal and nonverbal cues that provoke specific reactions from others.

Trolling Sending false information and extreme viewpoints for the purpose of watching others' reactions.

U, V

Unknown self Information unknown to self and others.

Upward communication Workplace interactions that subordinates have with their supervisors and others higher in the organizational hierarchy.

Vocalics Also known as paralanguage; the study of how we use our voices and vocal qualities to communicate nonverbally.

W, X, Y, Z

Wholeness The most fundamental concept in systems theory, suggesting that individual parts of a family cannot be viewed apart from the whole they create together.

Whorf-Sapir hypothesis The idea that language helps shape our understanding of reality.

Chapter Notes

Chapter 1

1. The opening case study is based on the couple written about in R. Francine, "When Love Is Mixing It Up: More Couples Are Finding Each Other Across Racial Lines—and Finding Acceptance," *Time* 158 (November 19, 2001): 22. Although based on the real couple in the article, some of their story has been changed or created for the purposes of the case study.

2. G. Yancey, "Who Interracially Dates: An Examination of the Characteristics of Those Who Have Interracially Dated," *Journal of Comparative Family Studies* 33 (2002): 179–196; J. Wilensky, "Relationships: What Factors Affect the Occurrence of Interracial and Interethnic Relationships Among Adolescents?" *Human Ecology* 30 (2002): 16–19; and D. Knox, M. Zusman, C. Buffington, and G. Hemphill, "Interracial Dating Attitudes Among College Students," *College Student Journal* 34 (2000): 69–75.

3. Knox, Zusman, Buffington, and Hemphill, "Interracial Dating Attitudes Among College Students."

4. Yancey, "Who Interracially Dates."

5. Yancey, "Who Interracially Dates."

6. J. Gottman, *Marital Interaction* (New York: Academic Press, 1979); J. Gottman, *What Predicts Divorce?* (Hillsdale, NJ: Lawrence Erlbaum, 1994); and R. Lewis and G. Spanier, "Theorizing About the Quality and the Stability of Marriage," in *Contemporary Theories About the Family*, edited by W. Burr, R. Hill, F. Nye, and I. Reiss (New York: Free Press, 1979).

7. W. Cupach and D. Canary, *Competence in Interpersonal Conflict* (New York: McGraw-Hill, 1997).

8. M. Argyle, *The Psychology of Happiness* (London: Routledge, 1987); and J. Lynch, *The Broken Heart: The Medical Consequences of Loneliness* (New York: Basic Books, 1977).

9. F. Korbin and G. Hendershot, "Do Family Ties Reduce Mortality: Evidence from the United States 1966–68," *Journal of Marriage and the Family* 39 (1977): 737–745; and J. House, K. Landis, and D. Umberson, "Social Relationships and Health," *Science* 241 (1988): 540–546.

10. J. Sheehan, "Kiss and Well," *Longevity* 93 (1996): 50–51.

11. House, Landis, and Umberson, "Social Relationships and Health."

12. D. Spiegel, H. Kraemer, J. Bloom, and E. Gottheil, "Effect of Psychosocial Treatment on the Survival of Patients With Metastatic Breast Cancer," *Lancet* 2 (1989): 888–892.

13. H. Laswell, "The Structure and Function of Communication in Society," in *The Communication of Ideas*, edited by L. Bryson (New York: Harper & Row, 1948); and C. Shannon and W. Weaver, *The Mathematical Theory of Communication* (Urbana: University of Illinois Press, 1949).

14. Shannon and Weaver, *The Mathematical Theory of Communication*.

15. J. C. Pearson and P. E. Nelson, *Understanding and Sharing: An Introduction to Speech Communication*, 6th ed. (Dubuque, IA: Brown and Benchmark, 1994).

16. Pearson and Nelson, *Understanding and Sharing.*
17. Shannon and Weaver, *The Mathematical Theory of Communication.*
18. P. Watzlawick, J. Beavin, and D. Jackson, *Pragmatics of Human Communication: A Study of Interactional Patterns, Pathologies, and Paradoxes* (New York: Norton, 1967); and P. Watzlawick, *How Real Is Real? Confusion, Disinformation, Communication: An Anecdotal Introduction to Communication Theory* (New York: Vintage, 1977).
19. Shannon and Weaver, *The Mathematical Theory of Communication.*
20. S. Beebe, S. Beebe, and M. Redmond, *Interpersonal Communication: Relating to Others* (Boston: Allyn & Bacon, 2002).
21. J. Wood, *Interpersonal Communication: Everyday Encounters* (Belmont, CA: Wadsworth-Thomson, 2004), 22.
22. J. Stewart, *Bridges Not Walls: A Book About Interpersonal Communication,* 7th ed. (Boston: McGraw-Hill, 1999); and G. Miller and M. Steinberg, *Between People: A New Analysis of Interpersonal Communication* (Chicago: Science Research Associates, 1975).
23. Similar to interpersonal author/teacher John Stewart (1999), we believe that the original and highly cited work of Gerald Miller and Mark Steinberg (1975) needs to be altered slightly for application in the twenty-first-century global world. They originally proposed a definition of interpersonal communication using a continuum that put cultural knowledge at the far left as the most general knowledge, followed by social knowledge and then interpersonal-level knowledge on the far right. We believe that cultural identities and knowledge about another are actually more informative and personal than are the general "social" features and roles of an individual. Thus, our model—like that of Stewart and Logan—places cultural knowledge as more specific and closer to the end of the interpersonal continuum. See Stewart, *Bridges Not Walls* (New York: McGraw-Hill, 1999); and also see Miller and Steinberg, *Between People.*
24. D. Barnlund, "A Transactional Model of Communication," in *Foundations of Communication Theory,* edited by K. K. Sereno and C. D. Mortensen (New York: Harper & Row, 1970).
25. Watzlawick, Beavin, and Jackson, *Pragmatics of Human Communication.*
26. Watzlawick, Beavin, and Jackson, *Pragmatics of Human Communication.*
27. A. Vangelisti, "Family Secrets: Forms, Functions, and Correlates," *Journal of Social and Personal Relationships* 11 (1994): 113–135.

Chapter 2

1. For more information on how businesses are using techology to provide reasonable accommodation for employees, go to *http://janweb.icdi.wvu.edu.*
2. S. Freud, *Three Theories on the Theory of Sexuality* (London: Hogarth Press, 1953).
3. K. Marx, *Capital* (Chicago: Kerr, 1909).
4. C. G. Prado, *Starting With Foucault* (Boulder, CO: Westview Press, 2000).
5. G. N. Gordon, "An End to McLuhnancy," *Educational Technology* (January 1982): 39–45.
6. R. Brislin, *Understanding Culture's Influence on Behavior* (New York: Harcourt Brace Jovanovich, 1992). Also see M. Orbe, *Constructing Co-cultural Theory: An Explication of Culture, Power, and Communication* (Thousand Oaks, CA: Sage, 1998).
7. R. M. Shuter, "Revisiting the Centrality of Culture," in *Readings in Cultural Contexts,* edited by J. N. Martin, T. K. Nakayama, and L. A. Flores (Mountain View, CA: Mayfield, 1998).
8. Orbe, *Constructing Co-cultural Theory.*
9. R. M. Shuter, "Revisiting the Centrality of Culture."

10. D. Carbaugh, "Culture Talking About Itself," in *Cultural Communication and Intercultural Contact,* edited by D. Carbaugh (Hillsdale, NJ: Lawrence Erlbaum, 1990).

11. M. L. Andersen and P. H. Collins, eds., *Race, Class and Gender: An Anthology* (Belmont, CA: Wadsworth, 1998).

12. C. West, *Race Matters* (Boston: Beacon Press, 1993).

13. M. Hecht, R. Jackson, and S. Ribeau, *African American Communication: Exploring Identity and Culture* (Mahwah, NJ: Lawrence Erlbaum, 2003).

14. S. L. Bem, "The Measurement of Psychological Androgyny," *Journal of Consulting and Clinical Psychology* 42 (1974): 155–162.

15. D. Tannen, *You Just Don't Understand: Women and Men in Conversation* (New York: William Morrow and Company, 1990).

16. J. T. Wood, *Gendered Lives* (Belmont, CA: Wadsworth, 1999).

17. J. T. Wood, "A Critical Response to John Gray's Mars and Venus Portrayals of Men and Women," *Southern Communication Journal* 67 (2002): 201–210. See also D. J. Goldsmith and P. Fulfs, "You Just Don't Have the Evidence: An Analysis of Claims and Evidence in Deborah Tannen's *You Just Don't Understand,*" *Communication Yearbook* 22 (1998): 1–49.

18. D. Langston, "Tired of Playing Monopoly?" In *Race, Class, and Gender: An Anthology,* edited by M. L. Andersen and P. H. Collins (Belmont, CA: Wadsworth, 1995).

19. M. Houston and J. T. Wood, "Difficult Dialogues, Expanded Horizons: Communicating Across Race and Class," in *Gendered Relationships,* edited by J. T. Wood (Mountain View, CA: Mayfield, 1996).

20. V. C. McKay, "Understanding the Co-culture of the Elderly," in *Intercultural Communication: A Reader,* edited by L. A. Samovar and R. E. Porter (Belmont, CA: Wadsworth, 1997).

21. D. O. Braithwaite and C. A. Braithwaite, "Understanding Communication of Persons With Disabilities as Cultural Communication," in *Intercultural Communication: A Reader,* edited by L. A. Samovar and R. E. Porter (Belmont, CA: Wadsworth, 1997).

22. T. Steinfatt and D. M. Chistophel, "Intercultural Communication," in *An Integrated Approach to Communication Theory and Research,* edited by M. B. Salwen and D. W. Stacks (Mahwah, NJ: Lawrence Erlbaum, 1996).

23. G. A. Yep, "My Three Cultures: Navigating the Multicultural Identity Landscape," in *Readings in Intercultural Communication: Experiences and Contexts,* edited by J. N. Martin, T. K. Nakayama, and L. A. Flores (New York: McGraw-Hill, 2002).

24. J. D. Hamlet, "The Reason Why We Sing: Understanding Traditional African American Worship," in *Our Voices: Essays in Culture, Ethnicity, and Communication,* edited by A. Gonzalez, M. Houston, and V. Chen (Los Angeles: Roxbury, 2000).

25. B. Bate and J. Bowker, *Communication and the Sexes* (Prospect Heights, IL: Waveland Press, 1997). Also see N. Josefowitz, *Pathways to Power Reading* (Reading, MA: Addison-Wesley, 1980).

26. A. Rich, "Prepartiarchal Female/Goddess Images," in *The Politics of Female Spirituality,* edited by C. Spretnak (Garden City, NY: Doubleday/Anchor, 1982).

27. Josefowitz, *Politics of Female Spirituality.*

28. Josefowitz, *Politics of Female Spirituality.*

29. J. R. P. French, Jr., and B. Raven. "The Bases of Social Power," in *Studies in Social Power,* edited by D. Cartwright (Ann Arbor, MI: Institute for Social Research, 1959).

30. French and Raven, "Bases of Social Power."

31. L. P. Stewart, "Gender Issues in Corporate Communication," in *Women and Men Communicating: Challenges and Changes,* edited by L. Arliss and D. Borisoff (Prospect Heights, IL: Waveland Press, 2001).

32. D. Borisoff and L. Merrill, *The Power to Communicate: Gender Differences as Barriers* (Prospect Heights, IL: Waveland Press, 1992).

33. J. Wicklein, *Electronic Nightmare: The New Communications and Freedom* (New York: Viking, 1981).

34. G. C. Armas, "Report: More Than Half of All Americans Go Online," *Kalamazoo (MI) Gazette* (February 9, 2002): A6.

35. See *http://www.cnn.com/2000/tech/computing/09/25/unwanted.access.idg/index.html.*

36. M. McLuhan, *Understanding Media: The Extensions of Man* (New York: Signet Books, 1964).

37. G. Gerbner, L. Gross, M. Morgan, and N. Signorielli, "The 'Mainstreaming' of America: Violence Profile No. 11," *Journal of Communication* 30 (1980): 10–29.

38. S. Hall, "Cultural Studies and Its Theoretical Legacies," in *Cultural Studies*, edited by L. Grossberg, C. Nelson, and P. Treichler (New York: Routledge, 1992).

Chapter 3

1. See *http://www.cnn.com/US/9601/teen_pregnancy/self_esteem/index.html.*

2. M. H. Kuhn and T. S. McPartland, "An Empirical Investigation of Self-Attitudes," *American Sociological Review* 19 (1954): 68–76.

3. G. E. Cooper and S. T. Murphy, "The Communicated Self: Exploring the Interaction Between Self and Social Context," *Communication Research* 26 (2000): 125–147.

4. M. H. Kuhn, "Major Trends in Symbolic Interaction Theory in the Past Twenty-five Years," *Sociological Quarterly* 5 (1964): 61–84.

5. G. H. Mead, *Mind, Self, and Society* (Chicago: University of Chicago Press, 1934).

6. Cooper and Murphy, "The Communicated Self."

7. Mead, *Mind, Self, and Society.*

8. C. H. Cooley, *Human Nature and the Social Order* (New York: Scribners, 1922).

9. Mead, *Mind, Self, and Society.*

10. J. T. Wood, *Gendered Lives: Communication, Gender, and Culture* (Belmont, CA: Wadsworth, 2002).

11. M. Sadker and D. Sadker, *Failing at Fairness: How America's Schools Cheat Girls* (New York: Charles Scribner's Sons, 1994).

12. M. Orbe, "'Remember, It's Always Whites' Ball': Descriptions of African American Male Communication," *Communication Quarterly* 42 (1994): 287–300.

13. N. Wolf, *The Beauty Myth* (New York: William Morrow, 1991).

14. R. Goldman, D. Heath, and Sharon L. Smith, "Commodity Feminism," *Critical Studies in Mass Communication* 8 (1991): 333–351.

15. M. Hecht, R. Jackson, and S. Ribeau, *African American Communication: Exploring Identity and Culture* (Mahwah, NJ: Lawrence Erlbaum, 2003).

16. J. Monahan and P. Lannutti, "Alcohol as Social Lubricant: Alcohol Myopia Theory, Social Self-esteem, and Social Interaction," *Human Communication Research* 26 (2000): 175–202.

17. D. Moon and G. Rolison, "Communication of Classism," *Communicating Prejudice*, edited by M. Hecht (Thousand Oaks, CA: Sage, 1998).

18. S. Mosley-Howard and C. B. Evans, "Relationships in the African American Family," paper presented at the Conference of the International Network on Personal Relationships, Oxford, Ohio, 1997.

19. J. Martin, R. Krizek, T. Nakayama, and L. Bradford, "Exploring Whiteness: A Study of Self Labels for White Americans," *Communication Quarterly* 44 (1996): 125–144.

20. M. Orbe and T. Harris, *Interracial Communication: Theory Into Practice* (Belmont, CA: Wadsworth, 2001).
21. Hecht, Jackson, and Ribeau, *African American Communication.*
22. G. Hofstede, *Culture's Consequences: International Differences in Work-Related Values* (Beverly Hills, CA: Sage, 1980).
23. Kuhn and McPartland, "Empirical Investigation."
24. P. McIntosh, "White Privilege and Male Privilege: A Personal Account of Coming to See Correspondences Through Work in Women's Studies," in *Race, Class, and Gender: An Anthology*, edited by M. L. Andersen and P. H. Collins (Belmont, CA: Wadswoth, 1995).
25. Orbe and Harris, *Interracial Communication.*
26. N. L. Dollar and B. G. Zimmers, "Social Identity and Communicative Boundaries: An Analysis of Youth Adult Speakers in a U.S. American Community," *Communication Research* 25 (1998): 596–617.
27. J. Luft, *Group Processes: An Introduction to Group Dynamics* (Mountain View, CA: Mayfield, 1984).
28. Aristotle, *On Rhetoric: A Theory of Civil Discourse*, edited and translated by G. A. Kennedy (New York: Oxford University Press, 1991).
29. H. Wintrob, "Self-disclosure as a Marketable Commodity," *Journal of Social Behavior and Personality* 2 (1987): 77–88.
30. I. Altman and D. Taylor, *Social Penetration: The Development of Interpersonal Relationships* (New York: Holt, Rinehart, and Winston, 1973).
31. Altman and Taylor, *Social Penetration.*
32. L.-N. Huang, "Family Communication Patterns and Personality Characteristics," *Communication Quarterly* 47 (1999): 230–243.
33. M. Nakanishi, "Perceptions of Self-disclosure in Initial Interaction: A Japanese Sample," *Human Communication Research* 13 (1986): 167–190.
34. W. B. Gudykunst, *Bridging Differences: Effective Intergroup Communication* (Thousand Oaks, CA: Sage, 1998).
35. J. Hale, R. Tighe, and P. Mongeau, "Effects of Event Type and Sex on Comforting Messages," *Communication Research Reports* 14 (1997): 214–220.
36. D. Canary and K. Dindia, eds., *Sex Differences and Similarities in Communication: Critical Essays and Empirical Investigations of Sex and Gender in Interaction* (Mahwah, NJ: Lawrence Erlbaum, 1998).
37. L. Pragg, R. Wiseman, M. J. Cody, and P. F. Wendt, "Interrogative Strategies and Information Exchange in Computer-Mediated Communication," *Communication Quarterly* 47 (1999): 46–66.
38. Pragg, Wisemand, Cody, and Wendt, "Interrogative Strategies."
39. M. Lea and R. Spears, "Love at First Byte? Building Personal Relationships Over Computer Networks," in *Under-Studied Relationships: Off the Beaten Track*, edited by J. T. Wood and S. Duck (Thousand Oaks, CA: Sage, 1995).
40. S. R. Stern, "Adolescent Girls' Expression on Web Home Pages: Spirited, Somber, and Self-conscious Sites," *Convergence* 5 (1999): 22–41.

Chapter 4

1. See *http://www.cnn.com/HEALTH/9911/02/elderly.fitness/index.html.*
2. L. Lazier and A. G. Kendrick, "Women in Advertisements: Sizing Up the Images, Roles, and Functions," in *Women in Mass Communication*, edited by P. Creedon (Newbury Park, CA: Sage, 1993).

3. J. T. Wood, "Gender and Moral Voice: Moving From Woman's Nature to Standpoint Epistemology," *Women's Studies in Communication* 15 (1992): 1–24.

4. M. Orbe and K. Warren, "Different Standpoints, Different Realities: Race, Gender, and Perceptions of Intercultural Conflict," *Qualitative Research Reports in Communication* 1 (2000): 51–57.

5. K. Warren, M. Orbe, and N. Greer-Williams, "Perceiving Conflict: Similarities and Differences Between and Among Latinos/as, African Americans, and European Americans," in *Brown & Black Communication: Latino and African American Conflict and Convergence in Mass Media*, edited by D. Rios and A. N. Mohamed (Westport, CT: Greenwood Press, 2003).

6. P. Orenstein, *School Girls: Young Women, Self-esteem, and the Confidence Gap* (New York: Anchor Books, 1994).

7. R. K. Merton, *Social Theory and Social Structure* (New York: Free Press, 1957).

8. F. Heider, *The Psychology of Interpersonal Relations* (New York: Wiley, 1958).

9. S. Asch, "Forming Impressions of Personality," *Journal of Abnormal and Social Psychology* 41 (1946): 258–290.

10. D. Hamilton, *Cognitive Processes in Stereotyping and Intergroup Behavior* (Hillsdale, NJ: Lawrence Erlbaum, 1981).

11. L. Sigelman and S. A. Tuch, "Metastereotypes: Blacks' Perceptions of Whites' Stereotypes of Blacks," *Public Opinion Quarterly* 61 (1997): 87–101.

12. T. Pettigrew, "The Ultimate Attribution Error: Extending Allport's Cognitive Analysis of Prejudice," *Personality and Social Psychology Bulletin* 5 (1979): 461–476.

13. A. Jesdanum, "Computers Get a Human Feel," *Kalamazoo (MI) Gazette* (January 21, 2001): C1–C2.

14. "Blacks Closing Gap in Use of Technology," *Kalamazoo (MI) Gazette* (March 11, 1999): A11.

15. "Net Gains," *Newsweek* (November 7, 2000): 82.

16. M. A. Paludi and W. D. Bauer, "Goldberg Revisited: What's in an Author's Name," *Sex Roles* 9 (1992): 387–390.

Chapter 5

1. See *http://www.cnn.com/WORLD/europe/9910/12yugo.kosovo.02/*.

2. H. Hoijer, "The Sapir-Whorf Hypothesis," in *Intercultural Communication: A Reader*, edited by L. A. Samovar and R. E. Porter (Belmont, CA: Wadsworth, 1994).

3. M. Fong, "The Crossroads of Language and Culture," in *Intercultural Communication: A Reader*, edited by L. A. Samovar and R. E. Porter (Belmont, CA: Wadsworth, 1994).

4. D. Hymes, *Foundations of Sociolinguistics: An Ethnographic Approach* (Philadelphia: University of Pennsylvania Press, 1974).

5. R. L. Birdwhistell, *Kinesics and Context* (Philadelphia: University of Pennsylvania Press, 1970).

6. J. Delia, B. O'Keefe, and D. O'Keefe, "The Constructivist Approach to Communication," in *Human Communication Theory*, edited by F. E. X. Dance (New York: Harper & Row, 1982).

7. C. Kitzinger, "How to Resist and Idiom," *Research on Language and Social Interaction* 33 (2000): 121–154.

8. G. Philipsen, "A Theory of Speech Codes," in *Developing Communication Theory*, edited by G. Philipsen and T. Albrecht (Albany: State University of New York Press, 1997).

9. J. T. Wood, *Interpersonal Communication Everyday Encounters* (Belmont, CA: Wadsworth, 1999).

10. H. Giles, A. Mulac, J. Bradac, and P. Johnson, "Speech Communication Theory: The First Decade and Beyond," *Communication Yearbook* 10 (1987): 13–48.

11. E. Morales, *Living in Spanglish: The Search for Latino Identity in America* (New York: St. Martin's Press, 2002).
12. L. Alvarez, "It's the Talk of Nueva York: The Hybrid Called Spanglish," *New York Times* (March 25, 1997): A1, B4.
13. J. C. Brown, "In Defense of the N Word," *Essence* (June 1993): 138.
14. C. Kramarae, *Women and Men Speaking* (Rowley, MA: Newbury, 1981).
15. P. Buzzanell, "Gaining a Voice: Feminist Organizational Communication Theorizing," *Management Communication Quarterly* 7 (1994): 339–383.
16. R. Maggio, *The Dictionary of Bias-free Usage: A Guide to Nondiscriminating Language* (Phoenix, AZ: Oryz Press, 1991).
17. C. K. Ogden and I. A. Richards, *The Meaning of Meaning* (New York: Harcourt, Brace, & World, 1946).
18. V. Shea, *Netiquette* (New York: Albion Books, 1994).

Chapter 6

1. *http://www.cnn.com/2000/tech/computing/03/17/email.business.idg/index.html*.
2. D. Moore, T. Kurtzberg, L. Thompson, and M. Morris, "Long and Short Routes to Success in Electronically Mediated Negotiations: Group Affiliations and Good Vibrations," *Organizational Behavior and Human Decision Processes* 77 (1999); A. Drolet and M. Morris, "Rapport in Conflict Resolution: Accounting for How Face-to-Face Contact Fosters Mutual Cooperation in Mixed Motive Conflict," *Journal of Experimental Social Psychology* (1999); and M. Mooris, J. Nadler, T. Kurtzberg, and L. Thompson, "Schmooze or Lose: Communication Media, Relationship-Building, and Negotiations," Stanford Graduate School of Business Research Paper #1583 (1999).
3. J. Devito, *The Nonverbal Communication Workbook* (Prospect Heights, IL: Waveland Press, 1989).
4. A. Mehrabian, *Silent Messages: Implicit Communication of Emotion and Attitudes* (Belmont, CA: Wadsworth, 1981).
5. V. P. Richmond and J. C. McCroskey, *Nonverbal Behavior in Interpersonal Relations* (Boston: Allyn & Bacon, 2004).
6. D. Buller and J. Burgoon, "Interpersonal Deception Theory," *Communication Theory* 6 (1996): 203–242.
7. M. Zuckermann and R. Driver, "Telling Lies: Verbal and Nonverbal Correlates of Deception," in *Multichannel Integrations of Nonverbal Behavior*, edited by A. Siegman and S. Feldstein (Hillsdale, NJ: Lawrence Erlbaum, 1985).
8. Richmond and McCroskey, *Nonverbal Behavior in Interpersonal Relation*; and R. E. Axtell, *Gestures: The Do's and Taboos of Body Language Around the World* (New York: John Wiley & Sons, 1991).
9. A. Wolf, "Emotional Expression Online: Gender Differences in Emoticon Use," *CyberPsychology & Behavior* 3 (2000): 827–834.
10. K. Milner Halls, "Emoticons: Say It With a Smile," *Child Life* 76 (1997): 26–27; N. Tamosaitis, "Face to Face in Cyberspace: Anonymity of E-Mail Can Tear Down Social Barriers," *Computer Life* 1 (1994): 137–139; and "Saying It With a Smile," *PC Magazine* (September 15, 1998): 41.
11. "Emoticons Give Way to Stand-Ins," *The Futurist*, 35 (2001): 2.
12. J. Streek, "Gestures as Communication: Its Coordination With Gaze and Speech," *Communication Monographs* 60 (1993): 275–299.
13. A. Mehrabian, "Significance of Posture and Position in the Communication of Attitude and Status Relationships," *Psychological Bulletin* 71 (1969): 359–372.

14. A. Mehrabian, *Silent Messages*.

15. Richmond and McCroskey, *Nonverbal Behavior in Interpersonal Relations*.

16. D. Leathers, *Successful Nonverbal Communication: Principles and Applications* (Boston: Allyn & Bacon, 1997).

17. P. Ekman, W. V. Friesen, and S. Tomkins, "Facial Affect Scoring Techniques: A First Validity Study," *Semiotica* 3 (1971): 37–58; and P. Ekman, W. V. Friesen, and P. Ellsworth, *Emotion in the Human Face: Guidelines for Research and an Integration of Findings* (New York: Pergamon Press, 1972).

18. P. Ekman and W. V. Friesen, *Unmasking the Face: A Guide to Recognizing Emotions From Facial Cues* (Englewood Cliffs, NJ: Prentice Hall, 1975).

19. J. D. Boucher and P. Ekman, "Facial Areas and Emotional Information," *Journal of Communication* 25 (1975): 21–29; Ekman and Friesen, *Unmasking the Face*; and H. G. Johnson, P. Ekman and W. V. Friesen, "Communicative Body Movements: American Emblems," *Semiotica* 15 (1975): 335–353.

20. D. Leathers, *Successful Nonverbal Communication*.

21. Knapp and Hall, *Nonverbal Communication in Human Interaction*.

22. Knapp and Hall, *Nonverbal Communication in Human Interaction*.

23. E. T. Hall, *The Silent Language* (Garden City, NY: Doubleday, 1959); and E. T. Hall, *The Hidden Dimension* (Garden City, NY: Doubleday, 1966).

24. DeVito, *The Nonverbal Communication Workbook*.

25. R. Sommer, *Personal Space: The Behavioral Basis of Design* (Englewood Cliffs, NJ: Prentice Hall, 1969); and G. R. Oldham and N.L. Rotchford, "Relationships Between Office Characteristics and Employee Reactions: A Study of the Physical Environment," *Administrative Science Quarterly* 28 (1999): 542–556.

26. Sommer, *Personal Space*; and Oldham and Rotchford, "Relationships Between Office Characteristics and Employee."

27. DeVito, *The Nonverbal Communication Workbook*.

28. Hall, *The Hidden Dimension*.

29. A. Mehrabian, *Public Places and Private Spaces: The Psychology of Work, Play, and Living Environments* (New York: Basic Books, 1976).

30. N. J. Stone, "Designing Effective Study Environments," *Journal of Environmental Psychology* 21 (2001): 179–200.

31. R. Sommer, "Sociofungal Space," *American Journal of Sociology* 72 (1967): 654–660; Oldham and Rotchford, "Relationships Between Office Characteristics and Employee Reactions"; and W. H. Moleski and J. T. Lang, "Organizational Goals and Human Needs in Office Planning," in *Behavioral Issues in Office Design*, edited by J. D. Wineman (New York: von Nostrand Reinhold, 1986).

32. D. P. Harner, "A Review of Research Concerning the Thermal Environment and Its Effect on Learning," Ph.D. diss., University of Mississippi, 1973; and P. Andersen, *Nonverbal Communication: Forms and Functions* (Mountain View, CA: Mayfield, 1999).

33. M. Eaves and D. Leathers, "Context as Communication: McDonald's vs. Burger King," *Journal of Applied Communication Research* 19 (1991): 263–289.

34. Andersen, *Nonverbal Communication: Forms and Functions*.

35. C. J. Boyatzis and R. Varghese, "Children's Emotional Associations with Colors," *Journal of Genetic Psychology* 155 (1994): 77–86.

36. M. Fink Vargas, *Louder Than Words: An Introduction to Nonverbal Communication* (Des Moines: Iowa State Press, 1986).

37. J. Burgoon and T. Saine, *The Unspoken Dialogue: An Introduction to Nonverbal Communication* (Boston: Houghton Mifflin, 1978).

38. J. K. Burgoon, D. B. Buller, and G. W. Woodall, *Nonverbal Communication: The Unspoken Dialogue* (Boston: McGraw-Hill, 1996).
39. "Hugs, Kisses Help Kids Later in Life," *American Health* (December 14, 1994): C5.
40. Richmond and McCroskey, *Nonverbal Behavior in Interpersonal Relations*.
41. T. Zeman and L. Howard, "Here's How the Presidential Candidates Really Measure Up," *Newsweek* (March 9, 1992); P. M. Sommers, "Is Presidential Greatness Related to Height?" *College Mathematics Journal* 33 (2002): 14–17; and C. Trillin, "The Tall and Short of It," *Time* 147 (May 27, 1996): 17–18.
42. "School Wins Right to Ban Objectionable Clothes in Supreme Court Case," *Curriculum Administrator* 37 (May 2001): 14.
43. R. Levine, "The Pace of Life," *Psychology Today* (October 1989): 42–46.
44. R. E. Axtell, *Gestures: The Do's and Taboos of Body Language Around the World* (New York: John Wiley and Sons, 1991); J. Martin and T. Nakayama, *Intercultural Communication In Contexts* (Boston: McGraw-Hill, 2004); and L. Samovar and R. Porter, *Intercultural Communication: A Reader* (Belmont, CA: Wadsworth, 2003).
45. E. Rogers and T. Steinfatt, *Intercultural Communication* (Prospect Heights, IL: Waveland Press, 1999).
46. E. T. Hall, *The Dance of Life: The Other Dimension of Time* (New York: Doubleday, 1983).
47. Rogers and Steinfatt, *Intercultural Communication*.
48. Rogers and Steinfatt, *Intercultural Communication*.
49. R. Birdwhistell, *Kinesics and Context: Essays on Body Motion Communication* (Philadelphia: University of Philidelphis Press, 1970).

Chapter 7

1. See *http://www.cnn.com/HEALTH/9904/21/trauma.counseling/index.html*.
2. M. Buckley, "We Listen a Book a Day; We Speak a Book a Week: Learning from Walter Loban," *Language Arts* 69 (1992): 622–626.
3. A. Wolvin and C. G. Coakely, *Listening* (Boston: McGraw-Hill, 1996).
4. H. Mackay, "Listening Is the Hardest of the 'Easy' Tasks," *Minneapolis Star Tribune* (Thursday, May 24, 2001); and *http://www.listen.org.pages/mackay.html*.
5. H. Beckman and R. Frankel, "The Effect of Physician Behavior on the Collection of Data," *Ann Intern Medical* 101 (1984): 692–696; M. Bowman, "Good Physician-Patient Relationship = Improved Patient Outcome?" *Journal of Family Practice* 32 (1991): 135–137; S. A. Cohen-Cole and J. Bird, "Function 2: Building Rapport and Responding to Patients' Emotions," in *The Medical Interview: The Three Function Approach*, edited by S. A. Cohen-Cole (St. Louis, MO: Mosby-Year Book, 1991); D. Goleman, "All Too Often, The Doctor Isn't Listening, Studies Show," *New York Times* (November, 13, 1991): C1; and A. Suchman, K. Markakis, H. Beckman, and R. Frankel, "A Model of Empathic Communication in the Medical Interview," *Journal of the American Medical Association* 277 (1997): 678–683.
6. Beckman and Frankel, "The Effect of Physician Behavior on the Collection of Data"; and Goleman, "All Too Often, the Doctor Isn't Listening, Studies Show."
7. S. Kaplan, S. Greenfield, and J. Ware, "Assessing the Effects of Physician-Patient Interaction on the Outcomes of Chronic Disease," *Med Care* 27 (1989): 110–127.
8. M. McKay, M. Davis, and P. Fanning, *Messages: The Communication Skills Book* (Oakland, CA: New Harbinger Publications, 1995).
9. R. Zeuschner, *Communicating Today* (Boston: Allyn & Bacon, 1997).

10. S. Bentley, "Listening in the 21st Century," *International Journal of Listening* 14 (2000): 129–142.
11. Wolvin and Coakley, *Listening*.
12. Bentley, "Listening in the 21st Century."
13. Bentley, "Listening in the 21st Century."
14. Bentley, "Listening in the 21st Century."
15. Bentley, "Listening in the 21st Century."
16. C. Kiewitz, J. Weaver, H. Brosius, and G. Weimann, "Cultural Differences in Listening Styles Preferences: A Comparison of Young Adults in Germany, Israel, and the United States," *International Journal of Public Opinion Research* 9 (1997): 233–248.
17. Bentley, "Listening in the 21st Century," 133.
18. C. Roach and N. Wyatt, *Successful Listening* (New York: Harper and Row, 1988).
19. Roach and Wyatt, *Successful Listening*.
20. J. Wood, "Mindful Listening," in J. Wood, *Interpersonal Communication: Everyday Encounters* (Belmont, CA: Wadsworth, 1999).
21. B. Bate, *Communication Between the Sexes* (New York: Harper & Row, 1988); C. Kramarae, *Women and Men Speaking: Frameworks for Analysis* (Rowley, MA: Newbury, 1981); J. Wood, "Engendered Relationships: Interaction, Caring, Power, and Responsibility in Close Relationships," in *Processes in Close Relationships: Contexts of Close Relationships*, edited by S. Duck (Beverly Hills, CA: Sage, 1993); and J. Wood, *Gendered Lives: Communication, Gender, and Culture* (Belmont, CA: Wadsworth, 2001).
22. Wood, *Gendered Lives*.
23. Wood, *Gendered Lives*.
24. Bate, *Communication Between the Sexes*.
25. L. Stewart, A. Stewart, S. Friedley, and P. Cooper, *Communication Between the Sexes: Sex Differences and Sex Role Stereotypes* (Scottsdale, AZ: Gorsuch Scarisbrick, 1990).
26. M. Asante and A. Davis, "Encounters in the Interracial Workplace," in *Handbook of International and Intercultural Communication*, edited by M. Asante and W. Gudykunst (Newbury Park, CA: Sage, 1989); and G. Smitherman, *Black Talk: Words and Phrases From the Hood to the Amen Corner* (Boston: Houghton Mifflin, 2000).
27. Asante and Davis, "Encounters in the Interracial Workplace."
28. B. J. Hall, *Among Cultures: The Challenge of Communication* (Belmont, CA: Wadsworth/Thomson Learning, 2002).
29. G. Chen and W. Starosta, "Listening Between Co-Cultures," (Chapter 9). *Foundations of Intercultural Communication* (Boston: Allyn & Bacon, 1998).
30. D. Carbaugh, "'Just Listen': 'Listening' and Landscape Among the Blackfeet," *Western Journal of Communication* 63 (1999): 250–270.
31. Carbaugh, "'Just Listen.'"
32. Carbaugh, "'Just Listen.'"
33. "Kill the Music if You Want Good Grades: Listening to Music Slows Writing," *New Scientist* 169 (2001): 17.
34. International Listening Association, *http://www.listen.org/pages/factoids.html*.
35. Wolvin and Coakley, *Listening*.
36. H. Lorayne and J. Lucas, *The Memory Book* (New York: Ballantine Books, 1974).
37. McKay, Davis, and Fanning, *Messages*.
38. B. Gunn, "Listening as a Feeling," *Strategic Finance* 82 (2001): 12.
39. McKay, Davis, and Fanning, *Messages*.
40. McKay, Davis, and Fanning, *Messages*.

41. E. T. Hall and M. R. Hall, *Understanding Cultural Differences* (Yarmouth, ME: Intercultural Press, 1989).

Chapter 8

1. See *http://www.CNN.com/US/9909/23/hate.crimes.gays/index.html*.
2. J. Gallagher, "Violent Times," *Advocate* 685 (July 11, 1995): 33–36; and A. J. Peters, "Isolation or Inclusion: Creating Safe Spaces for Lesbian and Gay Youth," *Families in Society: The Journal of Contemporary Human Services* 84 (2003): 331–340.
3. A. Goodell, "Organizational Climate: Current Thinking on an Important Issue," in *Readings in Organizational Communication,* edited by K. Hutchinson (Dubuque, IA: Brown Benchmark, 1992).
4. J. Gottman, *What Predicts Divorce? The Relationship Between Marital Processes and Marital Outcomes* (Hillsdale, NJ: Lawrence Erlbaum, 1994); J. Gottman, *Why Marriages Succeed or Fail?* (New York: Simon & Schuster, 1994); and S. Ting-Toomey, "An Analysis of Verbal Communication Patterns in High and Low Marital Adjustment Groups," *Human Communication Research* 9 (1983): 306–319.
5. W. Cupach and D. Canary, *Competence in Interpersonal Conflict* (New York: McGraw-Hill, 1997).
6. Gottman, *What Predicts Divorce?*
7. B. Spitzberg and W. Cupach, *Handbook of Interpersonal Competence Research* (New York: Springer-Verlag, 1989).
8. Cupach and Canary, *Competence in Interpersonal Conflict.*
9. M. Gannon, "Irish Conversations," in *Intercultural Communication: A Reader,* edited by L. Samovar and R. Porter (Belmont, CA: Wadsworth, 2000).
10. "He-Mails, She-Mails: Where Sender Meets Gender," *New York Times* (May 17, 2001): D1.
11. L. Dumas, "Talking With Kids About Tough Issues," *Children Now* and *The Henry J. Kaiser Family Foundation* (Menlo Park, CA: Henry J. Kaiser Foundation, 1996).
12. K. Galvin and B. Brommel, *Family Communication: Cohesion and Change* (New York: Addison Wesley Longman, 2000).
13. R. Adler and N. Towne, *Looking Out, Looking In* (Fort Worth, TX: Harcourt Brace, 2002).
14. K. Cissna and E. Sieburg, "Patterns of Interactional Confirmation and Disconfirmation," in *Interpersonal Communication: Readings in Theory and Research,* edited by M. Redmond (Fort Worth, TX: Harcourt Brace, 1995).
15. Cissna and Sieburg, "Patterns of Interactional Confirmation and Disconfirmation."
16. "Net Blamed for Marital Breakups" (April 15, 2002), *http://www.CNN.com/2002/TECH/internet/04/15/internet.breakup/index/html.*
17. A. Barbour and A. Goldberg, "Principles of Confirmation," in *Making Connections: Readings in Relational Communication,* edited by K. Galvin and P. Cooper (Los Angeles: Roxbury, 2000).
18. Gottman, *What Predicts Divorce?*
19. See *http://www.CNN.com/2001/career/trends/07/18/job.hunters.idg/index.html.*
20. See *http://www.CNN.com/2001/career/trends/07/18/job.hunters.idg/index.html.*
21. R. Lancaster, "Girlfriend Power: Communication Among African American Women," *Ebony* 56 (January 2001): 28.
22. J. Gibb, "Defensive Communication," *Journal of Communication* 11 (1961): 141–148.
23. K. D. Scott, "Broadening the View of Black Language Use," in *Our Voices: Essays in Culture, Ethnicity, and Communication,* edited by A. Gonzalez, M. Houston, and V. Chen (Los Angeles: Roxbury, 2000); and J. Wood, *But I Thought You Meant: Misunderstandings in Human Communication* (Mountain View, CA: Mayfield, 1998).

24. D. B. Bugental, "Communication in Abusive Relationships," *American Behavioral Scientist* 36 (1993): 288–309.

25. D. O. Braithwaite, "'Just How Much Did That Wheelchair Cost?' Management of Privacy Boundaries by Persons With Disabilities," *Western Journal of Speech Communication* 55 (1991): 254–275; D. O. Braithwaite and C. Braithwaite, "Understanding Communication of Persons With Disabilities as Cultural Communication," in *Intercultural Communication: A Reader*, edited by L. Samovar and R. Porter (Belmont, CA: Wadsworth, 2000); and D. O. Braithwaite and N. J. Eckstein, "How People With Disabilities Communicatively Manage Assistance: Helping as Instrumental Social Support," *Journal of Applied Communication Research* 31 (2003): 1–27.

Chapter 9

1. See *http://www.cnn.com/2000/HEALTH/09/05/self.mutilation/wmd/index.html*.

2. S. Levenkron, *Cutting: Understanding and Overcoming Self-Mutilation* (New York: W. W. Norton, 1998).

3. D. J. Canary, W. Cupach, and S. Messman, *Relationship Conflict: Conflict in Parent-Child, Friendship, and Romantic Relationships* (Thousand Oaks, CA: Sage, 1995).

4. J. W. Keltner, *Mediation: Toward a Civilized System of Dispute Resolution* (Annandale, VA: Speech Communication Association, 1987).

5. M. Trost and J. Alberts, "An Evolutionary View on Understanding Sex Effects in Communicating Attraction," in *Sex Differences and Similarities in Communication*, edited by D. Canary and K. Dindia (Mahwah, NJ: Lawrence Erlbaum, 1998).

6. J. Hoyce and W. Wilmont, *Interpersonal Conflict* (Madison, WI: WCB Brown & Benchmark, 1995).

7. S. McCorckle and J. Mills, "Rowboat in a Hurricane: Metaphors of Interpersonal Conflict Management," *Communication Reports* 5 (1992): 57–66.

8. L. A. Kurdeck, "Areas of Conflict for Gay, Lesbian, and Heterosexual Couples: What Couples Argue About Influences Relationship Satisfaction," *Journal of Marriage and Family* 56 (1994): 923–934.

9. M.-S. Kim and T. Leung, "A Multicultural View of Conflict Management Styles: Review and Critical Synthesis," *Communication Yearbook* 23 (2000): 227–269.

10. S. Ting-Toomey, "Managing Intercultural Conflict Effectively," in *Intercultural Communication: A Reader*, edited by L. Samovar and R. E. Porter (Belmont, CA: Wadsworth, 2000).

11. E. T. Hall, *The Dance of Life* (New York: Doubleday, 1983).

12. R. Cohen, *Negotiating Across Cultures: Communication Obstacles in International Diplomacy* (Washington, D.C.: U.S. Institute of Peace, 1991).

13. Ting-Toomey, "Managing Intercultural Conflict Effectively."

14. L. Sagrestano, C. Heavey, and A. Christensen, "Theoretical Approaches to Understanding Sex Differences and Similarities in Conflict Behavior," in *Sex Differences and Similarities in Communication*, edited by D. Canary and K. Dindia (Mahwah, NJ: Lawrence Erlbaum, 1998).

15. A. Filley, *Interpersonal Conflict Resolution* (Glenview, IL: Scott & Foresman, 1975). See also D. Cahn, "Intimates in Conflict: A Research Review," in *Intimates in Conflict: A Communication Perspective*, edited by D. Cahn (Hillsdale, NJ: Lawrence Erlbaum, 1990).

16. J. W. Pennebaker, *Opening Up: The Healing Power of Expressing Emotions* (New York: Guilford, 1997).

17. D. Goleman, *Emotional Intelligence* (New York: Bantam Books, 2000).

18. B. Burleson and S. Planalp, "Producing Emotion(al) Messages," *Communication Theory* 10 (2000): 221–250.

19. P. Shaver, S. Wu, and J. Schwartz, "Cross-cultural Similarities and Differences in Emotion and Its Representation: A Protoype Approach," in *Emotion*, edited by M. S. Clark (Newbury Park, CA: Sage, 1992).

20. Goleman, *Emotional Intelligence*.

21. M. Lewis, "Self-conscious Emotions: Embarrassment, Pride, Shame, and Guilt," in *Handbook of Emotions*, edited by M. Lewis and J. Haviland-Jones (New York: Guilford Press, 2000).

22. S. Westmyer, R. DiCioccio, and R. Rubin, "Appropriateness and Effectiveness of Communication Channels in Competent Interpersonal Communication," *Journal of Communication* 48 (1998): 27–48.

23. A. Landers, "Heartbroken Mother's Tale Is Only Half the Story," *Kalamazoo (MI) Gazette* (March 25, 1997): G4.

24. E. Langer, *Mindfulness* (Reading, MA: Addison-Wesley).

Chapter 10

1. See *http://www.cnn.com/2001/tech/internet/02/14/valentine.greetings.idg/index.html*.

2. L. Baxter, "A Dialectical Perspective on Communication Strategies in Relationship Development," in *Handbook of Personal Relationships*, edited by S. W. Duck, D. F. Hay, S. E. Hobfoll, W. Ickes, and B. Montgomery (London: Wiley, 1988); J. Wood, "Communication and Relational Culture: Bases for the Study of Human Relationships," *Communication Quarterly* 30 (1982): 75–84; and J. Wood, *Relational Communication: Continuity and Change in Personal Relationships* (Belmont, CA: Wadsworth, 2000).

3. D. Byrne, "An Overview (and Underview) of Research and Theory Within the Attraction Paradigm," *Journal of Social and Personal Relationships* 14 (1999): 417–431.

4. M. Rosenbaum, "The Repulsion Hypothesis: On the Nondevelopment of Relationships," *Journal of Personality and Social Psychology* 51 (1986): 1156–1166.

5. R. Singh and S. Y. Ho, "Attitudes and Attraction: A New Test of the Attraction, Repulsion and Similarity-Dissimilarity Asymmetry Hypotheses," *British Journal of Social Psychology* 39 (2000): 197–212.

6. R. Spellers, "Happy to Be Nappy! Embracing an Afrocentric Aesthetic for Beauty," in *Readings in Cultural Contexts*, edited by J. Martin, T. Nakayama, and L. Flores (Mountain View, CA: Mayfield, 1998).

7. G. Hofstede, "I, We, They," in *Readings in Cultural Contexts*, edited by J. Martin, T. Nakayama, and L. Flores (Mountain View, CA: Mayfield, 1998).

8. C. Wilkinson, "Expressing Affection: A Vocabulary of Loving Messages," in *Making Connections: Readings in Relational Communication*, edited by K. Galvin and P. Cooper (Los Angeles: Roxbury, 1999).

9. H. Kelley and J. Thibaut, *The Social Psychology of Groups* (New York: Wiley, 1978); J. Thibaut and H. Kelley, *The Social Psychology of Groups* (New York: Wiley, 1959); and M. Roloff, *Interpersonal Communication: The Social Exchange Approach* (Beverly Hills, CA: Sage, 1981).

10. I. Altman and D. Taylor, *Social Penetration: The Development of Interpersonal Relationships* (New York: Holt, Rinehart, & Winston, 1973).

11. D. Taylor and I. Altman, "Communication in Interpersonal Relationships: Social Penetration Processes," in *Interpersonal Processes: New Directions in Communication Research*, edited by M. Roloff and G. R. Miller (Newbury Park, CA: Sage, 1987).

12. L. Baxter and B. Montgomery, *Relating: Dialogues and Dialectics* (New York: Guilford, 1996).

13. J. Wood, "Communication and Relational Culture: Bases for the Study of Human Relationships," *Communication Quarterly* 30 (1982): 75–84.

14. B. Whorf, *Language, Thought, and Reality* (New York: MIT Press/Wiley, 1956).

15. Personal communication with Lynn Sessler-Schmaling, Japanese instructor, Clovis Grove School, Menahsa, Wisconsin.

16. C. Bruess and J. C. Pearson, "'Sweet Pea' and 'Pussy Cat': An Examination of Idiom Use and Marital Satisfaction Over the Life Cycle," *Journal of Social and Personal Relationships* 10 (1993): 609–615.

17. W. Betcher, "Terms of Endearment," *Self* (April 1994): 105–108.

18. R. Hopper, M. Knapp, and L. Scott, "Couples' Personal Idioms: Exploring Intimate Talk," *Journal of Communication* 31 (1981): 23–33.

19. Bruess and Pearson, "'Sweet Pea' and 'Pussy Cat.'"

20. E. Goffman, *Interaction Ritual: Essays on Face-to-Face Behavior* (Garden City, NY: Anchor, 1967).

21. J. Bossard and E. Boll, *Ritual in Family Living: A Contemporary Study* (Philadelphia: University of Pennsylvania Press, 1950).

22. L. A. Baxter, "A Dialectical Perspective on Communication Strategies in Relationship Development," in *The Handbook of Personal Relationships*, edited by S. W. Duck, D. F. Hay, S. E. Hobfoll, W. Ickes, and B. Montgomery (London: Wiley, 1988); and Baxter and Montgomery, *Relating: Dialogues and Dialectics*.

23. L. Bellak, *The Porcupine Dilemma* (New York: Citadel Press, 1970).

24. Baxter and Montgomery, *Relating*; and L. A. Baxter, "A Dialogic Approach to Relationship Maintenance," in *Communication and Relational Maintenance*, edited by D. Canary and L. Stafford (New York: Academic Press, 1994).

25. Baxter and Montgomery, *Relating: Dialogues and Dialectics*.

26. J. Wood, *Relational Communication: Continuity and Change in Personal Relationships* (Belmont, CA: Wadsworth, 2000).

27. Wood, *Relational Communication*; and J. Wood, *Who Cares: Women, Care, and Culture* (Carbondale: Southern Illinois University Press, 1994).

28. J. Wood, *Gendered Lives: Communication, Gender, and Culture* (Belmont, CA: Wadsworth, 1999).

29. Wood, *Gendered Lives*.

30. Wood, *Gendered Lives*.

31. See *http://www.CNN.com/2000/HEALTH/11/28/brain.listening/index.html*.

32. D. Canary and K. Hause, "Is There Any Reason to Research Sex Differences in Communication?" *Communication Quarterly* 41 (1993): 129–144.

Chapter 11

1. See *http://www.CNN.com/1999/US/12/24/mexico.orphanage/index.html*.

2. L. Turner and R. West, *Perspectives on Family Communication* (Boston: McGraw-Hill, 2002).

3. P. Noller and M. A. Fitzpatrick, *Communication in Family Relationships* (Englewood Cliffs, NJ: Prentice Hall, 1993); J. C. Pearson, *Lasting Love: What Keeps Couples Together* (Dubuque, IA: Wm. C. Brown, 1992); and V. Satir, *Peoplemaking* (Palo Alto, CA: Science & Behavior Books, 1972).

4. V. Satir, *The New Peoplemaking* (Mountain View, CA: Science and Behavior Books, 1988).

5. J. Gottman, *What Predicts Divorce?* (Hillsdale, NJ: Lawrence Erlbaum, 1994).

6. See *http://www.CNN.com/2000/HEALTH/08/18/working.wives/index.html*.

7. See *http://www.CNN.com/2000/HEALTH/03/15/divorce.suicide.wmd/index.html*.

8. All statistics, unless otherwise noted, are taken from the 2000 U.S. Census Bureau Report, *America's Families and Living Arrangements: Population Characteristics* (Washington, DC: U.S. Department of Commerce, Economics and Statistics Administration).

9. R. West and L. Turner, "Communication in Lesbian and Gay Families: Developing a Descriptive Base," in *Parents, Children, and Communication*, edited by T. Socha and G. Stamp (Mahwah, NJ: Lawrence Erlbaum, 1995); and S. Coontz, *The Way We Were: American Families and the Nostalgia Trap* (New York: Basic Books, 1992).

10. D. Demo, "Children's Experience of Family Diversity," *National Forum* 80 (2000): 16.

11. M. Wylie, "For Many Families, E-Mail Opens Communication," *Kalamazoo (MI) Gazette* (July 9, 2000): G2.

12. See *http://www.scarborough.com/scarb2002/press/pr_cellphone.htm.*

13. S. Liskow, "Wireless Culture Keeps Family Members Young and Old Connected," *Knight-Ridder/Tribune News Service* (August 7, 2001): K2341.

14. We adopt the same categorization scheme as in Turner and West, *Perspectives on Family Communication.*

15. See *http://www.CNN.com/2000/LAW/05/25/same.sex.marriages/.*

16. See *http://www.CNN.com/2000/CAREER/trends/10/04/domestic.partners./index.html.*

17. West and Turner, "Communication in Lesbian and Gay Families."

18. Demo, "Children's Experience of Family Diversity."

19. Demo, "Children's Experience of Family Diversity."

20. N. Sudarkasa, "Female-Headed African American Households: Some Neglected Dimensions," in *Family Ethnicity: Strength in Diversity*, edited by H. P. McAdoo (Newbury Park, CA: Sage, 1993).

21. Demo, "Children's Experience of Family Diversity."

22. T. DeLeire, and A. Kalil, "Good Things Come in Threes: Single-Parent Multigenerational Family Structure and Adolescent Adjustment," *Demography* 39 (2002): 393–412.

23. J. Lawrence, "Independence, Except From Gadgets: New Technology Enables Families to Keep Tabs on Seniors While Keeping Their Distance," *Washington Post* (December 18, 2001): F05.

24. D. Braithwaite, L. Baxter, and A. Harper, "The Role of Rituals in the Management of the Dialectical Tension of 'Old' and 'New' in Blended Families," *Communication Studies* 49 (1998): 101–120.

25. 2000 U.S. Census Report.

26. Turner and West, *Perspectives on Family Communication.*

27. D. Crary, "Boosting Marriage, Combating Divorce: Do States Have a Role?" *Kalamazoo (MI) Gazette* (February 2, 2001): D1.

28. Crary, "Boosting Marriage, Combating Divorce."

29. P. Tyre, "Giving Lessons in Love," *Newsweek* (February 18, 2002): 64.

30. J. Gottman, "What Predicts Divorce? The Relationship Between Marital Processes and Marital Outcomes," *Journal of Marriage and the Family* 56 (1994): 783–784.

31. Pearson, *Lasting Love.*

32. K. Galvin and B. Brommel, *Family Communication: Cohesion and Change* (New York: Addison, Wesley Longman, 2000).

33. C. Black, "Don't Talk: Communication Rules in the Alcoholic Family," in *It Will Never Happen to Me* (New York: Ballantine Books, 1987).

34. Galvin and Brommel, *Family Communication.*

35. D. Behrens, "Tying the Knot and Crossing the 'T': Prenuptial Pact Covers It All, From Budget to Bed," *Courier Journal* (February 14, 1996): A3.

36. P. Hartogs, "Study: Rules Improve Parent-Child Relationship," *http://www.cnn.com/2001/HEALTH/parenting/02/21/drugs.teens/index.html.*

37. Pew Internet & Merican Life Project (March 2000) Poll; and M. Wylie, "For Many Families, E-Mail Opens Communication," *Kalamazoo Gazette* (July 9, 2000): G2.
38. E. Allen, "Family Flame War," *Time* 156 (December 4, 2000): 179.
39. Satir, *The New Peoplemaking*.
40. J. Bossard and E. Boll, *Ritual in Family Living* (Philadelphia: University of Philadelphia Press, 1950).
41. R. Raskin, "Rituals for a New Age: E-mail and Family Life," *Family PC* 7 (2000): 60.
42. Raskin, "Rituals for a New Age."
43. Galvin and Brommel, *Family Communication*.
44. E. Stone, *Black Sheep and Kissing Cousins: How Our Family Stories Shape Us* (New York: Penguin Books, 1989).
45. N. C. James, "When Miss America Was Always White," in *Our Voices: Essays in Culture, Ethnicity, and Communication*, edited by A. Gonzalez, M. Houston, and V. Chen (Los Angeles: Roxbury, 1997).
46. F. Millar and E. Rogers, "A Relational Approach to Interpersonal Communication," in *Explorations in Interpersonal Communication*, edited by G. R. Miller (Beverly Hills, CA: Sage, 1976).

Chapter 12

1. L. Rosencrance, "Survey: Most U.S. Adults Without Web Access Don't Want It," *http://www.cnn.com/2000/TECH/computing/09/25/unwanted.Access.idg/index.html*.
2. G. J. Church, "The Economy of the Future?" *Time, http://www.time.com/time/magazine/printout/0,8816,31522,000.html*.
3. D. Price, "Workplace Snooping and Your Digital Shadow," *http://www.usatoday.com/careers/news/newsusa.ll.htm*.
4. See *http://www.PublicForumInstitute.com* and *http://www.rhimr.com/mr/dispatcher?file=/mr/eo_vol3_no2*.
5. T. R. Hinkin and C. A. Schriesheim, "Development and Application of New Scales to Measure to French and Raven (1959) Bases of Social Power," *Journal of Applied Psychology* 74 (1989): 561–567.
6. W. Z. Ford, *Communicating With Customers* (Cresskill, NJ: Hampton Press, 1999).
7. Ford, *Communicating With Customers*.
8. K. Davis, "Management Communication and the Grapevine," in *Intercom: Readings in Organizational Communication*, edited by S. Ferguson and S. D. Ferguson (Rochelle Park, NJ: Hayden Books, 1980); and S. Hellweg, "Organizational Grapevines," in *Readings in Organizational Communication*, edited by K. L. Hutchinson (Dubuque, IA: William C. Brown, 1992).
9. D. R. Eyler and A. Baridon, "A New Sexual Dynamic in the Workplace Can Be Beneficial," in *Male/Female Roles: Opposing Viewpoints*, edited by D. Bender and B. Leone (San Diego, CA: Greenhaven Press, 1994).
10. J. Hagberg, *Real Power: Stages of Personal Power in Organizations* (Salem, WI: Sheffield Publishing Company, 1994).
11. M. Gill, "Academic Sexual Harassment: Perceptions of Behaviors," in *Sexual Harassment: Communication Implications*, edited by G. L. Kreps (Cresskill, NJ: Hampton Press, 1993).
12. G. L. Blakely, E. H. Blakely, and R. H. Moorman, "The Relationship Between Gender, Personal Experience, and Perceptions of Sexual Harassment in the Workplace," *Employee Responsibilities and Rights Journal* 8 (1995): 263–275.

13. T. C. Fain and D. L. Anderson, "Sexual Harassment: Organizational Context and Status," *Sex Roles* 5 (1987): 291–311.
14. S. G. Bingham, "Sexual Harassment: On the Job, on the Campus," in *Gendered Relationships*, edited by J. T. Wood (Mountain View, CA: Mayfield, 1996).

Name Index

Subject Index